FOUNDATIONS OF MARKETING COMMUNICATIONS

A European Perspective

FOUNDATIONS OF MARKETING COMMUNICATIONS

A European Perspective

Patrick De Pelsmacker

Maggie Geuens

Joeri Van den Bergh

FT Prentice Hall
FINANCIAL TIMES

An imprint of **Pearson Education**
Harlow, England • London • New York • Boston • San Francisco • Toronto • Sydney • Singapore • Hong Kong
Tokyo • Seoul • Taipei • New Delhi • Cape Town • Madrid • Mexico City • Amsterdam • Munich • Paris • Milan

Pearson Education Limited

Edinburgh Gate
Harlow
Essex CM20 2JE
England

and Associated Companies throughout the world

Visit us on the World Wide Web at:
www.pearsoned.co.uk

First published 2005

ISBN 0 273 70386 2

British Library Cataloguing-in-Publication Data
A catalogue record for this book is available from the British Library.

Library of Congress Cataloging-in-Publication Data

Pelsmacker, Patrick de, 1957-
    Foundations of marketing communications : a European perspective / Patrick de
  Pelsmacker, Maggie Geuens, Joeri van den Bergh.— Rev. ed.
      p. cm.
    Rev. ed. of: Marketing communications. 2001.
    Includes bibliographical references and indexes.
    ISBN 0-273-70386-2
      1. Communication in Marketing—Europe.   2. Advertising.   I. Geuens, Maggie, 1969-   II.
  Bergh, Joeri van den, 1971-   III. Pelsmacker, Patrick de, 1957- Marketing communications.
  IV. Title.

HF5415.123.P45 2005
658.8'02—dc22   2005040119

10   9   8   7   6   5   4   3   2   1
09   08   07   06

Typeset in 10/12.5pt Sabon by 59
Printed by Ashford Colour Press Ltd, Gosport

The publisher's policy is to use paper manufactured from sustainable forests.

Dedication

This book is dedicated to all our students. They have always been a great source of inspiration.

Contents

About the authors

Patrick De Pelsmacker (b. 1957) holds a PhD in economics (University of Ghent, Belgium). He is Professor of Marketing at the University of Antwerp, Belgium. He is part-time Professor of Marketing at the University of Ghent. He has also worked at the University of Brussels (VUB). He is or has been a regular guest lecturer at various institutes, such as the Rotterdam School of Management (The Netherlands), the Swedish Institute of Management (Brussels, Stockholm), the China-Europe Management Centre (Antwerp), the Centre for Management Training (University of Warsaw, Poland), the Institute of Business Studies (Moscow, Russia) and the University of Venice (Italy). He also has teaching experience in management and marketing programmes in France, Thailand, Indonesia, the Philippines, Vietnam, the Czech Republic, Hungary and Romania. He has undertaken numerous in-company training and consultancy assignments.

His field of interest is mainly in marketing research techniques, consumer behaviour and marketing communications. He has co-authored textbooks on marketing research techniques, and has written over eighty articles in various journals, including *Applied Economics*, *International Journal of Research in Marketing*, *Journal of Advertising*, *Psychology and Marketing*, *International Journal of Advertising*, *Journal of Marketing Communications*, *Journal of International Consumer Marketing*, *Journal of Euro-Asian Economics*, *International Marketing Review*, *Educational and Psychological Measurements*, *Psychological Reports*, *International Journal of Marketing Research*, *Journal of Business Ethics* and *Journal of Consumer Affairs*. He has contributed to more than ten books and over sixty research reports and working papers on various marketing-related topics.

Maggie Geuens (b. 1969) holds a PhD in Applied Economics at the University of Antwerp, Belgium, where she also worked as an assistant professor. Currently she is Assistant Professor of Marketing at the University of Ghent. She also has teaching experience in Italy, Kazakhstan, Russia and Vietnam. She is involved in in-company training and consultancy on a regular basis.

Her main field of research interest is in advertising and consumer behaviour. She has co-authored books on marketing management and marketing communications, and has contributed to books and to over twenty working papers and research reports in this field, and has published in journals such as *International Journal of Advertising*, *Journal of Marketing Communications*, *Psychology and Marketing*, *International Marketing Review*, *Journal of Advertising*, *Advances in Consumer Research*, *Psychological Review*, *Educational and Psychological Measurement*, *International Journal of Marketing Research* and *Journal of Consumer and Market Research*.

Joeri Van den Bergh (b. 1971) holds a masters degree in marketing (University of Ghent and the Vlerick Leuven Gent Management School). He started his career as a researcher at the Marketing Communication Research Centre, and later became senior researcher, involved in the activities of this Centre, as well as the Kids and Teens Marketing Centre, and the Senior Consumer Marketing Centre. He is co-founder and managing partner of InSites Consulting, an internet research consultancy company. He is a regular teacher in various marketing programmes, has been involved in in-company training and consultancy, and is a Counsellor of the Board of Ancienne Belgique (AB), a large concert venue in Belgium.

His main field of interest is marketing communications, senior consumer marketing and especially kids and teens marketing and internet communications and research techniques. He has contributed to various books and to over thirty research reports in these fields. He has co-authored a book on marketing communications and published in journals including *International Journal of Advertising* and the *Journal of International Consumer Marketing*.

Preface

Marketing communications are not only one of the most visible and widely discussed instruments of the marketing mix, with an overwhelming impact on both society and business, they are also one of the most fascinating. Every private consumer and business executive is exposed to advertising. They make use of sales promotions, are a target of public relations activity, are exposed to sponsorship efforts, receive direct mail, telemarketing or research calls and visit stores in which no stone is left unturned to influence his or her buying behaviour.

Furthermore, an increasing number of consumers are regular users of the internet. Marketing executives constantly face the challenge of integrating their promotional effort into strategic management and marketing plans. They must integrate the various instruments of the marketing communications mix, build successful brands, try to find out how marketing communications can be instrumental in achieving company objectives, and how they can be applied in specific marketing situations.

This *Foundations of Marketing Communications* offers a comprehensive overview of the cornerstones, techniques and applications of marketing communications in a European context. We have added the subtitle, *A European Perspective*, to reflect this emphasis.

The market

This book is geared to undergraduate and postgraduate students who have attended introductory courses in marketing, and who want to extend their knowledge to various aspects of marketing communications. The book can also be used by marketing communication professionals who want an overview of the field and may find inspiration and new angles to their marketing communications practice in the many examples, cases and research results that are covered in this text.

Organisation

The book is organised as follows. Chapter 1 provides a global overview of marketing communications and discusses the crucial topic of the integration of marketing communications activity. Chapter 2 discusses the groundwork of all marketing communications activity. It is devoted to the intriguing question of how communications influence consumers.

In subsequent chapters the different steps in the marketing communications plan and the most important instruments and techniques of marketing communications are covered. Separate chapters are devoted to the definition of target groups (3) and objectives (4) and to budgeting issues (5).

Chapters 6–13 cover a number of important marketing communications instruments. Chapters 6–8 address advertising-related issues, including media planning and advertising research. Subsequent chapters each cover one tool of the marketing communications mix: sales promotions (9), direct marketing (10), e-communication (11) point-of-purchase communications (12) and public relations and sponsorship (13).

Pedagogy

To help reinforce key learning points, each chapter includes the following:

- Chapter Outline, which presents the contents of the chapter graphically.

- Chapter Objectives, Summaries and Review Questions assist the reader in understanding the important elements and help test one's knowledge.

- Main text organised in sections and sub-sections to help students digest and retain the information.

- Tables, figures, outlines and other illustrative material help the reader grasp the essential facts.

- Separate highlights throughout the text cover extended examples, mini-cases, interesting research results or more technical issues.

- Suggested further readings offer the opportunity to refer to other, more specialised or specific sources of information on many subjects.

- An extensive European or global case study in each chapter.

Distinctive characteristics

- This is not just a book about advertising, supplemented by a brief discussion of the other instruments of the marketing mix. Although advertising-related topics are thoroughly discussed, the book also covers the other major instruments of the marketing communications mix.

- The book has a consistent European focus. Although research results and examples from other parts of the world are covered, the main focus is the application of marketing communications concepts in a European environment.

- Every chapter contains an extensive European or global case study in a wide variety of industries, markets and countries. Most of these cases contain original and in-depth material, often provided by the marketing executives of the brands and companies discussed. Challenging case questions are designed to encourage the reader to apply the concepts from the chapter to the solution of the case at hand. Furthermore, many of these cases can be used with more than one chapter.

- A number of chapters focus extensively on particularly important and/or relatively new fields of interest related to marketing communications. This is the case for the chapters on how communications work and e-communications.

- Throughout the text, numerous examples, case studies and research results from various countries, industries and markets are given, to illustrate and make the concepts as practice-oriented as possible.

Authors' acknowledgements

While we assume full responsibility for the content of the whole book, important parts of it could not have been written without the help and support of numerous people. We would particularly like to thank the following people, and hope we have not forgotten anyone.

Bernhard Adriaenessens (World Federation of Advertisers)

Geert Ailliet

Malaika Brengman (Limburgs Universitair Centrum)

Frank Caron (Jouret Management)

Jean-Luc Charlier and Arnaud Demoulin, Valérie Van Geel, Jochem De Boer (Procter & Gamble)

Kristiaan Cloots (FreeMobility & CIA)

Danny Cools (Sony I.T.E.)

Laurent De Hauwere, Pia Steen Hansen, Vincent Maenhaut, Sandra Deblander (Tele Atlas)

Serge Dekoninck (Saatchi and Saatchi Business Communication)

Dimitri De Lauw, Sofie Huygelen, Wouter Van den Herreweghen, Fons Van Dijck (VVL/BBDO)

Geert Goessaert (Vlerick Leuven Gent Management School)

Mark Hofmans, Siegfried Högl (GfK)

Martin Kingdon (Retail Marketing In-Store Services)

Brian Kleppner (Ben & Jerry's)

Wim Lagae (Lessius Hogeschool)

Nigel Lawrence (Dunnhumby)

Pascal Libyn and Filip Eeckhoudt (RISC)

Klaus Lommatsch (Duval Guillaume)

Yuri Malinin (Mediafirst Russia)

Robin McCammon (General Motors)

Danny Meadows-Klue (IAB Europe)

Patrick Mertens (De Kie)

Marc Michils and Henk Ghesquière (Quattro Saatchi and Saatchi)

Marcel Moens

Geert Neutens (Artex)

Jorgen Nygaard Andreassen (Fedma)

Magdalena Ortendahl, Tariq Malik del Campo (Ericsson)

Josefien Overeem (CV News)

Veerle Ringoir (Bacardi-Martini)

Dirk Schyvinck (Dexia)

Katharina Thiessen, Benjamin Michahelles (Beiersdorf AG)

Freddy Vander Mijnsbrugge

F. Van Hoof (Pioneer Electronics)

Koen Van Hout (Mercedes-Benz)

Georges Van Nevel (DVN)

Theo van Roy (Hits)

Jan Verhaege (Etap Yachting)

Stefan Claeys and Maes Communications, Business to Business Concept & Tools

A number of reviewers: Paul Copley, University of Northumbria; Claude Pecheux, Les Facultés Universitaires Catholiques de Mons; Jane Underhill, University of Northumbria; Tania Van den Bergh, Arteveldehogeschool, Flanders, Belgium

Publisher's acknowledgements

We are grateful to the following for permission to reproduce copyright material:

Plate 1	Artex NV
Plate 2	Gesamtverband Werbeagenturen GWA & McCann-Erickson Europe
Plate 3	DaimlerChrysler
Plate 4	Gesamtverband Werbeagenturen GWA & J. Walter Thompson
Plate 5	Ben & Jerry's
Plate 6	Dexia Bank
Plate 7	Leo Burnett
Plate 8	VF Corporation
Plate 11	British Tourist Authority
Plate 12	Gesamtverband Werbeagenturen GWA & Abbott Mead Vickers BBDO
Plate 13	The Advertising Archives
Plate 14	Leo Burnett
Plate 15	Leo Burnett
Plate 16	Gesamtverband Werbeagenturen GWA & Euro RSCG Works
Plate 18	Federation of European Direct Marketing
Plate 19	Unilever, Inc.
Plate 20	Sony I.T.E.
Plate 21	Smart Center Antwerpen
Plate 22	Iglo-Ola, a Division of Unilever Belgium
Plate 24	DaimlerChrysler

We are grateful to Hilly Janes for permission to reproduce an extract 'From lad mag to dad mag' by Hilly Janes published in *The Guardian*, 9 April 2003 © Hilly Janes 2003.

Credits for tables and figures appear in situ.

Every effort has been made by the publisher to obtain permission from the appropriate source to reproduce material which appears in this book. In some instances we have been unable to trace the owners of copyright material, and we would appreciate any information that would enable us to do so.

Chapter 1

Integrated marketing communications

Chapter outline

The marketing mix
The communications mix
Integration of marketing communications
Factors leading to integrated marketing communications
Barriers to integrated marketing communications
Client–agency relations and integrated marketing communications
The integrated marketing communications plan

Chapter objectives

This chapter will help you to:

- Situate marketing communications in the marketing mix
- Get an overview of the instruments of the marketing communications mix
- Understand what integrated marketing communications mean, and their organisational implications
- Learn to know the factors leading to integrated marketing communications
- Understand why integrated marketing communications are not easily implemented
- Get an overview of the essential steps in the marketing communications plan

Introduction

The integration of the various instruments of the marketing mix is one of the major principles of sound marketing strategy. Obviously, this integration principle also applies to
the various instruments of the communications mix. In fact, integrated communications
have been practised by good marketing communicators for decades. The concept of
'integrated marketing communications' (IMC) has in recent years developed into one of
the basic new trends or buzz words in marketing communications. The integration of the
various instruments of the communications mix is favourably influenced and necessi-
tated by a number of important trends in marketing today. At the same time, barriers
to change, and to the successful implementation of IMC, remain strong. The latter may
explain why such an obvious concept as IMC, leading to a more homogeneous and
therefore more effective communications effort, has not been put into practice much
earlier. As a result, integrated communications have a number of practical and organisational consequences that influence the way in which communicators organise their
communications function, the way in which they deal with communications consultants such as PR and advertising agencies, and indeed the way in which communications consultants organise themselves.

Marketing and the instruments of the marketing mix

Marketing is the process of planning and executing the conception, pricing, promotion
and distribution of ideas, goods and services to create and exchange value, and satisfy
individual and organisational objectives.[1]

Given the marketing objectives and goals, the target segments and the market position that has to be defended, the tools of the marketing plan have to be decided upon.
The marketer has a number of tools to hand: the instruments of the marketing mix.
Traditionally, these instruments are divided into four categories, called the 4 Ps of the
marketing mix. In Table 1.1 some of the tools of the marketing mix are shown.

The product tool consists of three layers. The core product is the unique benefit
that is being marketed. In fact it is the position, the unique place in the mind of the

Table 1.1 Instruments of the marketing mix

Product	Price	Place	Promotion
Benefits	List price	Channels	Advertising
Features	Discounts	Logistics	Public relations
Options	Credit terms	Inventory	Sponsorship
Quality	Payment periods	Transport	Sales promotions
Design	Incentives	Assortments	Direct marketing
Branding		Locations	Point-of-purchase
Packaging			Exhibitions and trade fairs
Services			Personal selling
Warranties			Internet

consumer, that will be focused upon. Often the brand is a summary, a visualisation of this core benefit and all the associations it leads to. The core product has to be translated into a tangible product. Product features, a certain level of quality, the available options, design and packaging are important instruments by which a core benefit can be made tangible. Finally, the augmented product gives the tangible product more value and more customer appeal. The augmented product can be defined as the 'service layer' on top of the tangible product. It includes elements such as prompt delivery, installation service, after-sales service and management of complaints.

Price is the only marketing instrument that does not cost anything, but provides the resources to spend on production and marketing activity. The list price is the 'official' price of a product. However, discounts and incentives of all kinds can be used to make the product more attractive. Systems of down payments and payment periods, combined with attractive interest rates, can also be used to make the offering more attractive and ensure that the immediate budget constraint is less of a problem for the consumer. The price instrument is an ambiguous tool. On the one hand, price cuts are an effective way to attract consumers. On the other, price cuts mean losing margin and profit. Furthermore, the customer gets used to discounts and may gradually be educated to buy on price and be a brand-switcher. The regular use of the price instrument is incompatible with building a strong position and a strong brand on the basis of product characteristics or benefits. Therefore good marketing can be defined as avoiding the price tool as much as possible.

By means of place or distribution the company manages the process of bringing the product from the production site to the customer. This involves transporting the product, keeping an inventory, selecting wholesalers and retailers, deciding on which types of outlet the product will be distributed in, and the assortment of products to be offered in the various outlets. Distribution strategy also implies maintaining co-operation between the company and the distribution channel, and finding new ways to distribute products, such as infomercials (programme-length advertising and selling) and e-commerce.

Promotion, or marketing communications (MC), is the fourth and most visible instrument of the marketing mix. This involves all instruments by means of which the company communicates with its target groups and stakeholders to promote its products or the company as a whole. The instruments of the communications mix are introduced in the next section.

Good marketing is integrated marketing. Two principles are important when designing and implementing a marketing mix, i.e. interaction and synergy. Marketing instruments have to be combined in such a way that the company's offering is consistently marketed. In other words, all marketing instruments have to work in the same direction, and not conflict with each other. The ice cream brand Häagen-Dazs is positioned as a high-quality treat for sophisticated young adults. This core product or basic positioning is reflected in the whole marketing mix. The product itself is of excellent quality and made from the best ingredients. The brand name sounds – at least to an American public – exotic, maybe Scandinavian. The price is high, emphasising the exclusive character and the top quality of the brand. Distribution is relatively exclusive. The product is available in special shops or in separate freezers in supermarkets. Marketing communications reflect the sophistication and special, erotic atmosphere of the brand positioning. Similarly, a watch, the basic benefit of which is low cost, will be a very simple product with no special features or design. No strong brand name will be developed, and the basic marketing instrument will be price. The watch will have to be widely available, especially in discount stores and hypermarkets. Promotion will be limited to in-store communications or a simple presentation of the product in the retailer's advertising campaign.

The second important principle is interaction. Marketing mix instruments have to be designed in such a way that the effects of the tools are mutually reinforcing. A brand will become stronger if it is advertised and available in the appropriate distribution outlets. Sales staff will be more successful if their activities are supported by public relations activity, price incentives or advertising campaigns. The effect of sponsorship will be multiplied if combined with sales promotion activity and public relations campaigns generating media exposure of the sponsored event. Intensive distribution will be more effective when combined with in-store communications and advertising, etc. Successful marketing depends on a well-integrated, synergetic and interactive marketing mix.

The communications mix

Often advertising is considered a synonym of marketing communications because it is the most visible tool of the communications mix. But, of course, a large variety of communications instruments exists, each with its own typical characteristics, strengths and weaknesses. The tools of the communications mix were presented in the last column of Table 1.1.

Advertising is non-personal mass communication using mass media (such as TV, radio, newspapers, magazines, billboards, etc.), the content of which is determined and paid for by a clearly identified sender (the company).

Sales promotions are sales-stimulating campaigns, such as price cuts, couponing, loyalty programmes, competitions, free samples, etc.

Sponsorship implies that the sponsor provides funds, goods, services and/or know-how. The sponsee will help the sponsor with communications objectives such as building brand awareness or reinforcing brand or corporate image. Sports, arts, media, education, science and social projects and institutions, and television programmes can be sponsored. Events are often linked to sponsorship. A company can sponsor an event or organise its own events, for instance for its sales team, its clients and prospects, its personnel, its distribution network, etc.

Public relations consist of all the communications a company instigates with its audiences or stakeholders. Stakeholders are groups of individuals or organisations with whom the company wants to create goodwill. Press releases and conferences, some of the major public relations tools, should generate publicity. Publicity is impersonal mass communication in mass media, but it is not paid for by a company and the content is written by journalists (which means that negative publicity is also possible).

Point-of-purchase communications are communications at the point of purchase or point of sales (i.e. the shop). It includes several communications tools such as displays, advertising within the shop, merchandising, article presentations, store layout, etc.

Exhibitions and trade fairs are, particularly in business-to-business and industrial markets, of great importance for contacting prospects, users and purchasers.

Direct marketing communications are a personal and direct way to communicate with customers and potential clients or prospects. Personalised brochures and leaflets (with feedback potential), direct mailings, telemarketing actions, direct response advertising, etc. are possible ways of using direct marketing communications.

Table 1.2 Personal versus mass marketing communications

	Personal communications	Mass communications
Reach of big audience		
■ Speed	Slow (selling), faster (DM)	Fast
■ Costs/reached person	High	Low
Influence on individual		
■ Attention value	High	Low
■ Selective perception	Relatively lower	High
■ Comprehension	High	Moderate–low
Feedback		
■ Direction	Two-way	One-way
■ Speed of feedback	High	Low
■ Measuring effectiveness	Accurate	Difficult

Personal selling is the oral presentation and/or demonstration of one or more sales-persons aimed at selling the products or services of a company. It is a personal contact between a company representative and a prospect or client.

The internet offers new ways to communicate interactively with different stakeholders and, together with e-commerce, combines communicating with selling.

Marketing communications try to influence or persuade the (potential) consumer by conveying a message. This message transfer may be directed to certain known and individually addressed persons, in which case it is called personal communications. The message transfer may also take place to a number of receivers who cannot be identified, using mass media to reach a broad audience. This is called mass communications. Personal communications are mainly direct and interactive marketing actions and personal selling. All other promotional tools are mass communications. Table 1.2 compares personal and mass marketing communications using different criteria. This comparison does of course generalise. The practical implications of the selection mix depend on the situation and the creative implementation and execution of the communications instruments. A bad mailshot could also lead to higher selective perception and lower attributed attention.

Apple: combining personal and mass communications

The following illustrates the difference between personal and mass communications by apply-ing both to a marketing communications strategy for the Apple Imac computer.

Personal communications
An Apple salesperson demonstrates the new Apple Imac to a group of clients or prospects. It will take some time before he has visited a large group of prospects (slow speed). To reach one prospect, the company will have to pay the labour costs of half a day (costs per person reached are high). Once the salesperson has made an appointment, the chance of the mess-age being skipped or avoided is low and he or she will have the attention of the audience. He or she will be able to give a clear explanation and will know straightaway if the prospect has questions to ask or has not understood everything. The salesperson will be able to answer questions and listen to the needs of the prospect (two-way communication). The speed of

▶

feedback is very high: the prospect will or will not buy. As a consequence, effectiveness is easy to measure: sales/number of sales visits, etc.

Mass communications
Apple uses advertising on TV and in magazines to promote its new Imac computer. With TV advertising in prime time it reaches millions of viewers in a few seconds (high speed). Although advertising is not cheap, the cost per contact will be substantially lower than in the case of the salesperson. The attention TV viewers attribute to advertising is a lot lower: they may be talking with family members, reading, leaving the room for refreshments, etc. Selective exposure is high: zapping TV commercials, skipping ads in magazines, etc. It is difficult to transmit a clear message to everybody in 30 seconds or in one print ad. Ad viewers may have questions but cannot respond (one-way communication). The speed of feedback is low, and effectiveness may be assessed only later by looking at sales figures or brand-awareness scores. Effectiveness is often difficult to measure: market research is needed and is often subject to inherent methodological weaknesses.

Another way of categorising marketing communications instruments is to differentiate between theme or image communications and action communications.

In **image** or **theme communications** the advertiser tries to tell the target group something about the brand or products and services offered. The goal of image communications could be to improve relations with target groups, increase customer satisfaction or reinforce brand awareness and brand preference. This might eventually lead to a positive influence on the (buying) behaviour of the target group. Theme communications are also known as above-the-line communications, as opposed to below-the-line or action communications. This difference (the line) refers to the fee an advertising agency used to earn. All above-the-line promotional tools used to lead to a 15% commission fee on media space purchased. Consequently, above-the-line communications are synonymous with mass media advertising (TV, radio, magazines, newspapers, cinema, billboards, etc.). Below-the-line or **action communications** tools were communications instruments for which the 15% rule was not applicable. This terminology has since lost its importance because most agencies now charge a fixed fee or hourly fee rather than using the commission system.

Action communications seek to influence the buying behaviour of target groups and to persuade the consumer to purchase the product. The primary goal is to stimulate purchases. In practice, theme and action campaigns are not always that easy to discern. Sometimes the primary goal of advertising is to sell, as in advertisements announcing promotions or direct response ads. Visits from sales teams may also have the purpose of creating goodwill rather than selling. Theme promotions such as sampling gadgets to increase brand awareness are also used.

Integration of marketing communications

Integrated marketing communications have been defined in a number of ways, stressing various aspects, benefits and organisational consequences of IMC. Putting it very generally,

> 'it is a new way of looking at the whole, where once we saw only parts such as advertising, public relations, sales promotion, purchasing, employee communication, and

so forth, to look at it the way the consumer sees it – as a flow of information from indistinguishable sources'.[2]

It is the integration of specialised communications functions that previously operated with varying degrees of autonomy. It is seamless, through-the-line communication.[3] The American Association of Advertising Agencies uses the following definition of IMC:

'a concept of marketing communication planning that recognises the added value of a comprehensive plan that evaluates the strategic roles of a variety of communication disciplines, e.g. general advertising, direct response, sales promotion and public relations – and combines these disciplines to provide clarity, consistency and maximum communication impact'.[4]

The various definitions incorporate the same core idea: communications instruments that traditionally have been used independently of each other are combined in such a way that a synergetic effect is reached, and the resulting communications effort becomes 'seamless' or homogeneous. The major benefit of IMC is that a consistent set of messages is conveyed to all target audiences by means of all available forms of contact and message channels. Communications should become more effective and efficient as a result of the consistency and the synergetic effect between tools and messages. In other words, IMC has an added value when compared with traditional marketing communications.[5]

The rationale behind this new way of looking at marketing communications – and certainly the most relevant issue in the whole IMC discussion – is the consumer point of view. The consumer does not recognise the subtle differences between advertising, sponsorship, direct mailing, sales promotions, events or trade fairs. To him or her, these are all very similar and indistinguishable ways a company employs to persuade the consumer to buy its products. Therefore, it is very confusing and less persuasive to be confronted with inconsistent messages. Consumers may be more sensitive to commonalities and discrepancies among messages than to the specific communications vehicles used to transmit them.[6] IMC may therefore also be defined from the customer's point of view. The receiver is offered sources, messages, instruments and media in such a way that an added value is created in terms of a faster or better comprehension of the communication. Integration occurs at the consumer or perceiver level. It is the task of the communicator to facilitate this integration at the consumer level by presenting the messages in an integrated way.[7] In fact, there is a need to manage each point of contact between the consumer and the product or organisation.[8]

Integrated marketing communications do not happen automatically. All the elements of the communications mix have to be carefully planned in such a way that they form a consistent and coherent integrated communications plan. As a consequence, IMC can only be implemented successfully if there is also a strategic integration of the various departments that are responsible for parts of the communications function. Indeed, advertising, public relations, sales promotions and personal selling in most companies are traditionally managed by separate divisions that seldom communicate with each other, let alone take account of each other's priorities or integrate their efforts. Successful IMC rests on the existence of one communications manager who has the authority to supervise and integrate all the specialised communications functions of the organisation. Often this will imply a radical change in the structure of the organisation, and that may be the most important reason why IMC has not been implemented in most companies.

Perception of IMC in the US motor carrier industry

In a study of the perception of US motor carrier marketing managers, 192 respondents were asked to report for which communications functions they used each of the marketing communications tools they employed. The subjects framed five communications functions as the steps of the individual-level new product adoption model. Sixteen marketing communications tools were mentioned. The map below was generated by means of correspondence analysis on the basis of the number of times a communications tool was assigned to a specific communications function. It is a graphical representation of how appropriate the marketing managers perceive the role of each tool in each stage of the new product adoption process. The horizontal axis of the map primarily represents the various stages in the adoption process. All mass communication tools are clustered in the left-hand side of the map, close to the first stages of the adoption process (awareness and interest). Internet and e-mail are positioned close to the interest and evaluation stages. Telemarketing is more closely associated with generating trial, while personal selling is more closely associated with gaining adoption. Although integrated marketing communications advocates consistency in all the communications tools used, each tool still has a specific role to play in the communication strategy accompanying the launch of a new product.[9]

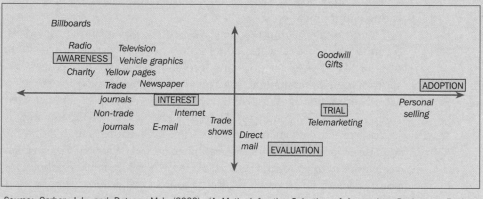

Source: Garber, L.L. and Dotson, M.J. (2002), 'A Method for the Selection of Appropriate Business-to-Business Integrated Marketing Communications Mixes', *Journal of Marketing Communications*, 8(1), 1–18.

In Table 1.3, some major differences between 'classic' communications and integrated communications are summarised.[10] In this overview the focus is on the changing nature of communications and the changing attitude of the consumer. Both necessitate a seamless integration of communications instruments. Traditional communications strategies are based on mass media, delivering generalised transaction-oriented messages. Integrated communications are much more personalised, customer-oriented, relationship-based and interactive. They are not only aimed at changing awareness and attitudes, but also at directly influencing behaviour. Integration is not synonymous with relationship marketing, satisfaction management or interactive communications. These principles may well be put in practice by means of a 'classic' communications strategy. However, by means of integrated communications the key objectives of modern marketing can be reached much more effectively.

Table 1.3 Classic and integrated communications

Classic communications	Integrated communications
Aimed at acquisition	Aimed at retention, relationship management
Mass communications	Selective communications
Monologue	Dialogue
Information is sent	Information is requested
Information provision	Information – self service
Sender takes initiative	Receiver takes initiative
Persuasive 'hold up'	Provide information
Effect through repetition	Effect through relevance
Offensive	Defensive
Hard sell	Soft sell
Salience of brand	Confidence in brand
Transaction-oriented	Relationship-oriented
Attitude change	Satisfaction
Modern: linear, massive	Postmodern: cyclical, fragmented

Based on: van Raaij, W.F. (1998), 'Integratie van Communicatie: vanuit de zender of vanuit de ontvanger' (Integration of Communication: Starting from the sender or the receiver?), in Damoiseaux, V.M.G., van Ruler, A.A. and Weisink, A., *Effectiviteit in Communicatiemanagement (Effectiveness in Communication Management)*. Deventer: Samson, 169–84.

Combining marketing communications tools to create synergies

Integrating the various tools can lead to synergies in a number of ways. Here are some examples:

- The sales team have an easier job if their product or company is well known as a result of sponsorship or advertising.
- In-store or point-of-purchase communications that are consistent with advertising are much more effective.
- A promotional campaign that is supported by advertising is generally more successful.
- Direct mailing is more effective when prepared by an awareness-increasing advertising campaign and supported by a sales promotion campaign.
- Public relations, corporate advertising and sponsorship can have synergetic effects on company image-building.
- Websites will be more frequently visited when announced in mass media advertising.
- Advertising for a trade show will be more effective if an incentive to visit the stand is offered.

Factors leading to integrated marketing communications

A number of important changes and trends have created the need and urge to integrate marketing communications and to facilitate them. In Table 1.4 key IMC drivers are listed.

Table 1.4 Key drivers of integrated marketing communications

- Loss of faith in mass media advertising
- Media cost inflation
- Need for more impact
- Need for more cost-effectiveness and efficiency
- Media fragmentation
- Audience fragmentation
- Increased reliance on highly targeted communication methods
- Low levels of brand differentiation
- Increased need for greater levels of accountability
- Technological evolutions
- Greater levels of audience communications literacy
- More complex decision-making units
- Need to build more customer loyalty
- Move towards relationship marketing
- Globalisation of marketing strategies

There is a widespread belief that mass media communications are becoming increasingly less effective. Communications clutter, resulting from increasing advertising pressure, leads to increased irritation and advertising avoidance behaviour and to a situation in which advertising in traditional, undifferentiated and impersonalised media is less and less capable of attracting attention, let alone of convincing consumers. As a result of more and more advertisers claiming media time and space, mass media are increasingly expensive. Furthermore, traditional mass media communications are primarily capable of stimulating awareness and attitudes, but much less of stimulating or directly influencing demand. The need for marketing strategies influencing behaviour directly has further eroded the attractiveness of traditional mass media. Using more media and more channels and tools to reach the consumer effectively increases the need for integration of these tools.

New forms of communications: advertorials and infomercials

Traditional mass media can be used to create new forms of communication to escape from message clutter. One of these new types is the advertorial (advertisement + editorial). For instance, a television programme can take viewers into department stores to introduce them to the latest fashion and beauty trends. At a certain moment in time, the show directs the customers to certain brands, the marketers of which have sponsored the programme. The viewers only learn about the sponsors at the end of the show. After the show, consumers are offered the opportunity to order a newsletter containing information about the featured products. Similarly, the Walt Disney Studios sponsor an entertaining movie news show. At the end of the show it is revealed that it was paid for by Buena Vista (Disney's film distribution company). Of course, most consumers are not aware of the close link between Disney and Buena Vista.[11] As becomes clear from the examples, these new forms of communication may raise some serious ethical questions.

Another type of creative communication on television is the infomercial (information + commercial) or programme-length advertising. During an 'informative programme' a product

▶

is presented and demonstrated to the consumer, who is urged to order it by telephone. Infomercials are very behaviour-oriented and try to bridge the gap between not knowing the product and ordering it in half an hour's time.[12]

The recession at the beginning of the 1990s increased cost-awareness and the need for more cost-effective and efficient marketing. The time horizon of companies became more short-term-oriented. As a result there is a greater need for directly effective marketing strategies and for instruments the effectiveness of which can be assessed and can be assessed instantaneously. There is, in other words, a growing need for increased levels of accountability. Consequently, mass media are supplemented with, or replaced by, other communications tools with allegedly more impact, that focus much more on influencing the behaviour of individual consumers directly, and the effectiveness of which can be measured precisely, such as direct marketing and interactive marketing communications. Adding more and more diversified tools to the communications mix leads to more media being used and more fragmented media, and increases the need for integration of marketing communications. As a spin-off from this integration of fragmented communications tools, it becomes less and less relevant to measure the effect of one single element in the communications mix, such as advertising. The measurement of communications effectiveness will have to focus on techniques such as monitoring and tracking, which assess the effectiveness of a total campaign at the brand level.

Audiences and markets tend to become more and more fragmented, making mass media less effective and increasing the need for more specialised and fragmented media. Communications tend to become customised for narrower and narrower markets, and customer contact is established by means of multimedia methods. There is an increasing reliance on highly targeted communications methods, such as database techniques and boutique channel (highly targeted television channel) advertising.[13] Integrated marketing communications are about co-ordinating multiple and diverse tools targeted at multiple and diverse audiences.[14]

New creative ways to reach target audiences

Marketers are constantly looking for new, efficient and creative ways to reach their audiences. Here are some examples.

Extremely short ads
Master Lock, the American lock company, produced a 'zap-proof' and 'snack-proof' ad: the one-second commercial. The goal of such extremely short ads is to prevent consumers using the commercial break to zap to another channel. Although one can question whether it is possible to convey any information in just one second, Master Lock is convinced that it is sufficient on the condition that the advertising company is well known and uses a very familiar logo or image. Between June and August 1998, Master Lock aired 400 one-second ads. So far, no other company has announced similar campaigns.[15]

Free products in exchange for commercial messages
The Californian multimedia company Free-PC offered a free computer to 10,000 consumers.[16] In exchange for a Compaq with internet access, the consumers have to accept that almost half of the 4.2 gigabyte hard disk is occupied by advertisements. The banners appear on the side

▶

of the screen and are frequently adapted when the user is online. The advertising companies choose which messages the user receives. Well-known companies such as Disney, credit card company MBNA, and internet car dealer Autobyte! seemed to have a lot of faith in this project and enlisted as advertisers. Whether advertisers are really willing to pay for the costs of the PCs remains to be seen. However, this is not so inconceivable since it seems to be part of a trend that can already be witnessed in the mobile phone market. More and more phone providers offer free telephones in exchange for subscribing to their network. The same goes for internet providers. British Telecom and LineOne announced that they were dropping their subscription fees. Furthermore, phone companies are offering free phone calls as long as the consumer is willing to accept that his or her phone call will be interrupted by an advertising message every five minutes. Again, although free phone calls to friends seem to be an attractive offer, the future will show whether the consumer is willing to take the advertising messages that accompany it.

Troopers

Sometimes it is difficult to motivate people to go to a musical or a play because they live too far away, or are not in the habit of going. The Belgian company Music Hall tries to change this by hiring 'Troopers'.[17] Troopers are preferably people who are very sociable and have lots of friends and acquaintances. The goal is that every Trooper tries to motivate his or her friends to go and see, for example, *Les Misérables* together. In exchange, the Trooper receives a price reduction on each ticket, the total of which he or she can keep for him or herself or split with the group. The advantage for Music Hall is obvious: they can reduce their advertising budget and reach people who would not otherwise have bought a ticket.

Advertising for animals

In January 1999 the first commercial for animals was aired on the British channel ITV.[18] Whiskas announced it in the media and asked the British people to observe their cat's responses. According to a first test, 60% of cats paid immediate attention to hearing the mice and bird sounds, and a minority approached the TV to sniff and pat the screen. The goal of the advertising agency, Saatchi and Saatchi, seems to have been obtained: 'Sell to the one that does not consume. Be consumed by the one that does not buy'. Whiskas' research department was overwhelmed with responses and the question from, amongst others, Japanese production houses to extend the campaign.

Stealth tactics

The New York advertising agency Big Fat Inc. organises campaigns that can be labelled as undercover, stealth or guerrilla marketing. Key influencers of the target group promote products or brands by means of so-called real life product placement. For instance, a group of young and attractive role models are paid to hang around in trendy bars, to order a new drink, say vodka-mineral water, and to talk about it in such a way that the other visitors of the bar are positively exposed to the new drink in a real-life situation. Nestlé organises wake-up calls for students. Fifteen minutes after the wake-up call, someone rings the doorbell to offer the student a cup of Nestlé coffee. The technique as such is not new. Years ago, the cognac brand Hennessy hired people to order Hennessy in bars.[19]

High exposure

The Dutch agency MediMountain sells advertising space on ski lifts in the Alps. Millions of tourists are exposed to the commercial messages on 650 ski lifts in 165 ski areas in Switzerland, France, Austria, Italy and Slovenia. Advertising on ski lifts has an enormous advantage for the advertiser: forced and unchallenged exposure is high during a substantial amount of time.[20]

Most markets in well-developed countries are mature. This means that a lot of products and brands are of similar quality. Low levels of brand differentiation increase the need to make the difference by means of communications. Therefore, some argue 'that the basic reason for [the increased attention for] integrated marketing communications is that marketing communications will be the only sustainable competitive advantage of marketing organisations in the 1990s and into the twenty-first century'.[21]

Mainly as a result of technological evolutions and innovations, new marketing and marketing communications tools are becoming available. Scanning and database technology allow more in-depth knowledge of the consumer and especially a more personalised and direct approach of the consumer. Interactive media, such as the internet, have contributed to a situation in which the relationship between the sender and the receiver of messages is less unidirectional. Direct marketing and direct response communications also lead to a situation in which communications become more and more receiver-directed.[22] Together with increased communications literacy on the part of the consumer, this leads to a market situation in which much of the power is at the receiving end, i.e. the receiving consumer decides what he or she will be exposed to and how he or she will react to it. Indeed, the marketing situation has gradually shifted from a situation in which all the power of knowledge and control was in the hands of the manufacturer to a market in which the retailers are the strongest party. Today the balance is shifting towards a market in which the consumer is the most powerful agent.[23] In fact, one could argue that integration is mainly technology-driven. New technologies and applications, such as the internet, make the consumer less accessible, and force companies into a more integrated approach towards a fragmented and increasingly interactive communications situation which will make marketing communications more credible and more convincing.

Decision-making units are increasingly complex, implying that they have to be reached by means of different communications tools and channels.

One of the trends in marketing today is the increasing importance of building customer loyalty instead of attracting and seducing new customers. This trend towards relationship marketing implies a much more 'soft sell' approach. Integrated marketing communications focus upon building a long-term relationship with target groups by means of consistent interactive communications, rather than aggressively persuading the consumer to buy a company's products.

Finally, markets are becoming increasingly global. Phenomena such as the internet, but also the globalisation of mass media and the increasing exposure of consumers and stakeholders to international communication stimuli, increase the need for consistency in everything the company communicates in all countries in which it markets its products.[24]

Barriers to integrated communications

Integrated marketing communications are far from a reality in most companies. A number of strong barriers prevent IMC being implemented quickly and efficiently. They are listed in Figure 1.1.

Over many years companies have grown used to extreme specialisation in marketing communications. The various instruments of the communications mix are managed by separate individuals or departments. Traditionally, the strategic power is the exclusive

Figure 1.1 Barriers to integrated marketing communications

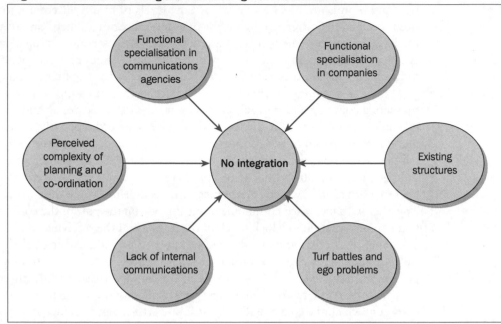

domain of advertising, PR is largely reactive, and sales promotion and personal selling are mainly tactical. Specialisation is rewarded and highly regarded, and the need for, or benefits of, integration are overlooked.

The various instruments of the communications mix have traditionally been managed by different organisational entities as discrete activities. Financial structures and frameworks have been in place for many years.[25] Often the idea of IMC is incompatible with traditional hierarchical and brand management structures. These structures may or may not be changed easily. Ideally, integrated marketing communications can best be effected when all communications activities are physically integrated into one department. But people are generally conservative and reluctant to change. Turf battles and ego problems are important barriers to IMC. The parochialism of managers and their fear of budget cutbacks in their areas of control, and of reductions in authority and power, lead to defending the status quo. PR departments especially are reluctant to integrate because they often consider IMC as the encroachment of ad people on PR professionals and a form of marketing imperialism.[26]

If not all communications activities of a company are integrated into one department, at least the sharing of information, the communications across divisions and the co-ordination of all communications activities have to be organised. Often, the combination of lack of internal communication and the perceived complexity of planning and co-ordination are important barriers to the organisation of IMC.

Finally, the functional specialisation of external communications agencies and their fragmentation in overspecialised disciplines make the full integration of communications even more cumbersome. The role of communications consultants is discussed in the following section.

Client–agency relations and IMC

Communications agencies are traditionally as functionally specialised as the various departments of the companies that hire their expertise. Besides advertising agencies there are direct marketing consultants, PR agencies, sales promotion agencies, media planning companies, internet experts, designers, etc. Companies that want to engage in integrated communications face the difficult task of choosing an agency that can offer all these fields of expertise 'under one roof' or work with a multitude of specialised agents, in which case they face the task of integrating their advice and activities. Ideally, one would expect advertising or PR consultants to evolve to 'full service' agencies that can provide all communications support in an integrated way. Although the need for an integrated approach is increasingly recognised by agencies, and more and more different communications tasks are expected from them, there are a number of structural problems. Research shows that in integrated agencies, often the advertising function is in command. In other words, the agency is not really integrated, but rather an advertising agency that accepts other communications tasks.[27] Advertising agencies and PR agencies in particular seem to perceive conflicts of interest that hamper the integration of communications functions.[28] Furthermore, there seems to be a (perceived) trade-off between the level of integration of an agency and the level of expertise provided. Companies seeking top quality expertise in different fields of marketing communications may be better off using specialised agencies and integrating their advice themselves.[29]

The question as to how the client–agent relationship in the perspective of IMC is managed at present and will be managed in the future is a matter of uncertainty and debate. Several models can be assumed:

- The company plans its integrated communications and subsequently seeks specialised external experts for each communication instrument.
- The company develops a communications plan and contacts an integrated communications agency that carries out the plan.
- The company works with one integrated communications agency. The strategic communications plan is jointly developed and the agency carries out the whole plan.
- The company develops a plan, in co-operation with one (specialised) agency (e.g. an advertising agency), and the agency subcontracts specialised PR, sales promotion, direct marketing, etc. experts.

Research does not provide an answer as to the way in which these client–agency relationships are generally organised now, or how they will evolve in the future. Each of the scenarios mentioned can be found in different companies.[30]

The integrated communications plan

The different communications tools will be used in an integrated marketing communications mix, according to a communications plan that will have to be integrated into the strategic marketing plan. The essential steps in the communications plan are shown in Table 1.5.

Since marketing communications have to be embedded in the strategic marketing plan, the first step is to analyse the marketing communications environment and the

Table 1.5 The communications plan

- Situation analysis and marketing objectives: *Why?*
- Target groups: *Who?*
- Communications objectives: *What?*
- Tools, techniques, channels and media: *How and where?*
- Budgets: *How much?*
- Measurement of results: *How effective?*

marketing strategy, and assess where the marketing communications activity should fit in. From this analysis, target groups and objectives and goals of the marketing communications effort can be derived. Next, which instruments, techniques and media to use and to what extent will be agreed. On the basis of this plan a budget can be established, and the communications plan can be implemented. Finally, the effectiveness of the campaign has to be assessed.

Summary

Integrated marketing communications are the integration of formerly specialised communications functions into one organisational system that conveys a consistent set of messages to all target audiences. Integrated marketing communications manage each point of contact between the consumer and the product or the organisation. Several key drivers of IMC can be identified, such as loss of faith in mass media advertising, the need for enhanced cost-effectiveness, media and target audience fragmentation and overlap, more complex decision-making units, the need to build customer loyalty, relationship marketing and, last but not least, the evolution of technology. The slow evolution towards IMC is caused by a number of important barriers to integration, such as the functional specialisation in companies, existing structures, the lack of internal communications and the perceived complexity of planning and co-ordination. The client–agency relationship and agency structures are profoundly impacted by the evolution towards IMC. In integrated marketing communications many instruments are used. They are embedded in a communications plan that has to be integrated in the strategic marketing plan.

Review questions

1 Give a brief overview of the instruments of the communications mix.
2 What are integrated marketing communications and in what way do they differ from 'classic' communications?
3 What are the factors that reinforce the need for integrated marketing communications, and how can the latter provide an answer to contemporary marketing communications problems?
4 What are the barriers to integrated marketing communications?
5 In what way can the communications activities of companies and external communications consultants be integrated?

Further reading

Duncan, T. (2002), *IMC. Using Advertising and Promotion to Build Brands*. McGraw-Hill Higher Education.

Gronstedt, A. (2002), *The Customer Century: Lessons from World Class Companies in Integrated Communications*. London: Routledge.

Schultz, D.E. and Kitchen, P.J. (2000), *Communicating Globally: An Integrated Marketing Approach*. Lincolnwood IL: NTC Business Books.

Case 1

Marie Jo and PrimaDonna: when luxury meets quality

Van de Velde SA, founded in 1919 in Belgium, is a famous supplier of figure-enhancing, high-quality women's lingerie. It has production operations in Hungary and Tunisia, and subcontractors in China, France and Germany. Van de Velde is market leader in the Benelux countries in the luxurious lingerie market, is one of the three main market players in the other EU countries, and is also present in the US and Southeast Asia. Perfection and quality have always been the key characteristics of Van de Velde's products. However, from the late 1970s, Van de Velde started to combine its sense of perfection and quality with elegant creativity. Since 1981 the creative line 'Marie Jo' successfully tapped into the trend of seeking for individual experiences and paying attention to one's personal charisma. The lingerie that women burnt in the 1960s became the symbol of the 'new' independent, assertive female. Meanwhile three new brands have been added: in 1990 PrimaDonna was taken over, in 1997 Marie Jo L'Aventure was launched and in 2001 Marie Jo L'Exclusive was introduced, leading Van de Velde into the top segment of the luxury lingerie market. Van de Velde believes that luxury products create their own markets:

> 'It is a characteristic of mankind to distinguish oneself through luxury, beauty and originality. Linked with quality, luxury is a hard to beat competitive advantage. This is also true or even truer when the economy is not doing very well.'

The excellent results of Van de Velde can be considered as proof of the above statement. The company realised a turnover of more than €90 million in 2002, which is an increase of 7.7% compared to 2001. Sales of Marie Jo and Marie Jo L'Exclusive increased by 6%; those of Marie Jo L'Aventure and PrimaDonna by 7.5% and 10% respectively. Except for Germany, the company is doing very well in Europe, with an average increase in turnover of 11%. In France, an increase of 17% was realised and in the US revenues were 12% higher. The most important competitors of Van de Velde in the luxury market are La Perla, Lise Charmel, Aubade, Barbara, Simone Pérèle, Chantelle and Lejaby.

Brand positioning

The luxury lingerie market in Belgium, the Netherlands, France, Germany, Switzerland, Austria and the Scandinavian countries is estimated to consist of about 40 million women, representing a market potential of about €1.5 billion. In this segment, consumers pay an average price of between €50 and €90 per item. However, even in the segment of the luxury lingerie market, subsegments can be discerned. Therefore, Van de Velde designs, produces and commercialises different brands, of which each has its own unique style and each is clearly positioned in different subsegments of the market (see Case Table 1.1).

In 2002, Marie Jo accounted for 42% of the company's revenues; PrimaDonna for 41%, Marie Jo L'Aventure for 17% and Marie Jo L'Exclusive for 1%. Every year 300 new products are introduced under these four brand names. All of the products are consistently communicated with the value propositions shown in Case Table 1.1, season after season, year after year.

Integrated marketing communications

Van de Velde uses through-the-line communications to try to reach both specialty lingerie retailers and the end consumer. About 8% of the turnover is spent

Case Table 1.1
Van de Velde's brand portfolio

Marie Jo	Refined, luxurious and fashionable. Women mainly buy it to please themselves, but partly also to please their partner. It is a brand for self-conscious, ambitious and assertive women. It is the *accessible luxury* product line.
Marie Jo L'Aventure	*Pure and minimalist*, without frills, represents a young and dynamic lifestyle. It is a brand for extrovert, energetic, spontaneous and pure young women looking for *sober lingerie*.
Marie Jo L'Exclusive	Extreme creativity and glamour, it is a chic, extravagant product line. It reflects distant, unattainable luxury and *glamour*.
PrimaDonna	*Fashion* and luxury *for larger cups* (up to H cups). Besides luxury and fashion, fit and comfort are the main benefits.

on marketing communications. The communication objectives can be defined as creating awareness for its products by means of informing the consumer about new collections as well as building a strong brand by creating a unique brand image. Throughout Europe a consistent marketing communications approach is used: both the same message and the same MC tools are employed. Obviously different tools are used depending on the two broad target groups: retailers and consumers.

Retailer communications. Thirty-eight sales representatives have direct contact with 4,000 specialty lingerie retailers. To keep the retailers motivated, their concerns are always taken into account. For example, instead of using the website to sell lingerie, Van de Velde lists the retailers' addresses where Van de Velde products are for sale. Moreover, Van de Velde prints brochures on which the retailer can put his or her address before it is distributed to the consumers. Retailers receive 1,500 free brochures to distribute amongst their (potential) customers. If they want more than 1,500 they have to pay for them. For every brand and every season a different brochure is produced.

Besides brochures, Van de Velde's communications mix directed to retailers consists of mailings, point-of-sales material (such as posters, pancartes, books), support in local advertising, retailer contests and retailer visits by the sales representatives. For example, twice a year a multi-brand mailing containing a Newsmagazine per brand is sent to all 4,000 retailers. This way retailers are informed in advance of when, where and what will appear in the media, in the brochures and POS communication. In between the winter and summer seasons, another mailing is sent. This means that at least four times a year, every retailer receives some information on the Van de Velde brands. Van de Velde tries to establish close relationships with its retailers and tries to be as prominent in the stores as possible. In the luxury lingerie market women first decide on which store to visit, and afterwards they decide on the brand. Therefore, in-store communications and being present with as many brands as possible is very important. Even so, it is not profitable to try to build a good relationship with every store. In view of the size of the retailer group and the costs involved in establishing good relationships, Van de Velde segments its retailers according to their value to the company. First of all, an individual retailer value is calculated based on the retailer's turnover, age of customers, number of employees, size of window, location, etc. Next, a product value is computed: how much of the individual Van de Velde brands are sold by the retailer, how much of the collection is sold, etc. Thirdly, a communication value is computed on the basis of the retailer's response to diverse marketing communications actions undertaken by Van de Velde, such as previous direct mail actions, Van de Velde's newsletter, whether point-of-sales material was actually used or not, etc. This segmentation is taken into account for fine-tuning the MC support: the higher the value of the retailers to Van de Velde, the higher the marketing communications investments.

Consumer communications. Van de Velde's main communications tool is its brochure. This is used both as a tool for action (purchase response on seeing the new collection) and image (brand building) communication. Besides distributing brochures by means of the retailers, Van de Velde uses its brochures to advertise in women's and lifestyle magazines. In this case, a brochure is inserted in a magazine or a gatefoldencart (showing retailer pictures and addresses) is used. In France and Finland this brochure contains all four brands instead of just one brand. For this type of magazine advertising, Van de Velde opts for reach instead of frequency, meaning it reaches many women of the target group once instead of reaching a limited part of the target group frequently. Moreover, the choice of magazines is also very important. Van de Velde opts for magazines that are selective on the target group, meaning that they avoid mass magazines but go for magazines of which the readers resemble Van de Velde's target group of the upper-upper-class (see Case Table 1.2).

Another communications tool targeted at the end consumer is the website. The website is mainly used as an information channel to support the brand and the collection. Therefore, every season the site is updated. However, the website is also an interactive communications tool in the sense that visitors can send e-cards (with nice pictures of models wearing one of Van de Velde's brands) or can order gift cheques. For the gift cheques visitors can click through to local dealers. Moreover, men who would like to give their partner a nice lingerie gift, but do not know her size, can find some tips on the site for calculating the right size.

Of Van de Velde's total communications budget, about 60% is spent on the brochures and consumer advertising, 20% goes to retailer communication (direct mailings) and another 20% is spent on point-of-sales communications and local media to support retailers.

Communications effectiveness

Van de Velde realises that the way to achieve effective communications is using the same claims, the same tone of voice, the same positioning and the same values for the same brand, season after season, year after year. Moreover, every communications tool, be it a poster, a brochure, a website or a magazine ad, has to be consistent with the brand's value proposition. Although every year 300 new products are launched under the Marie Jo, Marie Jo L'Exclusive, Marie Jo L'Aventure and PrimaDonna brand names, the style is very recognisable to consumers. Every Marie Jo picture, for example, is shot in the studio, and the model will always look into the camera, while every PrimaDonna ad is shot on an external location, stressing more the fashion and creative appeal (Plate 1). This integrated marketing communications approach clearly pays off. In 1998 the impact of a Marie Jo booklet in *Feeling* was compared to an average Belgian print ad. The Marie Jo insert was well recognised, people's knowledge of which brand the booklet was for was above average (attribution), the booklet was liked, and was considered original and informative (see Case Figure 1.1).

In other countries the communications also seem to be effective. A 2002 communications analysis carried out by the German magazine *Brigitte* reveals that over the years Marie Jo has increased in awareness, liking and actual purchase (see Case Figure 1.2).

The fact that Van de Velde uses the right advertising appeal for its target groups is also evident from the 2003 impact scores of two ads that appeared in *Gala*. Nine out of ten French consumers had seen at least one of the two ads. Moreover, the ad really made the consumers want to buy Marie Jo (see Case Table 1.3).

This case study shows the power of integrating marketing communications tools targeted at retailers and consumers and doing this in a consistent way over the years.

Case Table 1.2
Magazine use in selected countries

Country	Magazines used in 2002
Austria	Cosmopolitan, Marie Claire, Elle, Gala, Brigitte, Amica
Belgium	Gael, Feeling, Weekend Knack, Nouveau, Elle, Cosmopolitan, Marie Claire, Loving You
Denmark	Cosmopolitan Inland, Marie Claire Inland, Elle Inland, Gala, Femina, Eurowoman
France	Gala, Madame Figaro, Point de Vue
Germany	Brigitte Inland, Cosmopolitan Inland, Marie Claire Inland, Elle Inland, Gala
Luxemburg	Femmes Magazine, Info Magazine
Netherlands	Nouveau, Elle, Cosmopolitan, Marie Claire, Feeling, Loving You, Body Perfection
Switzerland	Femina
UK	Elle, Cosmopolitan

Case Figure 1.1 Impact scores of a 1998 Marie Jo booklet in *Feeling*

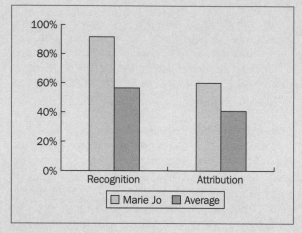

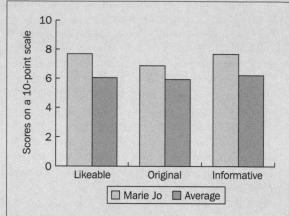

Case Figure 1.2

Brand potential of Marie Jo in Germany

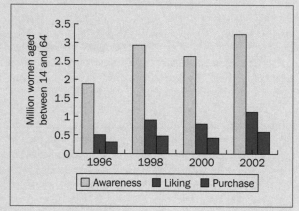

Questions

1 Evaluate the communications mix Van de Velde uses to reach its consumers. What do you think of the type and number of different communications tools that are used?

2 Considering the four brands in Van de Velde's portfolio, would you advise the company to use a different communications mix for some of the brands? Would some or all of the brands benefit from another approach?

3 Should Van de Velde try harder to establish a relationship with the end consumers? If so, how could it do that?

4 Does Van de Velde use an appropriate marketing communications mix to communicate with its retailers? What are the strong and weak points of its approach?

5 Do you think it was a good idea to extend the Marie Jo brand (Marie Jo L'Exclusive, Marie Jo L'Aventure) or would it have been better to launch the latter products under a completely different brand name?

Sources: http://profiles.wisi.com/profiles/scripts/corpinfo.asp?cusip=C056C8040; Annual Report 2002; www.mariejo.com; Information provided by Geert Neutens, Artex Marketing & Communication.

Case Table 1.3 Impact scores of *Gala* ads

Ad	Seen	Read	Like	Ad fits magazine	Makes me want to buy
Marie Jo 1	88	48	81	84	73
Marie Jo 2	85	50	92	88	85
Average apparel	84	46	66	80	50
Average all sectors	80	43	62	78	48

* Cells are percentages.

References

1 American Marketing Association (1985).

2 Schultz, D.E., Tannenbaum, S.I. and Lauterborn, R.F. (1992), *Integrated Marketing Communication: Putting it Together and Making it Work*. Lincolnwood, IL: NTC Business Books.

3 Duncan, T.R. and Everett, S.E. (1993), 'Client Perceptions of Integrated Marketing Communication', *Journal of Advertising Research* (May/June), 30–9.

4 Duncan, T.R. and Everett, S.E. (1993), 'Client Perceptions of Integrated Marketing Communication', *Journal of Advertising Research* (May/June), 30–9.

5 Payne, A. and Holt, S. (2001), 'Diagnosing Customer Value: Integrating the Value Process and Relationship Marketing', *British Journal of Management*, 12, 159–82.

6 Englis, B.G. and Solomon, M.R. (1996), 'Using Consumption Constellations to Develop Integrated Communication Strategies', *Journal of Business Research*, 37, 183–91.

7 Schultz, D.E. (1996), 'The Inevitability of Integrated Communication', *Journal of Business Research*, 37, 139–46.

8 Englis, B.G. and Solomon, M.R. (1996), 'Using Consumption Constellations to Develop Integrated Communication Strategies', *Journal of Business Research*, 37, 183–91.

9 Garber, L.G. and Dotson, M.J. (2002), 'A Method for the Selection of Appropriate Business-to-Business Integrated Marketing Communications Mixes', *Journal of Marketing Communications*, 8(1), 1–18.

10 Based on: van Raaij, W.F. (1998), 'Integratie van Communicatie: vanuit de zender of vanuit de ontvanger?' ('Integration of Communication: Starting from the sender or the receiver?'), in Damoiseaux, V.M.G., van Ruler, A.A. and Weisink, A., *Effectiviteit in Communicatiemanagement (Effectiveness in Communication Management)*. Deventer: Samson, 169–84.

11 Zinkhan, G.M. and Watson, R.T. (1996), 'Advertising Trends: Innovation and the Process of Creative Destruction', *Journal of Business Research*, 37, 163–71.

12 Evans, C.R. (1994), *Marketing Channels. Infomercials and the Future of Televised Marketing*, Englewood Cliffs, NJ: Prentice Hall.

13 De Pelsmacker, P. and Roozen, I. (1993), 'Trends in Marketingtechnieken van Vandaag' ('Trends in Marketing Techniques Today'), *No Ideas No Marketing, congresverslagen 12e congres van Stiching Marketing*, 75–88.

14 Stewart, D.W. (1996), 'Market-Back Approach to the Design of Integrated Communications Programs: A Change in Paradigm and a Focus on Determinants of Success', *Journal of Business Research*, 37, 147–53.

15 'Televisiepubliciteit in één knipoog' ('TV Advertising in one Eye Glance'), *De Morgen*, 20 August 1998.

16 'Gratis computers in ruil voor reclame' ('Free Computers in Exchange for Advertising'), *De Morgen*, 15 February 1999.

17 'Gezocht: publiek dat zichzelf vermenigvuldigt' ('Wanted: Audience that Multiplies Itself'), *Het Nieuwsblad*, 3 October 1998.

18 'Als het aan de kat lag, keek ze televisie' ('If it Depends on the Cat, then she Watches Television'), *De Morgen*, 28 January 1999.

19 *De Morgen*, 4 August 2001.

20 *De Morgen*, 22 February 2003.

21 Schultz, D.E., Tannenbaum, S.I. and Lauterborn, R.F. (1992), *Integrated Marketing Communications: Putting it Together and Making it Work*. Lincolnwood IL: NTC Business Books.

22 Low, G.S. (2000), 'Correlates of Integrated Marketing Communications', *Journal of Advertising*, 40, 27–39; Liechty, J., Ramaswamy, V. and Cohen, S.H. (2001), 'Choice Menus for Mass Customisation: An Experimental Approach for Analysing Customer Demand with an Application to a Web-based Information Service', *Journal of Marketing Research*, 38, 183–96.

23 Schultz, D.E. (1996), 'The Inevitability of Integrated Communication', *Journal of Business Research*, 37, 139–46.

24 Schultz, D.E. and Kitchen, P.J. (2000), *Communicating Globally: An Integrated Marketing Approach*. Lincolnwood IL: NTC Business Books.

25 For a discussion of the structural relationship between PR and advertising departments in organisations, see Grunig, J.A. and Grunig, L.A. (1998), 'The Relationship Between Public Relations and Marketing in Excellent Organisations: Evidence from the IABC Study', *Journal of Marketing Communications*, 4(3), 141–62.

26 Hutton, J.H. (1996), 'Integrated Marketing Communication and the Evolution of Marketing Thought', *Journal of Business Research*, 37, 155–62.

27 Mitchell, H. (1997), 'Client Perception of Integrated Marketing Communication', in De Pelsmacker, P. and Geuens, M. (eds), *The Changing World of Corporate and Marketing Communication. Proceedings of the 2nd International Conference on Marketing and Corporate Communication*. Antwerp: RUCA, 197–204.

28 Ewing, M.T., De Bussy, N.M. and Caruana, A. (2000), 'Perceived Agency Politics and Conflicts of Interest as Potential Barriers to IMC Orientation', *Journal of Marketing Communications*, 6(2), 107–19.

29 Gronstedt, A. and Thorsen, E. (1996), 'Five Approaches to Organise an Integrated Marketing Communication Agency', *Journal of Advertising Research*, (March/April), 48–58.

30 Borremans, T. (1998), 'Integrated (Marketing) Communication in Practice. Survey among Communication, Public Relations and Advertising Agencies in Belgium', in Kitchen, P.J., *The Changing World of Corporate and Marketing Communication: Towards the Next Millennium. Proceedings of the Third International Conference on Marketing and Corporate Communication*. Glasgow: Strathclyde Graduate Business School, 66–75.

Chapter 2
How marketing communications work

Chapter outline

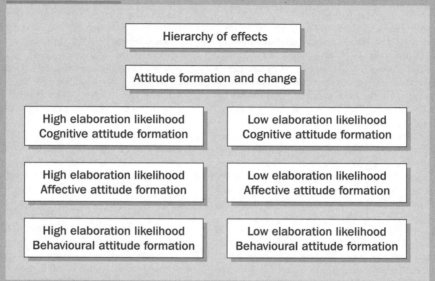

Hierarchy of effects

Attitude formation and change

High elaboration likelihood
Cognitive attitude formation

Low elaboration likelihood
Cognitive attitude formation

High elaboration likelihood
Affective attitude formation

Low elaboration likelihood
Affective attitude formation

High elaboration likelihood
Behavioural attitude formation

Low elaboration likelihood
Behavioural attitude formation

Chapter objectives

This chapter will help you to:

- Get an idea of how hierarchy-of-effects models describe how communications works
- Understand the importance of attitude formation in the consumer persuasion process
- Distinguish the basic types of attitude formation and change processes and marketing communications models
- Learn about the importance of elaboration likelihood and cognitive, affective and behavioural processes for marketing communications

Introduction

Often it is hard to predict how a consumer will respond to advertising or how someone will process a communications message. Several factors have an impact on this: consumer goals, the product type, the situation the consumer is in (hurried or distracted by others, for example), involvement in the product category, and social, psychological or cultural factors. In this chapter an overview of the different ways in which a consumer might process marketing communications is given. One type of explanatory framework that has dominated the marketing communications literature for decades is the hierarchy-of-effects models. Later, modifications of these models were presented, and the focus has shifted towards attitude formation models of response to marketing communications. Consumer involvement and cognitive, affective and behavioural aspects of message processing have been studied intensively. One thing we have learnt so far is that no single theory can explain it all. Some models are applicable in some situations for some kinds of people and for some categories of products.

Hierarchy-of-effects models

Hierarchy-of-effects models[1] are some of the oldest marketing communications models. The first was published in 1898, and their influence on marketing thought remained important until the 1980s. In general, a hierarchy-of-effects model assumes that things have to happen in a certain order, implying that the earlier effects form necessary conditions in order for the later effects to occur.[2] According to these models, consumers go through three different stages in responding to marketing communications, namely a cognitive, an affective and a conative stage, or a think–feel–do sequence. During the **cognitive stage** consumers engage in mental (thinking) processes which lead to awareness and knowledge of the brand communicated. In the **affective stage** emotional or feeling responses occur which are associated with the advertised brand and attitudes towards the brand are formed. A difference with the previous stage is that consumers may become aware and gather information continuously and effortlessly, while affective reactions may only be formed when the need for an evaluation arises. The **conative or behavioural stage** refers to undertaking actions with respect to the advertised brand, such as buying it.

Consumers are assumed to go through the three stages in a well-defined sequence. The majority of the hierarchy models claim a cognitive–affective–conative sequence. In other words, consumers should first learn or become aware of a brand such as Fitness breakfast cereal, for instance. Afterwards they develop affective responses or form an attitude towards Fitness, which might be that Fitness is tasty and healthy. Finally, this feeling or attitude makes the consumers want to buy Fitness. The task of marketing communications is then to lead the consumers through these successive stages. Table 2.1 gives some examples of hierarchy models that follow this traditional sequence. The Lavidge and Steiner model is the one most frequently referred to in the literature.

However, a lot of disagreement exists regarding the sequence of the different stages, and several researchers have developed alternative models. An example is the 'low

Table 2.1 Hierarchy-of-effects models

Year	Model	Cognitive	Affective	Conative
1900	AIDA, St Elmo Lewis	Attention	Interest, desire	Action
1911	AIDAS, Sheldon	Attention	Interest, desire	Action, satisfaction
1921	AIDCA, Kitson	Attention	Interest, desire, conviction	Action
1961	ACCA (or DAGMAR), Colley	Awareness, comprehension	Conviction	Action
1961	**Lavidge and Steiner**	**Awareness, knowledge**	**Liking, preference, conviction**	**Purchase**
1962	AIETA, Rogers	Awareness	Interest, evaluation	Trial, adoption
1971	ACALTA, Robertson	Awareness, comprehension	Attitude, legitimation	Trial, adoption

Based on: Barry, T.E. and Howard, D.J. (1990), 'A Review and Critique of the Hierarchy of Effects in Advertising', *International Journal of Advertising*, 9, 121–35.

involvement' hierarchy according to which consumers, after frequent exposure to marketing messages, might buy the product, and decide afterwards how they feel about it (cognitive–conative–affective hierarchy). Another possibility is that consumers' affective responses towards a product lead them to buy it and, if necessary, they reflect on it later. This would suggest an affective–conative–cognitive sequence.

Vaughn[3] proposed an integration of the different sequence models and presented a model, known as the Foot–Cone–Belding (FCB) grid. Four different situations are distinguished, based on two dimensions, i.e. the high–low involvement and the think–feel dimension. **Involvement** can be defined as the importance people attach to a product or a buying decision, the extent to which one has to think it over and the level of perceived risk associated with an inadequate brand choice. The **think–feel** dimension represents a continuum reflecting the extent to which a decision is made on a cognitive or an affective basis. Here Vaughn takes into account that for certain products such as sugar, mineral water, paper towels, soap and banks, cognitive elements are important, while for products such as cakes, ice cream and perfume, affective elements seem to have more impact on the buying decision process. For example, consumers may wonder whether they are running out of water, or whether they will need paper towels during the next week. This is in contrast to considerations such as what to buy the children for a treat: Kinder Delight or chocolate mousse? In Figure 2.1 the different sequences in each of the four situations are shown.

Purchase decisions in quadrant one are characterised by high involvement and rational decision criteria. Here, the consumer first wants to learn about the product. This could be the case for deciding on an insurance policy or a loan or for buying a new computer or major household appliances. In this quadrant the classical hierarchy of effects would hold. The second quadrant concerns product decisions of high involvement, but for which less information is needed. In this case, the consumer first wants to be emotionally attracted by the brand image, then he or she collects information, and finally undertakes some action. Jewellery, perfume, fashion and holidays may be

Figure 2.1 The FCB grid

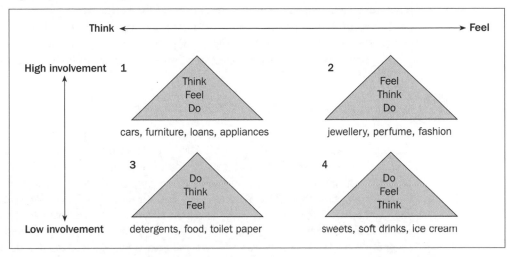

Based on: Vaughn, R. (1980), 'How Advertising Works: A Planning Model', *Journal of Advertising Research*, 20(5), 27–33. Reproduced with permission of ARF, New York.

examples that fit in this category. In the third quadrant product decisions are located that require a minimum of cognitive effort and tend to become routinised because of habit formation. The assumed sequence is first buying the product, then learning what its major advantages and disadvantages are, and finally developing an attitude after product or brand usage. Toilet paper, sugar, paper tissues and detergents are expected to be bought without much reflection and only after product experience will an attitude be formed. The fourth quadrant reflects decision-making regarding products which can be termed 'life's little pleasures'. The assumed sequence here is: buy the product, experience an affective response and gather product knowledge afterwards. Examples that fit this category might be soft drinks, ice cream and chocolate bars. For example, consumers buy cake or pizza, eat it and realise that they are really fond of it, but learn afterwards that it makes them fat.

The Rossiter–Percy Grid is an alternative to, or a modification of, the FCB grid which again classifies products and buying decisions in four categories, based on the dimensions high–low involvement and fulfilling a transformational or informational buying motive.[4] Transformational buying motives consist of positive motivations, such as sensory gratification, social approval or intellectual stimulation, while informational buying motives refer to reducing or reversing negative motivations such as solving or avoiding a problem, or normal depletion. Examples of products for which transformational motives prevail are products that give consumers pleasure such as ice cream, cosmetics and perfume. Examples of products purchased on the basis of informational motives are detergents, babies' nappies and insurance products.

The advantage of hierarchy-of-effects models and related frameworks is that they incorporate what is their most important contribution, i.e. the recognition of the importance of brand awareness. Hierarchy-of-effects models consider brand awareness as a prerequisite for brand attitude formation. They correctly assume that affective responses cannot be formed or that a purchase cannot take place without having an awareness of the brand. In this respect, it should be mentioned that most companies strive to reach Top-of-Mind Awareness (TOMA) in consumers. TOMA indicates which brand is most salient within a product category. It reflects the first brand that comes to mind when thinking of a particular product category. It is generally acknowledged that brands that are top of mind are more likely to be purchased.

Stabilo goes for image instead of price

The felt pen manufacturer Stabilo, whose margins were being squeezed, carried out a European study among youngsters aged between 12 and 24 years old to investigate its brand awareness and brand image. Contrary to expectations, felt pens did not appear to be a low involvement product, but are considered as an expression of one's personality. Youngsters appeared to consider the possession of the Point 88 as a status symbol. The latter made clear that joining the competitors in a price war would be a poor choice for Stabilo. Instead Stabilo decided to invest in reinforcement of the brand. The fact that Stabilo had not run any communications campaigns for several years was an advantage since youngsters saw this as a sign of self-confidence and superiority. Stabilo decided to use a coded language in its advertising. The product was never shown. In this way the message may not have been comprehensible to non-targets, but it made the message more appealing to the opinion leaders in certain communities. Stabilo's turnover increased by 30% due to its successful campaign.[5]

Notwithstanding the important contribution of the classical hierarchy models, several shortcomings have been formulated. A major critique is that empirical support for the fact that consumers go through each stage is still lacking. Significant relations have been observed between ad characteristics and recall, and between ad characteristics and attitudes and purchase intentions, but not between recall and attitudes. This leads to the conclusion that, empirically, no hierarchy of cognitive, affective and conative effects can be observed.[6] Furthermore, hierarchy models do not allow interactions between the different stages, which is very unlikely. Purchase will lead to experience, which will have an important impact on beliefs and attitudes, for example. Therefore, to base marketing communications on hierarchy-of-effects models may not be the most effective or relevant strategy.

Attitude formation and change

Since the 1980s, attitudes have received more and more attention. Attitudes can be defined as a person's overall evaluation of an object, a product, a person, an organisation, an ad, etc. In this view, an attitude towards a particular brand (Ab) can be considered as a measure of how much a person likes or dislikes the brand, or of the extent to which he or she holds a favourable or unfavourable view of it. The reason for this interest in, for example, brand attitudes is the belief that the more favourable brand attitudes are, the more likely a purchase of the brand becomes. Although brand attitudes are relatively stable, they can be changed over time. So, the ultimate challenge for marketing communications is to change attitudes in favour of the company's brand.

Figure 2.2 Attitude components

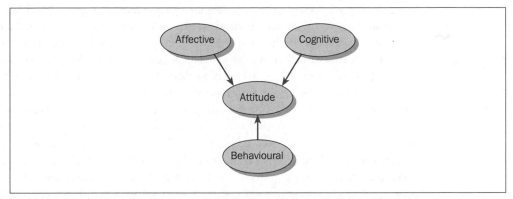

Attitudes play an important role in hierarchy-of-effects models too, but in these models they are primarily defined as affective reactions in a hierarchical setting. In fact, an attitude can be assumed to consist of three components (Figure 2.2).[7] The **cognitive component** reflects knowledge, beliefs and evaluations of the object; the **affective component** represents the feelings associated with the object; and the **behavioural component** refers to action readiness (behavioural intentions) with respect to the object.

An example may clarify the distinct components. You may love Timberland shoes (affective component) because you know they are durable and convenient to wear (cognitive component) and that's why you intend to buy Timberland the next time you go shopping (behavioural component). To change attitudes, marketeers might concentrate on changing one of the three components. Gap might stress the fact their clothes are neat, cool and stylish, thereby trying to influence the feelings associated with it by image-building. Communications campaigns trying to influence the consumer on an affective basis often use emotional ads containing no or very few product arguments. Miele might address the quality and durability of its appliances to change consumers' beliefs and evaluations. Marketing communications will probably use many and strong arguments to illustrate the numerous benefits of Miele. Coca-Cola might run a promotion campaign in which consumers can receive a fabulous Coke mobile phone or a Coke sofa in return for a certain amount of cola caps, to induce consumers to buy (a lot of) the brand.

As mentioned before, consumers follow different processes. Not surprisingly, a lot of communications models have been developed, most of them giving an adequate explanation for particular situations only. These different communications models regarding attitude formation and attitude change can be classified along two dimensions.[8] The first refers to the way attitudes are formed – primarily cognitive, affective or behavioural; the second is about the level of elaboration of a message, or central-route versus peripheral-route processing.

Broadly stated, these dimensions are comparable to the ones used in the FCB grid, but no hierarchical conclusions are derived from them. The think–feel dimension of the FCB grid is transformed into a distinction between cognitive, affective and behavioural attitude formation. The involvement dimension of the FCB grid is extended to motivation, ability and opportunity (MAO). By **motivation** a willingness to engage in behaviour, make decisions, pay attention, process information, etc. is meant. Motivation is to a large extent influenced by consumer needs and goals. Consumer needs can be categorised as functional, symbolic or hedonic.[9] Functional needs can be compared to the informational motivation dimension of the Rossiter–Percy Grid and pertain to solving consumer problems. Consumers buy detergents to clean dirty clothes and hire a baby-sitter because they cannot leave their baby unattended. Symbolic needs relate to how we see ourselves and how we would like to be perceived by others. Youngsters may wear Calvin Klein jeans to show they are trendy. Hedonic needs reflect consumers' desires for sensory pleasure. Many tourists buy Belgian chocolates when visiting Belgium because of the delicious taste. Needs/goals can also be classified as approach or promotion goals, and avoidance or prevention goals.[10] The former pertain to positive outcomes while the latter relate to avoiding negative outcomes. For example, consumers can decide to shop at Carrefour because it offers them a nice shopping experience (= approach, promotion) or because they do not have to drive far (= avoidance, prevention). A consumer who plans to buy a new car is probably motivated to process marketing communications on cars. However, the needs or higher order goals that this particular consumer is pursuing have an important impact on information processing and the benefits he or she is receptive to.[11] If the consumer is mainly driven by functional needs, he or she may want clear information on price, safety, fuel consumption, etc., while a status appeal or an ad showing driving sensations may be more effective when symbolic or hedonic needs prevail. The same goes for approach/promotion goals and avoidance/prevention goals: when the former are prevalent then marketing communications should bring a message focussed on positive outcomes (you feel the excitement when driving this car), while for the latter goals a message should emphasise negative outcomes (the excellent air bags will protect you during a crash). So, in order to be persuasive, marketing communications should tap into consumers' motivational concepts and marketers need to understand what goals consumers are trying to accomplish by buying the product.[12]

Although someone is motivated to do something, he or she may be unable to do it. **Ability** refers to the resources needed to achieve a particular goal. One may be motivated to process a computer ad, but when it is full of technical details one may not be able to process and understand it because of a lack of technical knowledge. A person may be motivated to buy a particular house, but after learning what it is going to cost after renovation, stamp duty, land registration fees, etc. might be unable to buy it because of insufficient money.

Finally, **opportunity** deals with the extent to which the situation enables a person to obtain the goal set. A consumer may be motivated to buy Danette of Danone, but if the supermarket runs out of Danette, the consumer does not have the opportunity to buy it. A consumer may be motivated to process the information of a particular ad, but if the phone rings, he or she does not have the opportunity to pay attention to it. Also, when the ad contains little or no information, it does not provide the opportunity to elaborate on it.

The effects of the MAO factors on attitude formation and marketing communications processing are presented in the **Elaboration Likelihood model** (ELM) (Figure 2.3).[13] If motivation, ability and opportunity are all high, the elaboration likelihood is said to be high and consumers are expected to engage in central-route processing. This means that they are willing to elaborate on the information, to evaluate the arguments

Figure 2.3 The Elaboration Likelihood model

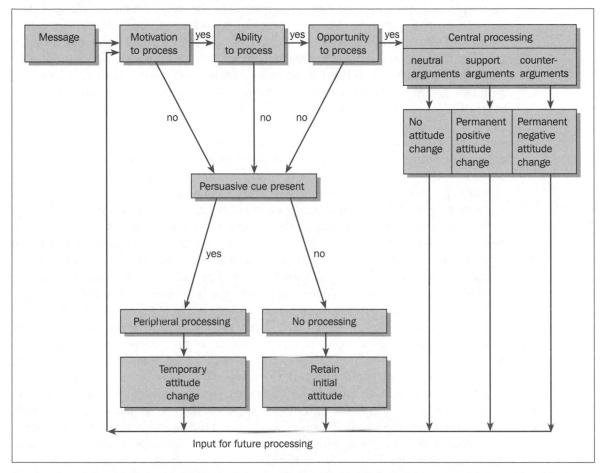

Based on: Petty, R.E. and Cacioppo, J.T. (1986), 'The Elaboration Likelihood Model of Persuasion', *Advances in Experimental Social Psychology,* 19, 123–205. Reproduced with permission of Elsevier.

and find out what the information really has to offer. Depending on the quality and credibility of the arguments, consumers will react by producing counter-, support or neutral arguments, which induce a negative, positive or no attitude change, respectively. For example, when thinking of McDonald's consumers might think of how good McDonald's burgers and fries taste: a support argument. On the other hand, consumers might also think of how unhealthy fast food is: a counter-argument. Furthermore, consumers might just think of the red and yellow colours of a McDonald's restaurant: in effect, a neutral argument. Attitudes formed via the central route prove to be good predictors of later behaviour and are fairly resistant to other persuasive messages.

On the other hand, if one or more of the MAO factors is/are low, consumers are more likely to process the information peripherally. The result of the latter is no real information processing, but an evaluation based on simple, peripheral cues, such as background music, humour, an attractive source or endorser, the number of arguments used, etc.[14] In other words, a favourable brand attitude might be formed because the consumer liked the music in a Levi's commercial or the erotic setting in a Häagen Dazs ad or because the consumer is fond of the polar bears in the Coca-Cola commercial, or because he or she assumed that the high price of the Miele washing machine is a sign of superior quality, or that French wine is invariably good. However, such attitudes do not necessarily last long. If Pepsi launches a campaign with a cute animal, a celebrity or a nice song, consumers may forget about Coca-Cola's nice polar bears and switch their attitude in favour of Pepsi. The reason why consumers start paying more attention to peripheral cues is that in many ads peripheral cues form the only processable information under circumstances of low motivation, limited ability or limited opportunity. Ads without attractive peripheral cues, but with an easy-to-process, product-related message might also work under low MAO, simply because the cognitive resources to form counter-arguments are lacking.

At first sight, the above might suggest that the central route pertains to cognitive attitude formation (people carefully think about the substance of the message), while peripheral route processing is more likely to give rise to affective attitude formation (people rely on how the ad makes them feel instead of what the ad really tells). However, reality reveals a more complicated picture. The ELM assumes that under different MAO conditions, both arguments and affect may give rise to peripheral and central (and even biased) processing. It is not so much the MAO factors, but consumers' goals that might determine whether consumers rely on the substance of the message (i.e. the strength of the claims, the compellingness of the product attributes, etc.) to form a judgement or on their affective responses (i.e. ad-evoked feelings, aesthetic of the product design, charisma of the endorser, etc.). How exactly the message substance or affective responses are processed is likely to depend on consumers' elaboration likelihood. Therefore, we distinguish six types of marketing communications models based on two dimensions (see Table 2.2). The first dimension pertains to elaboration likelihood which can be either high or low. The second dimension is related to the attitude component on which attitude formation is mainly built, i.e. cognition, affect or behaviour.

Table 2.2 Six types of attitude formation and change

		Elaboration likelihood (EL) based on motivation/involvement, ability and opportunity	
		High Elaboration *central-route processing*	*Low Elaboration* *peripheral-route processing*
Attitudes based on:	*Cognitions*	■ Multi-attribute models ■ Self-generated persuasion	■ Heuristic evaluation
	Affect	■ Feelings-as-information model	■ Ad transfer ■ Feelings transfer ■ Classical conditioning ■ Mere exposure effect
	Behaviour	■ Post-experience model ■ Perception–Experience–Memory Model	■ Reinforcement model ■ Routinised response behaviour

Multiple attribute models

Multiple attribute models are relevant if the consumer's motivation, ability and opportunity are high and especially when cognitive elements are important for attitude formation. An example is someone who is going to buy a home video installation and tries to compare objectively the different brands available on several attributes (price, sound quality, etc.) before making a decision.

The most famous multiple attribute model is no doubt the Expectancy-Value model, or Fishbein model.[15] In this model brand attitudes are made up of three elements: relevant product attributes, the extent to which one believes the brand possesses these attributes, and the evaluation of these attributes or how good/bad one thinks it is for a brand to possess these attributes. More specifically, brand attitude is represented by the sum of the products of brand beliefs and attribute evaluations:

$$A_o = \sum_{i=1}^{n} b_{oi} e_i$$

where: A_o = attitude towards object o
b_{oi} = belief of object o possessing attribute i
e_i = evaluation of attribute i
n = number of relevant attributes

In other words, since not all product attributes are equally important for a consumer, product beliefs are weighted by the importance that the consumer attaches to the different product attributes. Table 2.3 shows an example of an attitude towards going to university and going to a polytechnic. In this case, beliefs and evaluations are measured by means of a 7-point Likert scale. An example of a 7-point (going from 1 to 7 or from −3 to +3) Likert scale, is:

To what extent do you think it is difficult to succeed at university?

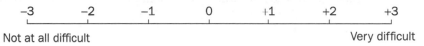

Not at all difficult   Very difficult

Table 2.3 An illustration of the Fishbein model

| | | Attitude towards going to a university/polytechnic | | | |
| | | University | | Polytechnic | |
Attribute	e_i	b_i	$e_i \times b_i$	b_i	$e_i \times b_i$
Difficulty	2	+2	+4	+1	+2
Prestige	6	+2	+12	0	0
High cost	3	+1	+3	0	0
Quality of teachers	7	+1	+7	−1	−7
Number of friends	5	−1	−5	+2	+10
High study time	3	+2	+6	0	0
Business-oriented	5	−1	−5	+1	+5
Attitude			22		10

e_i is measured on a 7-point bipolar scale (1 = bad, 7 = good)
b_i is measured on a 7-point unipolar scale (−3 = unlikely, +3 = likely)

In this example the quality of the teachers is most valued (e = 7) and the perception that it is difficult to get a degree seems to be the least important attribute (e = 2). Multiplying these evaluations by the beliefs regarding universities and polytechnics as possessing these characteristics gives the results in the fourth and sixth columns. Summing these products results in a more positive attitude towards going to a university. So, if all relevant attributes are measured and correctly evaluated, a university would eventually be chosen.

The Theory of Reasoned Action (TORA) is an extension of the Expectancy-Value model.[16] The model was developed to provide a link between attitude and behavioural intention. The latter is not only determined by attitudes, but also by subjective norm. A subjective norm is comprised of the belief one holds regarding what different reference groups consider as socially desirable behaviour, weighted by the consumer's need or willingness to behave according to the norms of the particular reference group. The latter is referred to as social sensitivity. Certain personalities are more sensitive to social pressure and, as a consequence, are more willing to comply with the rules, norms and beliefs of reference groups than others. An example of socially influenced behaviour is that, even though a child might not be particularly fond of piano lessons, it might take these lessons to please its parents. And although a teenager might not hold a favourable attitude towards smoking, he or she might do so because his or her friends regard it as 'cool' to smoke. Again, some teenagers will be more likely to let themselves be led by the opinions of others. Table 2.4 gives an illustration of how a subjective norm can influence the choice between going to university and going to a polytechnic.

The reference group valued most highly is the friends at school (ss = 6), while the sensitivity or motivation to comply with the opinion of current teachers is the lowest (ss = 3). Multiplying social sensitivity by the opinions of significant others for the different reference groups, and summing all these products, results in a subjective norm of +35 for going to university and +1, for going to a polytechnic. In view of these results as well as the results of Table 2.3, the attitude towards a university is more favourable than the attitude towards a polytechnic.

Table 2.4 An illustration of subjective norm effects

| | | Subjective norm = social sensitivity (ss) × others' opinions (oo) | | | | |
| | | University | | | Polytechnic | |
Reference group	ss_i	oo_i	$ss_i \times oo_i$		oo_i	$ss_i \times oo_i$
Friends at school	6	+2	+12		−1	−6
Friends in youth club	5	0	0		+1	+5
Friends in sports club	5	−1	−5		+1	+5
Parents	4	+2	+8		−2	−8
Family	4	+1	+4		0	0
Current teachers	3	+2	+6		0	0
Business	5	+2	+10		+1	+5
Subjective norm			**+35**			**+1**

ss_i is measured on a 7-point bipolar scale (1 = low, 7 = high)
oo_i is measured on a 7-point bipolar scale (−3 = negative, +3 = positive)

The Theory of Reasoned Action has been further extended into the Theory of Planned Behaviour (TPB).[17] This extension was necessary to be able to deal with behaviours over which people have incomplete volitional control. Indeed, behavioural intention can result in actual behaviour only if the consumers themselves can decide to perform or not perform the behaviour. For many consumer behaviours this prerequisite does not pose a problem (for example, choosing between Coke Vanilla or Coke Lemon), but often behaviour also depends on non-motivational factors, such as resources (time, money, skills, infrastructure, etc.). For example, a consumer may be willing to go to work by means of public transport, but when he or she lives in a remote village in which hardly any public transport facilities are available, this may be difficult to do. Or, a consumer and his or her significant others may hold very favourable attitudes towards buying a Lamborghini, but when this consumer lacks the money, a cheaper car will be bought in the end (so, in fact, the extension resembles the 'ability' and 'opportunity' factors of MAO). That behavioural control as perceived by the consumer is more predictive of behaviour than actual behavioural control is very important. Perceived behavioural control can be defined as 'the perceived ease or difficulty of performing the behaviour and it is assumed to reflect past experience as well as anticipated impediments and obstacles'.[18] Two individuals enrolling for a foreign language course may have equally strong intentions to learn the foreign language, but if one feels more confident than the other that he or she can master it, he or she is more likely to persevere than the one who feels less confident. Therefore, not actual control but perceived behavioural control is added to TORA to build the Theory of Planned Behaviour. Perceived behavioural control is computed by multiplying control beliefs by perceived power of the particular control belief to pose the behaviour, and the resulting products are summed across the salient control beliefs. For example, for jogging, salient control beliefs appeared to be 'being in poor physical shape' and 'living in an area with good jogging weather'. Figure 2.4 presents the TPB model graphically.

Figure 2.4 The Theory of Planned Behaviour (TPB)

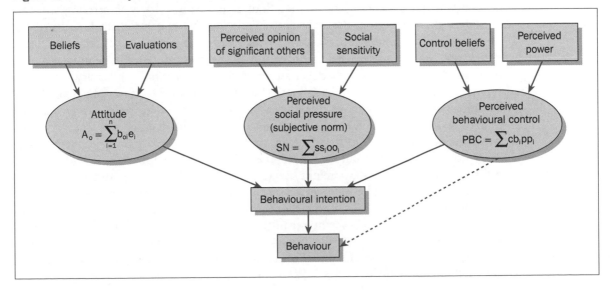

Figure 2.5 Marketing communications and the TPB model

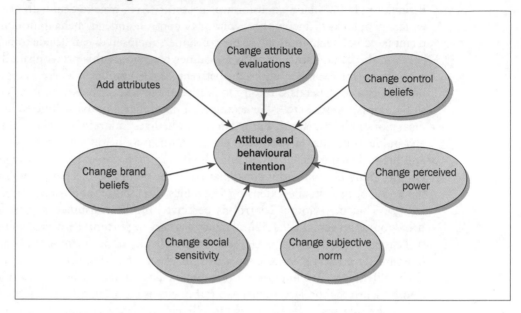

The Theory of Planned Behaviour has received considerable attention in the literature.[19] These studies deal with a variety of activities, from predicting choice of travel mode, eating and leisure behaviour, healthy lifestyle, condom use, loosing weight, etc.[20]

Based on the TPB model, marketing communicators can try to change consumers' attitudes and influence their behaviour in several different ways (Figure 2.5). First, they can try to change brand beliefs. For example, suppose a university has a reputation for granting degrees too easily and not taking the education task seriously enough. If an independent quality control committee finds that this university is offering students a good quality education, the university might use this conclusion in an advertising campaign in order to influence existing beliefs. A second possibility is changing attribute evaluations. For example, when people have the impression that a large university has to be good since it is able to attract so many students, a small university can try to change this evaluation by emphasising the benefits of small classes (more personal contact, more time per student, greater supervision, etc.). Finally, attitudes can be changed by adding attributes. For example, suppose a university has an exchange contract with foreign universities so that foreign students can take part of the courses while own students can follow courses abroad, the university can emphasise the multicultural environment. By doing so, it might create an additional attribute students take into account when choosing between universities. When Levi's, for example, saw its market share decline, it emphasised Levi's pioneering role in the jeans market and tried to add the fact that Levi's was the first jeans brand as a product attribute that consumers might consider when buying jeans. An example in the beer market is Labatt Ice which underscores the freshness of the beer rather like Cola Light claims 'you have never been refreshed like this before'.

Besides trying to change attitudes, marketers can focus on **changing the opinion of others**. To counter the increase in smoking of young girls, for example, the UK government tried to change the opinions of youngsters by means of a communications campaign of which the main message was that smoking makes you less attractive for the opposite sex. One ad pictured two pairs of kissing lips with the message 'Ever kissed a non-smoker? Taste the difference.' Changing the opinion of others is also prevalent in several children's advertisements. Marketers try to influence children's attitudes so that they start nagging for the product. For example, Kraft tries to show children that Lunchables is a cool school lunch and having it will make all other children jealous. Raising or lowering social sensitivity for specific significant others is another possibility. For example, while buying a new car used to be a decision made by the parents, Opel stresses how comfortable, exciting and cool Opel Safira is perceived by children, hoping that parents will take the opinion of their children into account when choosing a particular type and brand of car. Finally, perceived behavioural control can be influenced. Marketers could **change control beliefs** by showing how easy or convenient to use certain products are. For example, MasterCard uses the slogan 'North. South. East. West. No card is more accepted' to indicate you can pay everywhere with MasterCard (see Plate 2). Another possibility is to focus on **increasing perceived power** or the confidence of consumers that they can master the activity. Nike stresses 'Just do it', meaning that everyone can be an athlete.

Heuristic evaluation

When one of the MAO factors is low, the consumer concentrates on peripheral cues. The consumer will try to make inferences on the basis of the cue in order to form a cognitively based attitude. For example, when consumers do not have the time to compare all available brands on relevant attributes, they may infer from a high price that it is a high-quality brand and therefore form a positive attitude towards the brand. This process is called heuristic evaluation.[21] When MAO is low, central information processing is very unlikely to occur and consumers will probably process the communication peripherally. This means that they do not elaborate on the message, but try to make inferences on the basis of ad characteristics. In other words, peripheral cues in the ad are used as a heuristic cue to evaluate the quality of the message and to form a general evaluation of the brand advertised. These inferential beliefs have a significant influence on the attitude people form towards the brand. Heuristic evaluation has also been referred to as the satisficing choice process.[22] Since consumers' MAO factors are not optimal, they lack the motivation, ability or opportunity to gather and process information to find the best choice. They are not looking for direct evidence of performance superiority in this case, but settle for a satisfactory or acceptable brand choice. Therefore, they seek for reassurance or credibility in heuristic cues such as brand name reputation, experts endorsing the brand, price level, etc. Table 2.5 summarises a few ad characteristics that can be used as a heuristic cue.

Another example is the use of celebrities. The heuristic in this case might be 'if Kim Clijsters uses Sanex skin care it has to be a good brand' or 'if Anna Kournikova wears a Shock sportsbra because "only the ball should bounce", it has to be a comfortable and good bra'. However, using this approach can give rise to problems. A famous Dutch

Table 2.5 Potential heuristic cues

Characteristics	Peripheral cue	Heuristic
Source	Attractiveness Expertise Status Number of sources	The more attractive, the better The more expertise, the better The higher status, the better The more, the better
Message	Number of arguments Repetition Layout	The more, the better The more, the better The more attractive, the better
Product	Price Design Country of origin	The higher, the better The more attractive, the better German is good (cars) The Netherlands is good (cheese) Italian is good (fashion, leather)

Based on: Pieters, R. and van Raaij, F. (1992), *Reclamewerking (How Advertising Works)*. Leiden/Antwerp: Stenfert Kroese Uitgevers.

actress, Monique van de Ven, claimed in a TV commercial that she had a mortgage with FBTO, one of the largest Dutch insurance companies. Some insurance agents did not believe her, and after an investigation they found out that she had her mortgage at Aegon, FBTO's competitor. Needless to say, this created a big to-do in the Netherlands which not only harmed the image of FBTO and the actress, but may also lead to negative knock-on effects for the corporation as a whole when it seeks to advertise again. Furthermore, the practice of using false statements in advertising is actionable in court. Therefore, care should be taken that if, for example, Ronaldo announces that he always plays football wearing Nike boots, he in fact always wears Nike, for training as well as for matches. The foregoing illustrates that credibility is crucial to evoke positive cognitive responses, and as a consequence change attitudes in a favourable way.

Dolmio's use of country of origin as a peripheral cue

When Dolmio introduced its sauce to the British market in 1986, Italian food was still a novelty. By 1994, Dolmio had become market leader with a market share of 40%. Dolmio positioned its products on quality, based on the belief 'only the best will do'. However, when own-brands (private labels) were introduced with comparable, cheaper product lines, Dolmio's market share quickly fell to 33%. Meanwhile, these sauces had become more generic and more British. Research showed that it might be a good move for Dolmio to stress its Italian values. A new campaign was launched 'Take Italian Lessons', which was flexible enough to allow for new products while giving the existing products a younger image. The commercials picture an Italian family who without any doubt attach high value to product quality. The family likes to eat good and tasty food, but do not always have the time to cook. The ad shows how the Italians enjoy their meals without featuring Italian stereotypes. In 1997 Dolmio spent about €6 million increasing its market share to 36%. In 1998 Dolmio's share went up to 39%.[23]

Affect-as-Information model

Affect has long been considered as a peripheral cue, having an impact only when people have low involvement. However, it is increasingly recognised that affect may play a fundamental role in decision-making. People may judge objects by monitoring their subjective feelings to the target. The Affect-as-Information model posits that consumers may use feelings as a source of information to form an overall evaluation of a product or brand, not by means of a simple association, but through a controlled inferential process or, in other words, in an informed, deliberate and high-elaboration manner.[24] A feeling-based inference often referred to is the 'how-do-I-feel-about-it' model. According to this model, consumers evaluate brands/objects by imagining the brand in their minds and asking themselves 'How do I feel about this brand/object?' Next they infer like/dislike or satisfaction/dissatisfaction from the valence of their feelings.[25] Consumers may even infer the strength of their preference from the strength of the feelings the brand or object evokes.[26] Note that we are talking about real feelings (i.e. 'subjective experiences of affective states and responses with a somato-visceral component'), not about affective or hedonic beliefs (such as 'It would be great to spend a weekend in Stockholm').[27] These feelings can be evoked either integrally by looking at the product or imagining the product, or by a pre-existing or contextually-induced mood.[28] However, a prerequisite of the Affect-as-Information model is that when people inspect their feelings to judge a brand or object, they do not inspect their mood states at that moment, but their feelings in response to the brand or object. So, if consumers decide not to go to the movies, it is because the thought of going to the movies makes them feel unpleasant, not because they happen to be in a bad mood. As a consequence, for feelings to influence the product evaluation, they must be perceived as representative of the product, i.e. consumers must be convinced that these feelings are genuine affective responses to this product. Moreover, feelings need not only be representative, they also have to be relevant for the evaluation at hand.[29] For example, when a consumer has made an appointment to go to the dentist, the fact that he or she does not feel happy about going may not be considered to be relevant by this person, and he or she might still go. In fact, when consumers' purchase motivations are hedonic rather than functional, the likelihood that they will perceive their feelings as relevant and follow the 'how-do-I-feel-about-it' model is much more likely.[30]

It should be obvious that feelings should not be assigned a heuristic or peripheral role here. Under high elaboration likelihood, people use their feelings because they believe they contain valuable information. When consumers closely scrutinise the arguments in a message, mood and ad-evoked emotions can be considered as an argument or a central cue.[31] One way to elicit strong ad-evoked feelings is to make consumers think of pleasant things in the past, such as the birth of a baby, a wedding, a first romance, etc. Another way is to use nostalgic ads. Nostalgic ads make use of music, movie stars, fashion products, symbols or styles that were popular during a consumer's youth. Research has indicated that early experience performs a determining role in shaping subsequent preferences and that they actually can influence consumers' lifelong preferences.[32] For example, it has been shown that consumers retain a lifelong attachment to the styles of popular music they experienced in their late teens and early twenties.

Aad and feelings transfer

While central-route processing and cognitively based attitude formation predominated in the 1960s and 1970s, models characterised by peripheral processing of mainly affective elements have received a lot of attention in the 1990s. The attitude towards the ad (Aad) and feelings transfer, classical conditioning and the mere exposure effect are some models that have been frequently referred to in the literature.

From the 1980s onwards, research on low involvement, affective processing has boomed. The conclusion of this research was that both brand attitude (Ab) and purchase intention were influenced not only by brand beliefs, but also to a great extent by the attitude towards the ad. When consumers feel indifferent towards the available brands as a consequence of low brand differentiation or insignificant consequences of a non-optimal choice, their choice goal is likely to be to buy the first brand that they like.[33]

Ad likeability might be an important factor because of its ability to attract attention and facilitate information processing. Peripheral cues such as humour, music, animals and children may attract attention, induce curiosity which lead consumers to watch the whole ad, and induce a favourable Aad which can lead to a favourable Ab.

Japp pushes you further

One of the commercials for the snack Japp features a reggae man singing in his small truck, while driving on a mountain road. Suddenly he sees a man doing stretching exercises while putting his hands on his new, red Porsche. The Porsche is parked near a canyon and the hands on the car give the impression that the man is pushing the car. The reggae man, helpful as he is, stops his truck and gives the stretching man a hand, the result of which is that the Porsche falls into the canyon. The reggae man thinks he has done the man a big favour, gets back into his truck satisfied, and happily proceeds on his way eating a Japp. The baseline is 'Japp. Pushes you further'. The accompanying music, the faces of the participants and the end result make the ad very funny. These peripheral cues may lead people to like the ad, and this favourable evaluation might transfer to the brand, increasing the likelihood of buying Japp.

The Aad transfer model receiving most empirical support is the **dual mediation model** (Figure 2.6).[34] According to this model the evaluation of the ad not only has an immediate impact on the evaluation of the brand, but also an indirect effect on brand attitude via brand cognitions.

The reasoning behind this model is that consumers who hold a positive attitude towards the communication are more likely to be receptive to arguments in favour of the brand advertised. For example, if you like the Frisk commercial in which a cook accidentally drops a Frisk in an aquarium, a fish eats it and gets so much energy out of it that he jumps into the next aquarium, then the next and at the end out of the window, you might be less inclined to think of counter-arguments, or you might find yourself thinking of more support arguments (e.g. Frisk gives energy, Frisk is refreshing) because you think the commercial is clever, original and humorous.

Figure 2.6 Dual mediation hypothesis

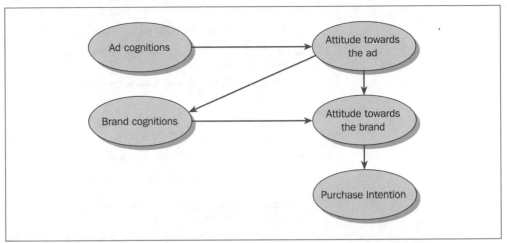

Based on: MacKenzie S.B., Lutz, R.J. and Belch, G.E. (1986), 'The Role of Attitude Toward the Ad as a Mediator of Advertising Effectiveness: A Test of Competing Explanations', *Journal of Marketing Research*, 23, 131. Reproduced with permission of American Marketing Association.

The power of ad likeability

The conclusions of a study in which consumer responses were measured to all ads that were on air in Belgium in two consecutive years are:[35]

■ Emotions are more effective than information.

■ If consumers see emotions, they will feel your ad.

■ If they feel something while they see your commercial, they will like it.

■ If they like your ad, they will like you.

■ If they like you, they will buy you.

In line with the foregoing, some researchers suggest that the feelings an ad evokes may be transferred to the attitude towards the ad, the brand attitude and the purchase intention without much deliberation.[36] Why consider ad-evoked feelings? Several studies show that people in a positive mood make decisions more quickly, use less information, avoid systematic processing, evaluate everything more positively, accept a persuasive message more easily and pay less attention to details.[37]

A study investigating 23,000 responses to 240 advertisements shows that ad-evoked feelings (pleasure, arousal, dominance) explained 3% to 30% of the variance in brand interest and purchase intention while brand knowledge and beliefs explained 2% to 13%.[38] The magnitude of the influence of ad-evoked feelings depends on the product category advertised, the specific feelings that are evoked and the type of ad that is tested.

Emotional conditioning can be considered an extreme case of feelings transfer, and is based on Pavlov's classic conditioning theory.[39] When dogs see food they begin to salivate. This is called an unconditioned response since it happens automatically. By frequently pairing a conditioned stimulus (a bell) with an unconditioned stimulus (meat

Figure 2.7 Emotional conditioning at work

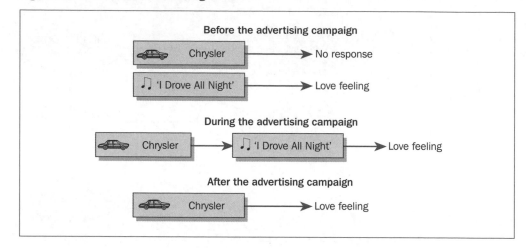

powder), Pavlov was able to get dogs salivating just by hearing the bell (conditioned response). In a marketing context, communications practitioners sometimes try to pair a brand with an emotional response. Figure 2.7 illustrates a DaimlerChrysler approach. Being aware of the fact that Celine Dion is a very popular singer, DaimlerChrysler paid Celine Dion between US$10 million and US$20 million to use songs such as 'I Drove All Night' in a three-year 'Drive and Love' campaign. Chrysler hopes that by frequently pairing Celine Dion's songs with the brand, the love feeling that the songs of Celine Dion evoke will be transferred to Chrysler and will make the brand classy again.[40] Research shows that on the premise of a high exposure frequency and strong emotional content, attitudes towards saturated brands are said to be predominantly formed on the basis of emotional conditioning.[41] Examples of brands that try to benefit from emotional conditioning are Martini, Bacardi Breezer and Häagen-Dazs, which try to associate sexual arousal with their brands.

Emotional conditioning worked out well for Häagen-Dazs

Häagen Dazs has used erotic advertising for several years. One of its campaigns features a couple indulging in sexual foreplay. The ice cream is their main attribute, which is put on each other's body and licked off by the other. By frequently combining the ice cream with foreplay, the ice cream itself has sexual connotations for some people. This is illustrated by the statements of some university students who completely identify Häagen Dazs with sex. In an interview one of those students said:[42]

'. . . it was very nice ice cream, we really enjoyed the ice cream and the advertising had a lot of sexual connotations in it and I think we basically liked the connotations of the ads and we liked the idea of that and we believed the idea that Häagen Dazs was sexy because the ads told us it was sexy, so when we had the ice cream in front of us we felt that the pot was very sexy, a sexy pot.'

Furthermore, when the students had a date, they always made sure to buy Häagen Dazs in advance. Today, Häagen-Dazs is still positioned on pleasurable experiences, but the source of the pleasure (the sex) has been replaced by New Age spirituality.[43]

Mere ad and brand exposures can increase liking of the ad and the brand, and can make it more likely that the advertised brand enters consumers' consideration set.[44] In other words, the mere exposure of consumers to a particular ad, without the consumer actively elaborating on the ad, can influence consumer preferences and behaviour. Indeed, studies show that respondents who were exposed to an ad more than once, as compared to respondents who saw the ad for the first time, appeared to evaluate the ad as more favourable and less dull.[45] For a while, it has been assumed that prior exposures to stimuli acquaint consumers with the stimuli and that this familiarity causes the more positive attitude towards the stimuli. However, several studies indicate that the mere exposure effect on brand attitude does not occur through a subjective feeling of familiarity. When a respondent has been exposed to a particular stimulus before, this exposure can result in a more positive stimulus evaluation even if the respondent cannot remember having seen the stimulus before.[46] A more recent explanation of the mere exposure effect is that prior exposure increases processing fluency at the time consumers have to make a judgement.[47] The fact that consumers have been frequently exposed to a certain ad or brand results in a representation of this stimulus in consumers' memory. When consumers later on want to evaluate the stimulus, for example during a shopping trip, the representation of the stimulus in their memory will facilitate the encoding and processing of the stimulus. As a consequence, processing of the stimulus will be easier and more fluent. Since consumers often do not realise that prior exposures increase processing fluency, they misattribute the source of the processing fluency (i.e. the previous exposures) to liking, truth or acceptability of the ad or brand. Of course, the mere exposure effect is limited and should be seen as a function of learning and satiation.[48] The more novel a stimulus, the more consumers can learn and the more positive the affective response will be.[49] When consumers are confronted too often with a particular message or ad, there is no learning opportunity anymore and they get bored. This can have a boomerang effect on ad and brand attitude. The latter effect is called wear-out and indicates that there is a certain threshold of exposures after which additional exposures result in negative instead of positive communications effects.

Post-experience models

The theories discussed above have often been tested for hypothetical products and/or hypothetical brands, which make them more relevant for new than for established brands. Although using hypothetical stimuli is ideal for eliminating research biasing effects such as brand knowledge, the extent to which the brand has been advertised in the past and the influence of previous campaigns, it disregards a source of information that might have important consequences for the way a consumer processes and evaluates a new marketing message, more specifically personal brand experience through previous brand usage. Post-experience models assume central-route processing of prior brand experiences. So, in this case the consumers are motivated, willing and able to think of previous brand experience and will take this into account in forming an attitude towards the brand, as well as in deciding what brand to buy in the future.

Although incorporating the influence of brand experience is a much more realistic approach to consumer information processing, brand experience has been neglected by most researchers. As a consequence, only a few communications models exist that try to explain its effect on the communications process. However, it is straightforward that brand satisfaction or dissatisfaction will have an impact on the next purchase. For example, if you have been driving a Nissan for six years and you are really satisfied with its design, petrol consumption and after-sales dealer service, the probability that you will buy a Nissan next time is much higher than if you find out that your Nissan consumes much more petrol than your friend's Mazda, spare parts are more expensive than a Ford's, and your Nissan broke down five times in six months. Another example is that when you buy Lay's crisps you expect them to be fresh, otherwise you are very likely to switch brands.

What is the role marketing communications can play for first buys on the one hand, and for other than first-time purchases on the other? The Perception–Experience–Memory model (see Figure 2.8) tries to formulate an answer to this.[50] When consumers do not have brand experience yet, the main function of advertising consists of framing perception. Framing can affect consumers' expectation, anticipation and interpretation. Expectation is concerned with notifying consumers that a particular brand in a certain product category is available and putting the brand in a frame of reference so that the consumers expect to see it. Next, marketing communications should try to create anticipation or hypothesis generation. Research indicates that exposing consumers to an attribute-based ad before brand trial makes consumers more curious about the brand ('Would Red Bull really energise my body and mind, and give me wiiiiings?'), it helps consumers to formulate hypotheses about the brand ('Red Bull will give me a kick'), and it induces the consumers to test their hypotheses during a subsequent trial experience.[51] Besides expectation and anticipation, pre-experience communications may offer an interpretation or a rationale for the anticipation the brand generates. For example, an unfamiliar computer brand could use the Intel Inside logo to assure consumers that it is a trustworthy and high-quality brand.

Figure 2.8 The Perception–Experience–Memory model

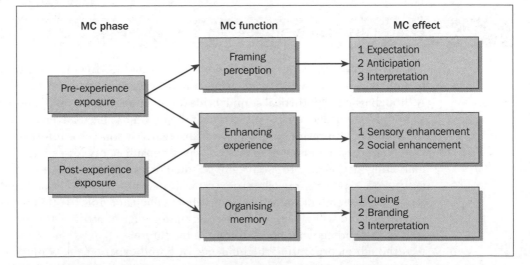

Based on: Hall, B.F. (2002), 'A New Model for Measuring Advertising Effectiveness', *Journal of Advertising Research*, 42 (March/April), 23–31.

A next critical function of both pre-experience and post-experience communications is enhancing sensory and social experience. Products may taste better, function better or look nicer and the service may be perceived as friendlier or more knowledgeable just because consumers expect to experience this and anticipate the experience.[52] Moreover, consumers may focus their brand trial evaluation on attributes that they would not have used without the pre- or post-experience advertisement (instead of evaluating Red Bull on taste, carbonation, sugar level, etc. it may be evaluated on the uplifting experience it gives because of the advertising campaign), or marketing communication may change the weight that the advertised attributes receive at evaluation (valuing the uplifting experience as more important than taste, refreshment, etc.). On the basis of experiments in which respondents were exposed to an ad alone, to an ad and a product trial, or to a product trial alone, it appeared that a pre-experience ad combined with brand trial resulted in significantly more favourable brand responses than either a brand trial alone or an advertisement alone. More specifically, when an ad and brand trial were combined, the pre-trial ad led consumers to process the brand trial information in a more focussed and meaningful way, resulting in more confidently held brand beliefs, a higher expectancy value from the brand (as measured by the Fishbein model) and higher purchase intentions. Moreover, ads appeared to be better in fostering confidently held beliefs about non-experiential attributes (such as the number of calories), while trial was more powerful in creating confidently held experiential attribute beliefs (such as taste).[53] Also, post-experience ads have been shown to enhance the experience of a previous brand trial. This happens when a consumer evaluates his or her brand experience as more favourable when he or she has been exposed to advertising after brand usage as compared to the situation when no advertising followed the brand experience. For example, if you have had Fitness for breakfast and afterwards you see an ad for Fitness which shows all the ingredients and stresses the fact that no sugar is added, it might improve your evaluation of Fitness as a healthy breakfast choice.

A second role of post-experience communications is to organise memory. It offers verbal and visual cues such as jingles, slogans, user imagery, etc., enriching the brand schema and making it more likely that afterwards the brand will be recalled. Increasing brand recall and top-of-mind awareness can increase the possibility that consumers stop buying the competitor's brand and change to the company's brand; in other words, it can stimulate brand-switching. Pepsi, for example, tried to change taste beliefs by stressing 'nothing else is a Pepsi'. On the other hand, post-experience communications may also prevent consumers switching to the competitor's brand.[54] Finally, post-experience communications also helps consumers to interpret their experiences. 'The advertisement not only influences the consumer to feel that the sensory or social experience was a good one, but it also provides reasons to believe that it was.'[55] It is important to remember that marketing communications really is able to improve and reshape objective sensory experience. In an era in which consumers have the feeling that in the majority of product categories brands are converging instead of becoming more distinct,[56] post-experience advertising may offer the extra element for a brand to be perceived as better or more unique than the rest.

In some cases at least one of the MAO factors is low, making well thought through processing less likely. Consumers will rather concentrate on elements of previous brand experience to form an attitude and purchase intention. A typical model for this low-involvement–behavioural-oriented processing is Ehrenberg's **reinforcement model**.

According to this model, awareness leads to trial and trial leads to reinforcement. Product experience is the dominant variable in the model, and advertising is supposed to reinforce habits, frame experience (see previous section) and defend consumers' attitudes.[57] A similar model is called **routinised response behaviour** and assumes that a large number of product experiences can lead to routinised response behaviour, especially for low involvement, frequently purchased products such as toilet paper, toothpaste, paper tissues, mineral water or chewing gum.[58] In this case, consumers do not spend much time on deciding which brand to buy, but buy a particular brand out of habit. In other words, previous behaviour guides future behaviour. Although the initial brand choice may have been thoroughly elaborated, routinised response behaviour is characterised by no or very low cognitive effort in which very few possibilities are considered. The fact that routinised response behaviour is a frequently used purchase strategy is illustrated by a study observing consumers who were buying detergents in a supermarket:[59] 83% of the 120 consumers observed took only one brand while no more than 4% picked up more than one brand to investigate them a bit closer. It took the consumers on average 13 seconds to walk down the aisle and choose a detergent. Obviously, no extended problem-solving was used here. Building brand awareness and trying to become top of mind is very important here in order to be included in the limited set of brands that a consumer is willing to consider, to retain brand loyalty and to enhance brand-switching to the own brand.

As becomes obvious from previous sections, a lot of communications models have been presented and all of them found empirical support in some circumstances. However, the key seems to be to define which variables influence the way a consumer deals with marketing communications. Motivation, ability and opportunity certainly are very important variables, although an even more important factor – previous brand experience – has been neglected most of the time.

Summary

How marketing communications persuade consumers is largely a black box process that can be explained in many ways. In hierarchy-of-effects models, the consumer is assumed to go through a hierarchical process of cognitive, affective and behavioural responses to communications stimuli. Depending on the type of product and buying situation, this hierarchy may differ. A crucial role in this persuasion process is the formation and change of attitudes. The extent to which attitudes are formed in a stable or less stable way depends on the elaboration likelihood of information processing, which in turn depends on the motivation, the ability and the opportunity to process information. If one of these factors is not present, consumers may be convinced by peripheral stimuli, such as the colours in the ad or the celebrity endorsing the product, rather than by rational product information. The way in which attitudes are formed and changed depends on the high or low likelihood of elaboration on the one hand, and whether attitudes are primarily based on cognitive, affective or conative factors on the other. As a result, six types of attitude formation and communications models can be distinguished. Among the most important of these models are the cognitively based high elaboration likelihood model of Fishbein–Ajzen and the theory of planned behaviour, the affectively oriented feelings-as-information and feeling transfer models. The perception–experience–memory and the routinised response behaviour models focus on the behavioural aspects of attitude formation.

Review questions

1 What are the contributions and shortcomings of hierarchy-of-effects models, such as the Lavidge and Steiner model and the FCB grid?

2 How are attitudes formed and changed? How can the ELM model explain how communications work?

3 How can the elements in the Theory of Reasoned Action be used in marketing communications?

4 What is heuristic evaluation and how can it be used in marketing communications?

5 How can the feelings-as-information theory be used in marketing communications?

6 What is the importance of ad-evoked feelings and emotional conditioning in marketing communications?

7 What is the mere exposure effect?

8 How can pre- and post-experience advertising influence brand choice?

Further reading

Ajzen, I., 'Theory of Planned Behavior: A Bibliography', online (http://www.unix.oit.umass.edu/~aizen/tpbrefs.html)

Davidson, R.J., Scherer, K.R. and Goldsmith, H.H. (2003), *Handbook of Affective Sciences.* Oxford: Oxford University Press.

Forgas, J.P. (2001), *Handbook of Affect and Social Cognition.* Hillsdale, NJ: Lawrence Erlbaum Associates.

Haddock, G. and Maio, G. (2003), *Theoretical Perspectives on Attitudes for the 21st Century.* Philadelphia, PA: Psychology Press.

Ratneshwar, S., Mick, D.G. and Huffman, C. (2000), *The Why of Consumption: Contemporary Perspectives on Consumer Motives, Goals and Desires.* New York: Routledge.

Case 2

Jealous as Axe

Unilever was founded in 1930 when the British soapmaker Lever Brothers and the Dutch margarine producer Margarine Unie joined forces. By now, Unilever has become one of the world's leading suppliers of fast-moving consumer goods with sales of almost €49 million in 2002 in foods and in home and care products offered all over the world. Leading brands in the food market are Knorr, Iglo (called Findus in Italy and Bird's Eye in the UK), Bertolli, Becel (called Flora in the UK), Ben & Jerry's, Magnum and Lipton. In the home care market Unilever holds leading brands such as Brilhante, Cif, Comfort, Domestos, Omo, Skip and Snuggle. Famous personal care brands in Unilever's portfolio include Axe (known as Lynx in the UK), Dove, Lux, Pond's, Rexona, Sunsilk and Calvin Klein. Deodorants are one of Unilever's fastest growing product categories, with its major brands holding strong positions in all regions. These brands have been carefully nurtured throughout the years, one of Unilever's major strengths. Ever since William Lever launched Sunlight, the world's first packaged, branded laundry soap, in the late nineteenth century, backing it with a large-scale innovative and competitive advertising campaign, Unilever has been at the forefront of advertising trends. An early presence in commercial television, whenever and wherever it came on stream, and innovative marketing campaigns have played their part in maintaining awareness of the company's brands. In 2002, total expenditure on advertising and promotions reached €6.839 billion.

Marketing situation

When launched, Axe created a new product category: deodorant body spray for men. Over and above the classical deodorant promise of odour prevention (e.g. Mennen), Axe also offered fragrance, which allowed it to be positioned as 'a seduction tool, a rite of passage brand, easing the transition from adolescence to manhood'. From then onwards, Axe has established itself as the leading male toiletries brand in Europe. Central to the brand's success was its innovative character, creating its own category, which situated it at the leading edge of fashion. However, ten years on, the brand seemed to have aged with its initial consumers and was no longer at the forefront of youth fashion trends. Research indicated that the 'Axe man' was seen as dated – 'James Bond in a safari suit' – and executions had become too predictable. The communications format was unable to tap into the current values of the core youth target.

Advertising objectives and target group

The first communications objective was to make Axe trendy again by improving the brand image to get it back in tune with 15–24-year-old youth values and attitudes. A second behavioural objective was to transform 15–24-year-old non-users into brand-users. The targeted youth have grown up with Axe advertising and, while they find them 'naff', they still love the unique Axe fantasy of 'the woman making the first move'. Young men in this age group are eager for their first experience of women. They dream about being able to seduce women without too much effort, because deep down they are not as confident as they seem. Their main topics of interest are sex, music, football and having a laugh. They are extremely media

literate, adore irreverent advertising/films which communicate in the second degree or play with market codes (Diesel, *Pulp Fiction*, etc.).

Creative strategy

The strategy had to build on the brand heritage, while rejuvenating Axe's image to make it contemporary. Passive seduction was still a real and motivating consumer insight. The lads want to be seductive without being seen to try too much. Having women show an interest gives them the confidence to go on. However, since all brands in this segment talk about seduction, Axe had to impose its own point of view in a clever and motivating way. The execution had to be new and different; it had to make a break with conventional scenarios. Humour could be used, but taking care not to risk derision or make a joke of the core promise, as seduction is considered a serious business. The setting and protagonists used should be relevant and aspirational to the target audience. This involves moving from the traditional exotic surroundings and rugged male role model to an aspirational environment, close to the consumer's reality. Similarly, characters with whom the target can identify more readily had to be used, capturing today's relationship in today's world. The creative idea was to present the brand promise in a striking, humorous and innovative way. The idea was to show the seductive effects of Axe on women, regardless of who is wearing it. A plot was worked out, in which a young woman in a hurry grabs her husband's Axe deodorant by mistake. Wearing the deodorant, she leaves the house, remarking that all the women she encounters seem attracted to her in a strange way. Suddenly aware of the seductive effect on women of her husband's Axe deodorant, she rushes home in a fury, jealously demanding some explanation from her husband.

Media strategy

The powerful and distinctive medium of television was used to convey the advertising message. Focus was placed on weekends and on youth-relevant environments (e.g. sports, music, etc.). Axe had to be placed in a young environment to move from a wide target of men below 50 years old to the core target of 15–24-year-old men. In order to be able to recruit this core target, the brand had to be made more youthful. Cinema was also used as a medium, to reach maximum proximity and complicity with the target.

Results

The success of the 'Jealousy campaign' has been endorsed by both qualitative and quantitative studies. Pre-test results reveal that 'Jealousy' scored higher than previous Axe ads and better with the younger core target everywhere it has been tested. Pre-tests gave scores well above average in terms of enjoyment, memorability, understanding and brand linkage (France, Germany, Mexico, Chile) (see Case Tables 2.1 and 2.2).

Qualitative studies have shown Jealousy to appeal strongly to the target market, and move the brand forward in terms of image and appeal.

DRSM – Spain: *'Most (especially non-users) found the change welcome and the brand more relevant (younger).'*

Research International – Germany: *'Jealousy is met with high acceptance among young consumers. It is seen as an idea that is new, strongly attention getting and unique in the field of fragrance/care products.'*

Studio Pavan – Italy: *'Jealousy has the capability of extending Axe's image. The language is clearly directed at a "young", modern, attentive public: the X Generation that has an always greater need for excitement and new sensations that can be immediately enjoyed.'*

Research International – Denmark: *'Jealousy positions Axe in a young, modern and high speed environment. This could be the beginning of a new style of Axe advertising and a renewal of the Axe image.'*

Research International – Sweden: *'Jealousy revitalises the brand, makes it more of a brand for the 90s. The film doesn't exclude any part of the target group . . . Our belief is that the Swedish market is ready for a change when it comes to Axe commercials and would appreciate a different kind of film, which Jealousy is a good example of.'*

DRSM European Brand Audit 1997: France, Germany, UK, Italy: *'Despite differences exposed between regions, the soul of the brand is consistent across markets. The opportunity for a common pan-European expression remains realistic due to the broad appeal of Jealousy.'*

Tracking and post-tests have demonstrated significant improvements in impact, brand proximity and persuasion to buy (Case Tables 2.3, 2.4 and 2.5).

Market shares show that Jealousy has had a measured sales impact in most countries. In Italy Axe deodorant reached its highest market share ever. But in other countries too, such as Germany, Sweden, Greece and Portugal, significant increases were attained (Case Table 2.6).

Case Table 2.1 Pre-test results of the Axe campaign

	France		Germany		Mexico		Chile	
	Jealousy ad	Previous Axe ads	Jealousy ad	Previous Axe ads	Jealousy ad	Previous Axe ads	Jealousy ad	Previous Axe ads
Enjoyment	3.60	3.30	3.63	3.24	4.05	3.68	4.05	3.75
Memorability	3.03	2.71	3.20	2.97	3.41	3.97	6.90	–
Understand	3.36	3.33	3.37	3.56	3.58	3.60	3.41	3.24
Brand linkage	4.05	3.73	4.18	3.96	3.98	4.00	4.10	3.75

Figures in cells represent average evaluation scores on a five-point scale.

Case Table 2.2 Pre-test results of the Axe campaign per age group

	Germany 16/24 vs 25/40		France 16/24 vs 25/40		Mexico 16/30 vs 31/45	
Enjoyment	3.63	3.63	3.78	3.42	4.28	3.79
Memorability	3.25	3.18	3.12	2.84	6.98	6.80
Understand	3.47	3.32	3.36	3.35	3.40	3.45
Brand linkage	4.22	4.16	4.13	3.87	4.17	4.02

Figures in cells represent average evaluation scores on a five-point scale.

Case Table 2.3 Post-test results of the Axe campaign (Germany)

		Axe Jealousy	Standard (budget > 1.5 DM/ month, millions)	Standard Body Care
Impact	TV awareness	47%	44%	40%
	Product aided	12%	11%	10%
	Brand aided	36%	33%	30%
Recall	Specific scores	31%	19%	15%
	Related scores	32%	25%	23%
	Recognition	65%	53%	50%
Sympathy	Likes	79%	53%	50%
	Dislikes	10%	23%	24%
Persuasion	Recognition	20%	–	–
	Buying international total	17%	–	–

Case Table 2.4
Post-test results of the Axe campaign (France)

	14 April 1996	11 May 1996
Ad recognition	9%	33%
Attribution	60%	76%
Think brand different	2.25/5	3.70/5
New info	1.75/5	2.60/5
More likely to buy	2.00/5	3.02/5
Brand for you	1.75/5	2.91/5

Case Table 2.5
More post-test results for the German Axe campaign

	June 1996	March 1997
Consideration when buying	24%	44%
Brand proximity	17%	29%
Bought last	15%	24%
Use more often	16%	28%
Ever tried	53%	67%
Unaided brand awareness	64%	69%

Case Table 2.6 Market share (%) of Axe in selected countries

Country	Air date	Previous period	Following period	Previous year
Germany	06/96	8.7	9.6	8.6
Italy	06/96	6.7	8.1	7.3
Austria	08/96	11.2	12.1	11.1
Greece	05/96	17.4	20.0	17.0
Portugal	04/96	6.4	6.9	6.9
	10/96	6.7	7.9	6.8
Netherlands	07/96	5.6	6.4	5.9
France	04/97	8.6	11.5	–
Czech Republic	01/97	3.9	4.1	3.7
Slovakia	01/97	5.6	6.9	7.7
Sweden	11/96	18.8	23.1	19.6
Norway	10/96	19.4	23.3	19.9
Denmark	09/96	10.0	11.1	10.9

This exceptional advertising campaign was highly appreciated by the trade and the general public and has won several prizes. Jealousy was awarded a Silver Euro Effie in 1997 for its effectiveness and has won a Silver Lion at Cannes (creative award). It won the 'Strategies' Grand Prize, was elected Eurobest and received the Unilever International Advertising Award. Furthermore, the campaign was the winner in consumer magazine competitions in Germany and Italy.

Five years later, the 'seductive fragrance' appeal is still in vogue. An innovative website shows testimonials of the Axe effect from the UK, Iceland, Russia and Mexico. Also video clips can be downloaded in which the Axe effect is prominent. For example, one video shows a football game. When one of the football players (who happens to wear Axe) runs in close to the cheerleaders to catch the ball, one of the cheerleaders cannot control herself any longer, runs on the field and chases the football player. The site also features an automated matching system promising 'Axe can help you get the girl of your dreams'. Moreover, the importance of a good fragrance is tested in a 'Seduction Survey', of which the results show amongst others that 81% of the women would not sleep with a guy if he smelled bad and that 52% of women have approached a sweet-smelling stranger to tell him how good he smells. Finally, the site also contains a 'warning' section: 'The Axe effect is powerful and unpredictable, and could be harmful if used improperly'. Here, surfers find suggestions such as not to wear Axe in situations in which women should not be distracted (such as in a moving car), etc. (see Plate 19).

Five years after the campaign Axe is still hot as a sales growth in 2002 clearly proves. Axe is the number one male toiletries brand, is available in 53 countries and occupies a dominant position in Europe, South America and Australia. Recent innovations include modern fragrances, stylish packaging, and after shave lotions and shower gels.

Questions

1 In which cell of the FCB grid would you classify deodorant for men? What does this imply regarding the assumptions of information processing? Does deodorant fall into the same cell for all people? In which cell of the FCB grid can Axe be situated?

2 Which motive from the Rossiter–Percy Grid did Unilever have in mind when developing the Jealousy campaign? Is this a good choice in view of the target group?

3 Using the classification of attitude formation models depicted in this chapter, which models seem most relevant to explain the information processing of the Axe campaign? Explain.

4 In terms of the Theory of Reasoned Action, how is Unilever trying to change the attitude towards Axe?

5 Do you think aspects of post-experience models are relevant in this case? If yes, which ones?

Sources: http://www.unilever.com; Unilever press pack; Axe Jealousy, 1997. Euro Effie, Efficiency in Advertising, pp. 21–6; www.theaxeeffect. com/flash.html. Case prepared by Malaika Brengman, Limburgs Universitair Centrum, LUC. Reproduced with permission of EFFIE award vzw.

References

1 Barry, T.E. and Howard, D.J. (1990), 'A Review and Critique of the Hierarchy of Effects in Advertising', *International Journal of Advertising*, 9, 121–35; Barry, T.E. (2002), 'In Defense of the Hierarchy of Effects: A Rejoinder to Weilbacher', *Journal of Advertising Research*, 42(3), 44–47.

2 Vakratsas, D. and Ambler, T. (1999), 'How Advertising Works: What Do We Really Know?', *Journal of Marketing*, 63, 1 (January), 25–43.

3 Vaughn, R. (1986), 'How Advertising Works: A Planning Model Revisited', *Journal of Advertising Research*, 26(1), 57–66.

4 Rossiter, J.R. and Percy, L. (1997), *Advertising and Promotion Management*. New York: McGraw-Hill.

5 *Media Mix Digest* (1999), 34(4), 8.

6 Barry, T.E. and Howard, D.J. (1990), 'A Review and Critique of the Hierarchy of Effects in Advertising', *International Journal of Advertising*, 9, 121–35; Barry, T.E. (2002), 'In Defense of the Hierarchy of Effects: A Rejoinder to Weilbacher', *Journal of Advertising Research*, 42(3), 44–47.

7 Peter, J.P., Olson, J.C. and Grunert, K.G. (1999), *Consumer Behaviour and Marketing Strategy, European Edition*. London: McGraw-Hill.

8 Hoyer, W.C. and MacInnis, D.J. (2001), *Consumer Behavior*. Boston: Houghton Mifflin.

9 Hoyer, W.D. and MacInnis, D.J. (2001), *Consumer Behavior*, Boston NY: Houghton Mifflin; Park, C.W., Jaworski, B.J. and MacInnis, D.J. (1986), 'Strategic Brand Concept–Image Management', *Journal of Marketing*, 50 (October), 135–145.

10 Aaker, J.L. and Lee, A.Y. (2001), ' "I" Seek Pleasures and "We" Avoid Pains: The Role of Self-Regulatory Goals in

Information Processing and Persuasion', *Journal of Consumer Research*, 28 (June), 33–49; Higgins, E.T. (1997), 'Beyond Pleasure and Pain', *American Psychologist*, 52 (December), 1280–1300.

11 Huffman, C., Ratneshwar, S. and Mick, D.G. (2000), 'Consumer Goal Structures and Goal Determination Processes', in Ratneshwar, S., Mick, D.G. and Huffman, C. (eds), *The Why of Consumption: Contemporary Perspectives on Consumer Motives, Goals and Desires*, New York: Routledge, 1–35.

12 Baumgartner, H. (2002), 'Toward a Personology of the Consumer', *Journal of Consumer Research*, 29 (September), 286–292.

13 Petty, R.E. and Cacioppo, J.T. (1986), 'The Elaboration Likelihood Model of Persuasion', *Advances in Experimental Social Psychology*, 19, 123–205.

14 Petty, R.E. and Cacioppo, J.T. (1986), 'The Elaboration Likelihood Model of Persuasion', *Advances in Experimental Social Psychology*, 19, 123–205.

15 Fishbein, M. and Ajzen, I. (1975), *Belief, Attitude, Intention, and Behavior: An Introduction to Theory and Research*. Reading, MA: Addison-Wesley; Ajzen, I. (1991), 'The Theory of Planned Behavior', *Organizational Behavior and Human Decision Processes*, 50, 179–211.

16 Ajzen, I. (1991), 'The Theory of Planned Behavior', *Organizational Behavior and Human Decision Processes*, 50, 179–211.

17 Ajzen, I. (1991), 'The Theory of Planned Behavior', *Organizational Behavior and Human Decision Processes*, 50, 179–211.

18 Ajzen, I. (2002), 'Perceived Behavioral Control, Self-Efficacy, Locus of Control, and the Theory of Planned Behavior', *Journal of Applied Social Psychology*, 32, 665–83.

19 http://www-unix.oit.umass.edu/~aizen/tpbrefs.html

20 Bamberg, S., Ajzen, I. and Schmidt, P. (2003), 'Choice of Travel Mode in the Theory of Planned Behavior: The Roles of Past Behavior, Habit, and Reasoned Action', *Basic and Applied Social Psychology*; Baker, C.W., Little, T.D. and Brownell, K.D. (2003), 'Predicting Adolescent Eating and Activity Behaviors: The Role of Social Norms and Personal Agency', *Health Psychology*, 22, 189–198; Bamberg, S. and Schmidt, P. (2003), 'Incentive, Morality or Habit? Predicting Students' Car Use for University Routes with the Models of Ajzen, Schwartz, and Triandis', *Environment and Behavior*, 35, 1–22; etc. (see http://www-unix.oit.umass.edu/~aizen/tpbrefs.html).

21 MacInnis, D.J. and Jaworski, B.J. (1989), 'Information Processing from Advertisements: Toward an Integrative Framework', *Journal of Marketing*, 53, 1–23.

22 Baker, W.E. and Lutz, R.J. (2000), 'An Empirical Test of an Updated Relevance-Accessibility Model of Advertising Effectiveness', *Journal of Advertising*, 29(1), 1–14.

23 *Marketing Mix Digest* (1999), 34(4), 8.

24 Schwarz, N. and Clore, G.L. (1996), 'Feelings and Phenomenal Experiences', in Higgins, E.T. and Kruglanski, A.W. (eds), *Social Psychology: Handbook of Basic Principles*, New York: Guilford, 433–65.

25 Pham, M.T. (1998), 'Representativeness, Relevance, and the Use of Feelings in Decision Making', *Journal of Consumer Research*, 25(2), 144–60.

26 Gorn, G.J., Pham, M.T. and Sin, L.Y. (2001), 'When Arousal Influences Ad Evaluation and Valence Does Not (and Vice Versa)', *Journal of Consumer Psychology*, 2(3), 237–56.

27 Pham, M.T., Cohen, J.B., Prajecus, J.W. and Hughes, D.G. (2001), 'Affect Monitoring and the Primacy of Feelings in Judgment', *Journal of Consumer Research*, 28(2), 167–88.

28 Pham, M.T., Cohen, J.B., Prajecus, J.W. and Hughes, D.G. (2001), 'Affect Monitoring and the Primacy of Feelings in Judgment', *Journal of Consumer Research*, 28(2), 167–88.

29 Pham, M.T. (1998), 'Representativeness, Relevance, and the Use of Feelings in Decision Making', *Journal of Consumer Research*, 25(2), 144–60.

30 Pham, M.T. (1998), 'Representativeness, Relevance, and the Use of Feelings in Decision Making', *Journal of Consumer Research*, 25(2), 144–60.

31 Bagozzi, R.P., Gopinath, M. and Nyer, P.U. (1999), 'The Role of Emotions in Marketing', *Journal of the Academy of Marketing Science*, 27(2), 184–206; Forgas, J.P. (1995), 'Mood and Judgment: The Affect Infusion Model (AIM)', *Psychological Bulletin*, 117(1), 39–66.

32 Schindler, M.R. and Holbrook, M.B. (2003), 'Nostalgia for Early Experience as a Determinant of Consumer Preferences', *Psychology and Marketing*, 20(4), 275–302.

33 Baker, W.E. and Lutz, R.J. (2000), 'An Empirical Test of an Updated Relevance-Accessibility Model of Advertising Effectiveness', *Journal of Advertising*, 29(1), 1–14.

34 Brown, S.P. and Stayman, D.M. (1992), 'Antecedents and Consequences of Attitude towards the Ad: A Meta-Analysis', *Journal of Consumer Research*, 19, 34–51.

35 Gouden Gluon Onderzoek (1998), *De Kracht van Emoties*, (Golden Gluon Research, *The Power of Emotions*), PUB, 14, appendix.

36 Bagozzi, R.P., Gopinath, M. and Nyer, P.U. (1999), 'The Role of Emotions in Marketing', *Journal of the Academy of Marketing Science*, 27(2), 184–206.

37 Frijda, N.H. (1987), *The Emotions*. Cambridge: Cambridge University Press; Bower, G.H. (1991), 'Mood Congruity of Social Judgment', in Forgas, J. (ed.), *Emotion and Social Judgment*. Oxford: Pergamon, 31–53.

38 Morris, J.D., Woo, C., Geason, J.A. and Kim, J. (2002), 'The Power of Affect: Predicting Intention', *Journal of Advertising Research*, 42(3), 7–17.

39 Pavlov, I. (1927), *Conditioned Reflexes*, London: Oxford University Press.

40 Freeman, S. (2003), 'Celine Dion Sings "I Drove All Night" for Chrysler', *Wall Street Journal*, January 16.

41 Kroeber-Riel, W. (1984), 'Effects of Pictorial Elements in Ads Analyzed by Means of Eye Movement Monitoring', *Advances in Consumer Research*, 11, 591–6.

42 Elliott, R. and Ritson, M. (1995), 'Practicing Existential Consumption: The Lived Meaning of Sexuality in Advertising', *Advances in Consumer Research*, 22, 740–5.

43 Anonymous, (2001), 'Is Häagen-Dazs Shrewd to Drop its Sexy Image?', *Marketing*, 6 September.

44 Shapiro, S. (1999), 'When an Ad's Influence is Beyond Our Conscious Control: Perceptual and Conceptual Fluency Effects Caused by Incidental Ad Exposure', *Journal of Consumer Research*, 26 (June), 16–36.

45 Mano, H. (1996), 'Assessing Emotional Reactions to TV Ads: A Replication and Extension with a Brief Adjective Checklist', *Advances in Consumer Research*, 23, 63–9.

46 Zajonc, R.B. and Markus, H. (1988), 'Affect and Cognition: The Hard Interface', in Izard, C.E., Kagan, J. and Zajonc, R.B. (eds), *Emotions, Cognition and Behaviour*. Cambridge: Cambridge University Press, 73–102.

47 Janiszewski, C. and Meyvis, T. (2001), 'Effects of Brand Logo Complexity, Repetition, and Spacing on Processing Fluency and Judgment', *Journal of Consumer Research*, 28 (June), 18–32.

48 Hoyer, W.C. and MacInnis, D.J. (2001), *Consumer Behaviour*. Boston: Houghton Mifflin.

49 Berlyne, D.E. (1970), 'Novelty, Complexity, and Hedonic Value', *Perception and Psychophysics*, 8 (November), 279–86.

50 Hall, B.F. (2002), 'A New Model for Measuring Advertising Effectiveness', *Journal of Advertising Research*, 42 (March/April), 23–31.

51 Kempf, D.S. and Laczniak, R.N. (2001), 'Advertising's Influence on Subsequent Product Trial Processing', *Journal of Advertising*, 30(3), 27–38.

52 Hall, B.F. (2002), 'A New Model for Measuring Advertising Effectiveness', *Journal of Advertising Research*, 42 (March/April), 23–31.

53 Kempf, D.S. and Laczniak, R.N. (2001), 'Advertising's Influence on Subsequent Product Trial Processing', *Journal of Advertising*, 30(3), 27–38.

54 Deighton, J., Henderson, J.M. and Neslin, S.A. (1994), 'The Effects of Advertising on Brand Switching and Repeat Purchasing', *Journal of Marketing Research*, 31(2), 28–43.

55 Kempf, D.S. and Laczniak, R.N. (2001), 'Advertising's Influence on Subsequent Product Trial Processing', *Journal of Advertising*, 30(3), 27–38.

56 Clancy, K.J. and Trout, J. (2002), 'Brand Confusion', *Harvard Business Review*, 80(3).

57 Ehrenberg, A.S.C. (1974), 'Repetitive Advertising and the Consumer', *Journal of Advertising Research*, 14 (April), 25–34; Vakratsas, D. and Ambler, T. (1999), 'What Do We Really Know?', *Journal of Marketing*, 63 (January), 26–43.

58 Peter, J.P. and Olson, J.C. (1993), *Consumer Behaviour and Marketing Strategy*. Burr Ridge, IL: Irwin.

59 Hoyer, W.D. (1984), 'An Examination of Consumer Decision Making for a Common Repeat Purchase Product', *Journal of Consumer Research*, 11, 822–9.

Chapter 3
Target groups

Chapter outline

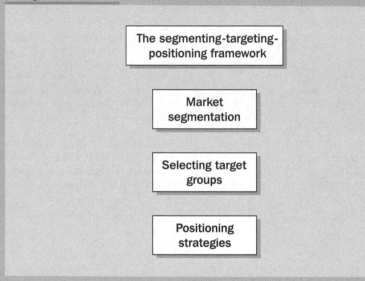

The segmenting-targeting-positioning framework

Market segmentation

Selecting target groups

Positioning strategies

Chapter objectives

This chapter will help you to:

- Understand the process of segmenting, targeting and positioning
- Get an overview of the criteria for segmenting markets
- Understand the requirements for good segmentation
- Distinguish the strategies for targeting market segments
- Choose positioning strategies

Introduction

In most circumstances a market has different groups of customers or prospects with different needs and subject to different trends. Identifying these different groups and deciding at which group(s) to target the marketing and communications efforts is a major task of communications planning.

Companies can define target markets in a number of ways, based on multiple criteria. Segmenting a market, deciding on target groups or segments to focus on, and establishing a position to defend vis-à-vis these target groups, are at the same time vital components of the strategic marketing plan and basic cornerstones of a communications strategy. The choice of well-defined target groups and positioning decisions should, later in the communications planning, be reflected in the selection of communications objectives, communications instruments, campaign execution and media planning.

The segmenting-targeting-positioning framework

In Table 3.1 the various steps in the segmenting-targeting-positioning (STP) process are shown. The STP exercise starts with a definition of potentially relevant factors on the basis of which a market can be segmented. Market segmentation should ideally lead to more homogeneous subgroups in that the members of one group should react in the same way to marketing stimuli and differ in their reactions to these stimuli from the members of other segments. In other words, it is not sufficient for men and women to be physiologically different. If there is no systematic difference between the two groups in the way they react to marketing stimuli, there is no sound reason to distinguish between them. For example, the furniture market includes different segments such as home and business markets. These segments can be further divided: home markets include student home furniture, design furniture, classic furniture etc.; business markets include, for instance, office furniture (for small/large companies), hotel furniture, etc.

In stage two of the STP process, segmentation variables can be combined to form segmentation profiles. In fact, by combining segmentation variables, multivariate segmentation takes place. Once segment profiles have been identified, their attractiveness can be assessed. Segment attractiveness will depend on the size and predicted evolution of sales, buying power and the amount of competition targeted at the same segment.

On the basis of this analysis of attractiveness the marketer will select a number of target groups to focus on, based on their attractiveness and for which the company has

Table 3.1 Segmenting, targeting and positioning

1 Definition of segmentation criteria
2 Definition of segment profiles
3 Assessment of the attractiveness of segments
4 Selection of target groups
5 Definition of the desired unique position in the mind of targeted consumers

relevant strengths. This is called **targeting**. All further communications objectives, strategies and tactics will be aimed at these specific groups. Hence, the promotional mix may differ depending on the different target markets a company is focussing on in its communications programme. For example, Ikea, the Swedish international 'takeaway' furniture distributor, could target the segment of young home users with a limited budget interested in designer furniture by offering a special designer furniture line. Or it could capitalise on the trend that tele-working and self-employment are increasing and develop a home office furniture line for this targeted segment.

Finally, the company has to define a unique and relevant position for its products in the mind of the target group. **Positioning** can be defined as the way a product is perceived by the target group on important attributes, the 'place in the mind' a product occupies relative to its competitors. Positioning is a core element of marketing strategy and hence of marketing communications. Indeed, marketing management can be defined as finding and sustaining a unique and defendable image or position for a product. Unlike imitating successful competitors, positioning attempts to claim exclusive 'ownership' of a benefit in the mind of the customer which differentiates it from the competition.[1] This position is the brand or product personality which should always be claimed and supported in the communications strategy.[2] Several examples of successful positioning can be given. Mercedes stands for luxury, Volvo for safety, Miele (dishwashers, washing machines, etc.) for quality, Levi's for the original American jeans, and Duracell batteries for power.

Market segmentation

Market segmentation is the process of dividing consumers into homogeneous groups, i.e. groups that share needs or react in a comparable way to marketing and communications efforts. Different variables or criteria can be used to segment a market. In Table 3.2, a framework and some examples of variables used to segment consumer markets are presented.[3] Objective segmentation variables are variables that can be measured objectively and straightforwardly. Inferred constructs have to be defined before people can be classified into groups. For instance, the construct 'lifestyle' has to be operationalised before any one consumer can be attributed to a lifestyle group.

General factors are segmentation variables that hold in all behavioural circumstances. A person is always male or female, no matter what buying situation he or

Table 3.2 Consumer market segmentation variables

	Objective	*Inferred (psychographic)*
General	Geographic Demographic (income, gender, age, education, profession, life cycle)	Social class Personality Lifestyle
Specific (behavioural)	Occasion Loyalty status User status Usage rate	Benefit Buyer readiness

she is in. On the basis of specific or behaviour-related variables, consumers can belong to different segments depending on the product class or buying situation concerned. For instance, a person can be a loyal buyer or a heavy user of chocolate or a chocolate brand, but an infrequent and brand-switching consumer of margarine.

Markets can be divided into different **geographic segments** such as continents, climate, nations, regions or neighbourhoods. Consumer behaviour and buying patterns often denote cultural differences and therefore the place consumers live may require other marketing mix approaches. For instance Inbev, one of the biggest international breweries, is selling its Stella lager as an ordinary lager in some European countries such as Belgium and as a premium and more expensive lager in countries such as the UK. This will also imply a different choice of communication tools: sponsoring pop music events to reach the population of students in Belgium while choosing stylish cinema events in Cannes and advertising in glossy trendy magazines such as *The Face* to support the different positioning in the UK. This segmentation method is often combined with other criteria. A marketing area is first defined geographically and subsequently other segments within this broad geographic area are identified.

Demographic segmentation divides the market on the basis of sex, age, family size, religion, birthplace, race, education, income or social class. These segmentation variables are frequently used, not only because they correlate with other variables such as consumer needs, but also because they are less difficult to measure than others.

For instance, Axe deodorant targets men, promising increased sex appeal in its communications campaign. Diamond targets women in the UK by offering a cheaper car insurance because women are better drivers and female accidents imply less severe damage. Colgate produces strawberry-flavoured toothpaste for children. BMW launched the Compact series for 'smaller' budgets.

Senior consumers are an increasingly important target group with specific characteristics. Here are a number of prejudices and misconceptions regarding seniors as a target group.

Seniors are one large group of non-active people
When marketers think of the mature consumer, they immediately think of hearing aids or false teeth. Of course, there is a part of the senior population, the more dependent part of 75+, who needs these products, but they form only 20% of the total senior population, leaving 80% of the 50+ market very interested in different products and services.

Seniors stop consuming
This is not true. In fact there are a lot of products with a higher penetration rate in the group of seniors than in other demographic groups. Examples are cosmetics (e.g. Nivea launched the Vital line to the 50+ers), but also financial and insurance services. Seniors also have more leisure time which they can use to take cruises or long vacations in 5-star hotels, or they rediscover an old hobby which prompts them to buy certain things. Every consumer market may have opportunities to the target market of mature consumers.

Seniors may harm the brand image
Marketers often fear harming the brand image by addressing it to senior consumers. This can be easily avoided. First, there are some very selective media to use, media that will not be noticed by other demographic groups, for instance *Viover60*, a magazine for seniors in Norway. Second, senior consumers abhor products 'typically directed to a group of seniors'. They explicitly do not want products for older people, because they do not feel old.

▶

Seniors are very brand-loyal

Another prejudice is that a brand should attract its consumers before they are 50, and that older people will not change their preferred brand. This means that marketing efforts to the over 50s will not have any influence and all efforts will be wasted. In a Belgian study among 935 senior consumers, it appeared that 35% of them were very brand loyal, but exactly the same number of them were brand-switchers: 43% indicated that they liked to try out new things. This confirms the findings of Uncles and Ehrenberg, who claim that older consumers are as open to trial or switching as their younger counterparts.[4]

Consumer markets can also be segmented on the basis of household life-cycle criteria. This concept is founded on the fact that family changes (for instance, marriage, birth and emancipation of children, break-up of the marriage, etc.) affect both income and expenditure of households.[5] Consequently each stage will imply different needs and therefore consumers can be segmented in this manner. Life-cycle segmentation and marketing is extremely popular in the financial sector where CRM software tools (customer relationship marketing) allow marketers to track changes in life cycles of clients as input for a targeted marketing campaign.[6] Studies revealed that the importance attributed to financial choice criteria and financial services varies as consumers pass through the life-cycle stages.[7]

Ninety per cent of men now attend not only their baby's birth, but also the first scan: evidence that men are more involved as parents than ever before. Research published by the equal opportunities commission shows that men undertake one-third of parental childcare in the UK, thanks mainly to the so-called 'swing door' phenomenon. In many families, when dad is home from work, mum is not. She will be out earning her share, leaving her partner in sole charge of the family. A survey in *Management Today* magazine found that three-quarters of men under 55 were likely to attach more importance to their work–life balance than their fathers did. But they are struggling to make that a reality. Almost half of them did not benefit from family-friendly policies at work; a third said that work seriously interfered with their private life; a quarter felt as if they had neglected their children recently.

Yet 50% said they would not trade career progression for more time with their family, reflecting, perhaps, feelings of insecurity in the job market. For similar reasons, 20% of fathers work more than 48 hours a week. A survey from the Department of Trade and Industry reveals that employers and working mothers are more willing to embrace flexitime than fathers. But this report coincides with the introduction of paid paternity leave, entitlement to unpaid time off for either parent with children under six, and the right for both sexes to ask employers for flexible work options, which policymakers hope will redress men's perception that work always comes first.

While men can find more objective guides to becoming a parent helpful, those written by female gurus, such as Penelope Leach or Gina Ford, tend to target the mother. Parenting magazines don't hit the spot either. The title of *Mother & Baby*, the bestseller at 80,000 copies a month, says it all. Even the more gender-neutral and culturally hip *Junior* is read largely by women. As for men's lifestyle magazines, there's little attention to self-improvement. Into the vacuum of this knowledge deficit comes *Dad*, created by Show Media, and edited by a founder of Fathers Direct, the national information centre on fatherhood. It is first a men's magazine, but for dads it is entertaining but informative. The first issue (April 2003) is a pilot, available on newsstands throughout the UK but also to be given away to fathers-to-be attending 12-week scans in selected hospitals. From September the distribution will go nationwide twice a year, reaching a potential 670,000 fathers annually, of which 40% are first-timers. Dad's first advertisers are upmarket – among them are Land Rover, Armani and Sony.[8]

Segmenting markets using lifestyle or personality criteria is called **psychographic segmentation**. Psychographic research was developed when traditional demographic segmentation was shown to have strong limitations in predicting consumer behaviour. Lifestyles describe how people organise their lives and spend their time and money. These external characteristics (playing sports, going to the theatre or a restaurant) are linked to a person's personality (for example, a risk-averse person won't take up dangerous sports). Lifestyle measurement is based on the activities, interests and opinions (AIO) of consumers. AIO combines internal and external characteristics to map the lifestyle of a consumer. Activities include how people spend their money and time, e.g. work, leisure, product use, shopping behaviour, etc. Interests can be in fashion, housing, food, cars, culture, etc. Opinions are attitudes, preferences and ideas on general subjects such as politics or economics, on more specific subjects or on oneself and one's family.

The New World Teen Study[9] found six different value segments for the global youth. It is the largest study of teen lifestyle sponsored by D'Arcy covering 26 countries with 6,400 interviews in the first phase and 44 countries and 27,600 interviews in the second phase. The segmentation is based on what high-school students (aged 15–19) around the world rate as the driving principles (values) that are important to them in life. Teens can be defined in the following groups:

Segment 1: 'Thrills and Chills' (18% worldwide)
This segment is somewhat the stereotype of the trying-to-become-independent hedonist. They have affluent and middle-class parents and have allowance money with which they love to buy 'stuff', not caring about the price for expensive items. They love to go out, meet in pubs and go dating or dancing. They constantly seek out the new, and experimenting is second nature. They are the popular kids in school, the trendsetters that other kids try to copy.

Segment 2: 'Resigned' (14% worldwide)
The resigned have very low expectations and exhibit an inescapable fatalism. They perceive that their lot in the world has already been determined and they are very pessimistic about their chances for economic success. Their looks resemble the ones from the Thrills and Chills segment (lots of body ornaments and colourful hair) but they tend to see the dark side. They come from blue-collar homes, with parents who are factory workers or clerks. The resigned do not participate in many activities outside school; for the resigned the world is grey, and boredom is a major factor.

Segment 3: 'World Savers' (12% worldwide)
This segment consists of the 'good kids', teens that really care about global and local causes, and altruism is the most significant attribute of this value segment. They are doing well in school and are club leaders that join many organisations. They attend the same parties as the Thrills and Chills kids but are not motivated by the new and exciting, rather they are more into romance, relationships and friendships. Grades and higher education are important not only to succeed in finding a better paying job but, more important, to provide careers like doctors, nurses, social workers, environmentalists.

Segment 4: 'Quiet Achievers' (15% worldwide)

Quiet Achievers value anonymity and prefer to stay in the shadows. These teens are the least rebellious of all groups; they study long hours, have strong family ties and realise that success reflects back upon the family. They avoid going to parties or drinking and have a singular purpose – to study hard and do well in school. Most of the Quiet Achievers live in Asia, especially Thailand and China. The parents of Quiet Achievers have some wealth and they will be keen on investing in computers and other technology that will help with homework.

Segment 5: 'Bootstrappers' (14% worldwide)

Bootstrappers are the starry-eyed optimists who cannot wait for adulthood so they can take the world for all it has to offer. Bootstrappers are highly family-oriented and enjoy spending time with relatives. Their key goal is achievement, but not exclusively scholastic. These teens have hopes and dreams that the world will improve in their lifetime and that they will contribute to this improvement. Geographically, many of the Bootstrapper teens come from emerging nations such as Nigeria, Mexico and India but also comprise 40% of Afro-American teens.

Segment 6: 'Upholders' (16% worldwide)

The Upholders are the most dreamy and childlike teens of the six segments. They are slow to make the leap to adulthood and live sheltered and ordered lives. They are different from the Quiet Achievers in that they do not have overwhelming ambitions to succeed. They are content to rest comfortably in the mainstream of life, remaining unnoticed. The girls want to get married and have families and the boys feel they are fated to have jobs similar to their fathers. Many of these teens will make up the middle-class of their countries. Upholders predominate in Asian countries such as Indonesia and Vietnam that value traditions and extended family relationships.

	Global	France	UK	Spain	Germany	Netherlands	Turkey	Russia
Thrills and Chills	**18%**	**24%**	**34%**	18%	**37%**	**32%**	**27%**	16%
Resigned	14%	**18%**	**21%**	21%	**27%**	**26%**	**21%**	12%
World Savers	12%	17%	14%	24%	11%	10%	12%	**20%**
Quiet Achievers	15%	9%	8%	7%	4%	7%	5%	**18%**
Bootstrappers	14%	4%	9%	9%	9%	10%	10%	10%
Upholders	**16%**	7%	7%	12%	5%	6%	8%	14%

Note that worldwide, 11% of teenagers could not be classified.

Source: Moses, E. (2000), *The $100 Billion Allowance. Accessing the Global Teen Market.* New York: John Wiley & Sons. © 2000 Wiley. This material is used by permission of John Wiley & Sons, Inc.

When a company divides its market into segments referring to product or brand preferences, or involvement with categories, it adapts a **behavioural segmentation**. Consumers can be segmented on the basis of the **occasion** in which they use a product or a brand. For instance, a brand of orange juice can be targeted at a segment of consumers drinking juice at breakfast, but there will also be a segment using orange juice in cocktails in the evening, etc.

Motivational segmentation of young smokers

According to research among 15- and 16-year-old smokers in Sweden, Austria, Poland, Belgium and Scotland, girls smoke to support relationships while boys are more individual smokers. Although many countries prohibit tobacco advertising and different anti-smoking campaigns were launched, the number of youngsters that can't resist a cigarette is still increasing. Remarkable in this evolution is that the growth specifically comes from the girls. People tend to smoke cigarettes to cope with negative emotions. For boys the predominant emotions they describe are often anger and stress, whereas girls mention a broader range of emotions: not only anger but also frustration, depression and feeling bad. Girls are also definitely more social smokers. They begin their smoking habit influenced by their female peers, share cigarettes to enhance group feelings and support relationships, and tend to smoke only in specific social situations that are linked to a relaxed and cozy atmosphere. The latter is explained by the stigma girls experience when smoking in public. Boys are more individual smokers. They start smoking on their own and don't consider it as a means to stimulate friendship. When asked for negative aspects about smoking, boys stress the effects on their physical fitness while girls feel ashamed that they are considered as 'smokers' and are concerned about the bad smell of cigarettes. The findings of this survey might influence the anti-smoking advertising campaigns. The majority of them focussed on how tobacco affects sporting performance but this study proves that this argument is not well targeted to the growing group of young women.[10]

Markets can also be divided into segments on the basis of **customer loyalty**. Customers can be loyal to one brand, loyal to a set of brands, or brand-switchers. Obviously, marketing communications efforts can be different when targeting these different groups. Brand-switchers are mainly influenced by material incentives. Sales promotions will therefore be an important tool to get them to buy a product. Brand loyals, on the other hand, do not have to be convinced. Advertising to keep the brand top-of-mind, and loyalty promotions will be the main communications instruments to be used with this group. Consumers that are loyal to a set of brands will have to be approached with a combination of communications tools. Advertising will keep the company's brand in their choice set, while in-store communications and sales promotions will make them choose the company's brand rather than competing brands.

Markets can also be segmented on the basis of the **user status** of customers. An individual can be a non-user, a potential user, a first-time user, a regular user or an ex-user. Non-users are consumers who will never buy a product. They should therefore be avoided in a marketing communications plan. Men, for example, will never buy sanitary towels for themselves. As a result, a communications plan should avoid talking to them as much as possible. Ex-users are more a target group for customer satisfaction research than for a marketing communications campaign. It will be very hard to regain a customer who has deliberately decided not to use the product anymore. Potential users need to be persuaded to try the product for the first time. Advertising, building awareness and attitude, trial promotions and in-store communications may convince them to have a go. First-time users should be converted into regular users. Advertising, building a favourable attitude and a preference for the brand, together with loyalty promotions, might do the job. Regular users should be confirmed in their favourable attitude and buying behaviour. They may be approached by means of advertising and loyalty promotions.

Markets can also be segmented on the basis of **usage rate**. Heavy users are of particular interest to the company because they make up the largest part of sales. Light users may be persuaded to buy and consume more of the product by means of special offers or 'basket-filling' promotions, increasing the number of items they buy.

Segmenting on the basis of **benefits** looked for by consumers can be done by researching all benefits applicable to a certain product category, e.g. a salty snack should be crunchy, taste good and not be expensive. For each of these benefits consumers preferring that benefit are identified and for each benefit products or brands offering that benefit are defined. This segmentation links psychographic, demographic and behavioural variables. A specific benefit for which a brand has a unique strength can be defined, and the communications effort can be targeted at the customer group preferring that particular benefit. As such, benefit segmentation is conceptually very close to positioning.

Finally, consumers can be divided into more homogeneous subgroups on the basis of their **buyer readiness**. When a potential customer is unaware of a brand, awareness-building advertising and sponsorship will have to be used. For a group of customers already aware of the product, attitude building campaigns are called for. People who are interested in and like the product should be persuaded to try it by means of sales promotions and in-store communications.

Similarly, variables that can be a basis for segmenting industrial or business-to-business marketing can be defined. They are summarised in Table 3.3.[11]

In stage two of the STP process, segmentation variables can be combined to form segmentation profiles. Segment profiles have to meet a number of requirements to be effective. Segments have to be **measurable**. It should be possible to gather information about segmentation criteria and about the size, composition and purchasing power of each segment. Segments have to be **substantial** enough to warrant separate and profitable marketing campaigns to be developed particularly for that segment. Segment profiles have to be **attainable**, i.e. accessible and actionable. The marketing manager must be able to identify the segment members and target the marketing action programme at them separately. Unless most members of the segment visit similar places, shop in similar supermarkets or read similar media, it will be difficult to reach them separately and develop specific stimuli for them. In other words, the chosen segments must be in reach of communications media and distribution channels. Finally, market segmentation should ideally lead to more **homogeneous subgroups** in that the members of one group should react similarly to marketing stimuli and differ in their reactions to these stimuli from the members of other segments.

Table 3.3 Business-to-business market segmentation variables

Demographics	Operating variables	Purchasing approaches
■ Industry	■ Technology	■ Purchasing function organisations
■ Company size	■ User/non-user status	■ Power structure
■ Location	■ Customer capabilities	■ Nature of existing relationships
Situational factors	**Personal characteristics**	■ General purchase policies
■ Urgency	■ Buyer/seller similarity	■ Purchasing criteria
■ Specific application	■ Attitudes towards risk	
■ Size of order	■ Loyalty	

Source: Bonoma, V. and Shapiro, B.P. (1983), *Segmenting the Industrial Marketing*. Lexington, MA: Lexington Books. Reproduced with permission.

Nike Goddess targeting active women

In its 30-year history, Nike has become one of the undisputed leaders in sport marketing. But although the company is named after a woman – the Greek goddess of victory – until recently 80% of Nike's sales figures came from male customers, even though the market of women's sports apparel had been skyrocketing. According to the NPD Group, women's sports apparel generated sales of more than $15 billion in 2001, $3 billion more than men's apparel. According to data from MRI, today's physically active women are more affluent and more educated than the average woman. Given that the girls who engage in sports or fitness activities at least twice a month are relatively well educated (most have at least a college degree and many have post-graduate degrees as well), it's not surprising that they tend to occupy professional, executive or managerial positions at work and have household incomes of more than €60,000. Not all active women are 18 years old, in fact the most active group of women is 25 to 34 years old.

Considering these evolutions and the increasing popularity of top female athletes, Nike decided to wake up to the women's business and start doing things differently. Until 2002 advertisement campaigns and sponsorship of female athletes weren't enough to target the segment of active women. Since 1986 Nike developed basket-ball shoes for female feet but with moderate success. Now Nike aims to augment sales to women to at least one-third of its yearly return. Nike Goddess initially began as a concept for a women's-only store because Niketown, the retail setting for which the company is best known, is also known to be a turnoff to female customers. The women's section is on the fourth floor. At each floor, women looking for workout shoes or a yoga mat have to wade through displays for basket-ball, golf and hockey to catch the next escalator up. The feel of the store is dark, loud and harsh. Women weren't comfortable in Nike's flagship stores. As women seem to be more comfortable in an environment that resembles their own homes, Nike Goddess stores have more of a residential feel, with furnishings. At the first Nike Goddess store, located in Newport Beach, California, the mood fits; it has light-blue and white colours, with dark wood floors. Milky-white mannequins with muscles fill the floor-to-ceiling windows. Shoes are displayed on tables or wooden shelves alongside pieces of pottery and white orchids. Overnight, the store can be overhauled to focus on a specific sport or trend – whatever is fashionable for the times.

Designing a new approach to retail was only one element in Nike's effort to connect with women. Another was redesigning the shoes and clothes. Nike's footwear designers worked on 18-month production cycles – making it hard to stay in step with the new styles and colours for women. The apparel group, which worked around 12-month cycles, was better at keeping up with fashion trends but that meant that the clothes weren't co-ordinated with the shoes – a big turnoff for women. The company appointed fashion designers to enlarge the collections and make them more female. On the product development side of the movement towards a more female positioning, Nike introduced the Air Kyoto, the first shoe for yoga (normally practiced in bare feet). Martin Lotti, the Swiss designer who created Air Max Craze and Spector was also the creative brain behind the Kyoto yoga shoe. The upper side of the shoe looks like both sides of a kimono and the sole is black with orange lines that reflect the sand in the Kyoto Zen garden. According to Lotti there are some differences in shoe design for women: the shape of women's feet is different (smaller heel) and as women weigh on average 20% less than men, the shoe soles must be softer and thinner. Darcy Winslow, Nike's global footwear director for women, says the Air Kyoto is the first step in a new journey for women's products at Nike – away from testosterone and a focus on competition and results.

▶

One key insight Nike understood is that for most women, high performance isn't about sports; it's about fitness and about a woman's active nomadic lifestyle. Women go from doing yoga in the morning, to work, to picking up the kids, to going for a run. Nike Goddess has to fit into that kind of life. That's why Nike designers and researchers have spent time scouring trendy workout spots like London's Third Space to pick up on new fitness trends that it calls the '21st-century gym'. And some of the company's designs don't involve workout gear at all, but everyday clothing.

The last step in the female repositioning was communicating the new values and style. For much of its history, Nike either treated women like men in advertising or didn't think much about them at all. Sometimes, though, Nike got the voice right. Back in 1995, the company ran a campaign titled 'If You Let Me Play' that struck a nerve with most women, who had grown up believing 'I could do anything boys could do'. The campaign featured female athletes talking about how sports could change women's lives, from reducing teen pregnancy to increasing their chances of getting a college education. Nike Goddess had to strike a similar chord with women and be more personal than Nike's traditional ads. Nike launched a dedicated website (www.nikegoddess.com, where apart from a forum, a 30-minutes workout mp3 mix is available for free downloading) and 'magalogs' (catalogues in a magazine format) with titles such as 'The Book of Lies', 'The Art of Contradiction' and 'The Encyclopedia of Addictions'. These 'magalogs' presented short picture stories with models wearing the Nike Goddess collection and became extremely popular among women because of their humourous and recognisable storylines in Bridget Jones style. For instance, one shows pictures of a girl looking at herself in the mirror of a dressing room and thinking: 'I've been sporting 35 minutes. I've spent 2 hours hesitating whether I would or would not sport tonight. So I've been busy with sporting for 2 hours and 35 minutes. A great improvement!'[12]

Targeting

After segmenting the market, opportunities for each segment should be singled out. The next stage in the process is targeting segments.[13] There are two decisions here: how many segments will the company target, and which segments are most attractive to that company?

Market concentration is used when the company chooses one segment and tries to be a market leader within that segment. Market differentiation involves directing the marketing effort to different segments with different marketing and communications strategies. Undifferentiated marketing is using the same strategies to all segments. There are five basic types of targeting strategies.

- **Concentration on one segment**: a company chooses one segment (one product for one market) and develops a marketing mix for that segment. This strategy has some positive aspects. The company will be able to build up expertise and enjoy learning effects. On the other hand, it will be dependent on a single segment (which could suddenly stop growing) and vulnerable to competitors. For instance, Jaguar was a company concentrating on one segment until it was acquired by Ford.

- **Selective specialisation**: a company chooses a number of segments that look attractive. There is no synergy between the segments but every segment looks profitable.

Activities in one segment can compensate for other, slower-growing segments. For instance, Richard Branson started with a music label (Virgin) which he sold while launching new services in different segments: travel (holidays, trains, flights and travel guides), entertainment (a new music label V2, virgin megastores, books, radio and internet service providing), telecom (mobile and fixed lines), lifestyle (soft drinks, wines, cosmetics and fitness clubs), energy (water, gas and electricity), finance (credit cards, loans, insurances . . .) and motoring (retailing of cars and bikes).

- **Product specialisation**: a company concentrates on one product and sells it to different market segments. For instance, a company can sell microscopes to companies, hospitals, universities, schools, labs, etc.

- **Market specialisation**: a company concentrates on one market segment and sells different products to that group of customers, e.g. a company selling microscopes, oscilloscopes, etc.

- **Full market coverage**: a company tries to target all customer groups with all the products they need. For instance, General Motors makes cars (in different classes), four-wheel drive cars, vans, agricultural machines, etc.

The second decision is to select the most attractive target groups. To evaluate segments companies have to look at four elements: size and growth of segments, structural attractiveness of a segment, objectives and budgets of a company, and stability of market segments. Current turnover, potential growth and profitability of segments are the first important conditions a marketer should evaluate for each segment. For small companies it could be wiser to target smaller or less attractive niche segments when competition is strong in the larger segments. Structural attractiveness can be analysed by using Porter's model. Current competitors, potential entrants, substitution products, and the power of customers and suppliers influence the attractiveness of segments. Some attractive segments may not fit with the strategic objectives or long-term goals of a company.

C&A, the Dutch clothing retailer active in 12 European countries, was traditionally positioned toward families. But at the end of the 1990s C&A had troubles competing in this segment with other, more trendy retailers such as the Scandinavian H&M. With the new millennium C&A decided to change strategies and repositioned internationally with new collections, a bigger product range and, since 2003, new store concepts: C&A kids, C&A Women and Clockhouse. The retailer now has 14 Clockhouse shops in Austria, Belgium, Switzerland and the Czech Republic, 29 Kids stores in Germany and Belgium and two Women stores in Germany. C&A Kids is targeted at young families with children up to 14 years old. Clockhouse targets 15–24 year olds. The new store concepts allow C&A to find good locations of smaller sizes (200–400 square metres), advantageous considering that it is hard to find the space for traditional C&A outlets of 2,000 square metres and the strategy of C&A to target smaller cities and villages. Clockhouse shops have dropped the umbrella brand C&A because the teenager segment is known to distance itself from parental habits and consequently avoids shopping in stores that are frequented by their parents. The new strategy seems to be working as C&A's sales have risen by 10% in 2001 and 2002 and the company was expecting growth of 5% in 2003.[14]

Positioning

Positioning a brand or product is differentiating it from competitors in the mind of consumers, e.g. Volvo is a safe car, Duracell batteries last longer, etc. Positioning means taking into account a complicated set of perceptions, feelings and impressions a consumer has about a brand or product. Consumers will position brands in certain associative schemes even if a company is not actively promoting the competitive advantage of its products.

A frequently used visual tool that helps companies position products and brands is 'mapping', based on axes representing the dimensions important to consumers. Every product or brand is given a score on both dimensions and the map shows which products or brands have the same characteristics. Figure 3.1 is a map of the salty snacks market. In the eyes of a consumer, there seems to be a big difference between peanuts and cocktail snack nuts. The latter are competing with fantasy snacks (snacks in different shapes). There's no product considered as natural and different. This is a hole in the market, but to be attractive it should be a profitable hole. There are a number of positioning strategies a company can use.[15] They are summarised in Table 3.4.

Figure 3.1 Mapping the salty snack market

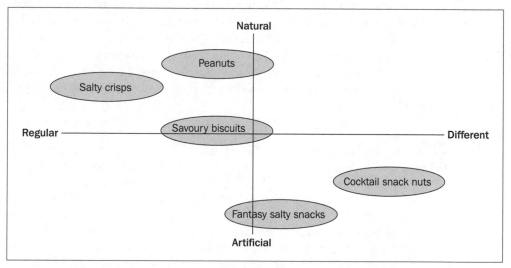

Table 3.4 Positioning strategies

■ Product attributes or benefits	■ Product user
■ Price/quality	■ Competitor
■ Use or application	■ Cultural symbols
■ Product class	

Positioning by product attributes and benefits is based on a unique selling proposition which makes a company's brand or product special for the target market. For example, Vidal Sassoon Wash&Go was the first shampoo (introduced by Procter & Gamble) offering a unique combination of shampoo and conditioner. Positioning by price/quality means offering the same or better quality at a lower price than competitors. For instance, Virgin Coke offers a 'good' coke with a brand image comparable to Coca-Cola and Pepsi but at a lower price. Positioning by use or application implies emphasising a specific use or application of the product. For instance, Kellogg's introduced cereals as a snack at hours other than breakfast by offering little variety packages that kids can take to school. Positioning by product class is an alternative to positioning against another brand, e.g. Eurostar offers a fast train connection as an alternative to airline connections. Positioning by product user is associating a product with a specific group of users, e.g. Aquarius, a thirst-quenching isotone drink for sporting men and women, is positioning a brand by a group of product users. In positioning by competitor, comparative advertising is often used. A well-known example is Avis, who use the slogan 'we try harder', to position itself against the market leader in car and truck rental, Hertz. 7-up was positioned as 'the un-cola' and became number three in the soft drinks market. Cultural symbols refer to brand personalities or branding devices such as Tony the Tiger (Kellogg's Frosties), Mr Clean, Captain Iglo, Bibendum (Michelin). These symbols are a visual way of successfully differentiating from competitors. The brand personality or cultural symbol often visualises the key benefit of a product. For instance, Mr Clean is a powerful, clean symbol. Tony the Tiger gives power and strength.

A company may possibly detect different competitive edges, in which case it will have to choose one or more competitive advantages for its positioning strategy. A company can focus on one single advantage for a target group. This exclusive Unique Selling Proposition (USP) will be easier to remember by the target group, especially in low-involvement buying situations. Other companies will stress more than one competitive advantage. This is necessary when two or more competitors claim to be the best in the same attributes. Volvo, for example, claims to be both safe and durable.

In 1950 Monte Goldman founded Eastpak, originally as Eastern Canvas Products, Inc. The company produced big durable bags that had to survive wars. When Mark Goldman joined his father's company, he convinced him to start making practical bags targeted to students. Not just school bags but comfortable bags for life, with padded backs and organiser pockets for all the things students carry with them through the day. The Eastpak brand name was introduced in 1979 with the mission statement 'to offer authentic, functional backpacks guaranteed for life with progressive designs for the mobile youth' and sold 1,000 pieces in the first year. In 2000 Eastpak sold almost four million backpacks in Europe accounting for €80 million sales. The Eastpak main target group is between 15 and 18 years old. Eastpak is the favourite backpack for the cool, progressive and trendsetting segment of skaters. About 60% of the skaters segment wants to own an Eastpak. Eastpak's brand values can be summarised as authentic, resistant, unique and naturally cool. In advertising campaigns (see Plate 8) the focus is always on the product and on the durability aspect. The target group itself is never incorporated in the ads because the group of teens does not have role models or popular celebrities. Advertising campaigns have always been on the edge: a cemetery full of backpacks, a skeleton wearing

▶

an Eastpak in the desert, dogs standing in a row to make love with the backpack, etc. Above-the-line communications only account for 45% of the brand's communications budget. All other marketing communications are strictly linked to the interest of the target group, for instance skating and BMX events.[16]

Summary

The segmenting-targeting-positioning process is one of the core elements of the strategic marketing plan. Market segmentation is the process of dividing consumers into homogeneous segment profiles. This can be done on the basis of one characteristic of potential consumers, or multiple characteristics can be combined. Segmentation criteria can be behavioural-related, such as buying occasion, loyalty status, usage rate, buyer readiness or benefit sought, or general, such as demographics and psychographics (lifestyle, personality, etc.). Market segments have to be measurable, substantial, attainable, different and large enough. The next stage in the process is to target one or more of these customer groups. Marketing communications can concentrate on one segment, specialise selectively, specialise in specific markets or products, or fully cover the market. Marketers have to define a unique position for their products in the mind of the consumer, based on product attributes or benefits, price/quality, use or application, product class, product users, competitors or cultural symbols. Developing, monitoring and adapting an appropriate position for a brand, a product or a company is a crucial prerequisite for effective marketing communications.

Review questions

1 What are the stages in the segmenting-targeting-positioning process, and what is the relevance of this process for marketing communications?

2 On the basis of what criteria can markets be segmented? How can market segmentation influence the communications mix?

3 What are segment profiles, and what are the requirements for effective segmentation?

4 Discuss the most important targeting strategies and the selection of target groups.

5 What positioning strategies can a company develop, and what are the consequences for communications strategies?

Further reading

Dibb, S. and Simkin, L. (1996), *The Market Segmentation Workbook. Target Marketing for Marketing Managers*. London: Routledge.

Hooley, G., Saunders, J. and Piercy, N. (2003), *Marketing Strategy and Competitive Positioning*. London: Financial Times Prentice Hall.

Ries, A. and Trout, J. (2001), *Positioning: The Battle for Your Mind*. New York: McGraw-Hill.

Wedel, M. and Kamakura, W. (1999), *Market Segmentation: Conceptual and Methodological Foundations*. Norwell, MA: Kluwer Academic Press.

Case 3

Mercedes' Baby Benz

In 1883 Karl Benz and Gottlieb Daimler each founded a company in Germany and started producing cars. For about 30 years the two companies competed against one another. In 1902 Daimler started to name his cars after his daughter, Mercedes, instead of Daimler. After the First World War, cars were still rare and considered a luxury good. The economic crisis in Germany made things even worse and the two companies merged in order to survive, founding the company Mercedes-Benz. In 1909 a patent was taken on the star, the symbol for the three motor divisions: motors for on land, on water and in the air. In November 1998 Mercedes-Benz merged with the American company Chrysler to form DaimlerChrysler. There is very little overlap in their main geographic markets (Chrysler has its largest market in the US and Mercedes in Europe) and their products are complementary. Today DiamlerChrysler is the third largest automobile manufacturer in terms of revenues, the sixth largest in terms of units built, and is amongst the most innovative and profitable in its industry. DaimlerChrysler employs 425,000 people around the world, has production facilities in 34 countries, and produces 4 million cars a year sold in 200 countries (Case Table 3.1).

Why design a compact car?

Traditionally, Mercedes is associated with large, prestigious sedan cars. However, the idea of an innovative compact car with Mercedes' standard safety and exceptional economy of space is something Mercedes engineers have been working on since the 1980s. Mercedes began researching a compact car, initially concentrating not just on the technical aspects, but more on the wishes of the customers, traffic analyses and the findings of sociological studies. Mercedes' market researchers talked to more than 1,000 male and female motorists in Europe and asked them about their visions of the car of the future. In general, there seemed to be a demand for an attractive design, compact exterior dimensions combined with a spacious interior, a high utility value and a high standard of all-round safety. In addition, people wanted low emission engines with high fuel efficiency. Mercedes concluded that the time had come for an innovative, extremely compact automobile taking up less space on the road, consuming less fuel and producing lower exhaust emissions. Two drivable prototypes were built, one electrically powered and one with an internal combustion engine. The Mercedes board presented them to the public at the Frankfurt International Motor Show in September 1993. Study A, as the prototype was called, got a lot of positive response. To the question of whether Mercedes should build this car, 90% of the visitors answered yes. Study A also became a major crowd-puller at the Tokyo Motor Show a few weeks later: 95% of those questioned said that they would like to see the innovative model going into production soon. Mercedes-Benz decided to go ahead with its A class.

Due to its concept, the A class defines a car segment of its own and can be said to combine characteristics of four existing segments (Case Figure 3.1). It is estimated to appeal to about 30% of both the sub-compact class and the compact class buyers.

Target groups

Mercedes' traditional car buyers are typical of an older age class, male, earn a relatively high income (the median of which ranges from €2,501 to €3,500 a month), and are in a later stage of their life cycle (grown-up children). The target group of the A class would look totally different. Mercedes-Benz undertook several studies to determine which segment would be best to target. One study concerned the family life cycle, the conclusion of which was that the consumer group consisting of two

Case Table 3.1
Leading world car manufacturers

Company	Country	Turnover ($bn)
General Motors Corporation	US	178.17
Ford Motor Company	US	168.48
DaimlerChrysler	Germany	134.54
Toyota Motor Company Ltd	Japan	102.67
Volkswagen AG	Germany	67.00

Case Figure 3.1
A class characteristics

'A car is the expression of one's personality.'
'A car makes me independent.'

By means of cluster analysis, eight consumer segments could be identified: individuals, conformists, aesthetics, possessive conservatives, comfort and safety, cost-conscious environmentalists, car advocates and functionalists. In order to define which segments to target, these groups were evaluated on the characteristics that Mercedes thought would best match with the profile of a Mercedes A class driver. The A class driver profile is as follows: quite young people with a relatively high income, who are progressive (independent and innovative with respect to style), have a strong personality (in the sense of standing out, being extrovert and having a higher social position), and whose decision on what make of car to buy depends on how easy it is to handle and to manoeuvre, how stylish, economic and reliable it is, and how multifunctional the car can be. Case Table 3.2 shows to what extent the eight segments possess these characteristics. The evaluation of each characteristic is multiplied with a weighting factor reflecting the importance of the characteristic, after which all products are summed to become a total score on 100. The higher the total score, the better the segment corresponds with the A class profile.

On the basis of the total scores, Mercedes decided to target three segments, specifically: the individuals, the aesthetics and the car advocates. Since the analysis was done across Europe, Mercedes also checked whether these segments were sufficiently represented

adults without children was the largest and seemed most suitable to target. Another study revealed that young women especially were interested in the Mercedes A class as a second car in the household.

In a more extensive study European consumers were asked to what extent they agreed with 18 statements. Examples of these statements are:

'I like cars with an exceptional styling.'
'I like beautiful cars.'
'I like to drive very fast.'

Case Table 3.2 Class A target groups

Evaluation criteria	Individuals	Conformists	Aesthetics	Possessive conservatives	Comfort and safety	Cost-conscious environmentalists	Car advocates	Functionalists
Relatively young	++	–	+	– –	–	+	+	+
High income	++	++	++	–	++	0	0	0
Progressiveness	++	– –	+	0	+	0	+	0
Personality	++	– –	– –	– –	+	++	0	++
Manoeuvrability	++	– –	+	–	–	+	0	0
Handling	0	+	0	+	0	0	+	0
Styling	++	–	+	–	0	–	0	–
Multifunctional	+	0	+	0	++	0	0	0
Economic	0	+	0	+	0	+	+	0
Reliable	+	+	+	0	+	0	0	++
Total (100)	83	39	64	40	56	52	65	51

Case Table 3.3 Positioning of Mercedes and its competitors

Brand	Mercedes-Benz	Smart	Chrysler	Jeep
Slogan	The future of the automobile	Reduce to the max	Engineered to be great cars	Jeep. There is only one
Key definition	Top offer in all targeted segments	Smart solution	Premium and expensive	Legendary American hero
Core character	Automotive leader in quality, innovation and fascination	Premium light in emotional, individual and intelligent solutions	American, expressive, athletic, refined	Distinctive, mastery, reach
Brand position	Leadership in comfort, safety, reliability, durability and resale value. Fascination from exclusive, elegant, and timeless design with recognisable MB styling elements	Intelligent, pure, clear, individual, unusual, original, innovative, future-oriented, young, urban	Enhanced driving experience, leading edge design, technical innovation, heritage and pride	Legendary American hero, go anywhere, do anything. Four wheel drive leader, innovative, mastery, power and performance. Security, reach, robust to refined, adventurous. Heritage and pride
Pricing	Top pricing	Light medium pricing in respective segment	Medium and upper price segments	Mid- and upper pricing in each segment

in the largest European markets (Germany, Italy, UK and France), which indeed proved to be the case.

Positioning
Positioning of the DaimlerChrysler brands are shown in Case Table 3.3.

This positioning perfectly fits the reasons German, British and French consumers give for buying a Mercedes: quality, brand image, reliability and safety (Case Table 3.4).

The challenge is to position the A class in a way that fits with the general Mercedes positioning as

Case Table 3.4 Reasons for buying of people interviewed (%)

	Mercedes	Audi	BMW	Lexus	Nissan
High-quality products	83	67	77	50	37
Makes very reliable cars	82	65	71	48	53
Brand with clear identity	81	56	82	25	32
Makes prestigious cars	80	47	75	25	11
Concerned about safety	77	59	66	33	35
Makes beautiful cars	72	48	72	19	23
Makes cars with character	59	41	66	19	18
Committed to good service	58	44	52	43	49
Is committed to driving enjoyment	57	37	66	27	25
Cares about the environment	45	34	35	12	18
Innovatively styled products	44	48	51	26	21
Has good advertising	42	36	39	19	27
Makes fast cars	38	31	63	22	12
Successful in motor sports	36	25	41	10	10
Influenced by advertising	11	12	10	4	14

Case Figure 3.2 The unique characteristics of the Baby Benz

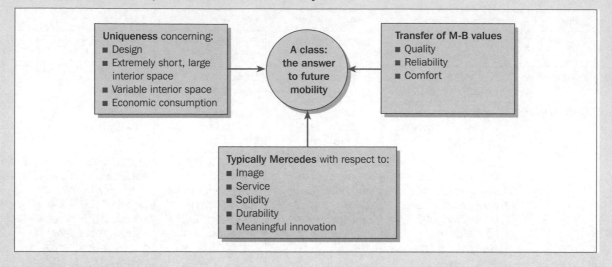

well as with the totally different car type and the totally different target group. Mercedes tries to position the A class as the answer to future mobility problems, stressing three important elements: the uniqueness, the transferred Mercedes-Benz values to this other type of car, and the basic Mercedes-Benz characteristics (Case Figure 3.2).

Marketing communications

In the summer of 1996 teaser ads for the A class were launched to make the Europeans aware of the notion of the Baby Benz. One of the ads read: 'Safety is not only a matter of size, but also of time – the new A class comes in 97'. The reasons for this early communication were fourfold. First, the customer usually hesitates for one or two years before purchasing a new car. Second, Mercedes is targeting a completely new customer segment. Third, the A class defines a completely new car concept. And fourth, the car is not like a Mercedes, as a consequence of which threshold fear had to be reduced. Starting one month before the launch at the Geneva car show in March 1997, an extensive marketing communications campaign started. The communications messages were characterised by a tone of voice consumers did not expect from Mercedes. It was a totally new form of communication for a totally new car. The communications broke with the prevailing Mercedes image, and tried to bring something sympathetic and challenging by using cartoons and puns. One ad, for example, shows a

few tips for remembering the name of Mercedes' new car: grab a cactus (Aaah!), look in the mirror (Aaah!), bang one's hand against a tree (Aaah!) and hold one's hand over a candle (Aaah!). Other ads mention words in which the letters A are replaced by a picture of the car, for example ✪CTION! (See Plate 3.)

Results

Pre-tests showed exceptional results for Mercedes, with most positive responses coming from young couples with one or two children, aged 30 to 45 years, 35% of whom were women. During the launch, test drives won excellent ratings and press comments were very positive in the sense of 'never was small so big', 'a subtle revolution', and 'a milestone', until the car tipped during the 'moose test' in Sweden, turning the Baby Benz into 'a problem child'.

Questions

1 Which segmentation variables did Mercedes-Benz use to segment the market?

2 Assess the positioning strategy of the Mercedes A class. Could other positions have been used?

3 What communications tools do you suggest Mercedes-Benz should use to address its primary target groups?

4 Do you think that the creative approach used by Mercedes-Benz so far matches its positioning strategy? If any, which positioning mistake may the company be making?

5 Do you think it is wise for Mercedes to build a car in this segment? What are the advantages and disadvantages?

Based on: Documents provided by Koen Van Hout, Manager Marketing & Distribution PKW, Mercedes-Benz Belgium; Emma Rylander and Ronald Charlajian, 1999; Paper prepared for the marketing communication course, Vesalius College, Spring 1999; Luc Wyns (1999) 'Marketing Strategy of Mercedes-Benz', paper prepared for the Marketing course, Postgraduate Programme in Management, Free University of Brussels, Belgium; *Automotive International*, 1998 and 1999 issues; *Autocar*, 1999 issues; 'Belangrijkste autobouwers' (Most important car constructors), 1999. *De Standaard*, 1 March; P. Stobart (1994), *Brand Power*, London: Macmillan, p. 109. Reproduced with permission of DaimlerChrysler, Belgium, Luxembourg.

References

1 Ries, A. and Trout, J. (1986), *Positioning: The Battle for Your Mind*. New York: McGraw-Hill.

2 Bovée, C.L., Thill, J.V., Dovel, G.P. and Wood, M.B. (1995), *Advertising Excellence*. Englewood Cliffs, NJ: McGraw-Hill.

3 See also Dibb, S. and Simkin, L. (1996), *The Market Segmentation Workbook. Target Marketing for Marketing Managers*. London: Routledge; Cathelat, B. (1993), *Socio-Styles. The New Lifestyles Classification System for Identifying and Targeting Consumers and Markets*. London: Kogan Page.

4 Uncles, M. and Ehrenberg, A. (1990), 'Brand Choice among Older Consumers', *Journal of Advertising Research*, 30(4), 19–22.

5 Redondo-Bellon, I., Royo-vela, M. and Aldas-Manzano, J. (2001), 'A Family Life Cycle Model Adapted to the Spanish Environment', *European Journal of Marketing*, 35, 5/6, 612–38.

6 Dumont, E. (2001), 'Is Life Cycle Marketing Outdated?', *Bank Marketing*, (April), 12–13.

7 Javalgi, R.J. and Dion, P. (1999), 'A Life Cycle Segmentation Approach to Marketing Financial Products and Services', *The Services Industries Journal*, 19 (July), 74–96.

8 *The Guardian*, 9 April 2003.

9 Moses, E. (2000), *The $100 Billion Allowance. Accessing the Global Teen Market*. New York: John Wiley & Sons.

10 *De Morgen*, 3 May 2003.

11 Bonoma, V. and Shapiro, B.P. (1983), *Segmenting the Industrial Marketing*. Lexington, MA: Lexington Books.

12 *De Morgen*, 26 October 2002; *Fast Company*, Issue 61, August 2002; *Active Marketer*, December 2002.

13 Kotler, P. (1994), *Marketing Management: Analysis, Planning, Implementation, and Control*. Englewood Cliffs, NJ: Prentice Hall.

14 *De Morgen*, 2 May 2003.

15 Aaker, D.A., Batra, R. and Myers, J.G. (1992), *Advertising Management*. Englewood Cliffs, NJ: Prentice Hall.

16 Geuens, M., Goessaert, G., Mast, G. and Weijters, B. *Case study: Eastpak & JanSport*. Vlerick Leuven Gent Management School, 2002.

Chapter 4
Objectives

Chapter outline

A hierarchy of marketing communications objectives

Stages in the product life cycle and marketing communications objectives

Chapter objectives

This chapter will help you to:

- Get an overview of the various goals and objectives of marketing communications campaigns
- Understand the relation between stages in the product life cycle (PLC) and communications objectives

Introduction

Once the target group of the marketing communications plan is well defined, it is crucial to the planning process to set the main communications objectives. These goals will determine the choice of the right communications and media mix and will consequently influence message and strategy development, budgeting and effectiveness research issues. Communications goals will always have to fit in with the marketing objectives such as market share, estimated return figures or market penetration goals. These marketing objectives, in turn, are formulated to contribute to the overall company goals, such as making profits, providing earnings for shareholders, etc. Formulating marketing communications objectives is also important in judging the effectiveness of a campaign. The question of whether an advertising campaign, promotional action or whatever other communications plan has been 'good' or 'effective' depends on the goals that were defined for that specific campaign. It is therefore impossible to judge campaigns or individual communications executions without a thorough knowledge of the objectives. Different categories and types of objectives can be distinguished. Furthermore, the product life cycle stage will also influence the marketing communications objectives.

Marketing communications objectives

Marketing communications objectives can be broadly divided into three categories: reach goals, process goals and effectiveness goals. The reach goal of communicating is to reach the target groups in an effective and efficient way. For this purpose a good segmentation and audience definition is needed, as well as insights into the media behaviour of the desired segments. The detailed considerations of media planning will be the subject of Chapter 7. Process goals are conditions which should be established before any communication can be effective. All communications should capture the attention of the target group, then appeal or be appreciated and last but not least be processed (and remembered). The third type of communications goals are the effectiveness goals. They are, of course, the most important ones, since reach goals only assure sufficient exposure, and process goals only ensure enough processing of the message to make the effectiveness goals possible.

Evidently, long-term sales and market share growth are the ultimate objectives of most marketing communications campaigns. However, sales are influenced by other marketing mix instruments, such as product quality, design, benefits, packaging, distribution and pricing strategies, as well as the market evolution, technology and innovations, and of course competitive action. Since the DAGMAR[1] (Defining Advertising Goals for Measured Advertising Results) model was published in 1961 by Russell Colley, communications goals have emphasised the current stage of the buyer or potential buyer in the purchase process rather than just immediate sales effects. This insight also helped marketers to use measurable goals since communications effects on sales were all but impossible to isolate due to interaction effects with other marketing mix variables.[2] The communications effects or goals that are distinguished in the DAGMAR model are shown in Figure 4.1.

Figure 4.1 Communications objectives: the DAGMAR model

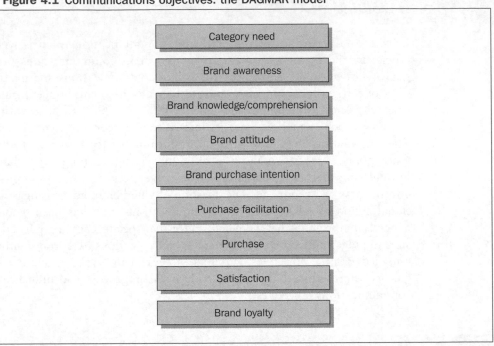

Source: Colley, R.H. (1961), *Defining Advertising Goals for Measured Advertising Results*. New York: Association of National Advertisers.

The DAGMAR model is essentially a hierarchy-of-effects model, similar to those discussed in Chapter 2. It is frequently used as a framework to define communications goals. To get a person or organisation to buy a product that was not bought before, or to increase the frequency or quantity of repeat buying, a consumer will normally go through the phases shown in Figure 4.1.

According to the DAGMAR model, during the communications process nine effects can be established. When a marketer is defining his or her communications strategies he or she will have to select the most appropriate communications effect or goals from the list above. Every promotional campaign should be organised with one of these communications objectives in mind. The choice of the right goals depends on the problems that have arisen in the preliminary situation analysis of the market, brand positions, competition, opportunities and threats. In that sense, communications objectives are only an intermediary way to reach marketing goals of a higher order, such as sales volumes, market share, distribution penetration, etc.

A good set of communications goals should have a number of characteristics. It should:[3]

- fit in with the overall company and marketing goals;
- be relevant to the identified problems and specific to cope with threats or to build on opportunities in the market;
- be targeted to different target audiences; this implies that different target groups (such as countries, socio-demographic groups, heavy and light users) could need different communications objectives;

- be quantified in order to be measurable which allows you to make a precise evaluation of the campaign results;
- be comprehensive and motivating to all involved persons but at the same time be realistic and achievable;
- be timed to enable specific scheduling of the campaign as well as planning of results evaluation;
- be translated into sub-goals when necessary.

The communications objectives are guidelines for everyone who is involved in campaign development and realisation: marketers, advertising agencies, PR officials and sales promotion agencies, media planners and buyers, and researchers. They are also fundamental to campaign strategy: all phases of the marketing communications plan, such as creative, media and budgeting decisions, should be built on the goals.

As communications objectives are also the criteria against which a campaign's success (or failure) is evaluated, it is important that they are well defined and quantified. Only when goals are measurable are they a management tool enabling you to gauge returns against investments.

Developing category wants

The first basic condition to be fulfilled by a brand is that it should fit within category needs and wants. If buyers cannot perceive the communicated product or brand as an appropriate answer to their needs and demands, they will not be motivated to buy it. Category wants or needs can be defined as the existence of one or more of these buying motives and the perception of the product category as a good means of meeting these motives. Of course, although category need is always necessary before other brand-related objectives work, it is clear that in most cases, i.e. when promotional actions and communications are targeted to category users, it can be considered as already present and thus can be ignored. Indeed, it can be assumed that category wants are already well developed in product categories such as food, detergents, insurances and cars. However, in product categories that are infrequently purchased or infrequently used, such as pain killers, communicating category needs to remind buyers of their present but forgotten need may be useful.

Using category need as a primary communications objective is a must for innovations. Consumers should first understand which need is satisfied by an innovation and the difference between the 'new category' and known categories should be stressed. When Sony invented the CD player, the first thing to communicate, before building awareness for the Sony brand, was the difference in sound quality compared with the record player. Creating category awareness is also an appropriate goal when non-category users are addressed. For instance, when telecom operators of cellular phone networks communicate to a group of non-owners of a cellular phone they will stress the need for mobile telephones. When they address owners they will stress other benefits such as special rates and special services. Sometimes a manufacturer repositions a product or service to meet other usage occasions or methods of use. Kellogg's introduced Variety cereals in small packages to broaden its cereal market from the breakfast moment to other snack and school moments and consequently takes part in the between-meals market. Category wants can be omitted, refreshed or actively used in market communications in the different situations described above. The following communications goals are not on a category level but focus on the brand.[4]

Brand awareness: recognition and recall

Brand awareness is the association of some physical characteristics such as a brand name, logo, package, style, etc. with a category need. There are three ways brand awareness can be defined. For example, if people think of a soft drink, they may spontaneously think of either Coca-Cola, Fanta or Lipton Ice Tea. This is their top-of-mind brand awareness. In an unaided context people may recall several brands spontaneously. This is brand recall or unaided spontaneous awareness. It is also possible that people recognise a brand by its package, colour, logo, etc. This is brand recognition or aided awareness. Aided brand awareness is of course less difficult to achieve. Less repetition and thus smaller investments are needed to establish it than brand name recall. Research has shown that the correlation between recall and recognition is on average 50%. Buyers will be better able to recognise brands than to recall brand names spontaneously.[5] On the other hand, brand recall is not a guarantee that the buyer will recognise the brand in a shop.

The question of which awareness goal should be aspired to by a marketer depends on the situational circumstances in which the product or brand is bought. If the purchase decision is made at another time and location than the point of sales (at the office, at home), or when a buyer has to ask explicitly for a certain product or service (e.g. at a drugstore or a pharmacist) brand name recall is needed. This is also true when a shopping list with preferred brand names for every category is made prior to going to a shop, or when somebody is making purchases by phone (airline tickets, courier services, etc.). When the purchase decision is made in the store, and the buyer can use visual cues such as packages, displays, colours, and logos, brand recognition is more important than brand recall.

All European countries are different in terms of market positions of the Eurocard/MasterCard compared to its major competition (Visa card, American Express, Diner's Club), resulting in a variety of marketing objectives and target audiences from one country to another. For instance, in central Europe Eurocard/MasterCard is still introducing the concept of credit cards (which will require stressing the category needs in advertising), while in Italy the notion of revolving credit is still unknown and in Germany first-time card applicants (youngsters entering the labour market) should be captured. This inevitably has meant that local media and tactics have been applied but all with the basic European advertising strategy that was first launched in Europe in 1998 in mind. Apart from the main advertising objective in this strategy, to build significant brand awareness, Eurocard/MasterCard discovered that its users are more family-oriented and less hedonistic than Visa users. They make the same purchases and spend similar amounts of money but are more in line with values such as personal balance and harmony than with materialistic values. Therefore Eurocard/MasterdCard's aim is to build a stronger emotional bond with the target audience in all countries to differentiate the card and its services from its main competitors. The core selling idea for the card is that Eurocard/MasterCard is the best way to pay for everything that matters. It is expressed by the 'Priceless' campaign stressing the fact that there are some things money can't buy – and for everything else there's Eurocard/MasterCard. As a result of this campaign unprompted brand awareness ▶

for Eurocard/MasterCard in its top nine European markets improved by 3% to 37% in April 2001, whereas Visa declined by 3% to 61%. Specifically, the major increases in awareness include Italy (+8%), Spain (+4%) and the UK (+3%).[6]

To stimulate brand recognition, showing the product package or logo in advertising and other communications in exactly the same colours and formats is crucial. The latter implies that media such as radio advertising are less appropriate for brand recognition goals. To build brand recall, repetition of the association between the category and the brand is necessary. Sign-off slogans should therefore always integrate category and brand name. In some cases a marketer should try to attain both brand recall and recognition. A consumer then recalls a brand at home and will search for it at the supermarket or store. For this search process to be successful, brand recognition is needed. Sometimes this dual brand awareness objective is required, since for many product categories consumers limit their search activity based on loyalty to a limited set of brands.

Every communications activity should take brand awareness into account. Even if brand attitude or other objectives are more dominant, it will still be important to support brand awareness. A brand can never have too much brand awareness. Brand awareness should also be established prior to brand attitude and the other communications objectives. If a brand is not known, it would be impossible to build an image, preference or attitude towards that brand. The effect of brand awareness on brand choice and brand purchases is substantial. If two brands are equally valued, the brand with the highest awareness will be purchased more often.[7]

Brand knowledge

Brand knowledge and comprehension mean that target consumers are aware of the most essential brand characteristics, features and benefits. They know the strengths of the brands as compared to competitive brands, they know why they should buy brand X instead of brand Y or Z. Essentially, consumers should be able to recall the brand's positioning. This knowledge may be based on very objective information, but also on brand image and lifestyle positioning. It is clear that what people know about a brand is very subjective and based on past experiences or on beliefs and perceptions. The knowledge and comprehension stage is strongly related to the next step in the DAGMAR hierarchy, in which a certain degree of like (or dislike) and preference is added to the information stored in a consumer's memory.

Brand attitude

Alldays Tanga: developing a positive attitude towards string panty liners

When Alldays, the Procter & Gamble brand of panty liner, introduced Alldays Tanga (a string panty liner) in May 2000 in markets where competitor Mölnlycke had already launched Libresse String, it was clear that the tried and tested formula of proclaiming a superior product feature which had led to a trusted but rather scientific brand image for the Alldays brand had to be put aside. String underwear became the most fashionable underwear at the beginning

▶

of the new millennium, particularly among young women. As research had shown Procter & Gamble that these young women were tired of advertising in the femcare category that took itself too seriously and Alldays Tanga needed to project a younger, more contemporary image, the company decided to shift perceptions of Alldays to a more cosmetic brand by using honest and straight-talking advertising without product demonstrations and scientific language. Alldays Tanga broke the advertising rules of the category by using humour. The TV spot showed a young woman in a club in Ibiza doing strange dance steps (imitated by the rest of the club to the tunes of Bob Sinclair's major club hit 'Can you feel it') because her string panty liner would not stay in place. Market research had showed Procter & Gamble that the only real issue involved with panty liners was the ultimate embarrassment for young women of having to deal with a dislodged panty liner while wearing the most fitted and glamorous clothes.

This campaign proved to reflect a well-liked brand imagery, with young women feeling that finally someone in the femcare category was speaking their language. It was also very successful in launching the Tanga product: in Germany, where it was the first major brand string launch, Alldays Tanga's share of the panty liner market was 65% at the end of December 2000, while the main competitor had only 14% share. In Greece where Alldays Tanga was second to market, the brand nearly matched the key competitor's value share six months after launch.[8]

If consumers are equally aware of a number of brands in a certain product category they will base their brand choice on an evaluation of the different brands. The result of this evaluation is called 'brand attitude'. Brand attitude is the perceived value of a brand to a consumer. Because a brand is stronger (and thus has more loyal customers) when the differentiation with another brand is bigger, brand attitude is an important communication objective.

A marketer should study the current brand attitudes and perceptions and then decide what to do. If there is no brand attitude, and people are unaware of brand benefits, a brand attitude should be created. If there is a moderately favourable brand attitude, the attitude should be reinforced through adapted communications. Improving attitudes among these benefit-aware target groups will lead to more frequent buying and hopefully make customers loyal. A very favourable brand attitude should be maintained to keep all loyal customers satisfied. In marketing practice there's no such thing as a permanently very favourable brand attitude because attitudes are liable to changes as a consequence of dynamic markets and competition power. When a certain brand attitude cannot be improved, it could be a strategic decision to switch to another attitude by repositioning the brand and perhaps finding a better brand proposition for the targeted market.

Existing brand attitudes can also be adapted to appeal to other and new target groups. For instance, Wolverine World Wide, the American company behind Wolverine shoes for workers and Hush Puppies, an American brand of casual footwear, began building the Caterpillar footwear brand in 1994 under licence from Caterpillar Inc., the heavy equipment and engine manufacturer. Caterpillar boots and shoes are now sold in 100 countries on six continents, reflecting the original brand attitude of Caterpillar in a totally different product category. In 1998 the company also acquired the licence from Harley-Davidson to transfer the legendary motorcycles brand image to shoes and boots; in 2000 Wolverine started to manufacture Stanley footwear, positioned as footwear helping workers to 'make something great', bringing the slogan of the well-known manufacturer of construction tools to life in a new category. If there is a negative prior brand attitude, changing the attitude is necessary. This is a very difficult objective to realise. It might be better – especially when the negative attitude is based on negative experiences – to modify the brand attitude and reposition the brand by appealing to different buying motivations.[9] In January 2003 Christian Dior had to change major elements of its advertising campaign for Dior Addict perfume and cosmetics. The TV spot for the fragrance originally showed a bikini model dipping her finger into a substance on a mirror and holding it up to her nose, then grabbing a bottle of Addict perfume while a voice whispers 'addict' and 'Will you admit it?'

The ad initiated the 'Addiction is Not Fashionable' protest campaign and boycott co-ordinated by Faces and Voices of Recovery and MOMStell, a group of parents concerned with addiction and recovery issues. In response to this protest Dior stopped using the tagline 'admit it' in its marketing communications and altered the ads to emphasise the full name of the product 'Dior Addict' instead of 'addict' as a single word.[10]

Purchase intention

The intention of the buyer to purchase the brand or the product or take other buying-related actions (going to the store, asking for more information) can also be enhanced. For low-involvement buying situations, purchase intention should not be stressed in communications. In this case, when a brand is known and a favourable brand attitude exists, this will in many cases lead to buying behaviour whenever the need for a certain category is aroused. In high-involvement situations, however, when perceived buying risks are high, the intention to buy is typically a necessary mediating step between a favourable attitude and the actual purchase. In this case generating purchase intention and trial is necessary.[11] Advertising and sales promotion can stimulate the consumer in that direction.

Purchase facilitation

Purchase facilitation is all about assuring buyers that there are no barriers hindering product or brand purchase. These barriers could be other elements of the marketing mix, such as price, product and place (distribution).

Sometimes availability or price is a problem preventing consumers from buying a product. Communications in this case should minimise the perceived problems. For example, if a certain brand is not widely available in all stores, a list of approved dealers might help the consumers.[12] Point-of-purchase communications may also help to facilitate purchases.

Purchase

Sales are, of course, the main marketing objective. However, in most circumstances it is difficult to use sales goals as a primary communications objective. Nevertheless, there are situations in which, due to the action-oriented context of communications tools, sales could be a good objective. For instance, the main objective of most sales promotions like couponing, price cuts and premiums is the short-term effect on sales. Some direct marketing tools such as direct-response advertising may be evaluated by generated sales. Indeed, in these situations direct sales is the main goal.

Satisfaction

When a consumer buys a product or service he or she has certain expectations about the purchase. When the product or service lives up to the required and desired benefits or surpasses the expectations, the consumer will be satisfied and thus inclined to choose the same brand whenever he or she buys the product again. Dissatisfied consumers will probably buy a different brand on the next occasion and will complain to relatives and friends. Most marketers are satisfied when consumers finally buy and stop communicating at that point. But it is clear that communications should also be directed to existing customers. The most important reason is that clients are advocates of the brand and products they buy. Word-of-mouth communications can be stimulated and approved by communicating with current customers. Moreover, it is important to reassure consumers about their choice. Cognitive dissonance, i.e. the fact that buyers start to have doubts about that choice, should be avoided to enhance brand loyalty.

Brand loyalty

Brand loyalty is defined as the mental commitment or relation between a consumer and a brand. But there are different types of brand loyalty. Repeat purchase is not the same as brand loyalty. The former is often the result of habit or routine buying rather than of brand preference or brand loyalty. Instead of evaluating alternatives and choosing a new brand for every new purchase, in low-involvement, fast-moving packaged goods consumers tend to buy the same brands again without having a commitment to the brand. This is how brand habits develop. By always using and buying the same brands a positive attitude towards those brands is initiated. Longitudinal tracking in the US, the UK and Germany has shown that brand loyalty is not a characteristic of a brand but of a product category. Brands with a higher market share in that category have a higher 'loyalty' because of their higher penetration rate and not necessarily because the emotional bond with the customer is better. Brand 'loyalty' can indeed be the result of habit formation.[13]

Instead of focussing solely on higher market penetration rates, many high-penetration brands are now using advertising campaigns to encourage their loyal consumers to use the brand more frequently, as well as suggesting new ways to use the brand or new situations in which it can be consumed. The more frequent use of a brand may be a much more cost-effective way to build sales. Recent publications have therefore argued that when dealing with brands with a high degree of market penetration, consumption intentions are more likely to capture consumption-related responses (and success of a campaign) than attitudes towards the brand or purchase intentions. Volume estimates would then best approximate the actual consumption of heavy users and likelihood estimates are best used with light users or with infrequently consumed brands.[14]

Of course, not all communications objectives should be present in a promotional plan or campaign. A marketer should choose which of the above goals is most appropriate in the market and communications situation. Marketers will therefore need a clear view based on situation analysis and prior research among the target audience to decide which goals a campaign should focus upon. If awareness levels are low, they should focus on that goal; if preference is a problem, the campaign should stress liking. Brand awareness and brand attitude will always be part of the goals, as both effects should be maintained in every promotional campaign. As these objectives should be quantified to make them measurable, marketing communications objectives could be: to increase the percentage of unaided recall or aided recognition among the target group; to increase the number of target consumers preferring the brand above the competitive brands; to stimulate current buyers to stay loyal and purchase the products again or buy them more frequently; and to encourage non-buyers to try the brand for the first time.

The DAGMAR model has the merit that, instead of sales goals which are hard to correlate with communications expenditures, other quantifiable measures for effectiveness, such as awareness and image ratings, are introduced. These other measures are assumed to be intermediate effects, and thus indicators for future sales. An increase in awareness and brand ratings would be ahead of sales increases. However, in practice it can be seen that awareness and image ratings are highly associated with usage, but that sales fluctuate sooner than awareness and image ratings. Attitude changes were even found to follow behaviour changes and can be considered to be caused by them.[15] This change in the communications effects hierarchy has been extensively described in Chapter 2 (e.g. the FCB grid).

Further criticism of the so-called traditional 'strong theory of communications', as presented in the DAGMAR model, was formulated by Ehrenberg.[16] He states that there is no evidence that consumers experience a strong desire or conviction before they purchase a product or a service. The traditional model is a conversion model, i.e. turning non-users into users, whereas advertising is directed at experienced consumers. Jones[17] and Ehrenberg present an alternative 'weak theory of marketing communications': the ATR model (Awareness → Trial → Reinforcement). Marketing communications first arouse awareness, then induce consumers towards a first trial purchase and then reassure and reinforce those users after their first purchase. According to Ehrenberg, involvement is basically product involvement and very rarely brand involvement. Consequently, the goal of marketing communications is to create or recreate brand awareness and to nudge brand choice during purchases. Marketing communications is almost never directed to so-called virgin non-users as is implied in the DAGMAR model, but rather to consumers with prior experience of different brands. This is also true in the case of price promotions. Most buyers have already bought the brand before. Even when new or unfamiliar brands are promoted, they are rarely chosen.[18]

Stages in the product life cycle and marketing communications objectives[19]

The choice of the most appropriate communications goals depends on a number of factors that originate in the marketing strategy and the situation analysis. One of the more important factors in choosing objectives is the phase of the life cycle of a brand or product. In this section different strategies for different life stages are explored. They are summarised in Figure 4.2.

Figure 4.2 Stages in the product life cycle and communications objectives

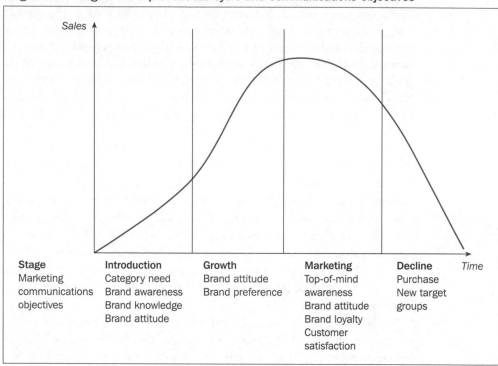

Stage	Introduction	Growth	Marketing	Decline
Marketing communications objectives	Category need Brand awareness Brand knowledge Brand attitude	Brand attitude Brand preference	Top-of-mind awareness Brand attitude Brand loyalty Customer satisfaction	Purchase New target groups

Introduction

A company that is marketing a completely new product will have to develop the market. Consumers will have to learn what the new product is about: which needs will be fulfilled by the product and what the differences are compared to the products the consumers were used to before the innovation or launch of the new product or brand. The major communications objectives in this market situation will be creating category need (explaining which needs are better fulfilled with the innovation), brand awareness and brand knowledge. With daily consumed goods consumers will have to be persuaded to try the new product. The communications strategy has to stress the basic selling points, i.e. the central functional advantages of the products.

Most introductions are new brand launches rather than real product innovations. Evidently, in this case it is not necessary to communicate the central functional product features as consumers are aware of them from their experience with other brands. Goals are to create brand awareness and support psycho-social brand image connotations. This is done by associating a brand with a certain projected lifestyle.

Nivea: changing communication in different stages of the product life cycle

When Nivea first launched the colour cosmetic sub-brand Nivea Beauté onto the European market in 1997, the objective was to utilise the Nivea core competencies of skin-care expertise and emotional values to build a care-based decorative cosmetic brand focussing on products offering gentle formulas and classic colours in the segments eye, nail, lip and face. By 2000 stronger focus had to be placed on category-specific drivers such as modernity, new colours, fashion trends and innovative products to cope with the continued pressure from local competitors, global heavyweight L'Oréal Perfection and the US number one brand Maybelline, using heavy advertising investments to support its global rollout after merging with Jade (Germany, Austria and Switzerland) and Gemey (France and Belgium). Apart from television ads spreading the 'the most beautiful me' message, the print communication was especially important in demonstrating colour and fashion competence. In Germany and France, Nivea Beauté was the only brand in 2000 notably to improve brand image values on all levels. Not only the core Nivea values but also category drivers such as 'colours are modern and up to date' saw improvements. Brand likeability, brand usage and brand awareness also improved after the campaign.[20]

Growth

In the growth stage a different situation leads to other strategies. Consumers are aware of the brand, the product and the most important characteristics and features. Other brands have entered the market with a comparable offer. Communications strategies in this stage of the product life cycle will be aimed at defending the brand's position against possible competitive attacks. Marketers will have to create brand preference by emphasising the right product features and benefits to differentiate the brand from competitors and position it as unique.

Relaunching the VW Sharan

The VW Sharan was the market leader in the MPV (multi-purpose vehicle) segment until it was overtaken by its identical twin the Ford Galaxy in 2000. In May 2000 both models were relaunched although there weren't any technological benefits in favour of the higher-priced VW Sharan. In Hungary VW Sharan's group cousin Seat Alhambra led the market and the VW Sharan was challenged by the Nissan Serena. In the Czech Republic the VW Sharan was market leader, followed by the Seat Alhambra until in January 2000, the Mazda MPV was relaunched and took over the lead. The challenge for the VW Sharan was to compete against its by far less expensive and, in some cases, identical rivals in very price-sensitive markets. The VW Sharan opted for a strongly emotional positioning that goes back to its origins: an active family car. While competition was communicating alternative spheres for use such as leisure, business and transportation, the VW Sharan focussed on the most important buyers, families, by using analogies from the animal world to visualise the various features of the car: strength, comfort, safety, etc. As a result, in Germany in February 2001 the VW Sharan was able to boost its share of the segment from 19% to 28.5%, recapturing market leadership from the Ford Galaxy. In Hungary the VW Sharan obtained a share of 35.5% in March 2001, almost identical to the Seat Alhambra lead position, and in the Czech Republic the rapidly declining VW Sharan was able to catch up with Mazda MPV sales.[21]

Maturity

A brand in the mature stage of its life cycle has to cope with strong competition in a market that is scarcely growing. This implies that an increase in the return of one manufacturer will be reflected in a decrease in a competitor's revenues. Communications strategies will focus on increasing the brand loyalty of consumers. Customers should be induced to be less open to the advantages of competing brands. There are six possible communications objectives in this particular PLC stage:

- high spontaneous brand awareness, top-of-mind awareness;
- claim a clear and unique brand benefit, a characteristic on which the brand is better than competing brands;
- if there are none or only small product differences, stressing a lower price might be a good strategy;
- get the attention by offering small product innovations;
- reinforce the psycho-social meaning for product categories such as cigarettes, beer and coffee. These brands differ very little in functional characteristics but the experience of the brands by its consumer groups might be very different. The strategy of these brands is positioning by supporting the transformational meaning of a brand;
- communications strategies could also be more defensive in this stage of the PLC. Current customers should be reassured of their choice and their positive experience and satisfaction of the brand.

Decline

When manufacturers are confronted with declining products or brands and decide to milk or harvest the brand, they will probably turn to sales promotions such as prizes and lotteries. If they decide to renew the life of the declining product or brand (and believe in life-cycle stretching), they can use the following strategies:

- communicate an important product adaptation or change;
- draw attention to new applications or moments of use (e.g. beer as a recipe ingredient instead of as a drink);
- increase the frequency of use;
- attract new target groups (e.g. Bacardi Breezer for youngsters).

Coral: reviving an old brand

Coral (Robijn in the Netherlands) is a light-duty detergent brand, long established in Germany, the Netherlands, Austria, Belgium, France, Switzerland and more recently in Sweden, Finland and Norway. Germany and the Netherlands represent two-thirds of global sales. Coral had a stable market share over time and nothing had been done to create a dynamic over the last decade, resulting in a drastically ageing consumer profile, with a core group of people of 50 years and over. To ensure a future for the brand, Coral had to recruit, and create a strong bond with, young European women of between 25 and 35 years old. This target group has absolutely no interest in washing, as they do not consider themselves mainly as housewives. Coral had to find another value that would speak emotionally to this young target group. Research showed Lever Fabergé, the company behind Coral, that clothes reflect personality, self-expression and self-confidence to young women. Hence, taking care of clothes is taking care of themselves. As black and dark clothes represent one-third of a modern woman's wardrobe, Coral decided to launch the first washing specialist for black clothes: Coral Black Velvet (Plate 4). In this way Coral was not a detergent anymore, but an essential fashion accessory helping young women

▶

to take care of their precious clothes. In order to demonstrate that Coral Black Velvet could be part of the strong emotional relationship between clothes and women, Lever used a media strategy that created contacts in locations where young women care about clothes, appearance and fashion: women's magazines, parties, fashion shows and bars. In Germany Coral's share of market moved from 3.8% to 6.2% in six months; in the Netherlands Robijn moved from a share of 9.6% to 14.2% in the same period. Coral Black Velvet was such a success in the fabrics market that the German market now has six me-toos.[22]

Summary

A marketing communications campaign can have several objectives that are consistent with the stages in the consumer decision-making process: stimulating product category need, increasing brand awareness and brand knowledge, improving brand attitude or image, increasing purchase intention and facilitating purchases, and maximising customer satisfaction and brand loyalty. Different objectives will require a different communications mix. The objectives of a communications campaign differ according to the stage in the product life cycle. While awareness-building is more important in the introduction and growth stages, brand image and brand preference-building will be crucial in the growth and the maturity stages, and purchase-directed objectives will prevail in the decline stage.

Review questions

1 Describe the various stages in the DAGMAR model. What is the consequence of this model for marketing communications objectives?

2 What are the characteristics of a good set of marketing communications objectives?

3 How does the definition of marketing objectives fit into the marketing communications plan?

4 In what circumstances is it useful to stress category needs and wants in marketing communications?

5 In what circumstances is brand recall rather than brand recognition the more important communications goal?

6 In what circumstances is the stimulation of purchase intention a good marketing communications objective?

7 What are the shortcomings of the DAGMAR model as a framework for marketing communications objectives?

8 To what extent should marketing communications objectives be adapted in the introduction, growth, maturity and decline stage of a product life cycle?

Further reading

Ehrenberg, A.S.C., Hammond, K.A. and Goodhardt, G.J. (1992), 'The After-Effects of Large Consumer Promotions', *Journal of Advertising Research*, 34(4), 11–21.

Jones, D.B. (1994), 'Setting Promotional Goals: A Communication Relationship Model', *Journal of Consumer Marketing*, 11(1), 38–49.

Jones, J., Slater, J. and Clarck, H. (2003), *What's in a Name: Advertising and the Concept of Brands*. Armonk, NY: M.E. Sharpe.

Joyce, T. (1991), 'Models of the Advertising Process', *Marketing and Research Today*, 19(4), 205–13.

Percy, L., Rossiter, J. and Elliott, R. (2002), *Strategic Advertising Management*. Oxford: Oxford University Press.

Case 4

Ben & Jerry's – Vermont's finest and the world's wackiest ice cream

After leaving college two friends, Ben Cohen and Jerry Greenfield, were wondering what to do. A conventional job was not their cup of tea and they thought of starting a pizza takeaway, but were deterred by the glut of competitors. Making their favourite bagels was another dream, but the initial investments were high (US$40,000) and when they saw an advertisement for a $5 Penn State correspondence course in ice cream making Ben & Jerry's was born. The two gathered $8,000, borrowed another $4,000 and opened their first ice cream shop in a renovated petrol filling station in Burlington, Vermont. The shop soon became popular for its innovative flavours of ice cream made from fresh Vermont milk and cream. In 1981 a first plant was established in Vermont. In 1985 the Ben & Jerry Foundation, a fund for community-oriented projects was initiated. Each year 7.5% of the pre-tax profits of Ben & Jerry's is donated to this fund to sponsor charities and not-for-profit organisations. In 1988 B&J entered the Canadian market. In 1992 they made their first move outside North America with scoop shops in Israel and Russia. Profits from the latter were used to support cultural exchange projects. Some years later the super-premium ice cream was also launched in the UK (1994), France (1995), the Netherlands (1996) and Belgium (1997). Internationally 1998 marks the introduction of Ben & Jerry's in Japan, with single-serve selections to suit Japanese taste and serving-size preferences. In 1999 Ben & Jerry's began distribution in Peru and from 2000 worked on strengthening existing foreign markets (UK, France, Benelux, Canada, Lebanon and Japan), instead of expanding them, by opening 52 new Ben & Jerry's scoop shops in these markets.

Net sales of Ben & Jerry's totalled $237 million in 1999, a 13.3% increase over 1998 sales. On 12 April 2000 Ben & Jerry's announced the company's acquisition by Anglo-Dutch corporation Unilever. Ben & Jerry's board of directors approved Unilever's offer of $326 million as well as a unique agreement in which Ben & Jerry's will operate separately from Unilever's ice cream business with an independent board of directors to provide leadership for Ben & Jerry's social mission and brand integrity.

Ben & Jerry's dedication to the concept of linked prosperity is consistent in three interrelated parts of the company mission. With regard to the product, B&J aims to make, distribute and sell the finest quality of all natural ice cream and related products in a wide variety of innovative flavours made from Vermont dairy products. Economically, the company operates on a sound financial basis of profitable growth, increasing value for the shareholders and creating career opportunities for employees. Socially, B&J searches for innovative ways to improve the quality of life of the wider community. Ben & Jerry's plants are often located in high unemployment areas. For its Chocolate Fudge Brownie ice cream, the company chose a bakery in New York which hired under-skilled workers and used its profits to house the homeless. B&J's Rainforest Crunch ice cream features nuts grown in South American rain forests. In 1999 in the UK Ben & Jerry's launched the Flying Friesian, a tour bus retrofitted for fun with a focus on fundraising for the children-in-need network, Childline and in 2002 partnered with the Dave Matthews band and SaveOurEnvironment.org in a campaign to fight global warming.

The ice cream market

Ben & Jerry's is active in the super-premium ice cream market, which is less than 10% of the ice cream market. The largest competitor of B&J is Häagen-Dazs which originates from the early 1960s and is owned by the Diageo group, a huge food and retail group that is also the parent company of Burger King restaurants and Guinness beer. The two manufacturers share around 82% of market share of the super-premium ice cream market. Häagen-Dazs is market leader with 43% and Ben & Jerry's takes 39% of the market. After the health-conscious consumer preferences of the early 1990s, consumers appear to be returning to taste. Low-fat products probably did not meet taste expectations: 83% of ice cream sold through grocery stores in 1997 was of the full-fat variety, 12% was reduced, light or low fat and only 5% non-fat. The frozen yoghurt category has been falling for the past two years. In 1998 it fell by more than 20%. Whereas ice cream was once a regional business with an outgrowth of local dairies, advances in distribution have led to the domination of national players in a consolidated ice cream business environment. The ice cream, frozen yoghurt and frozen dessert industry generally experiences the highest volume during the spring and summer months and the lowest volume during winter.

In most European countries, Ben & Jerry's main competitor Häagen-Dazs has been in the market since the early 1990s establishing a dominant market share in the super-premium ice cream market of around 90%. To reach its ambitious goal, Ben & Jerry's had to contend with a powerful rival in Häagen-Dazs, backed by its parent company Diageo PLC. Another problem for B&J in the European market is the Americanness of the super-premium ice cream. The quirky flavour names sometimes do not translate well in European countries.

The Ben & Jerry's marketing mix

Super-premium ice cream can be distinguished from the other categories in two ways: butterfat content and density. The butterfat content of super-premium ice cream is higher than any other category, at around 20%. Super-premium ice cream has much less air mixed in than ordinary ice cream which contains up to 50% air. Ben & Jerry's product is a combination of super-premium ice cream products and the social awareness created through bottom-up management, cause-generated marketing and PR efforts. The physical products include ice cream, frozen yoghurt and ice cream novelties. Its competitive advantage lies in both its variety and the uniqueness of flavours. The coolest and chunkiest flavours with wacky names such as Cherry Garcia (named after the late guitar player of The Grateful Dead, Jerry Garcia, a suggestion of one of B&J's consumers – something B&J likes to encourage) was for a long time the unique and primary strength of the company compared to the smooth standard flavours of Häagen-Dazs. When the latter cottoned on to the success of B&J's approach it decided to launch more complex flavours too. Today B&J only owns a flavour for about 60 days before imitations reach the market. In 1994 B&J introduced its line of smooth no chunks ice cream in response to market research indicating that a large portion of the super-premium consumers did not like chunks.

Ben & Jerry's uses pure, natural, hormone-free milk from Vermont's dairy farms. Its products are sold by the pint in recycled paperboard cups covered with colourful graphics and Ben and Jerry's photograph. It uses ear-catching names for its ice cream such as NY Super Fudge Chunk, Coffee Coffee Buzz Buzz Buzz, Chubby Hubby, Chunky Monkey, Phish Food, Wavy Gravy. The emphasis on the eclectic and euphoric nature of the product is quite different from Häagen-Dazs's traditional snob factor package. (See Plate 5.)

Co-branding appears to be the latest significant trend in the premium ice cream segment. Ben & Jerry's, for instance, has teamed up with the Dilbert Cartoon and the Heath candy bars to feature the Chocolate Heath Bar Crunch and the Dilbert/Totally Nuts flavour. Häagen-Dazs co-branded with Bailey's (a liquor marketed by its parent company) to deliver a new taste. In 2002 and 2003 more crazy flavours were introduced with names like Honey I'm Home, Karamel Sutra and The Full VerMonty.

Ben & Jerry's ice cream products are premium-priced at the high end of the ice cream market. This pricing strategy has been difficult to sustain in recent years as demand has shifted towards lower-priced and own-label products. Price elasticity has increased. Nearly half of all ice cream sold in 1998 was sold in some form of price or display promotion. Backed by a much larger parent company, Häagen-Dazs is capable of launching aggressive price promotion attacks. In certain parts of the US market Häagen-Dazs has two-for-one sales discounts. B&J has had to follow with price discounts and store coupons.

Ben & Jerry's ice cream is marketed through supermarkets, grocery stores, convenience stores, all-night shops and restaurants. Moreover, the company has more than 235 franchised ice cream shops and franchises. These shops all have a fun atmosphere with interior walls plastered with paintings of blue clouds, green grass and Vermont cows.

Because of its values and unconventional nature, Ben & Jerry's has traditionally had very little classic advertising to do. Media coverage (free publicity) was regularly guaranteed by its community involvement and socially conscious projects. The company's cause-related events included travelling shows in buses with solar-powered freezers. The largest part of Ben & Jerry's budget went to major Woodstock-style music festivals around the United States. The company-owned plant in Vermont is the number one tourist attraction, hosting 275,000 visitors a year. Word-of-mouth spread by extremely brand and company-loyal customers did the rest of the marketing communications job.

Questions

1 To reach the coverage goals of marketing communications, a good target group definition is essential. Describe the target group Ben & Jerry's is aiming at with its super-premium ice cream. Is its primary segment different from the one Häagen-Dazs is approaching? Do the two brands have the same positioning?

2 Imagine you were responsible for the launch of Ben & Jerry's super-premium ice cream in your country (make an abstract of the current market position and suppose B&J has to enter your local market). Which of the nine communications objectives would be most appropriate?

3 Now imagine you are in charge of Ben & Jerry's marketing communications strategy in the United States. Which communications goals would you include in your communications plan?

4 What do you think is more relevant for the Ben & Jerry's case: brand recognition or brand recall? Why?

5 Visit the Ben & Jerry's website (www.benjerry.com). How does the company try to communicate, and what kind of message is it trying to get across?

Based on: The Ben & Jerry's case developed by Joeri Van den Bergh for the marketing communications courses given at the Vlerick Leuven Gent Management School, 1994; Annual report Ben & Jerry's Homemade Inc. 1998; Wellman, D. (1999), 'Butterfat City: Industry Overview', *Supermarket Business*, January; *Wall Street Journal*, 7 August 1998; Markgraf, S. (1998), 'Indulgence Supreme; New Ice Cream Products for the Season. Annual Ice Cream Report; Product Announcement', *Dairy Foods*, March. Thanks to Bram Kleppner, International product manager of Ben & Jerry's Homemade USA. Reproduced with permission of Ben & Jerry's.

References

1 Colley, R.H. (1961), *Defining Advertising Goals for Measured Advertising Results*. New York: Association of National Advertisers.

2 Jones, D.B. (1994), 'Setting Promotional Goals: A Communication Relationship Model', *Journal of Consumer Marketing*, 11(1), 38–49.

3 Pickton, D. and Broderick, A. (2001), *Integrated Marketing Communications*. Essex: Financial Times Prentice Hall.

4 Rossiter, J.R. and Percy, L. (1997), *Advertising Communication and Promotion Management*. Sydney: McGraw-Hill.

5 Hefflin, D.T.A. and Haygood, R.C. (1985), 'Effects of Scheduling on Retention of Advertising Messages', *Journal of Advertising*, 14(2), 41–7.

6 Euro Effie, (2001).

7 Rossiter, J.R. and Percy, L. (1997), *Advertising Communication and Promotion Management*. Sydney: McGraw-Hill.

8 Euro Effie, (2001).

9 Rossiter, J.R. and Percy, L. (1997), *Advertising Communication and Promotion Management*. Sydney: McGraw-Hill.

10 www.jointogether.org

11 Rossiter, J.R. and Percy, L. (1997), *Advertising Communication and Promotion Management*. Sydney: McGraw-Hill.

12 Rossiter, J.R. and Percy, L. (1997), *Advertising Communication and Promotion Management*. Sydney: McGraw-Hill.

13 Franzen, G. (1998), *Merken en Reclame (Brands and Advertising)*. Kluwer Bedrijfsinformatie.

14 Wansink, B. and Ray, M. (2000), 'Estimating an Advertisement's Impact on One's Consumption of a Brand', *Journal of Advertising Research*, November/December, 106–13.

15 Joyce, T. (1991), 'Models of the Advertising Process', *Marketing and Research Today*, 19(4), 205–13.

16 Ehrenberg, A.S.C. (1992), 'Comments on How Advertising Works', *Marketing and Research Today*, 20(3), 167–9.

17 Jones, J.P. (1991), 'Over-Promise and Under-Delivery', *Marketing and Research Today*, 19(40), 195–203.

18 Ehrenberg, A.S.C., Hammond, K.A. and Goodhardt, G.J. (1992), 'The After Effects of Large Consumer Promotions', *Journal of Advertising Research*, 34(4), 11–21.

19 Floor, K. and Van Raaij, F. (1993), *Marketingcommunicatiestrategie (Marketing Communications Strategy)*. Houten: Stenfert Kroese.

20 Euro Effie, (2001).

21 Euro Effie, (2001).

22 Euro Effie, (2001).

Chapter 5
Budgets

Chapter outline

How communications budgets affect sales

Communications budgeting methods

Factors influencing budgets

Budgeting for new brands or products

Chapter objectives

This chapter will help you to:

- Understand how communications budgets may influence communications effectiveness
- Get an overview of theoretical and practical marketing communications budgeting methods
- Identify factors that influence budgeting decisions
- Decide upon a communications budget for a new product or brand

Introduction

Companies are continuously looking for new ways to economise. Restructuring and rationalisation have dominated companies' policies during the recession years of the new millennium. They tend to save most in those expenses that may be influenced in the short term. Hence, communications budgets are often first in line to be reviewed. However, the communications budget level is one of the determinants of the communications mix effectiveness and thus of company sales and profits. The allocation of funds for promotion is one of the primary problems and strategic issues facing a marketer. This chapter discusses the elements a marketer should consider when making budget allocations, and offers some insights into the relation between communications intensity and communications effectiveness.

How the communications budget affects sales

To be able to assess the size of the budget, it is important to understand how communications efforts influence sales. **Sales response models** depict the relationship between these two factors. In Figure 5.1, the S-shaped sales response model is shown.

This model assumes that initially, when the level of effort is low, there is no communications effect at all. Even if communications effort is zero, there will be a certain level of sales, and a minimum investment is needed to enjoy any results of the communications programme and to increase sales. When that level is reached, sales will start to increase with incremental communications expenditures. The higher the investments, the greater the additional sales. At point A increased investments start to lead to smaller changes in sales. It is impossible, even with very high communications investments, to exceed a certain saturation level of sales. This is due to the market, and the cultural and competitive environment. Exorbitant communications investments may even lead to negative effects, such as irritation and consumer resistance.[1]

Figure 5.1 The S-shaped sales response model

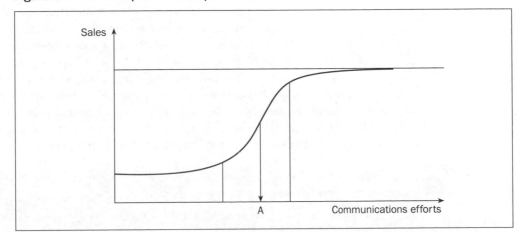

Estimating the relationship between the communications budget or effort and sales or market share is not easy. First of all, marketing communications are not the only marketing mix instrument influencing sales. Prices, product line decisions and changes in the distribution strategy will also influence sales. Furthermore, an effective marketing mix implies that synergy and interaction exist between the various marketing tools. In a well-designed marketing plan each tool reinforces the other. A communications plan may lead to better results if the distribution strategy is optimised or the price is lowered. A rearrangement of the product line may result in more effective communications, etc. As a result of this interaction, it is very difficult to isolate the effect of the communications budget on commercial results. Furthermore, sales response models do not take the effect of competitive actions and environmental factors into account.

Finally, and at least as importantly, communications efforts may have both an immediate short-term and a long-term effect on sales and market share. Traditional theories consider communications as a long-term investment in goodwill.[2] Cumulative investments are needed to lead to sales returns, and the long-term effects of communications efforts are much higher than the short-term effects.[3]

This traditional view is challenged by John Philip Jones,[4] who proposes a controversial theory on the short-term effects of advertising (STAS: Short Term Advertising Strength), claiming that paradigms stating that sales are mainly influenced by accumulated advertising campaigns of the past are mistaken. He tried to prove that immediate communications effects on sales exist. He used single-source data[5] relating advertising exposure (a test group with ad confrontation and a control group without ad exposure based on television viewing behaviour tracking) with scanner data of the same test subjects. Differences in purchases between the two groups were considered to be a measurement of ad effectiveness.

Based on these calculations Jones discovered that 70% of all ad campaigns were able to generate immediate advertising effects. Mostly these effects were small and temporary. When looking at the distribution in deciles of differential scores, 20% had good differential scores, 30% on average a positive score, 30% had no definite positive or negative score and 20% had a negative score and were not effective in beating competing ad campaigns. Only 46% of brands created a long-term effect, defined as an increase in market share compared to that of the previous year. He also came to the rather surprising conclusion that the first exposure of an ad causes the largest part of sales returns, and that additional exposures will only lead to small effects on sales. The most effective frequency of an ad campaign according to Jones is one single exposure.

Jones believes that long-term effects will only come about when an ad campaign is also effective in the short term and does not believe in the sleeper effects of marketing communications. This statement is radically opposed to the widespread belief that a higher ad frequency is needed to gain any effects on sales. Therefore, Jones's statements on short-term communications effects are very controversial, and may be an overreaction to the widespread belief that there are mainly carry-over effects of communications efforts. In reality, both short-term and long-term effects are important.[6]

A frequently used and simple sales response model, taking long-term and short-term effects into account, is the following (numbers are exemplary):

$$S_t = 250 + 1.4A_t + 0.6S_{t-1}$$

▶

where: S_t = sales in period t
        S_{t-1} = sales in period t–1
        A_t = advertising in period t
      250 = constant term expressing that even if there was no advertising at all in period t
            or in the past, sales would still be €250

The short-term effect of advertising is the coefficient of A_t. Every €1,000 invested in advertising results in €1,400 extra sales. The coefficient of S_{t-1} summarises the effect of all advertising efforts in the past. The long-term effect of advertising on sales is calculated as: 1.4/(1 – 0.6) = 3.5. This means that, in the long run, every €1,000 invested in advertising results in 3,500 extra sales.

Communications budgeting methods

In Table 5.1, the various communications budgeting methods are shown.

Marginal analysis

The basic principle of marginal analysis is quite obvious: to invest resources as long as extra expenses are compensated by higher extra returns. Marketers should invest in promotional or communications efforts as long as their marginal revenue exceeds the marginal communications cost. Profit is calculated as the difference between gross margin and communications expenditures. It is clear that sales and gross margin will increase with higher communications efforts, but will level off, which leads to lower profits and eventually loss. This analysis has the advantage of estimating the effect of advertising on profits, and derives a normative rule of optimal advertising efforts. However, the analysis remains largely theoretical because of the problems involved in estimating the sales response relation. As a result, marginal analysis is seldom used as a practical budgeting method.[7]

In addition to the theoretical marginal approach there are a number of techniques that are relatively easy to use without requiring difficult calculations. Some of the techniques that practitioners commonly use when developing communications budgets are the following.

Table 5.1 Communications budgeting methods

- Marginal analysis
- Inertia
- Arbitrary allocation
- Affordability
- Percentage of sales
- Competitive parity
- Objective and task

Inertia

The inertia method is nothing more than keeping budgets constant year on year, while ignoring the market, competitive actions or consumer opportunities. Needless to say, this is not a very strategic method.

Arbitrary allocation

Again, this is one of the most simple of all budgeting methods, but also one of the least appropriate. Whatever the general manager or managing director decides will be implemented. This very subjective way of deciding how to spend promotional funds does, of course, lack critical analysis and overall strategy. The technique is mostly used by small companies where the managing director's personal preferences (e.g. sponsoring a golf event) and contacts overrule more strategic processes that take the marketing and competitive environment and customer wants into account.

Affordability method

In this method 'leftover' resources, after all input costs (i.e. human resources, operational and financial costs), are invested in communications. This method is often used in small and medium enterprises. Marketing communications are considered to be a pure cost rather than an investment and are mostly not part of the strategic plan, nor are any concrete communications goals defined. As a result, it is a technique without any focus on strategic market or brand issues. This approach will never lead to optimal budgeting, since some opportunities will be lost because of lack of investment-proneness.

Percentage of sales

In this technique, budgets are defined as a percentage of the projected sales of the next year. An alternative to this technique is to take the communications outlays of the past year as a basis and then add a certain percentage, based on the projected sales growth of the following year. These techniques are very popular in many companies thanks to their ease of use. The percentages used by companies differ. Some sources indicate that they fluctuate around an average of 5%.[8] Other authors speak of percentages between 0.5% and 10%.[9] Although they are commonly used, and like the affordablity method ensure that costs do not threaten profits, these budgeting methods have some notable disadvantages. The percentage of sales method could lead to overspending in markets in which these kinds of investments are not needed and at the same time communications budgets might be too small where they might have had a major impact. Decreasing returns of sales will lead to smaller communications budgets, which will certainly not help to change the negative sales evolution. Communications budgets should not be the result of sales but rather should create demand and thus push up sales. This technique also defends the theoretical insight that sales are dominated by communications investments and that other marketing mix elements do not have an impact on sales. This technique does not consider any potential sales growth areas and will limit sales performance.

Another common way of using the percentage of sales method is to take the sales of the past year instead of projected sales, but that is even worse. This method uses past performance as a *ceteris paribus* situation. Therefore, it is unlikely that the company will make progress (unless a lucky wind changes the competitive environment or consumer demands in the right direction).

A last variant of this method is to take a percentage of profits instead of sales. This has the same disadvantages as an existing brand might need less advertising than a recently launched brand which is not making any profit at all during the first year. Losses will lead to cancelling communications budgets and thus to abandoning all hope instead of investing in brand communications to make them profitable again.

Competitive parity

Competitive parity means that companies look at the amount of money competitors spend on communications and then copy their budgets. The logic of this method lies in the fact that the collective behaviour of a market will not skew much of the budget optimum. The advantage of this method is that the market will not be destabilised by overinvestments or extremely low promotional budgets. This method is often used in fast-moving consumer goods where sales are believed to be highly influenced by advertising and communications spendings.

Nevertheless, the theoretical basis of this method has some disadvantages. The underlying assumption is again that promotional spendings are the only variable that influences sales. Furthermore, a company assumes that the competitor's communications budget was set in an effective and efficient way. Lastly, this method implies that resources, operational methods, opportunities and objectives of competitors used as a benchmark are exactly the same as those of our company. These are three quite dangerous assumptions. Companies may have other market definitions or other targets, leading to other activities and products in other stages of their life cycle which makes comparisons a difficult and unreliable technique for financial decisions. The parity method is also based on historical data and not on competitors' plans for the future. Believing that competitors will adhere every year to the same communications efforts is probably not the best analytical way to make marketing plans.

Some researchers have developed paradigms that are of practical use to marketers wanting to assess the effects of their share of voice (SOV) on their share of market (SOM). Share of voice is calculated as the ratio of own communications investments divided by the communications investments of all market players. A study on the impact of advertising of competitors with comparable products on market share, not taking the advertising quality or any formal or content characteristics of advertising into account, came to the following conclusions.[10] Ad spendings will only influence market share (SOM) when there is a different advertising intensity over a long period. Marginal budget changes do not affect SOM. If competitors aggressively augment their communications budgets, this can be countered by following with increasing communications expenditure. If, however, there is no reaction to this attack, the increase in share of voice will lead to a higher SOM. This means that market leaders will have to track the expenditures of competitors and react to changes to prevent them from gaining market share.

In Figure 5.2 a matrix is proposed with strategic recommendations for communications budgets in different market situations.

Figure 5.2 SOV effect and strategies for different market positions

High	**Offensive strategy:** ■ Find a niche and decrease SOV	**Defensive strategy:** ■ Increase SOV to defend position
Competitor's SOV	**Offensive strategy:** ■ Attack with big SOV premium to increase market share	**Defensive strategy:** ■ Keep a small SOV premium on competitors to keep SOM position
Low		

Based on: Schroer, J.C. (1990), 'Ad Spending: Growing Market Share', *Harvard Business Review*, 68(1), 44–8. One-time permission to reproduce granted by Harvard Business School Publishing.

Besides sales effects, the result of the marketing communications effort can also be measured in other terms, such as brand awareness. In the following graph the efficiency of the advertising campaigns of different banks is analysed. On the horizontal axis budgets are measured. The vertical axis shows top-of-mind awareness of bank names. For two consecutive years, the relationship between the two factors is shown. The more a bank moves to the upper left corner of the graph, the more efficiently it is spending its resources. The analysis also permits a comparison of the own company with competitors.

Top-of-mind awareness and advertising budgets

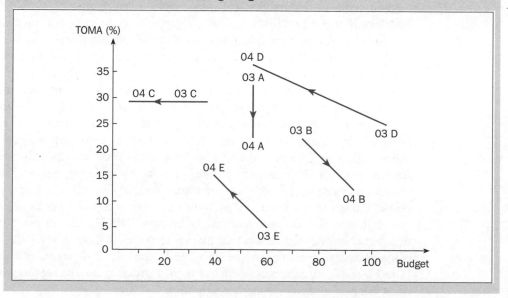

Objective and task method

This method is one of the least arbitrary methods which makes it a difficult technique to use. It differs from the other methods in that it starts from communications objectives and the resources that are needed to reach these planned goals. All needed investments are then added and this will lead to the overall communications budget. It requires more strategic planning and investment analysis and is therefore clearly superior to all the other methods. Moreover, budgets can be evaluated each year and this feedback will lead to improved decision-making and more efficient budgeting in the future. The difficulty in this method lies in the estimation of profit impacts of different communications actions and tactics. Therefore it is of the utmost importance that historical data on, for instance, sales promotion responses in each market are stored. But estimating all costs of every action needs some effort and often the final costs of an action are difficult to foresee.[11]

Percentage of sales is the most commonly used communications budgeting technique. It is likely that variants such as percentage on last year's returns and percentage on profits are also commonly used. Spending what is left after all other costs are covered is also popular and the arbitrary method is frequently used in smaller companies and business-to-business contexts.

Factors influencing budgets

A number of factors may influence the budgeting decision or may call for budget adjustments.[12] They are summarised in Figure 5.3.

The smaller the targeted markets, the easier it is to reach the targets in a cost-efficient way. Spending too much in small markets leads to saturation and overspends are likely to be ineffective. Larger markets imply more dispersed target groups which are more difficult to reach and thus more expensive. When particular markets have higher potential, it may be a good idea to allocate more money to these specific markets. Brands with smaller market shares and new brands require a high communications budget, larger well-established brands and 'harvested' brands in the maturity stage of their life cycle could do with a lower allocation of communications funds.

Some studies[13] show that companies and brands with larger market shares have an advantage in communications costs (such as better media space buying, synergy between different communications mix elements on different company brands, better media rental rates and lower production costs) and can thus spend less money on promotional activities while having the same or even better sales. However, other research[14] claims that there is no evidence that larger companies are able to support their brands with lower advertising costs than smaller ones. A number of organisational factors that have a potential influence on the budgeting decision can be identified:[15] the organisational structure (centralised vs decentralised, formalisation and complexity), the use of experts such as consultants, the organisational hierarchy, preferences and experiences of decision-makers and decision-influencers, and pressure on management to reach certain budgets.

Sometimes it is necessary to make adjustments to the planned budgets during the year or during the communications campaign. If sales and profits lag behind projected and budgeted figures (planning gap), cutting communications efforts is often the easiest

Figure 5.3 Factors influencing communications budgets

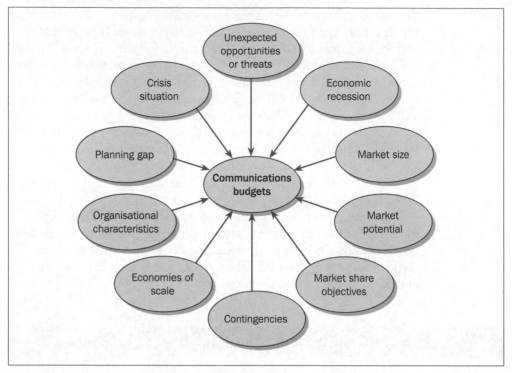

Based on: Belch, G.E. and Belch M.A. (1998), *Advertising and Promotion. An Integrated Marketing Communication Perspective.* New York: Irwin/McGraw-Hill.

and fastest way to increase profits. Of course, this will only have an immediate effect in the short term. In the long run this might lead to eroding competitive edges and market and brand positions. Crisis situations such as troubles with production or distribution might need exceptional investments in public relations and crisis communications. Other internal occurrences such as financial scandals, strikes, ecological catastrophes, etc. might also demand budget adjustments.

Unexpected opportunities or threats in the market might change strategic plans and communications budgets, as well as unexpected moves by competitors, new legislation, new media and changes in media costs.

Economic recessions will often have serious consequences for communications budgets. Consumers spend less money and shrinking markets mean stronger competitive battles in which price is a commonly used weapon. Companies may react in one of two ways with regard to their promotional spending. Some try to economise in every way possible. A substantial amount of all costs are fixed and cannot be lowered in the short term. Most companies are attracted by a budget that is quite easy to bring down: the communications budget. Other companies react by increasing their budget, believing that extra investment will drive sales up. A crisis is regarded as the ideal moment to establish their position. This is called anti-cycle budgeting. Market share is gained during recessions and then defended in periods of a booming economy. Some multinationals such as PepsiCo, Coca-Cola, General Mills, Kellogg's and Procter & Gamble have a strong belief in long-term investments in marketing communications.

Some companies prepare contingency budgets. These are reserve budgets provided for financing quick management actions as necessary. These crisis actions are planned in so-called contingency plans. They stipulate which actions must be taken, for instance, when significant drops in sales occur or when an important competitor switches to aggressive promotional actions or launches a new product. Reaction time will be substantially lower in such cases when all appropriate actions and budgeting have been foreseen.

Budgeting for new brands or products

Although budgeting for existing brands in established product categories is the most common task for marketers, often they are confronted with the problem of budgeting for a brand or product launch. This is even more difficult than the former. Historical data on the budget settings that have been successful are not available and consequently easy-to-use schemes as discussed above are not appropriate for estimating required budgets.[16]

The primary budgeting method for launching new brands or products should be the objective-and-task method. But given the uncertainty and lack of historical data, this is not only a difficult budgeting method but also one that is not risk free. Therefore, other methods are good back-ups to compare estimations made earlier. A marketer may, for instance, examine the industry advertising-to-sales (A/S) ratio (advertising intensity) for the market in which a brand is to be launched. He may decide to set a budget that is higher than the industry average in order to make an impact. Doubling the A/S ratio is considered a safe guideline for the first year of introduction. In the second year overspending the ratio by 50% should do. Of course, it could be even more informative to make comparisons with particular competing brands or products.

Peckham, a consultant with AC Nielsen, developed a rule of thumb for new fast-moving consumer good brands.[17] Peckham's 1.5 rule recommends setting the SOV of the brand to be launched at 1.5 times the desired SOM at the end of the brand's first two years. A limitation of Peckham's rule is that it is only applicable in markets or product categories for which there is a strong correlation between SOV and SOM. A study of 638 firms across 20 industries[18] found a strong relationship between SOV and SOM across a broad range of industries for consumer as well as industrial products.

Summary

Sales response models have been developed to describe the relationship between communications budgets and communications effects. However, the extent to which sales respond to advertising depends on a number of other factors, such as the product range, price and distribution strategies, the marketing environment and the competition. As a result, it is very difficult to decide on communications budgets on the basis of these models because the effects of communications efforts on sales cannot be isolated. Furthermore, traditionally, advertising is assumed to affect sales only in the long run (although this point of view is radically contradicted by the works of Jones), which makes it even harder to decide on budgets in terms of effectiveness. Therefore, companies often resort to more practical and easier, but not very relevant, budgeting methods such as inertia, arbitrary allocation, affordability and percentage of sales. In the objectives and task method, the communications needs are assessed, after which a task-related budget is defined. In the competitive parity method, companies analyse their market position and decide on their share of voice accordingly. Communications budgets are influenced by multiple factors, such as a crisis situation, contingencies, unexpected opportunities, economic recessions and other market and company factors, and companies should always be alert and prepared to adapt budgets to changing situations.

Review questions

1 What is a sales response model and why is it not easy to estimate it?

2 Discuss the various communications budgeting methods that are frequently used by practitioners.

3 What is the relationship between share of voice and share of market, and how does it affect budgeting?

4 What are the factors that influence the budgeting decision?

5 How should the communications budget for a new product launch be determined?

Further reading

Butherfield, L. (2003), *AdValue*. New York: Butterworth-Heinemann.

Jones, J.P. (2001), *Ultimate Secrets of Advertising*. London: Sage Publications.

Jones, J.P. and Slater, J.S. (2003), *What's In a Name? Advertising and the Concept of Brands*. Armonk, NY: M.E. Sharpe.

Case 5

Budgeting in the automobile industry

While analysts pointed to a stable situation for the world automotive industry in general, Western Europe clearly experienced recessive trends in its motor vehicle market during the year 2002. This reflected the rather weak performance of the European economy. The European Commission's consumer confidence indicator decreased in December 2002 for the third consecutive month and was at its lowest level for about six years. This was due to the deterioration of consumers' expectations about the general economic situation and the job market in particular.

The year 2002 ended with a total of 14.4 million passenger cars registered in Western Europe, reflecting a decrease of 2.9% compared to 2001. This slowdown came about despite the surge of auto sales that took place in December 2002, in particular in the Netherlands, Ireland and Italy. Looking at annual figures in detail, five countries posted increases, namely Denmark (+15.3%), Finland (+7%), the UK (+4.3%), Sweden (+3.2%) and Luxembourg (+1.4%). All other countries recorded decreases ranging from −11.4% in Portugal to −2.6% in Germany. Despite financial incentives, the Italian market experienced a fall of −6% on 2001 levels. While Germany also saw a decline in passenger car registrations, it remained the biggest individual European automotive market, accounting for about 23% of total registrations in the EU15.

Concerning market share figures, German and Japanese group brands had generally retained their position on the European market, while Italian and Korean makes had a marked decline in market share. In terms of new passenger car registration specifications, the diesel boom continues in Western Europe. The share of diesel-powered cars out of total new registrations rose from 36.6% in 2001 to 40.9% in 2002 (5.8 million units). As for new passenger car registrations by market segment, the highest share remains in the so-called 'small' segment, followed by the 'lower medium' segment. The 4 × 4 segments enjoyed a small increase in demand, accounting for 5.24% of new registrations in 2002 compared to 4.6% in 2001. Production of motor vehicles in Western Europe fell in parallel with the fall in demand. Latest figures from the CCFA (Comité des Constructeurs Français d'Automobiles – French Carmaking Association) indicate that production of passenger cars reached 14,810,460 units in 2002, a decrease of 1% compared to 2001.

In 2002 Belgium assembled 876,858 private vehicles for export. The figure has been decreasing for some years (for instance −22% compared to 1995). The main export countries for cars assembled in Belgium were Germany (17.6%), the UK (13.8%), Spain (11.2%) and France (8.8%).

In 2000 Belgian households spent 11.6% of their annual household budget on the purchase (4.8%) and use (6.8%) of their own transportation vehicles. At the end of 2002 Belgium had 4,724,856 passenger cars of which 55% ran on petrol, 43.4% on diesel and 1.2% on LPG. Petrol is becoming less popular as 64% of newly registered cars in 2002 had diesel engines compared to the 35.7% petrol registrations. The smallest engines (less than 1399cc) are also losing popularity and account for 23% of new cars compared to 31% in 1995.

Evolution of number of new passenger cars in Belgium

In 2002 a total of 472,630 new passenger cars were registered in Belgium: 40% were German car brands,

Case Table 5.1 Registration of new private cars in Belgium 1998–2002

Make	1998	1999	2000	2001	2002
VW, Audi	77,802	85,413	85,238	79,672	67,726
Peugeot	38,320	47,416	54,093	53,089	53,360
Renault	48,968	52,565	57,336	61,705	51,423
Citroën	32,878	34,508	39,401	45,761	48,853
Opel	43,615	51,854	54,405	51,017	48,194
Ford	29,871	31,140	32,106	26,834	22,850
Toyota	24,525	22,768	22,641	19,883	24,860
Mercedes-Benz	17,560	21,353	22,993	23,131	23,940
Smart	–	978	2,118	2,054	2,161
BMW	15,841	18,048	20,714	20,960	18,962
Fiat	15,895	16,085	19,422	14,461	14,750
Seat	10,444	11,944	13,831	12,008	10,512
Saab	2,947	2,607	2,966	2,426	2,548
Volvo	11,969	11,289	10,379	9,966	9,991
Lancia	2,535	2,875	3,693	2,489	1,176
Alfa Romeo	6,172	7,152	8,533	8,911	8,064
Nissan	14,334	11,821	10,903	8,990	7,205
Honda	6,644	6,187	5,203	3,224	3,605
Hyundai	3,548	4,393	4,910	4,471	6,342
Daewoo	4,228	4,934	7,030	3,197	3,213
Mazda	7,748	8,368	7,275	4,126	4,615
Mitsubishi	11,293	11,291	8,788	5,604	3,980
Suzuki	5,747	6,312	5,410	4,345	3,974
Skoda	3,892	4,360	5,325	7,198	6,462
Others	26,948	28,542	26,927	24,257	23,864
Total market sales	**463,724**	**504,203**	**531,640**	**499,779**	**472,630**

Case Table 5.2 Advertising budgets per year (all media) in Belgium 1998–2002 (€)

Make	1998	1999	2000	2001	2002
VW, Audi	15,809,170.35	20,656,093.90	18,656,745.01	21,807,961.13	20,044,759.61
Peugeot	10,888,469.30	10,105,524.48	8,524,046.24	9,129,936.45	6,276,534.71
Renault	17,591,736.11	17,934,047.18	17,819,656.61	16,232,637.81	19,188,633.74
Citroën	9,955,551.87	9,375,897.29	11,086,149.13	12,198,320.66	13,017,747.55
Opel	14,907,251.89	12,887,025.55	10,980,162.18	9,163,331.29	10,844,352.62
Ford	8,516,837.41	10,393,582.90	11,545,233.64	13,376,451.02	12,010,710.22
Toyota	9,847,257.74	8,201,152.66	10,621,321.61	8,332,861.58	10,008,409.60
Mercedes-Benz	6,940,913.10	5,560,698.14	8,399,114.65	9,517,310.76	12,191,168.81
Smart	3,123,118.59	2,783,227.05	1,582,280.81	1,616,182.46	1,460,899.11
BMW	5,032,418.82	6,095,307.88	6,184,385.56	6,621,779.61	7,189,418.45
Fiat	5,327,047.86	8,847,812.11	12,557,700.37	9,635,783.89	9,891,849.47
Seat	2,150,855.45	2,112,097.45	2,086,490.08	2,903,379.88	2,128,023.85
Saab	1,655,003.19	1,402,388.78	1,528,974.49	1,603,025.56	1,428,475.97
Volvo	3,897,299.15	4,839,459.85	5,571,333.04	2,070,494.60	3,015,340.12
Lancia	2,631,209.41	4,068,658.05	4,047,285.00	2,634,802.10	1,519,265.21
Alfa Romeo	3,047,275.74	3,431,974.87	4,454,473.31	4,282,977.24	5,025,305.25
Nissan	6,683,893.41	8,727,066.90	6,780,205.59	2,684,917.56	2,724,271.07
Honda	3,806,397.48	3,589,412.82	3,383,812.76	4,147,024.46	5,201,614.72
Hyundai	2,719,035.53	3,548,823.18	4,196,364.26	5,879,133.11	3,223,323.62
Daewoo	2,101,593.31	5,461,256.00	5,516,252.30	2,087,685.89	924,195.05
Mazda	4,709,351.67	4,273,819.94	3,516,591.18	171,247.30	2,496,149.14
Mitsubishi	6,437,979.05	6,814,626.93	4,254,547.97	3,271,787.78	3,573,022.81
Suzuki	2,320,588.39	2,308,655.19	2,486,431.69	1,389,115.14	1,768,284.50
Skoda	1,131,465.31	1,897,709.86	3,593,035.70	4,165,299.34	3,753,867.50
Others	10,385,608.41	12,246,897.46	13,167,123.96	14,286,180.37	17,857,026.20
Total market advertising	**161,617,328.54**	**177,563,216.42**	**182,539,717.14**	**169,209,626.99**	**176,762,548.90**

33% French and 11% Japanese. Italian makes represented 5% of the market of new cars and Swedish 3%. German brands were maintaining their strong market position, although in 1997 their share was even higher (46%), while French car makes were increasing their success (share of 24.5% in 1997). Japanese brands, on the other hand, were slightly losing their impact on the Belgian market (15.4% share in 1997). The average age of the Belgian passenger car is increasing: in 2002 it was 7 years, 7 months and 2 days, while in 1991 the average age was 6 years and 21 days.

Case Table 5.1 summarises the number of registrations of new private cars in Belgium for major brands in the period 1998–2002.

Evolution of advertising budgets of car brands in Belgium

The car industry is one of the largest advertising spenders in Belgium, together with government, financial services (banking and insurance), telecom, retail distribution and fast-moving consumer goods. Case Table 5.2 gives an overview of total advertising budgets spent by the major car makes in Belgium. They are an aggregation of all traditional above-the-line media: TV, radio, magazines, newspapers, billboards and cinema advertising.

Questions

1 Using Case Tables 5.1 and 5.2, carry out a share of voice/share of market analysis of the automobile industry for 1998, 2000 and 2002.

2 Study the figures of Swedish car manufacturers Saab and Volvo. What budgeting method would you assume they are using: a percentage of sales method or a competitive parity method? Why do you think this?

3 Suppose you want to launch the Smart brand on the Belgian market. Your goal is to capture a market share

of 1% by the year 2002. What budget would you suggest to reach this goal? Consider two methods: the A/S ratio method on the one hand and the Law of Peckham on the other.

4 What factors might influence advertising budgets in the car industry?

Sources: ACEA economic outlook 2003, www.acea.be; Febiac, www.febiac.be, 2003; NIS, Vervoer 2003; OMD, 2003 based on MDB/CIM figures. Thanks to Dimitri De Lauw, strategic planner of VVL/BBDO for providing advertising budgets of the car industry.

References

1 Longman, K.A. (1971), *Advertising*. New York: Harcourt Brace Jovanovich.
2 Jegers, M. and De Pelsmacker, P. (1990), 'The Optimal Level of Advertising, Considering Advertising as an Investment in Goodwill', *Ekonomicko Matematicky Obzor (Review of Econometrics)*, 26(2), 153–63.
3 Aaker, D.A., Batra, R. and Myers, J.G. (1987), *Advertising Management*. Englewood Cliffs, NJ: Prentice Hall.
4 Jones, J.P. (1995), *When Ads Work: New Proof that Advertising Triggers Sales*. New York: The Free Press/Lexicon Books.
5 Jones, J.P. (1995), Editorial, *Harvard Business Review*, (Jan.–Feb.), 53–66.
6 Dekimpe, M.G. and Hanssens, D.M. (1995), 'The Persistence of Marketing Effects on Sales', *Marketing Science*, 14(1), 1–21.
7 Belch, G.E. and Belch, M.A. (1998), *Advertising and Promotion. An Integrated Marketing Communication Perspective*. New York: Irwin/McGraw-Hill.
8 Aaker, D.A., Batra, R. and Myers, J.G. (1987), *Advertising Management*. Englewood Cliffs, NJ: Prentice Hall.
9 Kaynak, E. (1989), *The Management of International Advertising. A Handbook and Guide for Professionals*. New York: Quorum Books.
10 Schroer, J.C. (1990), 'Ad Spending: Growing Market Share', *Harvard Business Review*, 68(1), 44–8.
11 Fill, C. (1995), *Marketing Communication. Frameworks, Theories and Applications*. London: Prentice Hall.
12 Belch, G.E. and Belch, M.A. (1998), *Advertising and Promotion. An Integrated Marketing Communication Perspective*. New York: Irwin/McGraw-Hill.
13 Brown, R.S. (1978), 'Estimating Advantages to Large Scale Advertising', *Review of Economics and Statistics*, 60, 428–37.
14 Boyer, K.D. and Lancaster, K.M. (1986), 'Are There Scale Economies in Advertising?', *Journal of Business*, 59(3), 509–26.
15 Low, G.S. and Mohr, J.J. (1991), 'The Budget Allocation between Advertising and Sales Promotion: Understanding the Decision Process', *AMA Educators' Proceedings*. Chicago, 448–57.
16 Rossiter, J.R. and Percy, L. (1998), *Advertising Communication and Promotion Management*. Sydney: McGraw-Hill.
17 Peckham, J.O. (1981), *The Wheel of Marketing*. Scarsdale, NY: self-published.
18 Simon, C.J. and Sullivan, M.M. (1993), 'The Measurement and Determinants of Equity: A Financial Approach', *Marketing Science*, 12(1), 28–52.

Chapter 6
Advertising

Chapter outline

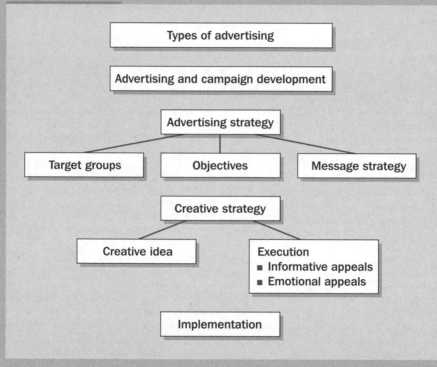

Chapter objectives

This chapter will help you to:

- Distinguish the various stages in advertising campaign development
- Learn about the information that is needed about the target groups of an advertising campaign
- Understand the various objectives of an advertising campaign and the characteristics of a good set of objectives
- Understand the importance of creativity in advertising
- Understand the effectiveness of emotional execution strategies such as humour, eroticism and warmth

Introduction

Advertising is one of the oldest, most visible and most important instruments of the marketing communications mix. Large sums of money are spent on advertising, and no other marketing phenomenon is subject to so much public debate and controversy. Huge amounts of research are devoted to the question of what makes advertising effective and to the role of advertising characteristics on its effectiveness.

As is the case with other communications instruments, special attention has to be devoted to the different steps in advertising campaign development and to the fit between the strategic marketing plan and the advertising campaign. The most crucial step in this process is translating the creative idea in an advertising execution. To this end, it is important to devote a lot of attention to different formal and content techniques and their effectiveness in advertising. But first of all, an overview is given of the different types of advertising.

Types of advertising

Advertising can be defined as any 'paid, nonpersonal communication through various media by business firms, nonprofit organisations, and individuals who are in some way identified in the advertising message and who hope to inform and/or persuade members of a particular audience'.[1] Advertising is a good marketing communications tool to inform and persuade people, irrespective of whether a product (Fitness of Nestlé keeps you slim), a service (Avis: We try harder) or an idea (Come up against cancer) is promoted. Not surprisingly, advertising is a commonly used tool, although major differences between the European countries occur, as Table 6.1 shows.

Different types of advertising can be distinguished on the basis of four criteria, as shown in Table 6.2. First of all, advertising can be defined on the basis of the sender of

Table 6.1 European advertising expenditures 2001

Country	Ad spendings (€ million)	Ad spendings per capita (€)	Rank	Ad spendings (% GDP)
Spain	11,543	292.5	1	1.74
UK	15,129	253.1	2	0.93
France	14,107	239.5	3	0.95
Austria	1,869	230.6	4	0.87
Ireland	871	230.0	5	0.75
Netherlands	3,446	216.4	6	0.79
Denmark	1,119	209.7	7	0.60
Germany	17,028	207.3	8	0.81
Portugal	2,015	201.3	9	1.60
Luxembourg	87	198.2	10	0.40
Sweden	1,646	185.5	11	0.69
Belgium	1,753	171.0	12	0.67
Norway	730	162.5	13	0.38
Greece	1,543	146.4	14	1.15
Italy	7,680	134.3	15	0.62

Based on: Media Digest (2002), Brussels: TMP/Omnimedia, Optimum/Mediateam. Reproduced with permission of OMD Belgium.

Table 6.2 Types of advertising

Sender	Message
■ Manufacturer	■ Informational
■ Collective	■ Transformational
■ Retailer	■ Institutional
■ Co-operative	■ Selective vs generic
■ Idea	■ Theme vs action
Receiver	**Media**
■ Consumer	■ Audiovisual
■ Business-to-business	■ Print
– industrial	■ Point-of-purchase
– trade	■ Direct

the message. Manufacturer or product advertising is initiated by a manufacturing company that promotes its own brands. If a government takes the initiative for a campaign, this is called collective advertising. Retail organisations also advertise. Sometimes two manufacturer companies, or a retailer and a manufacturer, jointly develop an advertising campaign. This is called co-operative advertising. Besides goods and services, ideas can be promoted, mostly by not-for-profit organisations.

The intended **receiver** of the advertising message can be either a private end-consumer or another company. In the latter case, the company may buy the products to use in its own production process (industrial advertising), or buy the products to resell them (trade advertising).

Different types of advertising can also be distinguished according to the **type of message** conveyed. The difference between advertising focussed on informational and transformational consumer motives was explained in Chapter 2. Institutional advertising is the term used to describe government campaigns. Selective advertising campaigns try to promote a specific brand, while a generic campaign promotes a whole product category, such as Dutch cheese, British beef or French wine. Theme advertising attempts to build a reservoir of goodwill for a brand or a product. Action advertising tries to stimulate consumers to buy a product immediately. Often, the latter is used in support of a sales promotion campaign.

Finally, different types of campaigns can be distinguished on the basis of the **medium** in which the ad is placed. Two main categories of traditional or above-the-line advertising can be distinguished: audiovisual and print. Other forms of advertising, such as direct marketing (Chapter 10) and in-store communications (Chapter 12), are called below-the-line.

Campaign development

Developing an advertising campaign, like any other communications plan, consists of a sequence of steps (Figure 6.1). The starting point is the marketing strategy, on the basis of which a specific advertising strategy needs to be developed. The three main points in the advertising strategy are: the target group (to or with whom are we going

Figure 6.1 Stages in campaign development

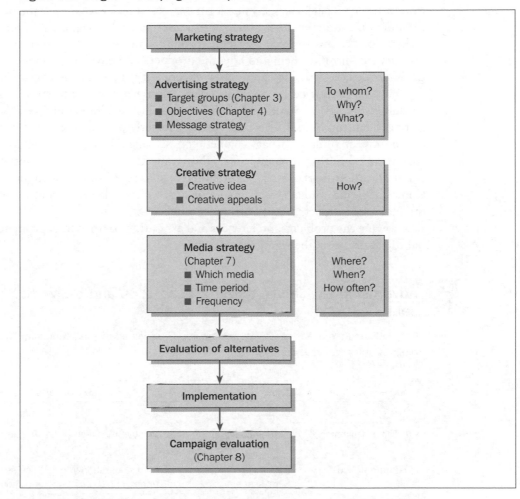

to communicate?), the advertising objectives (why are we going to communicate or what are we trying to reach?) and the message strategy (what are we going to communicate?). The most difficult step is translating the advertising strategy into a creative strategy or, in other words, going from 'what to say' to 'how to say it'. Afterwards the media strategy is developed. The different ideas will be evaluated on the basis of the creative brief and objectives stated, and the winning idea will be produced and implemented. In the process the ads in the campaign may be tested, and often the effectiveness will be assessed after the campaign. Target groups, objectives, media planning and campaign testing are discussed in Chapters 3, 4, 7 and 8 respectively.

Message strategy

What are we going to say to the consumers? The message strategy or advertising platform is a very important element of advertising strategy since it has to convince consumers. They have to know why they should buy the product, to learn in what way it is special, how it is beneficial or advantageous for them, how it can help them, what characteristics it has or what benefits, value it offers, etc. In order to answer the question 'what to communicate?' the advertiser has to know and understand the target group very well: he or she has to know what the product can do for the target group, what the product can mean to them and how the product can help the consumers to reach their goals. Indeed, advertising can only be effective if it benefits the consumer. Therefore, the message cannot be focussed on seller-objectives, but has to start from the target consumers' motives.[2] Some customers see a car just as a functional vehicle, a means of getting them from A to B. This target group can perhaps be convinced by communicating the brand's attributes (airbag, engine, etc.) or benefits (reliability, safety, etc.). Other customers do not want to buy a car, they want to buy an image, a status. Obviously, communications to the latter group should be different from those to the former group. Communicating a lifestyle, an image or a product's identity might be more suitable than telling customers about attributes or benefits.

Knowing the problems, preferences and aspirations of the target group may be essential for deciding on the right message.

Advertising to specific target groups: kids and teens and senior citizens

Both kids and teens and senior citizens require a specific advertising approach. The table below outlines some dos and don'ts.

Kids and teens		Senior citizens	
Dos	Don'ts	Dos	Don'ts
1 Tell a basic story	1 Long dialogues	1 Positive message	1 Remind of getting older
2 Entertain kids	2 Complex messages	2 Inter-generational approach	2 Use senior positioning
3 Surprise kids	3 Imitate kids' talk	3 Focus on cognitive age	3 Age labels
4 Use older models	4 Patronise	4 Promote benefits to overcome guilt	4 Make long story short
5 Remember mum and dad	5 Execution mistakes	5 Use symbols of their youth	5 Take physical consequences of getting older into account

Kids and teens want to hear a basic story (a product is a solution for a problem or a reward for good behaviour), but not a long dialogue or complex message. Children want to be entertained and surprised. They continually look for new experiences and details, and like the use of music, humour, animation, colours, jingles, games, puzzles, etc. Although they do like catchy slogans and are fond of slang and kids' talk, it is better for an advertiser to avoid using it since by the time you discover their sayings they are already out of date. The aspirational age of children is about four years older than they actually are, therefore it is better to cast

▶

older children to avoid reactions like 'This is not for me, this if for babies'. Kids hate being patronised, so do not pretend to be one of them or to know better than them. Although you want children to be fond of your brand, it is usually the parents who have to buy it. Therefore, make sure that your appeal is also attractive to parents by mentioning arguments pertaining to health, durability, lifetime value, values, etc. Finally, try to avoid 'wrong executions' such as showing children who are too young or the wrong gender (remember that boys have difficulty identifying with girl characters while girls can identify with both boys and girls) and not using enough visuals (children listen with their eyes!).[3] (Plates 6 and 7.)

Senior citizens know they are getting older and that this will bring inconveniences; they do not want advertising to remind them of this or to confront them with these negative life aspects. Rather, focus on what the product can do for them, what the main benefits are. Another possibility is to stress positive aspects of getting older such as friendships, children and grandchildren, a good financial position, wisdom and experience.[4] An inter-generational approach may tap into these perfectly, such as featuring grandparents enjoying a certain product or service with the rest of the family,[5] certainly much better than using a senior positioning. Seniors are not looking for a product 'ideal for seniors' because they still want to belong to society and do not want to form an isolated group, or as Ahmad put it: 'Older consumers like to be respected as people and not because they are old in terms of chronological age.'[6] Moreover, many seniors do not feel old (actually, at an age of 55 they feel about eight years younger than they are) and do not want to be addressed as old or senior citizens, certainly not if they have not reached the age of 65 yet. Unfortunately, in practice the age of 50 or 55 is often chosen as the boundary.[7] European seniors have lived through war situations and recessions and know what poverty and scarcity mean. As a consequence, many of them still feel guilty about spending money. Therefore, advertising should try to take away the feeling of being thrifty by providing them with good reasons to buy. Many senior citizens are rather critical and want objective, extended information and compelling reasons why they should buy the brand.[8] As mentioned in Chapter 2, nostalgic appeals showing symbols, heroes, music groups, etc. from the seniors' youth can be very powerful. Finally, although seniors do not like to admit it, they do encounter problems when ageing, for example sight and hearing problems. Therefore, it is better to use high contrast levels between text and background, a serif font not smaller than 10 points, and to use slower-paced TV and radio commercials, in which background noise is avoided.[9]

Furthermore, it is important not to confuse consumers. Therefore, most companies stick to promoting one unique benefit of their brand, which can be functional or non-functional. A functional benefit, also called a unique selling proposition (USP), usually refers to functional superiority in the sense that the brand offers the best quality, the best service, the lowest price, the most advanced technology. For example, Gillette is 'the best a man can get', there is 'no better washing machine' than Miele, Lee Casuals 'make any situation comfortable', Philips 'makes things better', Durex Avanti 'gives the most natural feeling', no card is more accepted than MasterCard, etc. A non-functional benefit usually reflects a unique psychological association to consumers and is referred to as an emotional selling proposition (ESP).[10] Dune of Dior is the essence of freedom, you buy L'Oréal because 'you are worth it', you buy your girlfriend a Chaumet watch because 'chaque instant est une émotion'. Other examples of brands that are promoted on the basis of non-functional benefits include Porsche, Rodania, Rolls-Royce, Louis Vuitton, and Van Cleef & Arpels.

In order to know which USP or ESP to go for, the advertiser needs to have a clear consumer insight. These are often revealed by qualitative research. For example, for Kraft a consumer insight was that mothers would not buy Lunchables for their kids because it is convenient (they do not have to prepare sandwiches in the morning, etc.), but they could be convinced if it made them feel like a good mother. Therefore, a child in the Lunchables commercial says 'Yes, yes, thank you Mama' when he discovers his mother gave him Lunchables for lunch instead of ordinary sandwiches. The Luxembourg fixed-line operator, TELE2 AB, was well aware of the fact that heavy phone users are sensitive about the cost the telephone represents in their monthly household budget. These heavy users would love to call more if they did not have to worry about the cost. Therefore, TELE2 positions itself on the promise of providing the 'best price offer' and the 'most simple and clear offer'. A pan-European campaign with the slogan 'TELE2, simply phone for less' proved to be very successful in France, Germany, Italy, Austria, Switzerland and Holland.[11]

Creative idea

Before an advertising agency can start thinking of a creative strategy, the advertiser must give them a creative brief. The necessary elements of a creative brief are summarised in Figure 6.2. The creative brief or the document that forms the starting point for the advertising agency should contain not only information on the target group, advertising objectives and message strategy, but also provide sufficient information concerning the background of the company, the product, the market and the competitors. This implies information concerning the past, present and future in order to give the agency as accurate a view of the brand and its environment as possible. Some examples of

Figure 6.2 The creative brief

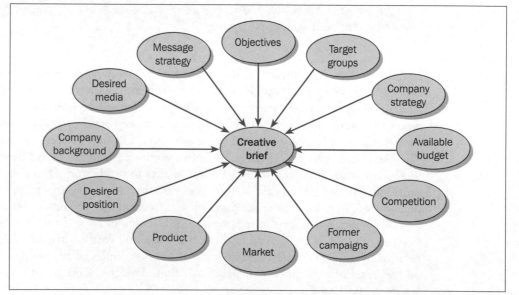

necessary elements are the long-term company and brand strategy, past, current and desired positioning, former advertising campaigns, message strategies and execution styles, desired media, available budget, and timing of the different steps (creative idea, execution strategies, campaign running, etc.).

The first step of the creative strategy is to develop a creative idea. But what is a creative idea? It is hard to give an accurate definition, but let's consider some attempts. A creative idea can be defined as an 'original and imaginative thought designed to produce goal-directed and problem-solving advertisements and commercials'.[12] According to others, a creative advertising idea has to be attention-grabbing and should work as a catalyst in the sense that it should create a 'chemical reaction' of immediately understanding the brand's position.[13] According to the jazz musician Charlie Mingus, 'Creativity is more than just being different. Everybody can play weird, that's easy. What's hard is to be as simple as Bach. Making the simple complicated is commonplace, making the complicated simple, awesomely simple, that's creativity.'[14] In essence, a creative idea seems to boil down to a proposition which makes it possible to communicate a brand's position in an original, attention-getting, but easy-to-catch way. Several researchers argue that creativity probably is the most important aspect of advertising.[15] An expert panel even held the opinion that 'the selling power of a creative idea can exceed that of an ordinary idea by a multiple of 10' (see Plate 8).[16]

A few examples may clarify what is meant by creative advertising ideas.

■ Miller beer has a screw cap instead of a crown cap. Miller promoted its beer in TV commercials with the slogan 'twist to open', showing a fat man in his underwear twisting in front of his bottle of Miller beer, pausing a moment to see whether his bottle had opened, and then starting to twist again.

■ Volkswagen promoted its Beetle with the slogan 'think small', turning the small size into a competitive advantage, just as Smart tried to do with 'reduce to the max'. Nissan did the opposite, promoting its new pick-up using print ads and billboards. To stress the size of the pick-up, a countryside picture features a man and, no, not his dog, but his hippopotamus playing with a stick. The baseline reads 'Think Bigger'. Nissan won a Gold Clio Award in 2003 for this campaign.

■ To make clear to the Spanish audience that children should watch less TV and play more, an ad was run in which a little boy is shown watching TV while his dog is watching him. After having waited a while to get a bit of attention, the dog turns away and starts packing its bags. With the bag in its mouth, the dog waits a few minutes in front of the boy, but when the boy does not even look up, the dog sadly leaves.

■ Oslo Sporveier wanted to encourage existing users to use public transport more often, as well as encourage new users to take up the habit of using public transport. To reach these objectives, public transport had to be made easier since at that time tickets could be purchased only at one place. Therefore, Oslo Sporveier started to sell season tickets through newsagents. The communications campaign promoting this season ticket featured a ticket collector on a bus. A smug-looking, self-satisfied woman holds her ticket ready for the collector. Just before the collector arrives, a punk seated next to the woman grabs the ticket, eats it, and then shows his season ticket to the collector. The pay-off slogan reads 'Smart people buy season tickets – not single tickets'.[17]

▶

- British Coal wanted to stop the decline in the use of coal as a heating fuel. In order to avoid the negative associations with coal, it was decided to concentrate on the sensual qualities of a lit fire. The ad shows a bulldog walking into a room and lying down by a roaring fire. Next, a cat follows, sits next to the dog and starts licking its ear. Finally, a mouse comes in, sits next to the cat and the two touch noses. In the background Shirelles' song 'Will you still love me tomorrow?' plays. The final frame says 'Now you know what people see in a real fire'.[18]

- Nicorette, a product to help smokers give up the smoking habit, received a Silver Euro Effie for its Beat Cigarettes campaign. Instead of showing quitters suffering cravings, they were shown beating a giant cigarette. In some ads the giant cigarette represented a boxing-ball; in others it was used as a battering-ram. All ads showed happy quitters in a humorous setting, while the baseline 'Beat cigarettes one at a time. You're twice as likely to succeed with Nicorette' summed it all up.[19] See Plate 12.

- Frisk Mints received a Gold Clio award for its campaign in which an imbecilic-looking guy is brought into a laboratory to test his response latency. In the laboratory, a real horse and a fictitious horse played by humans is shown. The imbecile first has to eat a Frisk and is then asked to distinguish between the real horse and the fictitious horse by pushing a button. Amazingly he succeeds in pressing the right button, after which the slogan 'Frisk sharpens you up' appears.[20]

Besides the need for a creative idea to develop effective advertising, one can question how creative the ad itself has to be. Indirect evidence of the belief in the success of creative ads might be the fact that advertising seems to be more creative than a few decades ago.[21] However, attention-grabbing, originality and imagination do not suffice. In the end advertising must help to accomplish marketing objectives. The few existing studies do not convey consistent results. One study[22] claims creativity has a positive impact on ad likeability, but two other studies could not find a relation between ad creativity and the attitude towards the ad.[23] Although it is clear that a creative idea is needed to express a brand's positioning statement attractively, the question remains as to how creative the ad itself should be, and whether the average consumer holds a similar opinion on what constitutes a creative ad to that of creative directors. It would not be the first time that consumers rank commercials differently to creative directors. The latter are often quite surprised that the public do not select the ads perceived as most creative by themselves. The foregoing illustrates that more research is called for to find out how important creativity is in the eyes of the consumers and what creativity means to them.

Creative appeals

In trying to generate the established advertising objectives, agencies or creatives can use a multitude of appeals, formats and execution strategies to express or translate their creative idea.[24] Broadly speaking, two different types of creative appeals can be distinguished: rational appeals and emotional appeals. Emotional appeals are advertisements whose main purpose is to elicit affective responses and to convey an image. Rational appeals, on the other hand, contain features, practical details and verifiable, factually relevant cues that can serve as evaluative criteria. Referring to the difference between action and image communications as discussed in Chapter 1, many image communications

Table 6.3 Creative advertising appeals, advertising formats and endorsers

Rational appeals	Emotional appeals
■ Talking head	■ Humour
■ Demonstration	■ Fear
■ Problem solution	■ Warmth
■ Testimonial	■ Eroticism
■ Slice of life	■ Music
■ Dramatisation	■ Etc.
■ Comparative ads	
■ Etc.	
Endorsers	
■ Expert endorsement	
■ Celebrity endorsement	

make use of emotional appeals, while most action communications use rational appeals. However, mixed appeals also exist, employing both rational and emotional elements. Both for emotional and rational appeals, different formats or execution strategies and different types of endorsers can be used (see Table 6.3). Also, it has to be added here that several of the formats that can be used for rational appeals could just as well be used for emotional appeals, although they are discussed only once. For example, a comparative ad can be purely factual describing own and competitive prices, but could also be humorous such as Virgin Atlantic's campaign featuring large billboards in airports with the message 'Enjoy your overpriced flight' (see Plate 9).

Rational appeals

Rational ads may contain one or several information cues (see also Plate 10). The most widely used classification system of information cues is the one presented in Table 6.4, which has been applied in more than 60 studies.[25] The classification consists of 14 different types of information.

Turning to the advertising formats noted in Table 6.3, a talking head refers to an ad in which the characters tell a story in their own words: monologue, dialogue or

Table 6.4 Resnik and Stern's advertising information classification

■ Price	■ Special offers	■ Safety
■ Quality	■ Taste	■ Independent research
■ Performance	■ Nutrition	■ Company research
■ Components	■ Packaging	■ New ideas
■ Availability	■ Warranties	

Based on: Abernethy, A.M. and Franke, G.R. (1996), 'The Information Content of Advertising: A Meta-Analysis', *Journal of Advertising*, 25(2), 1–17.

interview techniques could be used. For instance, talking heads are frequently used in Philadelphia cheese ads in which a woman talks about her lunch plans for the rest of the week.

In a **demonstration** consumers are shown how a product works. It is an easy way to focus on product attributes, tell about the benefits and product uses while demonstrating the product. For example, when Fébrèze was launched in Europe, ads showed consumers that the product could be used for preventing disturbing odours in clothes, sofas, curtains, cars, etc.

A **problem solution** shows how a problem can be solved or avoided. Problem solution is often combined with a fear appeal showing consumers what happens if the brand is not used.[26] For example, the ads for Head & Shoulders feature an elegant-looking business professional wearing a nice dark suit. Unfortunately he has a dandruff problem which clearly shows on the suit. Head & Shoulders can solve this problem.

A **testimonial** features ordinary people saying how good a product is. Typical products which are advertised in this way are detergents: 'I really was amazed, my clothes have never been so white'. SlimFast ('You really can') also used ads featuring local testimonials of how much weight people lost to introduce or relaunch the brand in the UK, Germany, France and the Netherlands.[27] Testimonials are often effective because they rely on the positive membership reference group effect. However, one should think twice when considering this advertising technique since research shows that testimonials often lead to irritation in consumers.[28]

Techies seeking for testimonials

After the 2000 dot-com crash, tech firms began using rather aggressive comparative ads, such as Sun Microsystems in 2001 with a direct aim at IBM 'Do you have the Big Blues over your IT infrastructure?' Also Oracle started using charts comparing the company with the competition. A year later, a new ad wave came over the tech market, consisting of testimonial campaigns. Hewlett-Packard mentions Amazon.com and DreamWorks as clients, Nasdaq mentions Starbucks, EDS mentions 7-eleven, and IBM mentions LL Bean, eBay and Saks. However, one wonders how effective these ads are in view of the volume of similar ads appearing at the same time. Moreover, customers are already assuming that these scenarios are a result of deals between the companies.[29]

Slice-of-life ads feature the product being used in a real-life setting, which usually involves solving a problem. The effectiveness of this type of ad is attributed to the fact that the product is shown in a real-life context the target group can relate to. An example would be a family putting picnic hampers, blankets, toys, etc., in their new Mercedes space van to go out for a picnic on a Sunday afternoon. Another example shows a boy playing soccer with his friends, then he comes home with his clothes so dirty you think they will never get clean again. Fortunately, the boy's mother has Dreft which cleans the clothes without a problem. Although slice-of-life is used quite often, research shows that such ads are more likely to cause irritation.[30]

A **dramatisation** is rather similar to a slice-of-life. Both first present a problem and afterwards the solution, but a dramatisation builds suspense and leads consumers to a climax. The difference between a slice-of-life, and for that matter a drama (which just tells a story), and a dramatisation lies in the intensity. The Alldays Tanga campaign is an example of a dramatisation. A young woman is dancing on a stage amidst a large crowd, wearing extremely close-fitting clothes. Suddenly, in front of everyone, her panty liner gets dislodged, causing her a lot of embarrassment while other girls make fun of her. The spot ends showing several other girls dancing without any worries. The solution becomes obvious in the base line 'Should've worn ALLDAYS TANGA'.[31]

Comparative advertising can be used as a means to differentiate a brand from a competitor. A direct comparative ad explicitly names the comparison brand (often a well-known competitive brand) and claims that the comparison brand is inferior to the advertised brand with respect to a specific attribute. An indirect comparative ad does not explicitly mention a comparison brand, but argues to be superior on a certain attribute compared to other brands ('Gillette, the best a man can get'). Taylor Nelson Sofres found in 2001 that two-thirds of UK consumers find comparable ads unacceptable; women were most opposed and youngsters between 16 and 24 minded least that brands criticise competitors.[32] Research in France in 2002 showed that direct comparative ads led to more positive brand attitudes than indirect or non-comparative ads.[33] However, French advertisers remain unconvinced of the effectiveness of comparative advertising on French consumers and do not intend to use it more often in the future.[34] Also in Spain comparative advertising does not seem to be well received. A study in 2003 revealed that the more intense the comparative claim was, the less consumers believed the propositions, the more counterarguments were formed, and the more negative attitudes and brand intentions became.[35] This seems to suggest that advertisers should be careful with using this technique in Europe.

Emotional appeals

Emotional advertising refers to advertising that tries to evoke emotions in consumers rather than to make consumers think. Emotional ads mainly consist of non-verbal elements such as images and emotional stimuli. It should be clear that there is a difference between the intended emotional content of a stimulus, or the emotional technique used, and the emotions experienced by a consumer as a result of being exposed to an ad. Emotional appeals do not necessarily evoke emotions in all people, although they are designed to do so.

Humour

Humorous advertising can be defined as an appeal created with the intent to make people laugh, irrespective of the fact that the humour is successful (people indeed perceive the ad as humorous) or unsuccessful (people do not think the ad is funny). Humour seems to be one of the most frequently used emotional techniques throughout the world. A survey in 1992 in 33 countries revealed that approximately 35% of all magazine and outdoor advertising contained humour.[36]

Are humorous appeals effective? No doubt most people appreciate a good joke, but can humorous ads convey a brand message? Or does it leave people remembering the joke, but neither the brand nor the brand message? Can humour be used for 'serious' products, or does a humorous approach make a clown of the advertising company? Humour has been studied by many researchers, and overall there is only one aspect on which agreement between the researchers can be found: humour attracts attention.[37] However, the question remains to what extent humour also attracts attention to the brand. As far as recall and recognition, creating positive ad and brand attitudes and increasing purchase intention are concerned, no conclusive results can be drawn.[38] This can partly be explained by several moderating variables.

Different types of humour exist, for example cognitive humour (see Plate 11). In this case there is an incongruity, an unexpected element as a result of which the consumer has to follow different lines of reasoning to solve the incongruity;[39] for example, the latest Amstel Light beer ad shows products that normally belong in the refrigerator in an unexpected spot because Amstel Light has taken their place in the refrigerator. One example features a woman who is sleeping in bed. When she wakes up and turns on the light, she screams when she finds a plate of meatloaf next to her in bed. The next scene shows the refrigerator where a 12-pack of Amstel Light is jammed into the meatloaf's position.[40] There is also sentimental humour, for example, a little kitten that tries to catch the ball in a football game on TV, a satire, meant to be funny and insulting at the same time, sexual humour, making fun of the other sex, etc. The different types of humour are appreciated by the target consumers to a different extent leading to different communications effects. While sentimental humour is quite innocent, satire or sexual humour is more aggressive, and not surprisingly not everyone finds the latter types of humour funny.

The effectiveness of humour also depends on the product type. The prevailing opinion seems to be that humour is more appropriate for low than for high-involvement products, and for transformational rather than for informational products and that humour, in any case, should be avoided for high-involvement/informational products, such as insurance.[41]

In general, humour seems to be more effective for existing and familiar brands than for new and unfamiliar brands.[42] In other words, building brand awareness is more difficult by using humour, since the humour might gain too much attention, leading to inferior brand attention. Humour that is in one way or another related to the product is more effective than unrelated humour. Finally, humour may have a detrimental effect when prior brand evaluations are negative.[43] In other words, if you are convinced that Lion tastes awful and sticks to your teeth, you are more likely to think that the company wants to be funny, but is not funny at all, while a positive brand attitude leads to more tolerance and acceptance.

Eroticism

Defined very broadly, an ad can be classified as erotic if one or more of the following elements are present: partial or complete nudity, physical contact between two adults, sexy or provocatively dressed person(s), provocative or seductive facial expression, and suggestive words or sexually laden music, etc (see Plate 13). Although some people seem convinced that eroticism is being used more and more in European advertising, content analyses show that this is only in the eyes of the beholder.[44]

How effective is an ad showing a seductive Claudia Schiffer in front of the Citroën Xsara, the erotic style of the Martini campaigns, the nude Sophie Dahl for Opium or the full-frontal nude model for Yves Saint Laurent's newest scent H7? Eroticism attracts attention. One may wonder, though, whether any attention is directed at the brand or the brand message. Indeed, most researchers agree that eroticism reduces brand and message recall.[45] Another negative aspect on which most researchers agree is that eroticism has a negative impact on the image of the advertiser.[46] For other communications objectives such as the attitude towards the ad or the brand, and purchase intention, mixed research results have been reported.[47]

An explanation can perhaps be found in a number of moderating factors. For instance, the more intense the eroticism or, in other words, the more overt the sex appeal in the form of nudity or suggestion of sexual intercourse, the more negative the responses to the ad become.[48] Research results reveal that the more the erotic appeal is related to the product, the more positive the responses to it become.[49] In other words, functional products such as underwear, bath foam, shower cream, etc. and romantic products such as perfume, aftershave, alcohol, cosmetics, etc. are expected to benefit more from an erotic appeal than other product categories such as coffee, a lawn mower, or a lathe, etc. Notwithstanding the foregoing, a recent study in which the effectiveness of eroticism for social marketing topics (as diverse as eating healthily, public library and museum attendance, HIV/AIDS prevention, etc.) was tested showed that sexual appeals were more persuasive than matched non-sexual appeals.[50]

Which target group can most effectively be addressed with an erotic appeal? Research shows that men respond significantly more positively to eroticism than women.[51] However, in most of the studies ads with seductive or naked women were used. Handsome men as product endorsers might have completely altered the picture. In fact, lately more and more advertisers are using men as sex objects to please women. Examples are the Cola Light 11.30 break commercial, the Australian ad for Underdaks men's underwear in which two female airport officers have a man stripped to his underwear by sounding a false alarm each time he passes through the control gate, the Gini ad in which a female passionately grabs a guy, starts opening the buttons of his shirt, unhooks his belt, pulls the belt out of his trousers and . . . uses the belt to open her bottle of Gini.

Warmth

Warm appeals can be described as advertising that consists of elements evoking mild, positive feelings such as love, friendship, cosiness, affection and empathy. Although warmth now seems to be used less than it was a few decades ago, it is still a frequently used emotional technique.[52] Is this frequent use of warmth justified? The answer is clearly, yes. Warmth leads to more positive affective responses, less negative feelings such as irritation, a more positive attitude towards the ad and towards the brand, and sometimes an enhanced purchase intention.[53] Target groups most responsive to warm appeals are females, emotional individuals and individuals with a lot of cognitive empathy (meaning that they can understand the situation of others).[54]

Fear

A fear appeal refers the consumer to a certain type of risk he or she might be exposed to and which he or she usually can reduce by buying (e.g. an insurance) or not buying (e.g. not drinking when driving) the product advertised. Typical risks that might be used in a fear appeal are:[55]

■ *Physical*: the risk of bodily harm, which is often used for burglar alarms, toothpaste, analgesics, etc. An example would be 'When are you going to install an alarm? After they break in?'

■ *Social*: the risk of being socially ostracised, often used for deodorants, dandruff shampoo, mouth wash, etc.

■ *Time*: the risk of spending a lot of time on an unpleasant activity while the activity can be performed in less time. During the introduction period of dishwashers, messages frequently read 'Do you realise that most people spend X years of their life washing the dishes?'

■ *Product performance*: the risk that competitive brands do not perform adequately. Dyson vacuum cleaners are promoted as having no bag, which makes them the only cleaner to maintain 100% suction, 100% of the time.

■ *Financial*: the risk of losing a lot of money, typically used by insurance companies.

■ *Opportunity loss*: pointing out to consumers that they run the risk of missing a special opportunity if they do not act right away. For example, the Belgian mobile phone provider Proximus ran a campaign with the following message: 'Subscribe now to the Proximus net, and pay nothing until April'.

Are fear appeals effective? Most studies point in an affirmative direction. Several studies confirm that fear appeals are capable of sensitising people to threats and of changing their behaviour.[56]

Music

Who has not caught themselves singing an ad jingle? – '. . . whenever there is fun, there is always Coca-Cola', 'I feel cointreau tonight', etc. or thinking about one of the songs used in a commercial? For example, Celine Dion's 'I Drove All Night' for DaimlerChrysler, Steppenwolf's 'Born to Be Wild' in the Ford Cougar ad, 'L'air du Temps' for the champagne brand Bernard Massard, Marvin Gaye's 'I Heard it through the Grapevine' in the California Raisin ad, etc. Music is extensively used in TV and radio commercials.

The major reasons why advertisers make use of music is because they believe that mucic can gain attention, create a mood, a sense of relaxation or can set an emotional tone that enhances product evaluations and facilitates message acceptance, send a brand message and convey a unique selling point, signal a certain lifestyle and build a brand personality, and communicate cultural values.[57]

Endorsers

Experts can be used to demonstrate the quality or high technology of a product. For example, toothpaste brands are often promoted by means of someone in a white lab coat to infer a dentist's opinion. The effectiveness of this type of ad is assumed to be based on the positive non-membership (aspirational) reference group effect. In contrast with testimonials, **expert endorsements** do not seem to be perceived as irritating. On the contrary, one study even suggests experts evoke more positive affective responses.[58]

Celebrities can also be used to endorse a product. Again, their effectiveness is based on the aspiration group effect. Examples of **celebrity endorsement** are Pamela Anderson for Pizza Hut, Naomi Campbell for the milk campaign, Justine Henin for Danette of Danone, Claudia Schiffer for Citroën, Rowan Atkinson for Barclaycard, etc. (See Plate 14.)

As is obvious, celebrities are used extensively. For example, one in four ads in the US and one in five UK campaigns feature celebrities.[59] But how effective are celebrity endorsements? They certainly attract a lot of attention, not only from the target group, but also from the media. The latter is very interesting since it can give rise to free publicity. For example, when the 'Won't Kiss Off Test' campaign for Revlon's Colorstay Lipsticks was launched, Cindy Crawford kissed reporters, leading to massive free publicity.[60] Moreover, several studies have shown that celebrities can have a direct positive impact on ad likeability and also an indirect effect on brand attitude and purchase intentions.[61] For instance, the management of Pepsi attributes its 8% increase in sales in 1984 to the Michael Jackson endorsement, while the Spice Girls were good for a 2% global market share increase in 1997.[62] However, not all celebrities are effective for all products or all situations. Several factors play a role.[63] According to the Source Credibility Model, the celebrity should be credible in the sense that he or she has expertise and is trustworthy. The trustworthiness of an endorser is defined as the degree to which the endorser is perceived to be honest and believable. Eric Cantona has proved that he has mastered how to play soccer, which makes him highly credible for promoting soccer shoes and sports wear. In a study in which both an actor and an athlete promote a candy bar and an energy bar, it was found that the ad featuring the athlete was more effective when an energy bar was promoted, while the type of endorser did not matter for the candy bar.[64]

Besides credibility, attractiveness may also be important. According to the Source Attractiveness Model, attractiveness refers in this context to the degree that the celebrity is known (awareness and familiarity), is perceived to be physically attractive and is liked by the target group. Although all adults agree that Sean Connery is a great movie star, Leonardo DiCaprio will no doubt have more impact on teenagers. Several studies found support for this model, although a recent study warns that one should be cautious about using highly attractive models. Using very thin models, for example, may reduce the self-image of the target group and evoke negative feelings both towards the celebrity and the product.[65]

According to the Product Match-Up Hypothesis, there should be an **appropriate fit** between the endorser's image, personality, lifestyle, etc. and the product advertised. In this respect, it should be added that the **behaviour of the celebrity** may turn against a brand he or she is associated with. Cantona, for example, was prosecuted for kicking a soccer fan. Although this could have been a disaster for Nike, Nike cleverly managed the problem and even succeeded in turning it to an advantage by starting to sell sports wear showing the word 'punished'. Youngsters who like rebels, and who still admire Cantona for his soccer skills, were extremely fond of these shirts. The potential risk of negative celebrity information is expected to be especially great for new or unfamiliar brands for which the celebrity is the primary cue on which consumers base their brand evaluations.[66]

Finally, 'Characters' (such as Tony the Tiger, Plate 14) or 'brand personalities' (such as the Marlboro Man, Plate 15) can also become celebrities.

Campaign implementation

After advertising agencies have come up with creative and executional ideas, the advertiser has to evaluate the different alternatives on the basis of the creative brief. This means that the idea ultimately chosen needs to be suited and appealing to the target group, be capable of reaching the advertising objectives, be a kind of catalyst, making the brand's position immediately clear in a simple, eye-catching manner. The idea must also fit with the company's and brand's long-term strategy and with previous campaigns. It has to be adaptable to the different media to be used, and financially implementable within the given advertising budget and within the given time limits.

When agreement is reached on the creative idea to be used for the different media, the advertisements need to be produced. Since advertisement production needs special skills, this job is typically carried out by technical experts. Photography, typography and sound recording needs to be well thought through, so that headline, baseline, copy, background music, packshots, presenters, characters, the set, etc. form an integrated and consistent advertisement. As soon as the advertiser approves of the advertisement proposal, the advertisements are produced and handed over to the media.

After the campaign has run, it has to be evaluated on its effectiveness. In order to be able to do this, it is very important to have clear, measurable objectives at the beginning of the campaign development process, as well as accurate data of the situation prior to the campaign launch. The important aspect of media planning is discussed in the next chapter. Advertising research is extensively covered in Chapter 8.

Summary

Advertising is any paid, non-personal communication through various media by an identified company. It is one of the most visible tools of the communications mix. Advertising campaign development consists of a number of stages. First, advertising strategy has to be decided on: Who are the target groups of the campaign, what are the objectives, and what messages are going to be conveyed? At the very core of the advertising process is the development of a creative idea. Companies have to write a creative brief before the advertising agency can start to do its job. Creativity is hard to describe, but bringing the message in an original, novel and appealing way comes close. In general, two broad types of creative appeals, rational and emotional appeals, can be used to develop a campaign, although mixed forms also exist. Emotional appeals are advertisements whose main purpose is to elicit affective responses and to convey an image. Rational appeals, on the other hand, contain information cues such as price, value, quality, performance, components, availability, taste, warranties, new ideas, etc. For both rational and emotional appeals different formats or execution strategies can be used. Rational appeals may, for instance, make use of a talking head, a demonstration, a problem solution, a testimonial, a slice-of-life, a drama or a (direct or indirect) comparison with competitors. Emotional appeals may be based on humour, fear, warmth, eroticism, music or the like. Rational and emotional appeals may further feature different types of endorsers: ordinary people, experts or celebrities. None of the execution strategies work in all situations and for all target groups; for example, although everyone agrees that emotional techniques are capable of attracting attention, it is by no means certain that they get the message across in the manner intended. Therefore caution should be taken to select the right technique.

Review questions

1 What are the various stages in advertising campaign development?

2 Is creativity in advertising important?

3 What are the necessary elements in a creative brief?

4 Are humorous advertising appeals effective? What about erotic ones?

5 To what extent are fear appeals effective advertising techniques?

6 On the basis of what criteria would you select a celebrity?

Further reading

Belch, M. and Belch, G. (2003), *Advertising and Promotion: An Integrated Marketing Communications Perspective. 6th Edition.* McGraw-Hill.

Cappo, J. (2003), *The Future of Advertising.* McGraw-Hill.

Journal of Advertising

Journal of Advertising Research

Journal of Marketing Communications

Lane, W. and Russell, J. (2001), *Advertising, A Framework.* Upper Saddle River, NJ: Prentice Hall.

Wells, W., Burnett, J. and Moriarty, S. (2003), *Advertising. Principles and Practice.* Englewood Cliffs: Prentice Hall.

Case 6

Launching the Citroën Xsara Picasso and relaunching the Volkswagen Sharan

By the year 2000, the market segment of so-called small MPVs (multi-purpose vehicles) had grown considerably and was already well established. The annual growth of sales in Europe was 1.3% in 1997 and 6% in 2000. The European car market is fiercely competitive and the competition in the MPV market segment has intensified. All across Europe the major car manufacturers have introduced their own version of the MPV: VW Sharan, Ford Galaxy, Seat Alhambra, Mazda MPV, Nissan Serena, Renault Espace, Peugeot 806, Citroën Xsara Picasso . . . The levels of advertising expenditure and the resulting levels of advertising clutter are very high. In 2000, one of the already well-established MPVs was the Volkswagen Sharan. Faced with increasing competition, which had led to losing its market leader position, Volkswagen decided to relaunch the model in May 2000. The Citroën Xsara Picasso was a latecomer into this market; it was launched in January 2000. Both car models are sold all across Europe. This case focusses on the campaigns in a number of selected European countries.

Citroën Xsara Picasso

Advertising objectives, creative strategy and media strategy

In January 2000 the Xsara Picasso was launched by means of a global campaign in 41 countries

Case Table 6.1

Share of voice of the Xsara Picasso campaign and its main competitors 2000 (%)

	Germany	France	UK	Spain	Italy
Xsara Picasso	2.0	3.5	2.5	1.8	2.2
Main competitor	3.0	2.5	4.6	2.8	3.0

worldwide, including 17 European countries. The main objectives of the campaign were as follows:

- To build a global campaign with advertising recognition and correct attribution above market average.
- To gain rapid awareness and desirability for the Xsara Picasso, and to attract younger and more family-oriented customers. The aim was to have a strong communication return on investments: to be the number two brand in product awareness within a year of launch.
- To rapidly build market share.

The Xsara Picasso is the first mass-produced car to carry the name of a famous painter. The invention of the product name was at the very heart of the creative strategy. From European research Citroën learned that customers attach a lot of importance to the 'badge' effect. A well-chosen name, and a communications campaign that links the values associated with this name to the values associated with the Citroën Xsara brand, can lead to rapid awareness and distinctiveness. Therefore, the creative strategy, developed by Euro RSCG Works, builds on the spirit of Picasso, using the concept 'Citroën Xsara Picasso, free your mind', making the car both distinctive and aspirational. The campaign did not focus at all on product attributes. At the same time, the campaign was placed in a familiar car environment, i.e. the car factory. The core element of the creative strategy was the 'Robot' television campaign, focussing around the name and the spirit of the new car. Robots in a car factory make a Picasso-like painting on a semi-finished Xsara Picasso. When they hear a noise, they rapidly clean the car and replace the drawing with the signature of Picasso (see Plate 16). Television was chosen as a primary campaign medium to clearly position the Xsara Picasso as a major challenger to the competition. Share of voice levels were reasonable, and in many countries close to those of the

market leader (see Case Table 6.1). A print campaign (magazines and newspapers) was also developed to provide more rational product information and posters and other point-of-sale materials were developed in synergy with the other campaign materials.

Campaign results

The campaign was among the best five tested by IPSOS since 1981. With 63% advertising recognition, the television campaign obtained the best IPSOS impact score in France ever, five times above the general average and 50% over the second score in all sections. In Case Figure 6.1, the correct attribution and the percentage of people liking the campaign of the Xsara Picasso campaign is compared with the average correct attribution and likeability scores of the foreign MPV car campaigns in five European countries. The correct attribution of the Xsara Picasso campaign is well above average in all five countries, and so are the likeability scores in at least three out of five countries. In Case Figure 6.2 the evolution of the prompted product awareness of the Xsara Picasso and its two major competitors in France is shown over the period November 1999 to March 2001. The Xsara Picasso occupies the second place, and has rapidly built awareness to levels close to those of the mental market leader.

A year and a half after its launch, the Xsara Picasso occupies the first position in the compact people carrier market segment in the UK with 29% market share, and in Spain with 24% market share. In France it occupies the second place with 28% market share.

The campaign has won various awards around the world. It won the Jury Grand Prize and the prize for the Best European Campaign at the European Automobile Film Festival 2000, the Best Brand Strategy at the Grand Prix Pubblicita 2000 in Italy, and the Grand Prize for Best Car Advertising Film at the Poznan Car Salon in Poland. In 2001 it won a silver Euro Effie award for its results in 2000.

Case Figure 6.1 Attribution and likeability scores of the Citroën Xsara campaign (%)

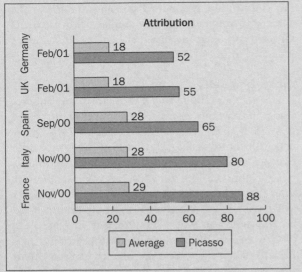
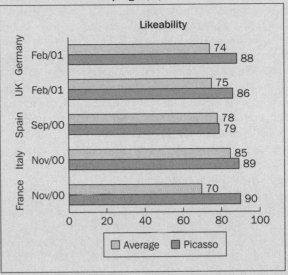

Case Figure 6.2
Prompted product awareness of the Citroën Xsara and its main competitors in France (%)

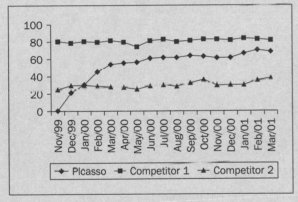

Volkswagen Sharan

The data in this section describe the situation, and the campaign details and results in three central European countries, i.e. Germany, Hungary and the Czech Republic. In Germany the Volkswagen Sharan was the market leader until it was overtaken by its identical twin, the Ford Galaxy, in early 2000. In Hungary the Seat Alhambra (Seat is a part of the Volkswagen group) was the market leader, and the Volkswagen Sharan was challenged for second place by the Nissan Serena. In the Czech Republic, the Volkswagen Sharan was market leader, followed by the Seat Alhambra, until it was overtaken by the relaunched Mazda in January 2000. All other competitors were also suffering.

Advertising objectives, creative strategy and media strategy

In early 2000 the VW Sharan was suffering from intense competition and was losing its leading market position. The challenge was to retake the lead against competitors that were in some cases identical, were often far less expensive and in markets that were very price-sensitive by means of a relaunch of the model. Germany is the major target market.

The advertising objectives were defined as follows:

- *Germany*: to recapture market leadership in the MPV segment within six months.

- *Hungary*: to catch up with the Seat Alhambra within six months, and to stop the rise of the Nissan Serena.

- *Czech Republic*: to recapture market leadership in the MPV segment within six months.

The original idea for MPVs was the 'active' family car. Gradually, MPVs have positioned themselves away from this original idea by emphasising other areas of use, such as leisure, business vehicle, transporting bulky loads, etc. The Sharan wanted to position the car 'back to its origins'. It wanted to become 'the family car in Europe'. This positioning should bring the car closer to what were still the most important buyers: families. Since the VW Sharan was much more expensive than its major, often identical, competitors, it could only be successful with a strong emotional positioning strategy. Apart from small children, animals were considered the best guarantee for high emotionalisation. They can arouse parently feelings in potential customers. Furthermore, the animal world offers a wealth of opportunities to visualise the strong points of the Sharan, such as strength, comfort, safety, etc. The 'Safari' campaign shows different animals and their babies in connection with the VW Sharan.

Television and cinema were used as the prime media. They are the most supportive for emotionalising campaigns aimed at a large family audience. Often the commercials were embedded in animal and other family-oriented programmes. Double- and single-page ads in consumer magazines supported the emotionalising positioning, supplementing it with rational product attribute arguments. Traffic at the dealership was enhanced by similar advertisements targeted at the trade channel. The campaign was launched in May 2000.

Campaign results
By September 2000, the VW Sharan was market leader in Germany again. In four months it increased its market share from 19% in April to 24%, overtaking the Ford Galaxy. By February 2001 the Sharan managed to increase its market share further to 28.5% (Case Figure 6.3). In Hungary, the VW Sharan more than doubled its market share from 14.9% in August 2000 to 35.3% in March 2001. The car almost closed the gap with the Seat Alhambra, and displaced the Nissan Serena from third to last position (Case Figure 6.4). In the second month after the roll-out of the campaign in the Czech Republic, the VW Sharan

Case Figure 6.3 Market share of the VW Sharan and its competitors in Germany (%)

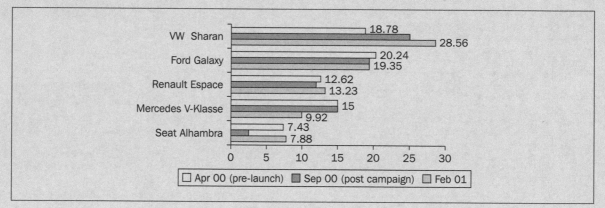
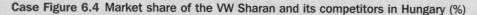

Case Figure 6.4 Market share of the VW Sharan and its competitors in Hungary (%)

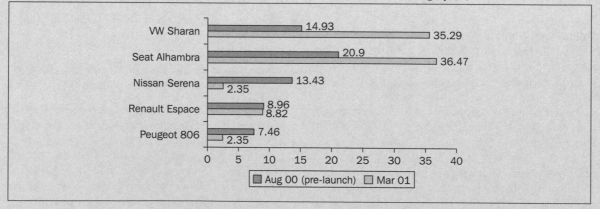

Case Figure 6.5 Market share of the VW Sharan and its competitors in the Czech Republic (%)

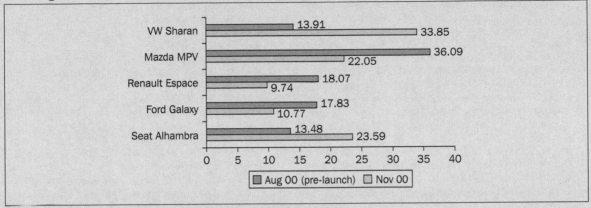

managed to sell twice as many cars as its main competitor, the Mazda MPV. In November, three months after the roll-out of the campaign, the VW had overtaken the Mazda (Case Figure 6.5).

The Volkswagen Sharan campaign was rewarded with a silver Euro Effie in 2001 for its effectiveness in 2000.

Questions

1 What are the main objectives, target groups and message strategies of the Xsara Picasso and the VW Sharan campaigns? Are they relevant and meaningful?

2 Compare the creative strategies of the Xsara Picasso and the VW Sharan. What do you think about the positioning strategies of the two car models?

3 Compare the execution strategies that were used in the two campaigns. What emotional and informational elements were used? Do you think they made the correct choices?

4 How can the competitors of the Xsara Picasso and the VW Sharan react? Which communications and creative strategies could they adopt?

5 Would the use of humour, eroticism or comparative advertising be appropriate for the Xsara Picasso or the VW Sharan, or any of their competitors?

6 Do you think the appropriate media strategy was used in the two campaigns?

7 Both campaigns appear to have been successful. Do you believe that the effectiveness claims made are legitimate and credible?

Based on: Euro Effie 2001 – efficiency in advertising 2001, Berlin, Gesamtverband Werbeagenturen GWA e.V; *See also:* www.citroen.com and country-specific Citroën sites; www.volkswagen.de and country-specific Volkswagen sites.

References

1 Bennett, P.D. (1995), *Dictionary of Marketing Terms*. Chicago: American Marketing Association.

2 Mitchell, A. (2001), 'Why the Old Advertising Model is Breaking Down', *Marketing Week*, 29 March, 34–35.

3 Mast, G., De Pelsmacker, P. and Geuens, M. (2002), 'How Family Structure Affects Parent–Child Communication Patterns', *International Journal of Advertising and Marketing to Children*, 4(2), 57–62; McNeal, J.U. (1999), *Kids Market: Myths and Realities*, Ithaca, NY: Paramount Market.

4 Weyters, B. and Geuens, M. (2003), 'Evaluation of Age-Related Labels by Senior Citizens', Working paper, Vlerick Leuven Gent Management School; Young, G.

(2002), 'Ageing and the UK economy', *Bank of England Quarterly Bulletin*, 42(3), 285–92.

5 Walker, M.M. and Macklin, M.C. (1992), 'The Use of Role Modeling in Targeting Advertising to Grandparents', *Journal of Advertising Research*, 32(4), 37–45.

6 Ahmad, R. (2002), 'The Older Ageing Consumers in the UK: Are They Really that Different?' *International Journal of Market Research*, 44(3), 337–60; Moschis, G.P. and Mathur, A. (1997), 'Targeting the Mature Market: Opportunities and Challenges', *Journal of Consumer Marketing*, 14(4), 282–93.

7 Weyters, B. and Geuens, M. (2003), 'Evaluation of Age-Related Labels by Senior Citizens', Working Paper,

Vlerick Leuven Gent Management School; Szmigin, I. and Carrigan, M. (2001), 'Time, Consumption and the Older Consumer: An Interpretive Study of the Cognitively Young', *Psychology & Marketing*, 18(10), 1091–1116; Barak, B., Mathur, A., Lee, K. and Zhang, Y. (2001), 'Perceptions of Age-Identity: A Cross-Cultural Inner-Age Exploration', *Psychology & Marketing*, 18(10), 1003–30.

8 Lewis, H.G. (1996), *Silver Linings: Selling to the Expanding Motive Market*. New York: Bonus Books.

9 Lumpkin, J.R. (1989), *Direct Marketing, Direct Selling, and the Mature Consumer: A Research Study*. Westpoint, CT: Quorum Books.

10 Kotler, P., Armstrong, G., Saunders, J. and Wong, V. (2001), *Principles of Marketing, European Edition*. London: Prentice Hall Europe.

11 Euro Effie (2001), Berlin: Gesamtverband Werbeagenturen GWA e.V.

12 Reid, L.N., King, K. and DeLorme, D.E. (1998), 'Top-Level Agency Creatives Look at Advertising Creativity Then and Now', *Journal of Advertising*, 27(2), 1–15.

13 Rossiter, J.R. and Percy, L. (2000), *Advertising Communication and Promotion Management*. New York: McGraw-Hill.

14 Centlivre, L. (1988), 'A Peek at the Creatives of the '90s', *Advertising Age*, 18 January, 62.

15 Otnes, C., Oviatt, A.A. and Treise, D.M. (1995), 'Views on Advertising Curricula from Experienced Creatives', *Journalism Educator*, 49 (Winter), 21–30.

16 *Management and Advertising Problems in the Advertiser–Agency Relationship* (1985). New York: Association of National Advertisers.

17 Ind, N. (1993), *Great Advertising Campaigns. How they Achieve Both Creative and Business Objectives*. London: Kogan Page.

18 Ind, N. (1993), *Great Advertising Campaigns. How they Achieve Both Creative and Business Objectives*. London: Kogan Page.

19 Euro Effie (2001), Berlin: Gesamtverband Werbeagenturen GWA e.V.

20 Anonymous (2003), 'Belgisch Regisseursduo Gooit Hoge Ogen op Amerikaans Reclamefestival' ('Belgian Producers Amaze at American Advertising Awards'), *De Morgen*, 22 May 2003.

21 Reid, L.N., King, K. and DeLorme, D.E. (1998), 'Top-Level Agency Creatives Look at Advertising Creativity Then and Now', *Journal of Advertising*, 27(2), 1–15.

22 Leather, P., MacKechnie, S. and Amirkhanian, M. (1994), 'The Importance of Likeability as a Measure of Television Advertising Effectiveness', *International Journal of Advertising*, 13(3), 265–80.

23 Biel, A.L. and Bridgwater, C.A. (1990), 'Attributes of Likeable Television Commercials', *Advances in Consumer Research*, 11, 4–10; De Pelsmacker, P. and Van den Bergh, J. (1998), 'Ad Content, Product Category, Campaign Weight and Irritation. A Study of 226 TV Commercials', *Journal of International Consumer Marketing*, 10(4), 5–27.

24 De Pelsmacker, P., DeCock, B. and Geuens, M. (1998), 'Advertising Characteristics and the Attitude Towards the Ad – A Study of 100 Likeable TV Commercials', *Marketing and Research Today*, 27(4), 166–79.

25 Abernethy, A.M. and Franke, G.R. (1996), 'The Information Content of Advertising: A Meta-Analysis', *Journal of Advertising*, 25(2), 1–17.

26 Brassington, B. and Pettitt, S. (2003), *Principles of Marketing, 3rd Edition*. Edinburgh Gate, Harlow: Pearson Education.

27 Ball, D. (2003), 'Unilever Sees Hefty Profit in SlimFast', *Wall Street Journal*, 23 April.

28 De Pelsmacker, P. and Van den Bergh, J. (1998), 'Ad Content, Product Category, Campaign Weight and Irritation. A Study of 226 TV Commercials', *Journal of International Consumer Marketing*, 10(4), 5–27; Aaker, D.A. and Bruzzone, D.E. (1985), 'Causes of Irritation in Advertising', *Journal of Marketing*, 49 (Spring), 47–57.

29 Wasserman, T. (2002), 'Techies Seek Testimony When Economy Falters', *Brandweek*, 43(44), 12.

30 De Pelsmacker, P. and Van den Bergh, J. (1998), 'Ad Content, Product Category, Campaign Weight and Irritation. A Study of 226 TV Commercials', *Journal of International Consumer Marketing*, 10(4), 5–27.

31 Euro Effie (2001), Berlin: Gesamtverband Werbeagenturen GWA e.V.

32 Brabbs, C. (2001), 'Two-thirds Find Comparative Ads "Unacceptable"', *Marketing*, 20 September, 4.

33 Dianoux, C. and Herrmann, J.L. (2001), 'The Influence of Comparative Advertising on Memorization and Attitudes: Experimentation in the French Context', *Recherche et Applications en Marketing*, 16(2).

34 Dianoux, C. (2002), 'What is the Future for Comparative Advertising in France?', *Décisions Marketing*, 25 (Janvier–Mars), 93.

35 del Barrio-Garcia, S. and Luque-Martinez, T. (2003), 'Modelling Consumer Response to Differing Levels of Comparative Advertising', *European Journal of Marketing*, 37(1), 256–74.

36 McCullough, L.S. (1992), *The Use of Humor in International Print Advertising: A Content Analysis*. Working paper, Miami University.

37 Weinberger, M.G. and Gulas, C.S. (1992), 'The Impact of Humor in Advertising – A Review', *Journal of Advertising*, 21(4), 35–59.

38 Geuens, M. and De Pelsmacker, P. (2002), 'The Moderating Role of Need for Cognition on Responses to Humorous Appeals', in Broniarczyk, S. and Nakamoto, K. (eds), *Advances in Consumer Research*, Provo, UT: Association for Consumer Research, 29, 50–56.

39 For a typology of humour types, see Speck, P.S. (1991), 'The Humorous Message Taxonomy: A Framework for the Study of Humorous Ads', *Current Issues and Research in Advertising*, 1–44.

40 Beirne, M. (2003), 'Heineken's Headlines are Humorous, but Amstel Light Spots are a Scream', *Brandweek*, 44(19), 8.

41 Spotts, H.E., Weinberger, M.G. and Parsons, A.M. (1997), 'Assessing the Use and Impact of Humor on Advertising Effectiveness', *Journal of Advertising*, 26(3), 17–32.

42 Weinberger, M.G. and Gulas, C.S. (1992), 'The Impact of Humor in Advertising – A Review', *Journal of Advertising*, 21(4), 35–59.

43 Chattopadhyay, A. and Basu, K. (1990), 'Humor in Advertising: The Moderating Role of Prior Brand Evaluation', *Journal of Marketing Research*, 27, 466–76.

44 De Pelsmacker, P. and Geuens, M. (1997), 'Emotional Appeals and Information Cues in Belgian Magazine Advertisements', *International Journal of Advertising*, 16(2), 123–47.

45 De Pelsmacker, P. and Geuens, M. (1996), 'The Communication Effects of Warmth, Eroticism and Humour in Alcohol Advertisements', *Journal of Marketing Communication*, 2(4), 247–62.

46 Ford, J.B., LaTour, M.S. and Lundstrom, W.J. (1993), 'Contemporary Women's Evaluations of Female Sex Roles in Advertising', *Journal of Consumer Marketing*, 8(1), 15–28.

47 De Pelsmacker, P. and Geuens, M. (1996), 'The Communication Effects of Warmth, Eroticism and Humour in Alcohol Advertisements', *Journal of Marketing Communication*, 2(4), 247–62.

48 Smith, S.M., Haughtvedt, C.P. and Jadrich, J.M. (1995), 'Understanding Responses to Sex Appeals in Advertising: An Individual Difference Approach', *Advances in Consumer Research*, 22, 735–9.

49 Geuens, M. (1997), 'Erotische Reclame: Een Effectieve Strategie?' ('Erotic Advertising: An Effective Strategy?'), *Tijdschrift voor Economie en Management*, 42(1), 57–79.

50 Reichert, T., Heckler, S.E. and Jackson, S. (2001), 'The Effects of Sexual Social Marketing Appeals on Cognitive Processing and Persuasion', *Journal of Advertising*, 30(1), 13–27.

51 De Pelsmacker, P. and Geuens, M. (1996), 'The Communication Effects of Warmth, Eroticism and Humour in Alcohol Advertisements', *Journal of Marketing Communication*, 2(4), 247–62.

52 De Pelsmacker, P. and Geuens, M. (1997), 'Emotional Appeals and Information Cues in Belgian Magazine Advertisements', *International Journal of Advertising*, 16(2), 123–47.

53 De Pelsmacker, P. and Geuens, M. (1998), 'Different Markets, Different Communication Strategies? A Comparative Study of the Communication Effects of Different Types of Alcohol Ads in Belgium and Poland', *International Marketing Review*, 15(4), 277–90; De Pelsmacker, P. and Geuens, M. (1996), 'The Communication Effects of Warmth, Eroticism and Humour in Alcohol Advertisements', *Journal of Marketing Communication*, 2(4), 247–62; Geuens, M. and De Pelsmacker, P. (1998), 'Feelings Evoked by Warmth, Eroticism and Humour in Alcohol Advertisements', *AMS Review*, www.ams.com; De Pelsmacker, P. and Van den Bergh, J. (1998), 'Ad Content, Product Category, Campaign Weight and Irritation. A Study of 226 TV Commercials', *Journal of International Consumer Marketing*, 10(4), 5–27.

54 Geuens, M. and De Pelsmacker, P. (1999), 'Individual Differences and the Communication Effects of Different Types of Emotional Stimuli: Exploring the Role of Affect Intensity', *Psychology and Marketing*, 16(3), 195–209.

55 Mowen, J.C. (1993), *Consumer Behavior*. New York: Macmillan.

56 Stephenson, M.T. and Witte, K. (2001), 'Creating Fear in a Risky World', in Rice, R. and Atkin, C.K. *Public Communication Campaigns*, Thousand Oaks: Sage, 88–102.

57 Braithwaite, A. and Ware, R. (1997), 'The Role of Music in Advertising', *Admap*, (July/August), 44–7; Alpert, J.I. and Alpert, M.I. (1990), 'Music Influences on Mood and Purchase Intentions', *Psychology and Marketing*, 7(2), 109–33; Bruner, G.C. (1990), 'Music, Mood and Marketing', *Journal of Marketing*, 54(4), 94–104.

58 Aaker, D.A. and Bruzzone, D.E. (1985), 'Causes of Irritation in Advertising', *Journal of Marketing*, 49 (Spring), 47–57.

59 Erdogan, Z., Baker, M.J. and Tagg, S. (2001), 'Selecting Celebrity Endorsers: The Practitioner's Perspective', *Journal of Advertising Research*, 41(3), 39–48.

60 Erdogan, Z., Baker, M.J. and Tagg, S. (2001), 'Selecting Celebrity Endorsers: The Practitioner's Perspective', *Journal of Advertising Research*, 41(3), 39–48.

61 Lafferty, B.A., Goldsmith, R.E. and Newell, S.J. (2002), 'The Dual Credibility Model: The Influence of Corporate and Endorser Credibility on Attitudes and Purchase Intentions', *Journal of Marketing Theory and Practice*, 10(3), 1–12.

62 Erdogan, B.Z. (1999), 'Celebrity Endorsements: A Literature Review', *Journal of Marketing Management*, 15(4), 291–314.

63 Erdogan, Z., Baker, M.J. and Tagg, S. (2001), 'Selecting Celebrity Endorsers: The Practitioner's Perspective', *Journal of Advertising Research*, 41(3), 39–48.

64 Till, B.D. and Busler, M. (2000), 'The Match-Up Hypothesis: Physical Attractiveness, Expertise, and the Role of Fit on Brand Attitude, Purchase Intent and Brand Beliefs', *Journal of Advertising*, 29(3), 1–13.

65 Bower, A.B. (2001), 'Highly Attractive Models in Advertising and the Women Who Loathe Them: The Implications of Negative Affect for Spokesperson Effectiveness', *Journal of Advertising*, 30(3), 51–63.

66 Till, B.D. and Shimp, T.A. (1998), 'Endorsers in Advertising: The Case of Negative Celebrity Information', *Journal of Advertising*, 27(1), 67–82.

Chapter 7

Media planning

Chapter outline

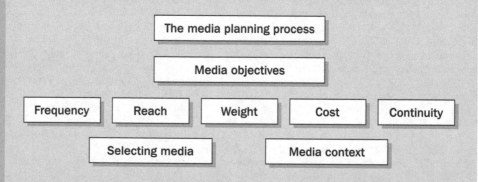

- The media planning process
- Media objectives
- Frequency
- Reach
- Weight
- Cost
- Continuity
- Selecting media
- Media context

Chapter objectives

This chapter will help you to:

- Distinguish the various steps in the media planning process
- Understand the technical details of media objectives, such as frequency, reach, weight, continuity and cost
- Learn on the basis of which criteria the media mix can be composed
- Understand the advantages and disadvantages of the different advertising media
- Get an overview of the criteria to be used in media planning
- Understand the importance of media context for advertising effectiveness

Introduction

Media planning is receiving more and more attention. This is not surprising since the cost of buying advertising time and space makes up 80%–90% of the advertising budget.[1] The latter also explains the recent attention paid to integrated marketing communications, the purpose of which is to use all advertising media, as well as other communications tools, as effectively and efficiently as possible. Media planning is not just a matter of selecting the appropriate media, given the target group of the advertising campaign and the characteristics of the different advertising media. It is also a technical issue in which the components of media objectives (such as frequency, reach, weight, continuity and cost) are calculated and compared. Both technical media objectives and criteria for selecting the media mix and characteristics of the different media are discussed in depth. Furthermore, creativity in the use of media and possible influences of the media context play a role in advertising effectiveness.

The media planning process

The purpose of media planning is to draw up an adequate media plan. A media plan can be defined as a document specifying which media and vehicles will be purchased when, at what price and with what expected results. It includes such things as flow charts, the names of specific magazines, reach and frequency estimates, and budgets.[2] Creating a media plan is a process which consists of different steps (Figure 7.1).

Just as an environmental analysis is necessary to formulate the marketing strategy and to create a marketing plan, the communications environment needs to be screened to formulate a media plan. First of all, media planners should be acquainted with all regulations and legal aspects, as well as with local habits. Is TV advertising allowed, do people watch predominantly TV, read magazines or listen to the radio, etc.?

Figure 7.1 Steps in media planning

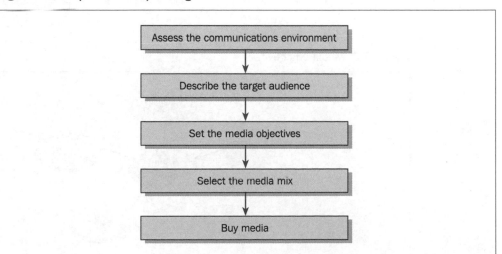

Second, media planners should be able to judge the communications efforts of the competition. In this respect, the following elements are important:[3]

■ **Category spending:** What is the advertising spending in the product category, and how has it evolved over the last five years? Did category spending increase, decrease or remain stable?

■ **Share of voice:** What is the relative advertising spending of the different competitive brands in the product category? Share of voice (SOV) is calculated by dividing a particular brand's advertising spending by the total category spending. Besides the share of voice, one should also investigate the share of market (SOM) and how share of voice relates to share of market. Some researchers assume that share of market follows share of voice, while others argue that the share of market should always be smaller than the share of voice in order to be able to maintain growth (see also Chapter 5 on budgets).

■ **Media mix:** Identify how each competitor divides its advertising spending across the different media and analyse the trend in media mix composition.

Target groups were extensively discussed in Chapter 3. Although all segmentation variables mentioned there remain valid, a variable that needs special attention at this stage is the media behaviour of the target audience. Do the target consumers listen to the radio or watch TV, and if so, which programmes do they listen to or watch, at what time, and on which days? Do the target consumers read newspapers or magazines, and if so, which ones do they read? Do the target consumers use electronic media, do they often go the cinema, etc.? This information is indispensable.

Media objectives

Media objectives are derived from the communications objectives, and ought to be concrete, measurable and realistic. Media objectives usually are formulated in terms of the characteristics shown in Figure 7.2.

Figure 7.2 Media objectives

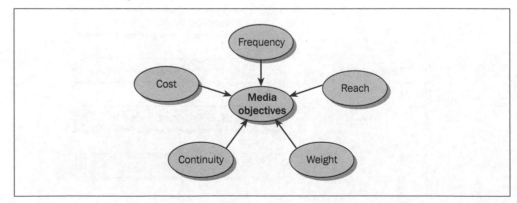

Frequency

Frequency indicates how many times a consumer of the target group, on average, is expected to be exposed to the advertiser's message within a specified time period. It is important to know that frequency is estimated on the basis of the number of times one could be exposed to the media vehicle, and not to the message itself. For example, if a consumer has a newspaper subscription and a certain campaign has one ad a week for six weeks in that newspaper, we could expect that the particular consumer will be exposed to the advertisement six times during the six-week period. However, if the consumer does not always read the full newspaper and occasionally omits the pages in which the ad appears, the actual number of times he or she will be exposed to the message will be lower than six.

When deciding on the objective of how many times the target group has to be reached, a first question that arises is how often should a consumer be exposed to a message for it to be effective? And how does a consumer respond to frequent exposures to the same message? Research shows that advertising repetition initially increases learning, but may lead to boredom and irritation later.[4] According to the **two-factor model**, an inverted-U relationship exists between the level of exposure on the one hand, and advertising effectiveness (cognitive responses, attitudes, purchase) on the other (Figure 7.3). Wear-in and wear-out effects explain the nature of this relationship.[5] At low levels of exposure, consumers develop rather negative responses (e.g. counterarguments) due to the novelty of the stimulus. After a few exposures, the reaction becomes more positive. This is referred to as **wear-in**. More frequent exposures again lead to more negative responses, a phenomenon called **wear-out**. Negative responses, such as irritation, can be expected to be the highest both at low and high exposure levels, while positive responses are

Figure 7.3 Ad frequency and ad effectiveness

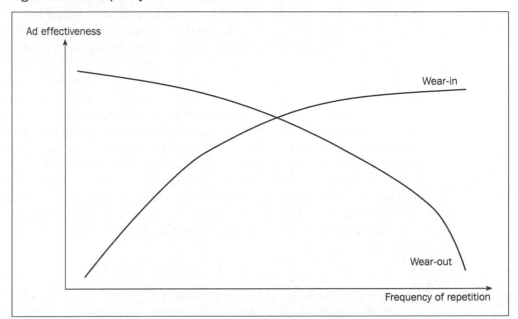

optimal at intermediate exposure levels. One way to counter or delay the wear-out effect is to make minor changes to the ad so that the consumer is not exposed to the same ad over and over again or to use executional cues that evoke positive emotional responses.[6] A recent study shows that in cases where consumers process messages in a superficial or shallow way (for example, when they are hardly aware of the fact that there is an ad), wear-out may not occur at all.[7]

Another way of thinking about advertising repetition is comprised in the economic signalling theory which assumes that consumers take advertising repetition as a signal of the quality of a brand. In this view, higher advertising costs signal greater manufacturer effort and higher manufacturer confidence and trust in quality.[8] Several reasons have been reported in the literature as to why a high (but not excessive) repetition level of advertising might be beneficial:

- It makes the message more memorable and raises brand recall.[9]
- It makes attitudes more accessible and raises consumers' confidence in their attitudes,[10] making them more resistant to attitude change and brand switching.
- It increases the believability of the ad claims.[11]
- It leads to a greater top-of-mind brand awareness.[12]
- It functions as a signal or cue for brand quality.[13]

However, the difficulty remains to determine the optimal frequency level, which is inevitably linked to the advertising objective, the type of message used, media clutter, the product category, the competition level, the target group and the media used. Controversy also exists concerning the frequency level that is sufficient to evoke the intended response in the consumer. This frequency level is also referred to as the motivational frequency or the effective frequency, defined as 'the minimum number of exposures, within a purchase cycle, considered necessary to motivate the average prospect in the target audience to accomplish an advertising objective'.[14] Some researchers think one exposure is sufficient, while others assume an effective frequency of at least three.[15] One exposure may be sufficient if you reach the consumer at the right moment, with the right message. For example, a consumer is driving home from work and a little stone makes the car window burst. One advertisement for Car Glass mentioning that it repairs car windows 24 hours a day may be very effective at that moment. On the other hand, a consumer may need to see a yoghurt ad 15 times before it becomes effective. Moreover, two exposures may be sufficient for market leadership or an established brand image, while at least four might be necessary for new campaigns targeted at infrequent users, if the objective is to increase the usage of a product or when medium clutter is high.[16] In other words, situational variables play an important role.

One technique to judge the effectiveness of media is the β-coefficient analysis, developed by Morgensztern, in which the relationship between the number of exposures and the degree of memorisation (i.e. the percentage of the target group that remembers the ad) is analysed. The mathematical form of the β-coefficient model is as follows:

$$M_n = 1 - (1 - \beta)^n$$

where: M_n = memorisation after n exposures
β: medium-specific memorisation rate

Figure 7.4 The β-coefficient: exposure and memorisation

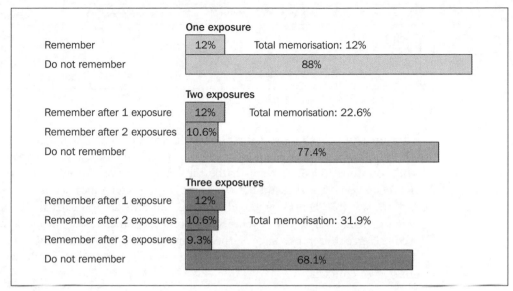

Figure 7.4 illustrates the evolution of memorisation, given a β-coefficient of 12%. As the figure illustrates, total recall increases decreasingly in function of exposure.

The β-analysis takes into account that memorisation of a message depends on the medium used. It is assumed that each exposure is able to make a constant percentage (β) of the consumers who previously could not remember the message of a campaign actually remember the message. Figure 7.5 shows the relation between the number of

Figure 7.5 The relation between exposures and memorisation for different media

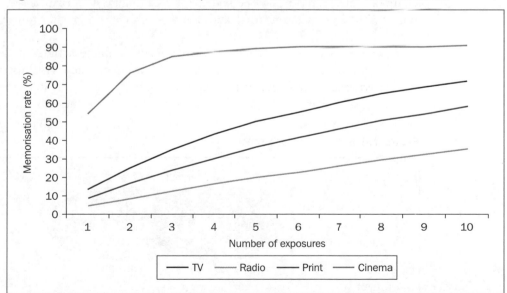

Source: JFC Informatique & média, Paris, France (2003). Reproduced with permission.

Table 7.1 Number of contacts for different media

Medium	Not enough contacts	Too many contacts	Suggested contacts
Radio	4	15	5–14
Press	3	10	4–9
Television	2	7	3–6
Cinema	1	3	2

Source: Quattro Saatchi, Brussels, Belgium (2003).

exposures and the memorisation rate for different media. Cinema advertising ($\beta = 70\%$) is by far the most effective medium to make people memorise your advertising message, while outdoor ($\beta = 2\%$) seems to be the least effective. Applying the formula shown above suggests that the number of people who have memorised a message after three exposures is 97.3% for cinema advertising, but only 27.1% for daily papers ($\beta = 10\%$).

Morgensztern not only developed different β-coefficients for different media, he also used these coefficients to suggest the minimum and maximum number of exposures for the different media in order for a message to be effective. Table 7.1 shows the suggested number of contacts.

Reach and weight

Total reach of a vehicle can be defined as the number or percentage of people who are expected to be exposed to the advertiser's message during a specified period.

The difference between total and **useful reach** is important. Useful reach is not about how many consumers will probably see the message, but how many consumers from the target group are likely to see the message in a specific vehicle. As was the case for frequency, only exposure to the media vehicle can be estimated, not to the message itself. Furthermore, one should realise that, although total reach may be higher for a TV campaign, useful reach may be higher for a campaign in specialised magazines. Even within the same medium, total and useful reach can differ enormously for different media vehicles.

When the same message comes in different media or multiple times in the same vehicle, a distinction can be made between gross reach and net reach. As illustrated in Figure 7.6, **gross reach** is the sum of the number of people each individual medium reaches, regardless of how many times an individual is reached. In other words, a person who is

Figure 7.6 Gross reach and reach

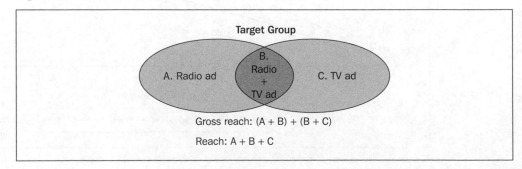

reached by medium x and medium y counts as two. **Reach,** also called net reach, is the sum of all people reached at least once (a person reached by x and y counts as one). In other words, reach equals gross reach minus the duplicated audience. Gross reach, expressed as a percentage of the target group, is referred to as gross rating points (GRPs). The **weight** of a campaign is typically expressed by GRPs. These GRPs can be realised by means of different media and different media vehicles.

A measure often used by media planners is **opportunity to see** (OTS). OTS is defined as the average probability of exposure that an average target consumer has. It is calculated by dividing gross reach by reach. The latter means that GRPs can be calculated in two different ways:

- By multiplying reach (in percentage) and frequency for the different media vehicles used:

$$GRP = \sum_{i=1}^{n} (f_i \times r_i)$$

where: n = number of media vehicles
  f_i = frequency of media vehicle i
  r_i = percentage reach of media vehicle i

- By multiplying reach (in percentage) and opportunity to see:

$$GRP = Reach \times OTS$$

where: reach = audience across different media vehicles minus duplicated audience

Effective reach is the number of target consumers who are expected to be exposed to the advertiser's message at an effective frequency level. Suppose an advertising campaign reached 60% of its target consumers with the frequencies reported in Table 7.2. If the consumer needs to be exposed at least three times to be effective, then the effective reach is 24.0% (11.5% + 6.0% + 3.5% + 1.8% + 1.2%).

Table 7.2 Reach and frequency distribution

Exposures	Reach
1	20.0%
2	16.0%
3	11.5%
4	6.0%
5	3.5%
6	1.8%
7	1.2%

Calculating gross reach, OTS and effective gross reach

A company defines its target group as all males between 30 and 40. The total size of the target group is 10 million consumers. The company plans a newspaper campaign. The newspaper has a total readership of 18 million and a useful readership of 5 million. Ten ads are placed in the newspaper. The table below gives the distribution of percentage reach in function of the exposure frequency.

▶

The reach of the campaign is 5 million or 50% of the target group. The weight of the campaign is 238 GRP ($5 \times 1 + 6 \times 2 + 3 \times 3 + 9 \times 4 + 8 \times 5 + 7 \times 6 + 6 \times 7 + 3 \times 8 + 2 \times 9 + 1 \times 10$). As a result, the gross reach is 23.8 million exposures (238% × 10 million). Opportunity to see is 4.76 (238/50 or 23.8/5). Effective rating points (ERP), or effective gross reach, defined as at least 3 exposures, is 221.

Frequency	Newspaper reach (% of target group)
1	5
2	6
3	3
4	9
5	8
6	7
7	6
8	3
9	2
10	1

Continuity

Concerning campaign continuity, advertisers have three possibilities: a continuous, a pulsing or a flighting schedule:

- A **continuous schedule** means that the advertiser spends a continuous amount of money throughout the whole campaign period. However, since most companies have budget constraints, a continuous schedule might result in too low expenditures per period to be effective.

- A **pulsing schedule** indicates that a certain level of advertising takes place during the whole campaign period, but during particular periods higher advertising levels are used.

- A **flighting schedule** is used when advertising is concentrated in only a few periods and not during the whole campaign period. This might be preferred due to budget constraints, for example. In other words, during some months no advertising takes place in order to be able to spend higher levels during peak demand months.

As mentioned before, some researchers argue that the most important thing is to reach consumers near the point of purchase. Jones[17] suggests that one exposure is sufficient and may have a much greater influence than frequent exposures. According to him, trying to reach as many people in the target group within the period near their purchasing is more effective than trying to reach a particular segment more frequently during the same time period. Ephron[18] shares this view and compares being off-air, as is the case with a flighting schedule, with being out-of-stock at the sales point. According to him, you reach this week's buyers with this week's advertising, and next week's buyers only with next week's advertising, and not with this week's advertising. Also, a recent study investigating the impact of 1,482 radio commercials reveals that media consistency and spending the advertising budget in complementary media and radio channels, i.e. focussing on reach rather than frequency of exposure (and, as a consequence, using a continuous rather than a flighting or pulsing schedule), is an important explanatory factor for both ad and brand recognition.[19] Others argue that both reach and frequency remain important.[20] When the purpose of advertising is to give information, frequent exposure can be important; when the objective of advertising is to remind people (e.g. in the case of mature products), one exposure may be enough.[21] But even in the latter case, a positive effect of frequent exposure can be measured.[22]

Another aspect worth considering when deciding on whether to use a continuous, pulsing or flighting schedule, is how long people remember the message. Too much focus on a certain period of time without any repetitions during the rest of the year can be detrimental, since people easily forget the communication they have been exposed to.

Two scheduling tactics worth mentioning are double-spotting and roadblocking.[23] With double-spotting, two spots are placed within the same programme to increase the likelihood of obtaining the effective frequency. Roadblocking refers to placing the same ad across many channels at the same time. In this case, reach can be seriously increased since everyone watching television at, for example, 9 p.m., will be confronted with the ad. Moreover, it is also a partial solution to the zapping phenomenon since even zapping will not help consumers to avoid the ad.

Cost

The cost of a medium is usually expressed as the cost per thousand (CPT), meaning the cost of reaching 1,000 people. Cost per thousand (CPT) is usually referred to as CPM, the 'M' referring to the Roman symbol for thousand. CPM is calculated by dividing the cost of the medium (the air cost of a 15- or 30-second commercial, the cost of a one-page magazine ad, etc.) by the medium's audience. More interesting to know is the cost per thousand people of your target market, also represented by CPM-TM. In this case, the cost of the medium has to be divided by the useful reach.

$$CPM = \frac{\text{Cost of the medium}}{\text{Total reach}} \times 1,000$$

$$CPM\text{-}TM = \frac{\text{Cost of the medium}}{\text{Useful reach}} \times 1,000$$

Suppose an Irish fashion chain wants to reach young females (between 16 and 30 years of age). An ad is inserted in three women's magazines, in a TV guide and in a special interest magazine. The following CPMs can be calculated. Although the CPM for *RTE Guide* is the lowest, calculation of the CPM-TM shows that for reaching the young female audience, *Woman's Way* may be more cost efficient.

Type of magazine	Magazine	Cost* (I£)	Total reach* (000s)	CPM	(Useful) reach**	CPM-TM
Women's magazines	*Woman's Way*	3,250	230	14.13	115	28.26
	Image	1,995	116	17.19	58	34.39
	U	1,800	106	16.98	53	33.96
TV guide	*RTE Guide*	3,900	585	6.67	117	33.33
Special interest	*Hot Press*	2,260	44	51.36	7	322.8

* *World Magazine Trends*, 1998/1999, Zenith Media, FIPP, Royal Mail.
** Fictitious numbers.

As was the case with the other concepts, only taking CPM and CPM-TM into account can lead to major errors. CPM and/or CPM-TM may be low just because the medium vehicle is very cheap and does not reach the target medium in an effective way. Using billboards near small roads does not cost a lot, but only a very small percentage of the target audience may be reached.

Selecting media

There is a difference between media and vehicles. Advertising media refer to types of communications channels that can distribute a message. Examples are newspapers, magazines, TV, etc. On the other hand, vehicles are particular programmes, magazines, etc., such as The Simpsons, The Osbournes, Pop Idol, *Cosmopolitan, Star*, etc. This section is mainly devoted to media, and not so much to specific vehicles.

In Europe, TV is the medium to which most of the advertising spendings are devoted (37%), followed by newspapers (29%) and magazines (19%). Radio and outdoor (7%) share the fourth place while cinema advertising (1%) comes in last.

Media mix criteria

Before deciding which media will and will not be included in the media mix, the different media should be evaluated on several criteria. These criteria can be categorised in quantitative, qualitative and technical criteria. Table 7.3 gives an overview of several potential criteria.

Table 7.3 Media mix criteria

Quantitative criteria	Reach Frequency Selectivity Geographic flexibility Speed of reach (delayed or not) Message life Seasonal influence
Qualitative criteria	Image-building capability Emotional impact Medium involvement Active or passive medium Attention devoted to the medium Quality of reproduction Adding value to the message (by means of the context) Amount of information that can be conveyed Demonstration capability Extent of memorisation of the message (β-coefficient) Clutter
Technical criteria	Production cost Media buying characteristics (lead time, cancellation, etc.) Media availability

Quantitative criteria deal with factors such as how many people can be reached, how often and how quickly the target group can be reached, whether the advertising message can be adapted for different geographic regions, whether the medium is more effective during certain periods of the year than during others, and how selective the advertising medium is.

Medium selectivity refers to the extent that a medium is directed towards the target group. Medium selectivity can be represented by a selectivity index showing how well the target group is represented in the medium reach, relative to the universe:[24]

$$\text{Selectivity index} = \frac{\% \text{ of the target group in total reach}}{\% \text{ of the target group in the universe}} \times 100$$

Selectivity index < 100: The target group is under-represented;
The vehicle is not selective on the target group
Selectivity index = 100: The target group is proportionally represented
Selectivity index > 100: The target group is over-represented;
The vehicle is selective on the target group

Qualitative criteria to evaluate different media are the extent to which the medium is capable of building a brand image and a brand personality, the impact the medium has on the audience, how involved the audience is with the medium, and as a consequence whether the audience is active or passive and whether the audience pays a lot or only minor attention to the messages conveyed by the medium. Qualitative criteria are also about whether or not the vehicle can add value to the brand or product due to the context in which the brand or product is shown (see also further in this chapter), whether or not the quality of reproduction is sufficiently high, how much and what type of information can be conveyed to the consumer (e.g. can the use and customer friendliness of the product be demonstrated?), how many exposures are needed to make consumers remember the message (β-coefficient) and whether or not the medium is characterised by a lot of advertising clutter resulting in a need for more exposures to become reasonably effective.

Calculating medium selectivity

Consider the Danish TV channels TV2 and ZULU. How selective are they for a target group consisting of young adults aged between 12 and 30?

Media vehicle	Population size young adults (12–30) (000s)	% young adults (12–30) of total TV population	Reach for young adults (12–30) (%)	% of young adults in total reach	Selectivity index (column 5/ column 3)
TV2	1,247	24.2	29.4	19.5	80.5
Zulu	1,247	24.2	3.9	41.0	169.4

Based on: IP Peaktime (2002), *Television 2002. European Key Factors*. Neuilly-sur-Seine, Cedex, Brussels: IP.

TV2 reaches 29.4% of the youngsters and Zulu only 3.9%. However, Zulu appears to be very selective for the target group of youngsters while TV2 is not. The latter can be explained as follows: TV2 has a large audience and although almost one in three youngsters watch this channel, other age groups are better represented. Zulu, on the other hand, has a very limited audience and although it reaches only 3.9% of the youngsters, youngsters are the age group that is most represented in Zulu's audience.

Technical criteria refer to the production costs of the message, often expressed as CPM or CPM-TM, the convenience or problems related to media buying (is it difficult to book media time or space, how long in advance do you have to book media time in order to be sure that you can distribute your message, can this media time or space be cancelled and if so, how long in advance, etc.?). Another criterion is media availability or what the penetration rate of the medium among the population is. If people do not own a TV or a radio, or never buy a newspaper, it is no use spending a lot of money advertising in these media.

The media buyer's task is to find out whether or not the vehicle audience matches the target group or whether or not the target group is sufficiently represented in the vehicle audience. Every vehicle is also related to its medium and inherits the characteristics associated with the medium. Therefore, the starting point for discussing the medium can be the advantages and disadvantages of each medium (see below). Knowing that the target group reads magazines every week is not sufficient; you need to know which magazines they read. If your target audience likes to watch TV which channels do they watch, at what time of the day do they watch, which programmes do they select, etc.? The different vehicles should be compared with each other within the same medium, between the different media and in relation to the target audience. The price must be understood in terms of value and not in terms of cost. Therefore comparisons are made to direct (other vehicles within the same medium) and indirect (vehicles within other media) competitors.

Care must be taken that media planning is more than just selecting the vehicles with the most promising results. The different media and vehicles must be considered in conjunction with each other. Is it wise, for instance, to plan the television campaign after the radio campaign, or vice versa? Is it better first to explain the message in more detail in magazines before the out-of-home campaign starts? How important is it to have several TV commercials during prime time in the first week of the launch of a new product? Research on β-coefficient issues is very important to get some insight into the consequences of planning one medium before the other, or to decrease the GRPs of radio to the advantage of television. Furthermore, for a media planner, media consumption should be far more important than GRP cost. The most important questions are: Which radio channel does a target consumer listen to in the morning? Which billboards does he or she come across on the way to work? Which magazines or newspapers are read in the evening? Which TV programmes are watched in the evening? Which events that can be sponsored does the target consumer go to? etc. The use, advantages and disadvantages of these media will now be discussed in more detail.

Outdoor

Outdoor advertising consists of media such as billboards, but also transit media in the form of messages on buses, trams, in stations, etc (see Plate 17). Outdoor advertising has the advantage of reaching a lot of people. As a consequence, effective reach can be very high. Not only reach, but also frequency can be quite high. The lifetime of a message is very long, and the same message can be seen over and over again. For instance, on the way to school or office you might encouter the Nokia message of 'connecting people' every day. The time period to reach the audience is very short and the costs are moderate. For certain types of billboards there is the obligation to work nationally, but for others a regional approach is obtainable.

However, people do not feel highly involved in billboards or transit advertising and usually do not pay a lot of attention to it. Furthermore, only a limited amount of information can be conveyed. Targeting or selective reach is not possible, since all kinds of people will see the messages. Usually, there is no context that can add value to the message.

Magazines

Magazines have the advantage that a large audience can be reached. Furthermore, special interest magazines or magazines directed at a specific target group, such as females or youngsters, create the possibility of a selective approach for different target groups. Depending on the type of magazine, a high-quality context can be offered, making it a good medium for image building (e.g. *Vogue*). Special interest magazines, such as computer magazines, also have the advantage of inducing a high involvement level and being perceived as highly credible, adding a certain value to the inserted ads. For magazines in general the quality of reproduction is high and a lot of information can be distributed. The message life is relatively long, people can process the messages at their own pace, and the same message or ad may be seen several times, since it is very likely that a reader does not read the magazine only once, but rather takes it up several times before he or she disposes of it.

Major disadvantages are that it is a rather slow medium, which leads to a delay in reach. People can buy a monthly magazine this week, but not read it for the next two weeks. Furthermore, the medium is not so flexible in the sense that last-minute changes are not tolerated and regional versions are impossible. Some magazines also suffer from high clutter, rendering an advertising message less effective.

Newspapers

The major advantage of newspapers is the number of people that can be reached in a very short period of time. Furthermore, it is a flexible medium in the sense that last-minute changes are possible in case the company's needs change or when the company wants to take advantage of, or make use of, recent events. Ads referring to recent events are called 'top topicals' and usually can count on more attention. The readers are usually highly involved in their newspaper, and the objective, informational context makes newspapers a credible medium with a high impact, not only for ads, but also for PR messages. Newspapers also provide the possibility of working regionally. In contrast with several other media, newspapers can convey large amounts of information.

Disadvantages of newspapers are the limited selectivity of the medium and the low quality of reproduction. Furthermore, it is a transient medium in the sense that the message has a very short life since a newspaper lasts only one day.

Compaq wins award for best use of newspapers

In 2002 Compaq won an award for best use of newspapers. Full-page newspaper ads were created that resembled actual news reports. The ads contained testimonials from leading businesses and governments indicating that Compaq had never been more dependable. For

▶

example, one of the headlines read 'Hong Kong SAR: Government Teams with Compaq to Deliver Online Public Services to Hong Kong Citizens'. Moreover, in some newspapers Compaq had fixed positionings on a certain day of the week, always featuring the same headline, for example 'BT: Business Tuesday from Compaq'. In the first instance, Compaq wanted to go for business magazines and information-technology trade magazines. In the end it chose newspapers because of their 'credibility and immediacy'.[25]

Door-to-door

Door-to-door advertising periodic publications (once a week, once a month, etc.) are distributed locally and free of charge. Advertisers in this medium are usually local merchandisers or local service organisations. Door-to-door publications have the advantage of being geographically flexible and of obtaining a fairly high reach. Furthermore, the medium provides the opportunity to deliver a lot of information at a fairly low cost. The promotional context in which the message appears may be useful for reaching consumers interested in promotional offers.

Limitations are that the medium is not at all selective and people may only be marginally involved in door-to-door publications and may not pay much attention unless they are interested in certain promotions. Furthermore, the quality of reproductions is often doubtful. Because of the overload of such publications, people often react negatively to this form of irresponsible use of paper and 'environmental pollution', and more and more people are putting a note on their mailbox stating 'no advertising please'.

Television

A clear advantage of television is the communication power of an audiovisual message which, in general, leads to a fairly high (especially emotional) impact. Television is a passive medium, making it ideal for transferring a brand image or brand personality. The context surrounding the message can also add value to the message by inducing in the audience a certain mood (e.g. by the programme or movie during which the message is shown). Furthermore, a lot of people can be reached in a fairly short period of time. Local TV makes it possible to exert a regional approach. Research on viewing habits reveals that different personalities and people with different lifestyles watch different programmes, creating the possibility of using TV as a selective medium.

Major drawbacks are the high production costs that are involved and the fact that it is not always possible to direct a message at a selective target group. Often, a lot of occasional viewers are reached, which results in a low effective reach. Furthermore, the lifetime of a message is extremely short: 15 or 30 seconds pass very quickly and often nothing is left of the message afterwards. Increasing advertising clutter further impedes the effectiveness of messages, making more exposures a necessity, which adds to total costs. Television also has a seasonal influence. During the summer more people spend time outdoors instead of spending their evenings in front of the television screen. In other words, during winter a TV commercial will reach a greater audience than in the summer.

Advertising in a cluttered environment

Advertising clutter is becoming a real problem.[26] Before you can convince consumers to buy, you have to build a brand. To build a brand, you need to create awareness. To create awareness, you need to attract attention. To attract attention, you have to find a way to break through the massive amount of other messages known as advertising clutter. One way to do this is to create original ads. Although this has been a long-held conviction by copywriters and art directors, only recently has the power of original ads to attract attention been empirically demonstrated.[27] Unfortunately, several advertisers do not opt for originality but react to the increasing clutter by outspending their competitors and launching even more ads. The result of all this is that in the UK, on television alone, 11,074,971 ads were broadcast in 2002, in Spain 2,045,113 were broadcast, in Germany 2,487,089, in France 1,147,652 and in Italy 1,022,351.[28]

Cinema

As is the case with television, cinema benefits from the audiovisuality of the message, leaving a greater impact on the audience. The impact of cinema advertising is even increased by the fact that the audience pays much more attention to the message than in any other circumstances, while distraction is less likely to occur. The surroundings and context further add to the value of the message, because of the mood and expectations of the audience. As will be discussed later in this chapter, a positive mood can lead a viewer to process all incoming information more positively than when the viewer is in a neutral or a negative mood. Going to the cinema is fun, people have a lot of expectations and are, in a sense, quite excited. This can lead to more positive processing of the advertising messages. Another important advantage of cinema advertising is the fact that this medium is fairly selective to a young and upmarket audience. Furthermore, this audience seems to like cinema advertising, and considers it as a part of their cinema visit that cannot be missed.[29]

The disadvantages are that the potential reach is limited, and that the speed and the frequency of reaching the audience is very slow. The lifetime of a message is very short. Furthermore, relatively high production costs are encountered.

Radio

The major benefit of radio advertising is that potentially a lot of people can be reached. Furthermore, the production costs are low and radio is a very dynamic medium. Different people (not only in terms of demographic characteristcs, but also in terms of lifestyle, etc.) seem to listen to different radio stations, making it a selective medium to target a specific consumer group.

Limitations are that the lifetime of a message is very short and that people use the radio as background noise. The latter means that the potential attention that will be paid to a message is fairly low.

For many years quantitative criteria such as reach, frequency, CPT, etc. have dominated media planning. Recently, more and more media planners are convinced of the importance of qualitative criteria such as the context, capacity of image building, creativity, etc. Creativity is very important because several media have become increasingly cluttered. Some advertisers

▶

succeed in running a very effective and efficient advertising campaign with relatively low costs thanks to creative use of the different media. Some examples are the following:

- Several years ago the newly launched Fiat Regata was promoted by attaching a life-size car to a billboard. In the press consumers were encouraged to walk near these billboards while filling out questions for a contest. The campaign received media exposure in the press worth five times more than the actual media investment.[30]

- In 1992 every time someone passed a tram shelter with a promotion for 3 Suisses, the billboard began to sing a Jacques Dutronc song 'J'aime les filles dans les abribus, j'aime les filles qu'on croise dans les trams . . .' (I love the girls in bus shelters, I love the girls I encounter on the tram). The campaign ran for seven days and was a huge success. It is said that some people were so surprised that they even forgot to get on the tram.[31]

- In Denmark Carlsberg used an Abribus campaign in 2003 where the ad looked different during daytime than at night-time. During the day a pint of Carlsberg was shown on a black background. The pint itself was 80% filled with white foam. At night-time, the same ad on the same black background was shown, but the pint was now 80% filled with the gold Carlsberg beer.[32]

- In 2002 Virgin Express used a similar approach with newspaper ads to Compaq. To promote the airline company, a full-page ad was created with different fictitious news reports. All reports mentioned the low attendance on occasions where normally many people are present. Headlines ran as follows: 'Problem of the traffic jams finally solved. Highways empty, except in the neighbourhood of the airport', 'Major peace manifestation attracts only 7 participants', 'Nobody attends erotica fair', 'Sudden idling swept our cities', and 'Members of Parliament play truant as never before'. In the middle of the page readers found the explanation for the situation: Virgin Express' extremely low fares to attractive cities such as Madrid, Milan, Nice, Rome, Athens, Barcelona, Lisbon, etc.[33]

- In 2002 Procter & Gamble's antidandruff shampoo, Head & Shoulders, was promoted by means of fragrance-emitting ads on bus shelters. The posters showed a happy young lady with the wind in her hair inviting consumers to press a button to dispense the scent of new citrus fresh.[34] By 2003 scent advertising is used more and more. In the Netherlands, the advertising agency Senta is completely devoted to scent advertising. It ran a magazine campaign for the fabric softener Robijn (also known as Snuggle and Cocolino). When consumers rubbed the ink, the scent was released. About 80% of readers noticed the ad and also seem to remember it.[35]

- Marketers also invent new media. In 2003 a London ad agency recruited university students to wear brand logos on their foreheads, turning their heads into living billboards. In exchange for wearing these ads in public places for three or four hours, students receive about €6.5 an hour.[36]

Media context

Advertising always forms part of a surrounding context. An advertising context consists of the receiver context and the medium context.[37] The receiver context refers to the situational circumstances in which a person is exposed to an advertisement (e.g. at home, in the company of friends, on one's way to work, when one is in a bad mood, etc.). The importance of the receiver's context (especially the psychological state)

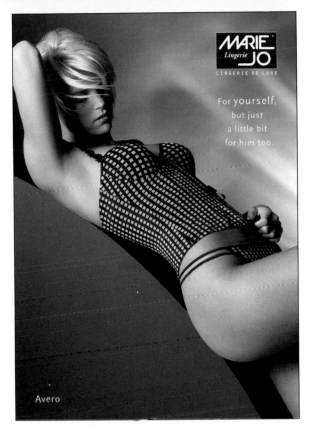

Plate 1 Marie Jo: when beauty meets luxury
(Reproduced with permission of Artex NV)

Plate 2 MasterCard: influencing perceived behavioural control
(Reproduced with permission of Gesamtverband Werbeagenturen GWA and McCann-Erickson Europe)

Plate 3 Mercedes A class: targeting new market segments with the Baby Benz

(Reproduced with permission of DaimlerChrysler)

Plate 4 Coral Black Velvet: innovations call for communicating category needs

(Reproduced with permission of Gesamtverband Werbeagenturen GWA and J. Walter Thompson)

Plate 5 Ben & Jerry's: Vermont's finest and the world's wackiest ice cream

(Reproduced with permission of Ben & Jerry's)

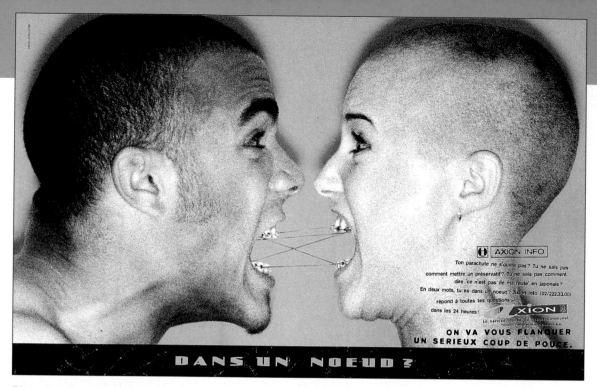

Plate 6 Axion: marketing bank products to youngsters

(Reproduced with permission of Gemeentekrediet, group Dexia)

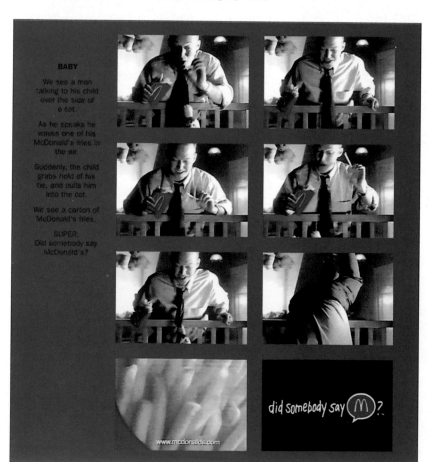

Plate 7 McDonald's: marketing to children requires a special approach

(Reproduced with permission of Leo Burnett)

Plate 8 Eastpak: the selling power of a creative idea

(Reproduced with permission of VF Corporation)

Plate 9 Virgin: an aggressive price challenger using humour

Plate 10 McDonald's: selling arguments have to be adapted to local culture

Plate 11 BTA: attracting tourists by means of cognitive humour

(Reproduced with permission of British Tourist Authority)

Plate 12 Nicorette: giving up smoking with a smile

(Reproduced with permission of Gesamtverband
Werbeagenturen GWA and Abbott Mead Vickers BBDO)

Plate 13 CKone: building a brand image by eroticising it

(Reproduced with permission of Advertising Archives)

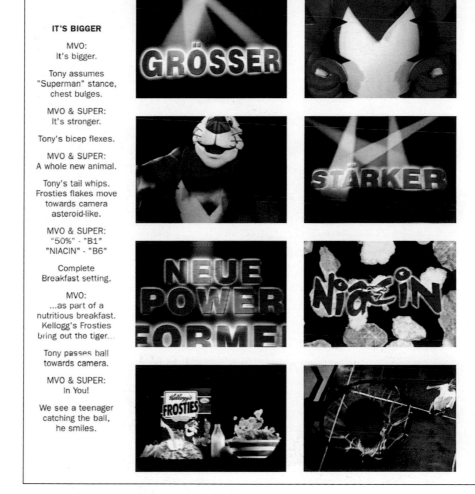

IT'S BIGGER

MVO:
It's bigger.

Tony assumes
"Superman" stance,
chest bulges.

MVO & SUPER:
It's stronger.

Tony's bicep flexes.

MVO & SUPER:
A whole new animal.

Tony's tail whips.
Frosties flakes move
towards camera
asteroid-like.

MVO & SUPER:
"50%" - "B1"
"NIACIN" - "B6"

Complete
Breakfast setting.

MVO:
...as part of a
nutritious breakfast.
Kellogg's Frosties
bring out the tiger...

Tony passes ball
towards camera.

MVO & SUPER:
In You!

We see a teenager
catching the ball,
he smiles.

Plate 14 Kellogg's Tony the Tiger: a 'character' becomes a celebrity
(Reproduced with permission of Leo Burnett)

Plate 15 The Marlboro Man: a personality symbol to support brand image
(Reproduced with permission of Leo Burnett)

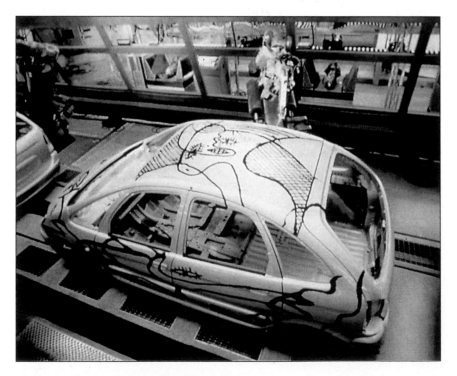

Plate 16 Citroën: Picasso paints the Xsara
(Reproduced with permission of Gesamtverband Werbeagenturen GWA and Euro RSCG Works)

Table 7.4 Impact of media context variables

Media context variable	Impact on ad effectiveness
Objective context variables	
■ Medium itself	Context effects more pronounced for TV
■ Vehicle content	Violence, humour and sex have a negative impact
■ Media clutter in vehicle	The more clutter, the less positive ad results
■ Type of ad block	Context effects more pronounced for interrupting than shoulder blocks
■ Sequence within ad block	Primacy and recency effects
■ Congruence between context and ad	Product involvement (PI) moderates impact: for low PI congruency is best, for high PI contrast is best
Subjective context variables	
■ Intensity of response	Mixed results, balance in direction of higher intensity, better ad results
■ Valence of response	Positive valenced context improves ad effectiveness

Based on: Moorman, M. (2003), *Context Considered. The Relationship Between Media Environments and Advertising Effects*, Doctoral Dissertation. Universiteit van Amsterdam, the Netherlands.

was dealt with in Chapter 2. The medium context refers to characteristics of the content of the medium in which an ad is inserted, as they are perceived by the individuals who are exposed to the ad.[38] TV commercials appear before, after or between TV programmes or other commercials, magazine or newspaper ads are inserted between articles, billboards are placed on the wall of a building or in a bus shelter, transit advertising forms part of the bus, tram, etc. Several studies indicate that the media context has an influence on how people perceive, interpret and process an advertising message. Since the effectiveness of the same ad may depend on the context surrounding the ad, it is useful for the advertiser to get a clearer view on what these context effects might look like.

The conclusions outlined in Table 7.4 are made on the basis of an extensive literature review.[39]

Context effects seem to be more prevalent in one medium than another. Although most studies so far focus on TV, there seems to be some evidence that context variables matter more in a TV than in a print environment.[40]

Besides the medium, the content of the medium vehicle also plays a role. Concerning how interesting and involving a programme is, a recent study found that violent and sexual programmes, as compared to neutral programmes, impair TV viewers' memory for television ads.[41] This was found to be the case for males and females, for all age groups and for people who like and dislike programmes containing violence and sex. One possible explanation for this finding is that sex and violence attract so much attention that there is not enough processing capacity left to process the embedded ads. Another explanation is that sexual and violent programmes evoke sexual and violent thoughts. Being occupied with thinking about sex and violence, consumers' memory for commercials could be seriously reduced. A similar conclusion also seems to hold for humorous programmes, although in the past comedies have been shown to lead to a higher ad recall than news or dramas.

As discussed earlier, **advertising clutter** has increased significantly in most media. A problem is that due to this enormous clutter, advertisements become less effective. The more clutter, the lower the motivation and opportunity to pay attention to an ad. Too many marketing messages compete for the attention of the consumer. As a consequence, less attention will be devoted to individual ads.[42]

Concerning **ad blocks**, a distinction can be made between interrupting blocks (a commercial block in the middle of the programme) or shoulder blocks (a commercial block between two different programmes). Although some researchers hypothesise that commercials in interrupting blocks are less effective because viewers do not want to be disturbed at that moment, this does not seem to be true. Intense and positive responses towards the context carry over more easily to ads in an interrupting break than in a shoulder break. An explanation for the latter is that during the programme viewers experience more arousal and interest than between programmes.[43]

As for the sequence within a block, the earlier an ad appears in the block, the higher the motivation to pay attention to the ad and process the information. Furthermore, the placement of an ad also determines the opportunity to pay attention to it. The primacy effect, suggesting that ads that come early in a magazine or early in a sequence of TV commercials are more effective, has been confirmed on several occasions.[44] However, for TV advertising the last position can also be beneficial since the consumer has more time to process the ad due to the fact that it is not followed by another ad, but by a short silence.[45] Because of inherent characteristics of the medium, certain places can raise the opportunity to pay attention; for example, the upper left corner of a magazine (people normally start reading from the left to the right), the right page (this is the flat page when a magazine is open) or the cover page.[46]

Studies on the impact of media style–ad style congruency reveal contradictory conclusions. Some researchers claim that the better the fit between the ad and the media context, the more motivated consumers will be to process the ad and the easier this job will be for them. A computer ad inserted in a computer magazine, for instance, increases the likelihood that the reader wants to pay attention and is willing to process the ad, since the computer magazine makes the need for a computer or information on computers more salient and this evoked need stimulates the motivation to pay attention to stimuli that are relevant to the need. Similarly, people reading a magazine that evokes transformational needs, such as a beauty magazine, are more likely to look for transformational cues in ads, such as the attractiveness of the hair after using a certain shampoo, while reading a health magazine is more likely to make people pay attention to cues such as the revitalisation of damaged hair.[47] According to the priming principle, an ad can be interpreted on the basis of schemas (knowledge structures) activated or primed by the context.[48] Congruency between the ad and the context means that the ad can be more easily interpreted since the relevant knowledge structures are already activated. However, some studies found no effects or even a positive impact associated with placing an ad in a style that is incongruent with the media context. This relation between ad-context congruency and ad effectiveness can be explained as follows: the novelty of the ad or the unexpectedness of the information given its context increases the attention to the ad because consumers see the ad as innovative and interesting. How can the contradictory results be explained and what should an advertiser go for: a context-congruent or a context-incongruent ad? The solution can be found in moderator variables.

Apparently, people react differently depending on how involved they are with the product category.[49] When product involvement is low, consumers go for the peripheral route of processing and it helps them that context and ad style are congruent. On the other hand, when product involvement is high, they are more likely to follow the central route. In this case, they are willing to expend more cognitive resources and they seem to appreciate a context-incongruent ad more.

Summary

In media planning the decision is taken what media and vehicles will be purchased, at what time and at what price. Media planning consists of a number of steps. After assessing the communications environment and describing the target audience, media objectives have to be set, and media vehicles have to be selected and bought. Media objectives refer to criteria, such as the frequency with which the target group has to be exposed to the message, and the reach or weight of a campaign, i.e. the number of desired contacts with the target group. Furthermore, the continuity or schedule of the campaign has to be decided on, and media costs have to be taken into account. Media selection is based on quantitative criteria, such as frequency, reach and seasonal influences, but also on qualitative criteria, such as image-building capacity, emotional impact, demonstration capacity and quality of reproduction. Technical criteria, such as production costs and media buying characteristics, also have to be taken into account. Each type of advertising medium (newspapers, magazines, television, radio, etc.) has its advantages and disadvantages. Furthermore, the media context can have a considerable impact on advertising effectiveness.

Review questions

1 What are the various steps in the media planning process?

2 How does ad message repetition affect advertising effectiveness?

3 How can the β-coefficient analysis be used to optimise message repetition?

4 What is the relationship between reach, gross and effective reach, opportunity to see, and gross and effective rating points?

5 How can media scheduling or continuity affect advertising effectiveness?

6 On the basis of which criteria should a media plan be composed?

7 What are the main advantages and disadvantages of print and audiovisual media?

8 Why is cinema advertising effective?

Further reading

Baron, R. and Sissors, J. (2002), *Advertising Media Planning*. McGraw-Hill.

Donelly, W.J. (1996), *Planning Media, Strategy and Imagination*. Upper Saddle River, NJ: Prentice Hall.

Jones, J.P. (2002), *The Ultimate Secrets of Advertising*. Sage Publications.

Katz, H.A. (2003), *The Media Handbook: A Complete Guide to Advertising Media Selection, Planning, Research and Buying*. Lawrence Erlbaum Associates.

Rossiter, J.R. and Danaker, P.J. (1998), *Advanced Media Planning*. Kluwer Academic Publishers.

Case 7

Relaunching Nizoral in Russia

The Russian economic, advertising and media context

Russia is a large country with a population of about 145 million (2001), more than 70% of which live in cities. Of these cities, Moscow and, to a far lesser extent, St Petersburg represent the economic heart of the country. The Buying Power Index (BPI), measured as a weighted average of the population share, consumer spends and share in national turn-over of each city is 21 for Moscow, 4 for St Petersburg and less than 1 for practically all other cities. The BPI of Moscow is 20% higher than the other 20 largest cities of Russia, St Petersburg included, taken together. Needless to say that, in these circumstances, any marketing campaign will have to focus heavily on the Moscow region.

Total ad spends in Russia were US$2,320 million in 2001, i.e. approximately US$16 per capita. They increase substantially every year. Television has a relatively stable market share of about 30%, print has a market share that has been decreasing slightly over the past few years, amounting to 27% in 2001. The share of outdoor advertising is increasing and equalled 16% in 2001. Radio has 3% market share, and direct marketing 6%. Top advertisers during the first half of 2002 were, amongst others, Procter & Gamble, Unilever, Nestlé, Mars, Henkel, Wrigley, Danone, Pepsico, Beiersdorf and Coca-Cola.

Nearly every Russian household has a television set. The top eight television channels attract more than 80% of the TV advertising investments. There are three national channels, ORT, RTR and NTV. They have a daily reach of 60%, 55% and 45% of the Russian population respectively. Their share of audience is approximately 30%, 20% and 15%, and they attract 32%, 25% and 26% of the ad spends on television in Russia. For each channel the list price per GRP is approximately the same, about US$2,800 per 30-second spot, and so is their cost per thousand

(CPT) of approximately US$5.5. Various types of Russian magazines can be distinguished: magazines for business managers, parents with young kids, teens and young adults (16–25), male adults and female adults (25–45 years old), and general interest magazines. The readership of these magazines differs from one title to another, and so does the CPT. The latter ranges from as low as US$27 to as high as US$550. The 10 largest newspapers reach a daily audience of about 23% of the Russian population. There are numerous radio stations in Russia, the majority of which are very focussed on a specific region and/or target group. The three largest national radio channels each reach about 18% of the population. Outdoor advertising is increasing, both in number of sites and in budgets. Tobacco brands constitute a major part of the investments in outdoor advertising.

The advertising and media briefing for Nizoral

Nizoral is a medicated antidandruff shampoo that is globally marketed by the pharmaceutical company Janssen-Cilag and its subsidiaries. Traditionally, Nizoral has tried to attract a mass market of consumers. As such it has a number of direct competitors in the inner market of pharmacy products (Freederm, Skin-cap, Vichy) and indirect competitors in the mass market of supermarket products (Head & Shoulders, Fructis, Schauma, Timotei, etc.).

The new marketing target group for the relaunch of Nizoral in 2003 has been defined as people concerned about dandruff, who regard it as a medical problem and seek a really effective, medical solution – people aiming for a high-quality, healthy and modern lifestyle. They choose only original products and the best quality: 'exclusive – really the only one that is effective'. An overview of the old and new positioning strategies is presented in Case Table 7.1. The marketing objectives of the 2003 relaunch were to reposition

Case Table 7.1 The old and new positioning strategies of Nizoral

	Target	Competitive framework	Rational benefit	Emotional benefit	Reason why	Brand character/ personality
Old	All antidandruff shampoo users Income average+	All antidandruff shampoos (Head & Shoulders, Schauma, Pantene Pro-V)	The most cost-effective medicated antidandruff shampoo (calendar)	Soft medicated shampoo (association with nature – green trees – beauty and health)	Impact on cause of dandruff Long-term effect (two weeks)	Soft, reliable care
New	Only medicated shampoo users Income average+	Medicated shampoos (Freederm, Skin-cap)	The only really effective antidandruff treatment	Luxurious, high-quality, healthy lifestyle	Contains medicine acting on cause of dandruff Recommended by specialists (pharmacists, dermatologists)	Brings the most valuable benefit to life

the brand and focus more heavily on the core market of Nizoral, those people who are seeking a high-quality medicated solution for their dandruff problem, to recruit new patients in the medicated segment and to protect existing users and market share. The objectives of the communications campaign were to explain the new positioning and benefits of the product, to reinforce the medical image of the brand and to justify its higher price.

Janssen-Cilag Russia specified the media planning tasks as follows:

- To create an effective and cost-effective communications mix.
- To identify the most relevant communications channels for the target audience.
- To provide maximum reach of effective frequency of the target audience.
- To provide a cost-effective reach of the target groups.

The target group of the campaign was described as people between 25 and 55 years old, of both sexes, but women in particular, with a monthly income of at least US$200, and predominantly highly educated.

The start of the campaign was planned in February 2003, and the total budget, all included, was US$800,000. A number of media agencies were asked to propose a media plan for this campaign. The proposal of First Media, one of the largest media planning agencies in Russia, is presented in the next section.

The media plan of First Media

The target group, as defined by Janssen-Cilag's Nizoral brand management, is of course the starting point of the media planning process: men and women aged between 25 and 55, with monthly income of at least US$200, and mostly with a higher income. Special emphasis should be put on frequent users of anti-dandruff shampoo, frequent users of medical shampoo and current users of Nizoral. In Case Figure 7.1, the demographic criteria as defined by Janssen-Cilag are combined with these user criteria to give a broader picture of the target groups. The affinity index represents the involvement of the various segments in the product category. However, according to First Media, the target group of the campaign cannot be defined on the basis of demographics and buying behaviour alone. The basic positioning of Nizoral is that dandruff is a disease that requires a special medical solution, and that Nizoral is the only product for those who recognise the problem sufficiently and want to get the best solution. Therefore, lifestyle and value considerations of the target groups should also be considered. On the basis of a psychographic analysis of the current and future target groups, First Media comes to the conclusion that the current consumers are mainly imprudent innovators and individualists that are ready to accept risks in buying new products. The basic psychographic characteristic of the new target consumers is, according to the agency, egocentrism: Nizoral should be targeted at independent and loyal consumers who are inclined

Case Figure 7.1 Demographic and behavioural definition of the target groups of the Nizoral campaign

Target Group Analysis
Users of Nizoral and its Category

Demographics		Frequently use antidandruff shampoo		Frequently use medicated shampoo		Current users of Nizoral		
		%	Affinity	%	Affinity	%	Affinity	
Gender	Male	53.0	118	30.7	68	51.2	114	
	Female	47.0	86	69.3	126	48.8	89	
Age	16–19	12.4	140	11.5	130	15.2	172	High % and affinity at stage of EGO* formation
	20–24	10.4	129	10.2	126	10.7	132	
	25–34	23.6	133	20.6	116	22.0	124	
	35–44	23.5	114	19.4	94	22.9	111	
	45–54	16.0	90	17.0	96	16.5	93	
	55–64	8.2	65	10.4	83	7.2	57	
	65+	5.9	41	10.8	76	5.5	39	
Income	Not enough money for food	3.1	64	3.5	72	2.7	55	Interesting in terms of potential investment in the future
	Enough money for food, but cannot afford clothes	18.6	79	20.4	86	13.3	57	
	Can afford food and clothes, but not expensive products	54.4	105	53.8	103	54.2	104	
	Sometimes buy expensive products, but cannot purchase anything they want	21.0	122	19.9	116	26.0	151	
	Can afford anything they want	1.0	103	1.1	111	1.9	197	Can be seen as additional target group for special projects
	Not available	1.9	131	1.4	94	2.0	138	

Nizoral target group – *men/women, 25–55 years with average + income (>$200)*

* EGO = a kind of lifestyle/personality variable that is measured in a large Russian media planning study.

Source: Gallup M'Index 2002/2.

towards a well-considered choice of the best solution for them on the market.

Based on this analysis, a media plan is composed. At first an analysis is made of the communications objectives, the consumer response sought, the target groups and the appropriate media types to support these objectives. The basis of this decision is an assessment of various media types. This analysis is based on a number of criteria. An importance weight is attached to each criterion, and each medium receives a score on each criterion. In Case Figure 7.2, an overview is given of the resulting 'value' of each medium type, i.e. the overall weighted average of importance

and performance scores. Case Figure 7.3 gives an overview of the perceived quality and use of different media types in the mind of the target group. Given the target groups of the campaign and the value and (perceived) characteristics of different types of media, the agency translates the communications objectives of the campaign to media solutions and to specific selected media types (Case Figure 7.4).

The agency then analyses the characteristics of specific television channels, magazines and newspapers to see whether they can reach the target groups effectively and efficiently. In Case Figure 7.5 the viewing share of the eight largest television

Case Figure 7.2 Value of media types

Available Media
Medium Value

Criteria	Weight	National TV Score	National TV Result	Regional TV Score	Regional TV Result	Magazines Score	Magazines Result	Newspapers Score	Newspapers Result	Radio Score	Radio Result	Outdoor Score	Outdoor Result	Cinema Score	Cinema Result	Internet Score	Internet Result
Reach-building potential	4	5	20	5	20	3	12	3	12	4	16	2	8	1	4	1	5
Geographic focus	4	1	4	4	16	2	8	3	12	4	16	5	20	5	20	1	1
Psychographic focus	4	4	16	4	16	5	20	5	20	3	12	1	4	2	8	2	8
Cost-efficiency	4	5	20	5	20	3	12	4	16	4	16	2	8	1	4	1	5
Frequency-building potential	2	4	8	5	10	3	6	3	6	5	10	2	4	1	2	2	8
Demographic focus	2	5	10	5	10	4	8	3	6	3	6	1	2	2	4	2	10
Visualisation	2	5	10	5	10	4	8	2	4	1	2	3	6	2	4	2	10
Detailed message	1	2	2	2	2	4	4	5	5	3	3	1	1	2	2	4	8
Prestige, image	1	5	5	5	5	4	4	3	3	3	3	2	2	2	2	1	5
Affordability	1	1	1	3	3	2	2	3	3	5	5	1	1	4	4	5	5
Totals:		37	96	43	112	34	84	34	87	35	89	20	56	22	54	21	65

Medium value

Weighted medium value

Case Figure 7.3 Perceived characteristics and use of media types by the target group

Available Media
Candidate Vehicles in the Minds of TG

Men/women, 25–54 years, average + income

Type of ad	Notice %	Notice Affinity	Trust %	Trust Affinity	Use %	Use Affinity
Newspaper ads	47.9	112	24.3	114	25.4	122
TV ads	58.0	107	19.4	106	18.3	112
Magazine ads	26.7	114	11.7	118	8.0	125
Radio ads	26.2	100	8.9	96	6.2	101
Ads in shop windows	18.6	114	6.0	116	3.9	116
Billboard ads	23.2	115	5.1	123	3.3	120
Direct mail sent to home	14.7	114	5.0	120	5.0	131
Ads on buses, trolleys and trams	22.3	111	3.0	103	2.0	116
Metro car ads	12.2	122	2.6	141	1.9	150
Direct mail sent to office	5.7	145	2.5	145	2.0	156
Advertising agents	5.1	112	2.5	107	2.6	125
Metro station ads	10.5	127	1.7	127	0.8	119
Internet ads	4.4	112	1.5	103	1.8	121
Roof ads	5.9	121	0.6	105	0.5	121

Source: Gallup M'Index 2002/2.

Case Figure 7.4 Communications objectives, media solutions and selected media types

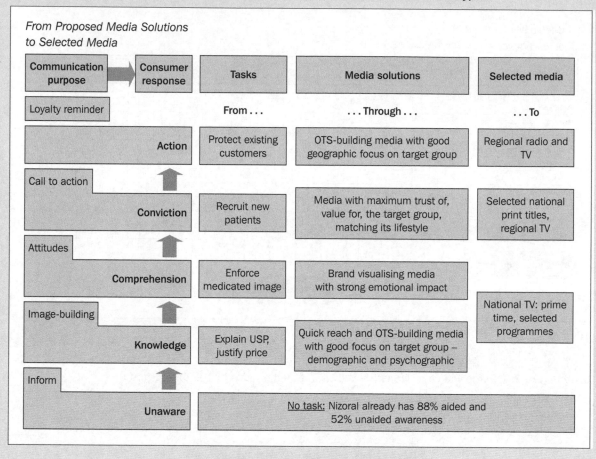

channels is shown. On the basis of this analysis the agency proposes a television rating point (TRP) mix of 55% ORT and 45% RTR. Magazines and newspapers are used as supplementary media for different reasons. Magazines are good media to build brand image and to carry over emotional messages and benefits, and to strengthen the emotional bond with the brand. On the other hand, newspapers are good media to objectively and rationally explain the details of the dandruff problem and the advantages of the Nizoral brand, and to persuade consumers. In Case Figure 7.6 the characteristics of a number of magazines are highlighted: percentage coverage of the target group, the affinity of the readers with the medium and their score on the 'egocentric' lifestyle values judged to be important in this campaign. The selection of the print media is based on the maximum coverage of the target group, with special emphasis on Moscow (7 *Day*, *Cosmopolitan*, *AIF*), maximum correspondence to the demographic and psychographic

profile of the target group, and the support to the image of the brand (*Men's Health*, *GEO*). On the basis of these considerations, First Media proposes a total media plan and budget (Case Figure 7.7).

Questions

1 What do you think about the media target group definition of Media First? Is it consistent with the marketing and communications brief of Janssen-Cilag?

2 Do you think that the assessments of the different types of media in Case Figure 7.2 and the target group's appreciation of these media (Case Figure 7.3) is correct? Would this appreciation be different in your country? Would it be fundamentally different in other segments of the population?

3 Is the translation of communications targets to media solutions and media types in Case Figure 7.4 correct? Could there have been other good solutions (other types of media)?

Case Figure 7.5 Viewing share of television channels

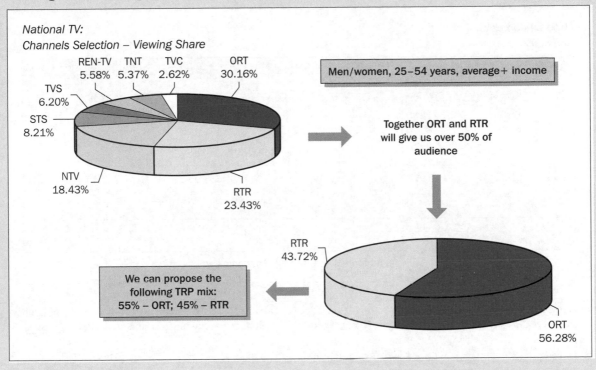

National TV:
Channels Selection – Viewing Share

Source: Gallup TV – Russia.

Case Figure 7.6 Characteristics of magazines

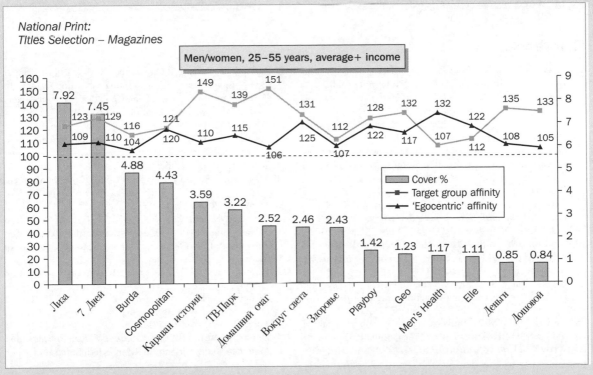

National Print:
Titles Selection – Magazines

Source: Gallup NRS July–October 2002, Media Ego.

Case Figure 7.7 Media plan and budget

National Campaign Summary

National Campaign			Jan	Feb	Mar	Apr	May	Jun	Jul	Aug	Sep	Oct	Nov	Dec
TV	Budget, $	$337,000		$104,500	$111,500							$121,000		
	TRPs	466		160	153							153		
	Spots	64		22	21							21		
Print	Budget, $	$149,928						$149,928						
	Insertions	16						16						

To be topped up with Regional Campaign

4 Do you think it is a good idea to split the TV budget between ORT and RTR, and to leave out NTV? Why or why not?

5 Based on the information in Case Figure 7.6, and using the various criteria to compose a media mix, do you think that the magazine choice is appropriate?

6 Do you think the media objectives (reach, frequency, weight, continuity, cost) of the campaign are reached?

Based on: Russian State Committee on Statistics, Central Bank of Russia, Russian Association of Ad Agencies, First Media, Taylor Nelson Sofres, Gallup Russia, Gallup M'Index 2002/2; see also: www.nizoral.com, www.janssen-cilag.com and country-specific sites.

References

1 Donnelly, W.J. (1996), *Planning Media, Strategy and Imagination*. Upper Saddle River, NJ: Prentice Hall.

2 Donnelly, W.J. (1996), *Planning Media, Strategy and Imagination*. Upper Saddle River, NJ: Prentice Hall.

3 Donnelly, W.J. (1996), *Planning Media, Strategy and Imagination*. Upper Saddle River, NJ: Prentice Hall.

4 Nordhielm, C.L. (2002), 'The Influence of Level of Processing on Advertising Repetition Effects', *Journal of Consumer Research*, 29 (December), 371–82.

5 Pechman, C. and Stewart, D.W. (1989), 'Advertising Repetition: A Critical Review of Wearin and Wearout', *Current Issues and Research in Advertising*, 12, 285–330.

6 MacInnis, D.J., Rao, A.G. and Weiss, A.M. (2002), 'Assessing When Increased Media Weight of Real-World Advertisements Helps Sales', *Journal of Marketing Research*, 39 (November), 391–407.

7 Nordhielm, C.L. (2002), 'The Influence of Level of Processing on Advertising Repetition Effects', *Journal of Consumer Research*, 29 (December), 371–82.

8 Kirmani, A. (1997), 'Advertising Repetition as a Signal of Quality: If It's Advertised so Much, Something Must Be Wrong', *Journal of Advertising*, 26(3), 77–86.

9 Newell, S.J. and Henderson, K.V. (1998), 'Super Bowl Advertising: Field Testing the Importance of Advertisement Frequency, Length and Placement on Recall', *Journal of Marketing Communication*, 4(4), 237–48.

10 Berger, I.E. and Mitchell, A.A. (1989), 'The Effect of Advertising on Ad Accessibility, Attitude Confidence, and the Attitude–Behavior Relationship', *Journal of Consumer Research*, 16 (December), 269–79.

11 Hawkins, S.A. and Hoch, S.J. (1992), 'Low Involvement Learning: Memory Without Evaluation', *Journal of Consumer Research*, 19 (September), 212–25.

12 D'Sousa, G. and Rao, R.C. (1995), 'Can Repeating an Advertisement More Frequently than the Competition Affect Brand Preference in a Mature Market?', *Journal of Marketing*, 59, 32–42.

13 Kirmani, A. (1997), 'Advertising Repetition as a Signal of Quality: If it's Advertised so Much, Something Must Be Wrong', *Journal of Advertising*, 26(3), 77–86; Nelson, P. (1974), 'Advertising as Information', *Journal of Political Economy*, 82(4), 729–54.

14 Donnelly, W.J. (1996), *Planning Media, Strategy and Imagination*. Upper Saddle River, NJ: Prentice Hall.

15 Katz, H. (2003), *The Media Handbook*. Mahwah, NJ: Lawrence Erlbaum Associates.

16 Donnelly, W.J. (1996), *Planning Media, Strategy and Imagination*. Upper Saddle River, NJ: Prentice Hall.

17 Jones, J.P. (2002), *The Ultimate Secrets of Advertising*. Sage Publications.

18 Ephron, E. (1995), 'More Weeks, Less Weight: The Self-Space Model of Advertising', *Journal of Advertising Research*, 35(3) (May/June), 18–23.

19 De Pelsmacker, P., Geuens, M. and Ghesquiere, H. (2001), 'The Importance of Media Planning, Ad Likeability and Brand Position on Ad and Brand Recognition in Radio Spots', *Proceedings of the 30th Annual Conference of the European Marketing Academy*, Bergen: Norwegian School of Economics and Business Administration, 8–11 May.

20 McDonald, C. (1997), 'From "Frequency" to "Continuity" – is it a New Dawn?' *Journal of Advertising Research*, 37(4), 21–25.

21 Newell, S.J. and Henderson, K.V. (1998), 'Super Bowl Advertising: Field-testing the Importance of Advertising Frequency, Length and Placement on Recall', *Journal of Marketing Communications*, 4(3), 237–48; D'Souza, G. and Rao, R.C. (1995), 'Can Repeating an Advertisement more Frequently than the Competition Affect Brand Preference in a Mature Market?' *Journal of Marketing*, 59 (April), 32–42.

22 Katz, H. (2003), *The Media Handbook*. Mahwah, NJ: Lawrence Erlbaum Associates.

23 Katz, H. (2003), *The Media Handbook*. Mahwah, NJ: Lawrence Erlbaum Associates.

24 De Landtsheer, D., Van Rensbergen, N. and Van Roy, T. (2001), Mediaplanning, Begrijpen en Benutten (Mediaplanning: Understanding and Using), Mechelen: Koncept.

25 Case, T. (2002), 'Media Plan of the Year', *Adweek*, 43(25), 34–36.

26 Ritson, M. (2003), 'Marketers Need to Find a Way to Control the Contagion of Clutter', *Marketing*, 6 March, 16.

27 Pieters, R., Warlop, L. and Wedel, M. (2002), 'Breaking Through the Clutter: Benefits of Advertisement Originality and Familiarity for Brand Attention and Memory', *Management Science*, 48(6), 765–81.

28 IP Peaktime (2002), *Television 2002. European Key Factors*. Neuilly-sur-Seine, Cedex, Brussels: IP; IP Peaktime (2002), *Radio 2002. European Key Factors*. Neuilly-sur-Seine, Cedex, Brussels: IP.

29 Magiera, M. (1989), 'Advertisers Crowd onto the Big Screen', *Advertising Age*, 60(40), 14–15.

30+31 Van Zeebroeck, T. (1996), *Media Creativiteit (Media Creativity)*. Antwerp: MIM Standaard Uitgevery.

32 www.afajcdecaux.dk

33 *De Morgen*, 11 May 2002.

34 White, E. (2002), 'Advertisers Hope Fragrant Posters Are Nothing to Sniff At – Firms Target UK Consumers With Ads That Sing and Spray', *Wall Street Journal*, 10 October.

35 Smets, F. (2003), 'De Geur als Wapen' ('Scent as a Weapon'), *De Morgen*, 22 March.

36 White, E. (2003), 'In-Your-Face Marketing: Ad Agency Rents Foreheads', *Wall Street Journal*, 11 February.

37 Moorman, M. (2003), *Context Considered. The Relationship Between Media Environments and Advertising Effects*, Doctoral Dissertation. Universiteit van Amsterdam, the Netherlands.

38 De Pelsmacker, P., Geuens, M. and Anckaert, P. (2002), 'Media Context and Advertising Effectiveness. The Role of Context Appreciation and Context-Ad Similarity', *Journal of Advertising*, 31(2), 49–61.

39 Moorman, M. (2003), *Context Considered. The Relationship Between Media Environments and Advertising Effects*, Doctoral Dissertation. Universiteit van Amsterdam, the Netherlands.

40 De Pelsmacker, P., Geuens, M. and Anckaert, P. (2002), 'Media Context and Advertising Effectiveness. The Role of Context Appreciation and Context-Ad Similarity', *Journal of Advertising*, 31(2), 49–61.

41 Bushman, B.J. and Bonacci, A.M. (2002), 'Violence and Sex Impair Memory for Television Ads', *Journal of Applied Psychology*, 87(3), 557–64.

42 Ha, L. (1996), 'Observations: Advertising Clutter in Consumer Magazines: Dimensions and Effects', *Journal of Advertising Research*, 36(4), 76–81.

43 Moorman, M. (2003), *Context Considered. The Relationship Between Media Environments and Advertising Effects*, Doctoral Dissertation. Universiteit van Amsterdam, the Netherlands.

44 Finn, A. (1988), 'Print Ad Recognition Readership Scores: An Information Processing Perspective', *Journal of Marketing Research*, 25 (May), 168–77; Pieters, R. and de Klerk-Warmerdam, M. (1993), 'Duration, Serial Position and Competitive Clutter Effects on the Memory for Television Advertising', in Chias, I.J. and Sureda, J. (eds), *Marketing for the New Europe: Dealing with Complexity*, Proceedings of the 22nd Annual Conference of the European Marketing Academy, Barcelona, 59–68.

45 Olson, D. (1994), 'The Sounds of Silence: Functions and Use of Silence in Television Advertising', *Journal of Advertising Research* (Sept./Oct.), 89–95.

46 Janiszewski, C. (1990), 'The Influence of Print Advertisement Organization on Affect Toward a Brand Name', *Journal of Consumer Research*, 17, 53–65; Finn, A. (1988), 'Print Ad Recognition Readership Scores: An Information Processing Perspective', *Journal of Marketing Research*, 25 (May), 168–77.

47 Park, C. and Young, M. (1986), 'Consumer Response to Television Commercials: The Impact of Involvement and Background Music on Brand Attitude Formation', *Journal of Marketing Research*, 23 (Feb.), 11–24.

48 Yi, Y. (1993), 'Contextual Priming Effects in Print Advertisements: The Moderating Role of Prior Knowledge', *Journal of Advertising*, 22 (1 March), 1–10.

49 De Pelsmacker, P., Geuens, M. and Anckaert, P. (2002), 'Media Context and Advertising Effectiveness. The Role of Context Appreciation and Context-Ad Similarity', *Journal of Advertising*, 31(2), 49–61.

Chapter 8

Advertising research

Chapter outline

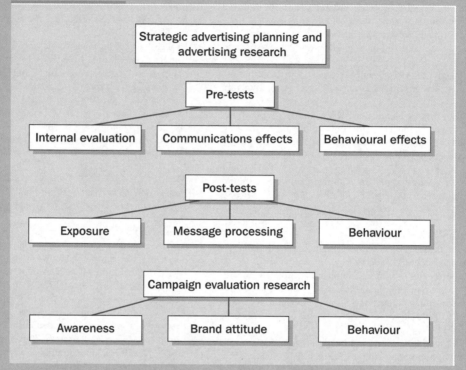

Chapter objectives

This chapter will help you to:

- Carry out strategic communications research in preparation of a communications campaign
- Understand the objectives, techniques and limitations of pre-testing advertising campaigns
- Understand the objectives, techniques and limitations of post-testing advertising campaigns
- Learn the techniques and procedures of advertising campaign evaluation research

Introduction

Advertising research is not always supported by those who are involved in the communications process. Creative professionals, for instance, are inclined to perceive research efforts as a potential threat and limitation to their creativity. Moreover, many marketing managers and other communications professionals believe that research cannot replace experience and intuition, and therefore is a waste of time and money. Finally, there is a widespread belief that the effects of communications efforts cannot be measured validly, and therefore one should not even try to do so. As in all prejudices, there is a core of truth, and a lot of ego defence and/or misunderstanding.

Obviously, advertising research should not lead to a situation in which all creativity is stifled, but should lead to more relevant, functional and, therefore, more effective creativity. Furthermore, research can never replace marketing knowledge, and even intuition, but should rather serve as an eye-opener and a correction to the 'marketing myopia' that is often mistakenly called 'experience'. There is more truth in the belief about the problem of measuring the effectiveness of communication efforts. Their effect on sales, market share or profits often cannot be isolated, and the commercial payoff of marketing communications is often only visible after a certain period of time. Therefore, in advertising research, very often 'intermediate' effects, such as brand awareness, brand knowledge, attitude, preference or purchase intention, are measured, and they are assumed to be predictors of commercial success.

Most of the research techniques discussed in this chapter have been developed for, and used in, an advertising context. Four basic types of advertising research will be discussed: preliminary or strategic communications research, pre-testing, post-testing and campaign evaluation research. Most of the techniques discussed can easily be transferred to other communications tools, such as public relations or in-store communications.

Strategic advertising planning and the role of research

Advertising research is used to improve decision-making in each stage of the advertising planning process. The various types of advertising research can therefore be linked to the stages in this process. This is illustrated in Figure 8.1. The starting point of a good advertising plan is a situation analysis or strategic research, on which the strategy can be built. On the basis of this research, objectives and target groups can be defined, and message and creative strategies can be developed. Following the development of an advertising strategy, a number of advertising tools (print advertisements, television spots, posters, etc.) will be developed and tested. This process is called pre-testing. After the development of the campaign, it is placed in the media. The impact of each of the tools can be assessed in post-tests. Finally, the results of the whole campaign can be compared with its objectives in campaign evaluation research. The results of the latter can serve as input for the development of subsequent advertising campaigns.

Figure 8.1 Stages in the development of an advertising campaign and the role of advertising and advertising research

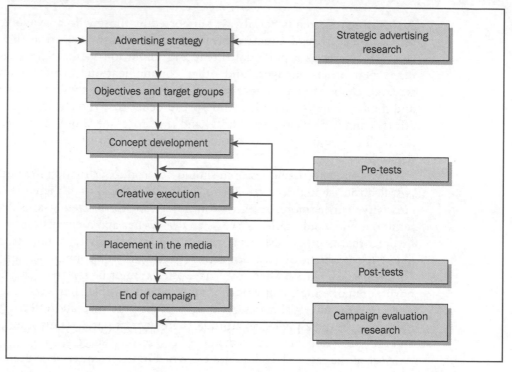

Strategic advertising research

Marketing communications, as one of the instruments of the marketing mix, have to be embedded in the overall marketing strategy of the company. Therefore, it has to be consistent with the overall marketing objectives, it has to be aimed at the desired market segments, and it should reflect the positioning strategy defined. Strategic communications research, and more particularly strategic advertising research, will therefore partially overlap with strategic marketing research. It enables the communications manager to establish a solid base on which the communications strategy can be built. Given the integrated nature of marketing communications, strategic research cannot be confined to advertising, but should cover the whole range of communications tools. Elements that have to be studied and prepared in this stage are:

- *Product*: what are its unique strengths and weaknesses, what is the unique selling proposition to be advanced, what is the advertising platform, i.e. the arguments with which to convince the target group, etc.?

- *Market*: market size evolution, market shares, market segments, competitors' strategies, consumer characteristics and behaviour, etc.?

- *Environment*: what are the legal restrictions, cultural and political trends, the economic situation, etc.?

Table 8.1 The communications audit

	Product A	Product B	Product C	Corporate
TV advertising				
Newspaper advertising				
Magazine advertising				
Sales promotions				
Direct mail				
In-store communications				
Front desk staff				
Public relations material				
Publicity				
Sponsorship				

Most of these issues can be studied on the basis of desk research and/or qualitative interviews. Apart from that, more specific analyses can be carried out to prepare the communications strategy, such as the communications audit, competitor communications strategy research, communications content research and management judgement tests.

In a **communications audit** all forms of internal and external communications are studied to assess their consistency with overall strategy, as well as their internal consistency. The audit can be carried out on the basis of an internal analysis, but should ideally be based on research with the various audiences and target groups of the company to determine the impact of all overt and non-overt communications. A framework for a communications audit is presented in Table 8.1. The consistency of the communications mix in this table should be assessed both vertically and horizontally, and the communications strategy for a number of products and/or instruments can be based on the results of this analysis.

Competitor communications strategy research is largely similar to the communications audit for the company. Competitive ads, promotions, PR material, etc. can be collected and analysed to judge competitive (communications) strategies in order to define target groups and positioning strategies more clearly for the company's own products. In addition, competitive media strategies and media mixes can be studied, not to copy them, but to get an idea of the competitors' communications budgets and shares of voice, target groups, positioning and communications strategies.

Communications content research is used to help communications creatives generate ideas about the content of new communications stimuli. When a new campaign is to be launched, brainstorming sessions can be organised, involving creatives, advertisers and consumers. Thought-starter lists, in which a multitude of potential benefits of the product are listed, may also be used to get the process underway. Finally, famous advertising gurus have issued their own sets of execution guidelines to be implemented in effective advertising. However, not only do they conflict in a number of ways, but they are also far too general to be implementable in each advertising strategy. The worst thing about these guidelines is that they lead to similar advertising executions and suffocate creative input.

If the advertising creative has too many ideas, they will have to be screened before including them in a campaign. These ideas can refer to headlines, slogans, illustrations, pictures, benefits (stated in different ways), endorsers, situations, advertising styles, etc. A sample of the target audience can be selected, and the various elements of the communications execution can be tested. The participants can be asked to order the headlines in terms of how convincing they are, the benefits in terms of their strength, the endorsers in terms of their likeability or similarity to themselves, etc., or they can be asked to rate each alternative on a scale. This *a priori* procedure is sometimes referred to as the Q-sort procedure.[1] It bears a lot of resemblance to the direct opinion measurement method in ad pre-testing (see below), but it is used before actual rough ad conception. Finally, in a management judgement test the ad execution proposals are presented to a jury of advertising managers, to check whether all the crucial elements of the strategic brief are correctly represented in the execution elements proposed. Again, this test bears a lot of resemblance to the internal analysis discussed in the pre-testing section.

Pre-testing of advertising

In a pre-test, advertising stimuli are tested before the ad appears in the media. The general purpose is to test an ad or different ads to assess whether or not they can achieve the purpose for which they are designed. The problems for which pre-testing can provide an answer are shown in Figure 8.2.

Often different concepts or executions of a new campaign are developed. Pre-testing helps with selecting the most effective one. As a final check a number of characteristics of a finished stimulus can be tested before media placement. As discussed before, consumers are assumed to go through a number of persuasion stages before buying a product or becoming loyal to a brand. Advertising, and communications in general, should serve as a guide to accompany the potential consumers through these stages. To that end, communications stimuli should generate a number of intermediate processes or communications effects, such as creating attention, carrying over information, evoking

Figure 8.2 Objectives of pre-testing

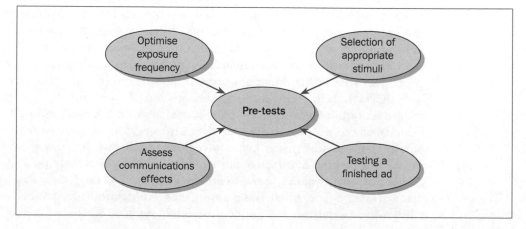

Figure 8.3 Pre-testing techniques

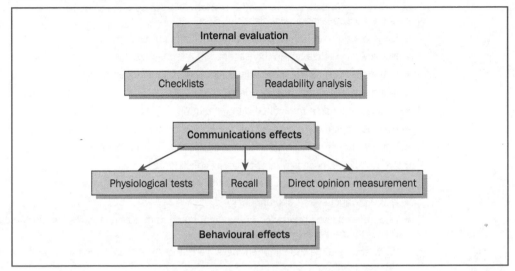

acceptance of the message, credibility, positive affective reactions about the ad and the brand, and purchase intention. In a pre-test the extent to which these intermediate effects are generated can be tested. Often, a campaign consists of a number of similar ads, i.e. different executions of the same basic communications strategy. Different executions are often used to keep the attention to the campaign alive by altering the format of the ad. Evidently, not all formats are equally appealing. A pre-test can help in establishing the extent to which some executions are more effective than others, and thus assist in deciding upon the frequency of placement of the various ads.

Three basic categories of ad pre-tests can be distinguished (Figure 8.3): a number of desirable characteristics can be tested internally, and samples of consumers can be used to test the communications or intermediate effects, or to test behavioural effects.

A campaign can be tested internally by the advertising agency and/or the advertiser by means of a checklist or readability analysis. Checklists are used to make sure that nothing important is missing, and that the ad is appealing, powerful and 'on strategy'. In Table 8.2 an example of a checklist for internal evaluation is given. Every ad can be qualitatively judged on each criterion. Obviously, not every criterion will be equally important for every campaign. For instance, the number of times the brand name is mentioned may not be important at all in an image campaign, and in a provocative campaign 'likeability' may not be all that important.[2]

Another type of internal test is the readability analysis. Good advertising copy is simple and easy to understand, especially since members of the target group are often paying only marginal attention to the text in an ad. This implies that advertising copy should be understood 'at first glance'. Several methods have been developed to test this 'readability'. For instance, a number of words in the text (e.g. every sixth word) can be removed, and a sample of consumers can be asked to fill in the missing words. The number of correctly reproduced words is an indication of the readability of the text.

Table 8.2 A checklist for qualitative internal ad pre-testing

- Is the ad appealing at first sight?
- Does the ad have impact, 'standout', 'stopping power'?
- Is the ad 'on strategy', i.e. consistent with the briefing?
- Is the essential selling proposition mentioned frequently enough?
- Is there a benefit-oriented headline?
- Is the brand name mentioned often enough?
- How appropriate and credible are the images, the characters, the storyline, etc.?
- What is the visual impression, is the ad likeable, is it pleasing aesthetically?
- Are headlines, captions and body copy consistent?
- Does the text tell the same story as the visual elements: is the ad cohesive?
- Is the product shown appropriately?
- Does the relative importance of the logo, brand name, slogan, pack shot in the ad correctly reflect their relative importance?
- What seems to be the intended message of the ad, and is it consistent with the objectives of the campaign?

Partly based on: Pickton, D. and Broderick, A. (2001), *Integrated Marketing Communications*. Harlow: Financial Times/ Prentice Hall.

Another technique is the Reading Ease (RE) formula of Flesch-Douma.[3] In this formula RE is defined as depending on the length of words and sentences:

$$RE = 206.8 - 0.77wl - 0.93sl$$

where: wl = number of syllables per 100 words
         sl = average number of words per sentence

A score between 0 and 30 means that the text is very difficult to read. A score close to 100 means that the text is very easy to understand. Research indicates that easy-to-read copy contains short sentences with short, concrete and familiar words, and lots of personal references.[4]

Communications or intermediate effects are measured in a sample of customers of the target group. The distinction can be made between physiological tests, recall tests, direct and indirect opinion measurement.

In a **physiological test** the reaction of the body to advertising stimuli is measured. Two types of physiological measurement can be carried out. The first involves the measurement of arousal, i.e. the activation of the nervous system, which is merely an indication of the intensity of the evoked affect by an ad. However, arousal measurement does not allow an assessment of the direction (positive or negative) of the affect, but is an indication of the primary affective reaction, which is assumed to trigger further processing of the ad.[5] Several techniques are used under very strict experimental conditions. For instance, the higher the arousal, the more the pupil of the eye dilates. Pupil dilation measurement is therefore used to assess the amount of arousal during, for instance, a television commercial. Another measure is the galvanic skin response. In this method, the varying humidity of the skin is measured by means of an electric current, on the basis of which the amount of arousal can be assessed. Other arousal measurement techniques are heartbeat and voice pitch analysis and electroencephalography. Most of these techniques are complicated and expensive, while the results are often difficult to interpret. Therefore, they are not frequently used.

Measuring attitudes indirectly: The Implicit Association Test

When social desirability limits the validity of explicit attitude measurement, implicit or indirect methods can be used. They measure a person's attitude without asking him or her for an explicit opinion. Implicit attitude measurements can to a certain extent predict behaviour that is spontaneous or uncontrolled. The Implicit Association Test (IAT) is an implicit attitude measurement technique that is based on the ease with which people make associations between attributes and target concepts. Images, words, logos, colours, etc. can be used as target concepts, while adjectives and nouns can be used as attributes, for instance likeable, dirty, etc. In the IAT people are asked to react as quickly as possible to a series of target concepts and attributes. If a person spontaneously and easily links a concept to an attribute, the speed with which he reacts to a combination will be higher. The opposite can be expected if the combination between the concept and attribute is less obvious or even appears contradictory to the individual. A careful analysis of reaction times provides insights into the attitude of individuals towards concepts and characteristics of these concepts. The IAT can be used to measure the reaction of individuals towards stimuli that may contain sensitive elements, or to test ads for sensitive products or issues, such as environmentally friendly buying behaviour, male/female stereotypes, hidden attitudes, racism, etc.[6] The results can be used to adapt elements of the creative execution of the ad, such as the models or arguments used, the combination between slogans and pictures, the type of appeal, etc.

For an advertisement to be effective, it has at least to be noted, and a minimum of information has to be carried over. The second type of physiological measurement tries to measure the potential of an ad to be seen. By means of a tachistoscope, print ads can be shown during a very short period of time. After exposure, the subject is asked to reproduce as many ad elements as possible. The element that is most recognised after the shortest exposure time is supposed to be the most effective one. Eye camera research[7] measures eye movements as a subject looks at a print ad or a television commercial. This technique registers what is looked at and for how long, and can be used to improve the structure or layout of an ad. It can also be used to test in-store communications tools and sponsorship activities.

In recall tests, such as the portfolio test, the extent to which an individual recalls a new ad or a new execution amidst existing ads is tested. The ad to be tested is put in a portfolio, together with the other ads. The subject is asked to look at the ads, and some time later (20 or 30 minutes), the recall test takes place. The subject has to name the ads and the brands, as well as the content of the ad that he or she can remember. Ads that are more frequently recognised are assumed to have drawn the attention better, and therefore are better ads.

Recall tests have a number of severe limitations. First of all, more than anything else, the memory of the individual as such is tested. People with a good memory will recall more ads and more of the content of the ads. This does not necessarily mean that the ads tested are good ones. Furthermore, product category involvement plays an important role. The more one is interested in a certain product (because one is planning to buy it in the near future, for instance), the more attention is paid to the ad, and the better it is recalled. Finally, very often the recall test is carried out very briefly after the exposure. The subject does not really have time to forget the ad. Ideally, the time between the exposure and the recall test should be as long as the time between the exposure and the buying situation in real life, but this can hardly be organised in a controlled experiment like the portfolio test.

In direct opinion measurement, a jury of customers is exposed to a number of ads, and they are asked to rate the ads on a number of characteristics. Most of the standardised ad testing procedures of advertising agencies, which enable them to compare test results over time, are of this type. Ad elements that can be tested are: clarity, novelty, evoked feelings, evoked attitude towards the ad and the brand, interest, quality of the information, the extent to which an ad induces the person to buy the product, etc.[8]

Direct opinion measurement of the attitude towards the ad

Many ad testing scales have been developed. Most of them test at least three dimensions by means of various items each: the affective reaction, the perception of informativeness, and the clarity of the ad. In the following scale, for instance, all statements have to be scored on 5- or 7-category scale items (completely disagree – completely agree).

This ad appeals to me.	It is clear what this ad tries to say.
This ad gives useful information.	It is not immediately clear who the sender of the message is.
This ad is interesting.	
This ad is beautiful.	The baseline is easy to understand.
This ad is believable.	You have to look at the ad a long time before you understand what it is about.
This ad draws the attention.	
This ad tells me something new.	This ad is confusing.
This ad fits the brand.	This ad is remarkable.
This ad is boring.	I think this ad is well made.
This ad gives me a positive impression of the brand.	I think this ad is original.

The subject may be asked to rate each ad on a number of scale items, to order them on the basis of a number of criteria, or to pairwise compare them on the basis of these criteria. The most important disadvantage of the direct rating method is that individuals are exposed to ads in a very unnatural environment. Therefore, they may be inclined to approach the ads too rationally compared to a real-life situation of ad exposure. They may even start to act and rate as 'instant experts', i.e. rating the ads from a professional advertiser's point of view, as they perceive it. This phenomenon is also known as the 'consumer jury effect'.

An example of an indirect opinion test is the theatre test. A group of test subjects is invited to a theatre to view a pilot programme of a new television show. On arrival, they are invited to choose a present from a number of available items (competitive products in the same product category). If the product tested is too expensive, a lottery is organised and subjects are asked to indicate what product they would choose should they win. After viewing the programme, in which the ad to be tested is also shown, the participants are asked to make their choice again, as an extra award or because 'we made a mistake the first time'. The difference between what participants choose before and after the programme is attributed to the effect of the ad tested. Apart from being expensive, this test is potentially invalid, given the unrealistic situation of the measurement and the fact that participants know they are being tested.

Finally, behaviour tests try to measure actual behaviour, as opposed to recall, arousal or attitudes. Apart from actual buying behaviour, the response to a direct response television commercial, to a direct mailing or to a direct response print ad can be measured. In a trailer test or coupon stimulated purchasing test, respondents are randomly recruited in an experimental and a control group. The members of the first group are shown a commercial that is being tested in a trailer in a supermarket car park. The control group has to answer a number of questions without being exposed to the commercial. Several experimental groups can be formed if different commercials have to be tested. Both groups receive a number of coupons as a reward for their co-operation. An individualised store card registers the items purchased. Ad effectiveness is measured by means of differences in redemption between the various coupons. Again, the participants know that they are being tested, and this might influence their buying behaviour.

A second example of a behaviour test is the split scan procedure, in which the split cable and scanner technology are combined to generate data on the effectiveness of advertising campaigns. In a split scan procedure television viewing behaviour of a panel of consumers is measured by means of a telemetric device. All members of the panel also receive a store card. The split cable technology allows different random groups of panel members to be exposed to different campaigns. By means of a store card, the actual purchase of the panel members can be measured, and in that way the effectiveness of the different commercials can be assessed. The split scan technology is very promising, because the actual behaviour can be measured of the same consumers that were exposed to the different ads in a controlled way (single source data). Furthermore, other parameters can be manipulated or controlled, such as the frequency of exposure and the exposure of specific target groups.[9]

Although pre-testing procedures are very valuable, they have some limitations that should be taken into account when interpreting their results (Figure 8.4). A pre-test

Figure 8.4 Limitations of pre-testing

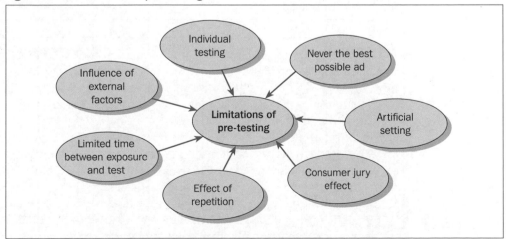

only offers the opportunity of selecting the best ad out of a series of ads tested. A pre-test will never lead to the best possible ad, but only to the best ad, given the executions tested. In that respect, pre-testing is only 'a guide to better advertising'. Pre-testing is only useful when the ads are tested in an individual interviewing procedure. Since ads are processed individually, they should also be tested individually, and not in a group setting in which the influence of the other members of the group invalidates the test rather than being synergetic. Most pre-tests take place in an experimental setting. Consumers may behave differently when exposed to an ad in a real-life situation. Some pre-test methods, especially the explicit ones such as the direct rating method, are susceptible to consumer jury effects. In most pre-tests the influence of external factors such as competitive action on the effectiveness of the ad is not measured. Often the effectiveness of the ad is measured almost immediately after exposure. The effect of the elapse of time on ad effectiveness is not assessed. Except for procedures like the split-scan method, the effect of repetition or frequency of exposure on ad effectiveness cannot be assessed.

Pre-testing a new campaign for a sauce mix

In a pre-test a number of elements can be measured that are considered to be important for the success of the campaign. However, before any judgement on the appropriateness of the campaign can be made, the results of the pre-tests should be benchmarked against other relevant campaigns. In the table below, the pre-test results of a new campaign for a prepacked sauce are given. Criteria such as attention, branding, communication, rational response and persuasion aspects are measured. The comparison is made between the new campaign and the average pre-test results of the same campaign in different countries, the average results of all other tested campaigns in the same country, and of all other food campaigns in this country. Furthermore, the pre-test results are benchmarked against normative action standards or pre-test objectives.

Pre-test scores of new campaign and benchmark campaigns for key criteria

		New campaign	Index against country average	Action standards	Country of campaign average	Country of campaign average food
Attention	Active	3.98	99	105	3.83	3.66
	Enjoyment	3.99	109	105	3.64	3.69
Branding	Brand linkage	4.18	109	110	3.90	3.88
Communication	Ease of understanding	3.73			3.65	3.70
	Specific criteria:					
	– Are practical to use	81%				
	– Have a very good taste	58%				
	– Are very good in quality	49%				
	– Are disposable in a large range of variety	71%				
	– Offer you something really new	63%				
Rational response	New information	3.15			2.59	2.67
	Different	3.23			3.15	3.30
	Relevant	3.06			2.85	3.02
	Believable	4.05			3.66	3.79
	Didn't tell you enough	2.89			2.88	2.89
Persuasion	Persuaded me	25%	120	110	12	

Post-testing of advertising

A post-test is a test of the effectiveness of a single ad after placement in the media. Post-tests are only meaningful if there is a before measurement or a control measurement as a benchmark. Three types of post-tests can be distinguished (Figure 8.5): measurement of exposure, communications effect tests and measurement of behaviour.

First of all, the extent to which an ad has reached its audience can be measured. Net reach, GRP, OTS and other **exposure measures** can be calculated. Normally, this type of effectiveness measurement is not only done after media placement, but also as a part of the media planning effort. Similarly, the amount of publicity generated in the press or sponsorship exposure can also be measured and expressed in terms of reach or GRP.

In measuring the communications or message processing effects of an ad, two types of tests are used: recall and recognition tests. A **recognition test** is a very obvious effectiveness test. A sample of ads are presented to a consumer, who is asked to indicate whether he or she recognises the ad or not. The underlying assumption is that ads can only be effective when they are at least noted. A well-known recognition test procedure for print ads is the **Starch method**. Some 75,000 advertisements in 1,000 issues of magazines and newspapers are assessed each year, using 100,000 personal interviews.[10] Consumers who say they have read a specific issue in a magazine are interviewed at home. The magazine is opened at a random page, and for each ad a number of questions are asked. The procedure leads to four percentage scores for each ad:

- *Non-readers*: the percentage of people who do not remember having seen the ad.
- *Noted*: the percentage of readers that claim to have seen the ad.
- *Seen/associated*: the percentage of readers that claim to have read the product and brand name.
- *Read most*: the percentage of readers that claim to have read at least half the ad.

Obviously the Starch test is very susceptible to the test subject's honesty. However, research reveals that high 'noted' scores are positively correlated with a positive attitude towards the brand (r = 0.43) and a positive intention to buy (r = 0.52).[11]

Figure 8.5 Post-testing techniques

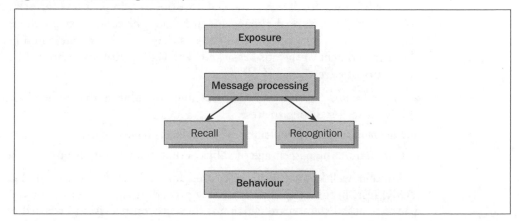

Figure 8.6 Masked identification test

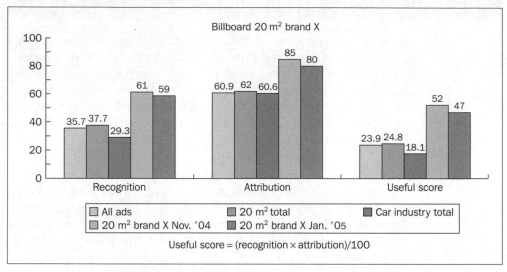

In a **masked identification test**, part of a print ad, usually the brand name, is covered. The subject is asked if he or she recognises the ad, and if he or she knows what brand it is for. Recognition and correct attribution scores can then be calculated. Obviously, brand confusion can be measured too. The combination of recognition and correct attribution scores leads to the useful score: the percentage of the consumer sample that both recognised the ad and attributed it correctly to the brand advertised. In Figure 8.6, an example of the results of a masked identification test of a billboard ad for a new car are shown, together with the results of a number of categories of control ads.

A second type of communications effect measurement is the **recall test**. In an unaided recall test consumers have to indicate which ads they remember having seen, in a specific magazine, on television or on billboards. In an aided recall test the consumer's memory is helped by means of clues such as: what car ads did you see on television yesterday? As such, the masked identification test can be regarded as an aided recall test. Unaided recall scores are usually lower than aided recall scores, which in turn are lower than recognition scores. Therefore they cannot be compared.

A well-known recall test is the **Gallup-Robinson Impact test** for print ads. First, the respondents have to read a magazine at home. The following day the respondents are called and asked to recall as many ads as they can. After that a number of questions about the content of the ads are asked. The Gallup-Robinson procedure leads to three indicators of advertising effectiveness:[12]

- *Proved name registration*: the percentage of subjects that remember an ad without having seen it during the test.
- *Idea penetration*: the extent to which subjects have understood the main idea in the ad.
- *Conviction*: the percentage of subjects that want to buy or use the product.

Another well-known recall test, used for audiovisual ads, is the **Day After Recall (DAR) test**. In this telephone interview procedure, a number of consumers are called. They are asked to indicate which ads they saw on television or heard on the radio the day before, within a certain product category. In the second stage, brand names are mentioned, and the respondent has to indicate if he or she remembers having seen or heard an ad for the brand. Additionally, a number of questions about the ad content are asked. The resulting percentages of correct recall are always compared with some kind of benchmark such as all commercials within the same product category, or all commercials of the day before. In the triple association test a product category and a selling proposition are given, and the respondent has to indicate a brand name, e.g. 'What brand of petrol puts a tiger in your tank?'

Finally, the effect of an ad can be tested by means of **behavioural measures**. Especially in the case of direct response advertisements, the number of people calling a free telephone number announced in the ad, sending back a coupon or actually buying the product can be considered a measure of the effectiveness of the ad.

Recall and recognition tests are useful and easy to carry out, but they have a number of severe limitations (Figure 8.7). In recognition tests, consumers can say what they like, they can lie, exaggerate or guess. This makes the results of recognition tests far from reliable. An ad that is part of a campaign of similar ads will be more easily recognised or recalled. In these circumstances it is very hard to isolate the effect of one single ad. The underlying assumption that recognition or recall of the ad eventually leads to buying the product may be erroneous. Recognising or recalling marketing communications may be a necessary condition to buy a product, but certainly not a sufficient one. Product involvement influences the results of the test. A consumer who is very interested in a certain product category will perform better in recognising ads for this product category. This does not imply anything about the effectiveness of that specific ad. Recall scores are very dependent on the time elapsed between exposure and recall measurement. Recall scores are nearly 100% immediately after exposure, but studies indicate that they drop to about 25% one day after, and to about 10% two days after exposure.[13] Rational mass appeals are recalled better than complex and/or emotional appeals, certainly after one exposure. Recall is in a number of cases an irrelevant indication of advertising

Figure 8.7 Limitations of post-testing

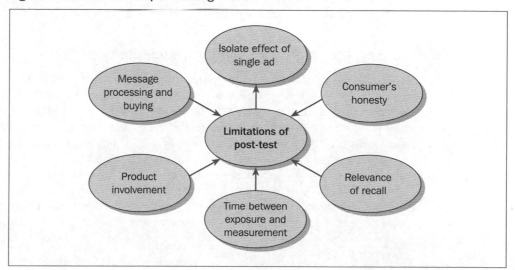

effectiveness. The only thing recall tests measure is whether the ad has been able to draw attention. Especially in cases in which it is sufficient for a consumer to recognise a picture or a brand in a shop to be inclined to buy the product, recognition tests are a much more valid and relevant measure of ad effectiveness than recall measurements.

Advertising campaign evaluation research

Contrary to post-tests in which the effectiveness of only one ad is assessed, campaign evaluation research focusses on the effectiveness of a whole advertising campaign. Campaign evaluation research tends to become increasingly more relevant than post-tests. Integrated marketing communications imply that it is very difficult or even irrelevant to assess the effects of one single medium or ad. Rather, the effects of the whole communications mix should be assessed.

In campaign evaluation tests, not ad-related responses, but brand-related effectiveness measures are focussed on. As in post-tests, a before or control measurement is necessary to assess adequately the effect of a particular campaign. Again, communications effects as well as behaviour effects can be measured.

Communications effects measurements can be structured following the hierarchy-of-effects logic: awareness, knowledge, attitude and intention to buy. Top-of-mind awareness (TOMA) measurement is an unaided awareness telephone test in which the consumer is asked which brand of a specific product category is the first one that comes to mind. Subsequently, the consumer is asked if he or she can name other brands in the same product category (again unaided awareness). Finally, a number of brands are mentioned, and the consumer has to indicate the ones he or she knows (aided awareness). The advertising campaign is not mentioned, but by comparing the awareness before and after a campaign, its effect on brand awareness can be assessed. Furthermore, brand awareness rates of competitive products are also measured, and can serve as a control measurement or benchmark.

Also attitude change or the change of the brand's image can be measured. Often a campaign aims at changing the target group's opinion about certain aspects or attributes of a brand. Scale techniques can be used to measure this change in image components.

Testing an image campaign for a telecom operator

In one European country[14] the mobile phone operator market is dominated by three competitors who's combined market share is almost 100%. The two largest companies have a combined market share of about 90%. The market splits into two important segments, i.e. pre-paid and post-paid. In terms of the number of clients, the pre-paid segment has grown much more rapidly than the post-paid segment. Initially, 100% of the market was post-paid. By 2002, two-thirds of the customers used prepaid cards. In 1996, the market leader had a relatively weak position in the pre-paid segment, and a very strong post-paid position. An image campaign was launched to build top-of-mind awareness, brand preference, emotional bonding and trust. Reliability and superior product quality (network, sound, number of clients, etc.) were stressed. Throughout the campaign, the campaign results were monitored. Chart 1 shows top-of-mind brand awareness of the three competing brands; in Chart 2 brand preference evolution is shown.

▶

Chart 1 Top-of-mind brand awareness

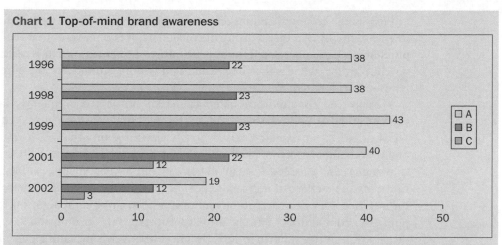

Chart 2 Brand preference

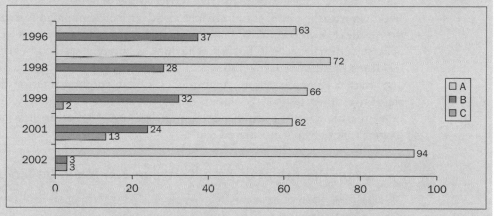

In Chart 3 the score of the market leader on a number of image attributes is given. The market leader has a better image than its competitors on all criteria measured.

Chart 3 Relative strengths of market leader

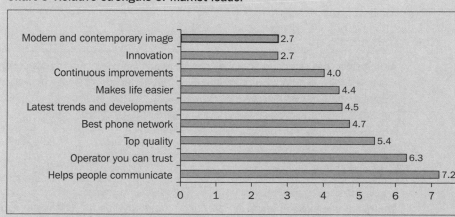

Finally, the communications effect of a campaign can be measured on the basis of the intention to buy of a target group of consumers. It is important that the question on the purchase intention is related to the near future or the next purchase, e.g.: 'The next time you buy coffee, what is the chance that you will buy brand X (as a percentage, or on a ten-point scale)?'

Most of the communications effect measurements are frequently used in tracking studies, in which comparable (random) samples of consumers are asked a standardised set of questions at regular intervals (e.g. every three months). As a result, the position of a brand and competing products can be tracked over time, and effects of subsequent campaigns can be assessed. As in all before–after measurements, problems of interpretation arise. The effect of a campaign cannot always be isolated. A deteriorating image, for instance, may be the result of, amongst others, a bad campaign, a price increase, bad publicity, competitors' actions, an inappropriate sales promotion campaign or a bad distribution strategy. Furthermore, the effect of advertising campaigns may only become visible after some time. The performance of a brand immediately after the campaign may therefore underestimate its true impact in the long run.

Obviously, the ultimate objective of an advertising campaign is to make people buy the product and eventually make a (better) profit. In behaviour tests the relation between advertising and buying behaviour is directly studied. Various behavioural measures of ad effectiveness can be distinguished, the most obvious ones being sales and market share evolution. Again, as in all campaign evaluation measurements, it should be noted that the evolution of market share and sales may be attributable to other marketing mix instruments than advertising. The effect of an advertising campaign cannot always be isolated easily.

How can the effect of an advertising campaign be isolated?

Isolating the effect of an advertising campaign is not always obvious. The following example illustrates this.[15]

A chain of do-it-yourself supermarkets launched a radio advertising campaign. The commercial results of the supermarkets look as follows (campaign in Year 2, Year 3 and Year 4):

	Year 1	Year 2	Year 3	Year 4
Sales	100	139	188	224
Annual growth of sales		+39%	+36%	+19%
Number of transactions	100	130	171	194
Ticket size	100	107	110	116

At first sight, this seems to be an impressive result. However, when a correction is made for the expansion of the number of supermarkets that increased in the period under consideration, the following picture emerges.

	Year 1	Year 2	Year 3	Year 4
Sales	100	131	159	183
Annual growth of sales		+31%	+21%	+15%
Number of transactions	100	128	165	189
Ticket size	100	106	110	118

The result still looks impressive, but not as impressive as the first set of figures in which the effect of a larger distribution network was included.

Apart from changes in sales, more specific behavioural effects can be measured, such as trial purchases and the degree of adoption of, or loyalty to, a brand.

The 'awareness–trial–retention' framework

An analysis combining awareness and behavioural measures to assess the effectiveness of advertising campaigns is the following. Three indicators are measured:

AR = AW/TG
TR = T/AW
ADR = A/T
AR awareness rate
AW number of target group members that are aware of the brand
TG number of people in the target group
TR trial rate
T   number of target group members that have purchased the brand at least once during a given period
ADR adoption rate
A   number of people that have purchased the brand at least a specific number of times during the same period

Evidently, the period under study and the number of times a consumer has to have purchased the product to be called a loyal consumer have to be determined in advance, and will depend upon the product category studied.

Suppose that for two competing brands the following results have been obtained after an advertising campaign:

	Brand A	Brand B
Awareness rate	70%	20%
Trial rate	40%	20%
Adoption rate	10%	70%

Obviously, the commercial end-result is the same for both brands: 2.8% of the target group have become loyal to the brand. However, the three indicators show a more differentiated picture. Brand B was not very successful in building awareness and trial. One might say that the advertising campaign was not very effective. On the other hand, the marketing strategy seems to be on target: most people who have tried the product have become loyal to it. Brand A has had a successful advertising campaign, but something seems to be wrong with the rest of the marketing strategy. Maybe the product is of bad quality, the price may be too high or the distribution strategy inappropriate. It could also be that the product is a luxury item, for which in the short run trial is more important than repeat purchase.

Most of the aforementioned measures of communications results are effectiveness measures, while marketers will also be interested in efficiency measurement, i.e. the extent to which the investment in an advertising campaign has had a commercial result. More specifically, marketers might want to know how many sales for every pound (or euro, or dollar) spent on communications has resulted. Over a longer period of time, data could be collected on advertising budgets and sales per time unit (three months, a year, etc.), and the relationship between the two may be estimated. This could result in the following:

$$S = 1.5 + 0.2 \times A$$

where: S = sales in € million
         A = advertising in € million

The conclusion would be that, over time, every euro invested in advertising has resulted in 0.2 euro of extra sales. Additionally, the cost function of the company may be modelled, in order to be able to calculate the profitability of the advertising efforts. However, advertising efforts usually have carry-over effects: the efforts of today do not lead to extra sales during the same period only, but also to extra commercial results in future periods. This effect may be modelled as follows:

$$S(t) = 1.5 + 0.2 \times A(t) + 0.8 \times S(t - 1)$$

where: S(t) = sales in period t
             A(t) = advertising investments in period t
         S(t − 1) = sales in period t − 1

The coefficient of S(t − 1) represents the effect of advertising investments in the past on this period's sales. This effect is assumed to decrease over time. The long-term effect of advertising can in this example be calculated as: 0.2/0.8 = 0.25. This implies that, in the long run, every euro invested in advertising leads to an increase in sales of 0.25 euro. The short-term effect of advertising on sales in the same period is only 0.20 euro.

Evidently, life is not so simple. First, sales are influenced by more than communications alone, so the model will have to be extended. Additionally, the competitors' efforts will have to be taken into consideration too. Consequently, estimating the profitability of advertising investments is a complicated task.[16]

Summary

Advertising campaigns can only be effective if they are accompanied by a well-structured research plan. Research can support the advertising activity in four stages of the advertising process. In strategic advertising research the advertising campaign is prepared by studying the marketing strategy, the competitive situation and the competitive environment it has to be embedded in. Techniques, such as the communications audit, competitor communications strategy research and communications content research are being used in this stage. During development of the advertising campaign, and before it appears in the media, the ads can be pre-tested. The major advantage of pre-testing is that it is a guide to better advertising. However, due to all kinds of limitations and the shortcomings of most of the techniques used, it can never lead to the best possible ad. Techniques used in pre-testing can be internal, such as the readability analysis, or external (with consumers), such as physiological tests, recall tests and direct or indirect opinion measurement. After a specific advertisement has been placed in the media, post-tests can be carried out, such as exposure, recall and recognition tests, and behavioural measures. Well known test procedures, such as the

Starch test, the Gallup-Robinson impact test and the Day After Recall tests are used in post-testing. Not just a single ad can be tested, but a whole campaign. Campaign evaluation tests focus on the brand-related effects of the campaign, such as brand recall and recognition, attitude towards the brand, purchase intention and, most importantly, behavioural or commercial measures, such as trial, repeat purchase, loyalty, sales and market share.

Review questions

1 What are the major techniques used in strategic communications research?

2 Discuss ad pre-testing techniques. What are the objectives and limitations of these measurement procedures?

3 Discuss ad post-testing techniques. What are the objectives and limitations of post-testing?

4 What measures of brand-related campaign evaluation techniques can be used?

5 How can advertising efficiency be measured? Why is it so difficult to judge the effectiveness and efficiency of an advertising campaign?

Further reading

Aaker, D., Kumar, V. and Day, G.S. (2001), *Marketing Research*. New York: John Wiley & Sons.

Malhotra, N. (1999), *Marketing Research, an Applied Orientation*. Upper Saddle River, NJ: Prentice Hall.

McDonald, C. and Vangelder, P. (1998), *ESOMAR Handbook of Market and Opinion Research*. Amsterdam: ESOMAR.

Case 8

Building added brand value for Smiths and transferring it to Lay's

The in-home snacking market

In Belgium, potato crisps are primarily eaten at home: 60% of crisp consumption is at home, after 6 p.m. In the 1980s and 1990s the in-home snacking market became increasingly competitive. Variation is an important driver in this product category. New competitors and appealing product concepts have emerged. As a result of the trend towards more healthy food, vegetables, cheese, olives, etc. have also become a part of the evening snacking habit. In Case Figure 8.1 the structure of the snacking market is presented. All potato crisp brands have basically the same product range, flat crisps and ribbed crisps, and they all have the same 'success flavours': salt, pepper, and pickles.

A commodity product, dominated by private labels

Case Table 8.1 shows the market share of the two most important manufacturer brands on the Belgian

Case Table 8.1

Market shares on the salty crisps market in Belgium, 1997

	Share of market (% volume)	Share of market (% value)
Smiths	28.8	38.1
Croky	23.5	29.7
Private labels	41.4	25.1
Other	6.4	7.1

Case Figure 8.1 The snacking market

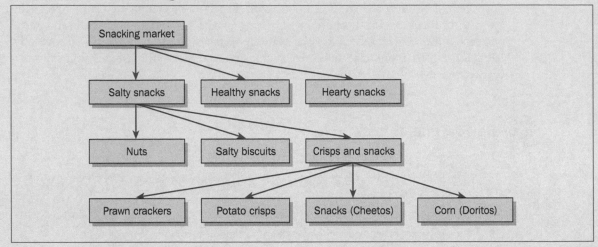

market and of the private label brands. Because of the price premium, Smiths (a FritoLay brand) is the market leader in value. Compared with some of the new successful products, the consumer perceives potato crisps as a low added-value product. Attempts to launch new crisp concepts in 1996 and 1997 failed. The consumer does not see the difference between the quality of manufacturer brands and private labels, and consequently is not prepared to pay more for a manufacturer brand. In 1995 only 16% of consumers agreed with the statement that Smiths crisps were worth paying more for, and only 12% that Croky chips were worth paying extra for. Marketing efforts traditionally focus upon sales promotions, but the production volume of Smiths has remained relatively stable over time. Between 1982 and 1997, the volume has only increased by 28%.

Building brand awareness, image, sales and market share

From 1998 onwards the Smiths brand has been supported by an image campaign, aimed at building brand awareness and brand preference, and stressing image components such as fun, modern, popular, irresistible, high quality, dynamic, and worth paying extra for. A series of humorous television and cinema spots was created. The ultimate goal was to strengthen the position of Smiths as a market leader. In 2000 it was decided to change the brand name to Lay's. From the beginning of 2001 onwards, this re-branding decision was implemented, and the objective

was to carry over the Smiths brand awareness and brand image to Lay's.

The communications objectives were as follows:

- Increase the relevant image parameters by 50% compared with 1995. Two types of image parameters were discerned:
  - *Expressive*: fun to eat, modern and popular brand
  - *Instrumental*: high quality, worth paying more for.

- The image gap with Croky should increase substantially.

- The day-after recall of each spot should score above product category mean.

- By the end of 2001 the aided brand awareness of Lay's should be at least at the same level as Smiths was at the end of 2000.

The commercial objectives can be summarised as follows:

Case Table 8.2
Market shares of Smiths/Lay's and its competitors

	Market share in volume (%)				
	1997	1998	1999	2000	2001
Smiths/Lay's	28.7	30.7	35.5	36.3	39.6
Croky	23.5	19.6	17.0	15.9	12.8
Private labels	41.4	44.3	42.4	43.1	42.6
Other	6.4	5.4	5.1	4.7	5.0

Case Table 8.3 Volume and value growth of total market and Smiths/Lay's

	Index volume growth		Index value growth	
Year	Market vs 1997	Smiths/Lay's vs 1997	Market vs 1997	Smiths/Lay's vs 1997
1997	100	100	100	100
1998	107	114	108	115
1999	107	133	113	135
2000	114	144	121	142
2001	126	174	137	177

Case Table 8.4 Day-after recall of Smiths/Lay's television spots and attitude towards the ad

Percentage of people:					
	Objective	Spot 1	Spot 2	Spot 3	Spot 4
Useful score (ad recognition and correct attribution of brand to ad)	30.2	35.0	34.0	32.0	31.0
Likeability	50.0	74.0	53.0	59.0	54.0
Percentage of people agreeing:					
	1995	Objective	Lay's 2001	Croky 2001	Gap
Makes good ads	7	Not given	42	14	28

- To increase volume market share to 35%, implying a growth of sales of 25%, and retain the market share after re-branding.
- To increase the market share gap with Croky.
- To stop the private label growth.
- The increased sales should not be the result of price cuts and promotions; volume and value growth should increase to the same extent.

All of these objectives should be reached by the end of 2001.

Results

In Case Tables 8.2 and 8.3 the commercial results are shown. In Case Table 8.2 market shares are presented. Case Table 8.3 shows the evolution of volume and value growth of both the total market and Smiths/Lay's. Not only did Smiths reach its objectives, it also claims that the whole product category revived as a result of the campaign. In Case Table 8.4, day-after recall results are shown of the various television spots. In Case Table 8.5 the evolution of brand awareness is shown, and Case Table 8.6 presents the evolution

of the image of Smiths/Lay's compared with the largest manufacturer brand, Croky.

The marketing management of the brand claims that these results should be exclusively attributed to the advertising campaign. There were no price changes during the campaign; the promotional activity remained the same (one sales promotion campaign per year); the R&D strategy did not change; the distribution coverage remained the same. The difference was made as a result of active brand-building by means of an image advertising campaign. Smiths/Lay's won a bronze Effie Award in Belgium in 2002.

Case Table 8.5
Evolution of brand awareness of Smiths/Lay's, end 2001

	Objective (%)	Result (%)
Top-of-mind	Not given	16.0
Unaided	53.0	50.1
Aided	85.0	97.7

Case Table 8.6 The evolution of the brand image of Smiths/Lay's and Croky

	Percentage of people agreeing				
	1995	Objective	Lay's 2001	Croky 2001	Gap
Expressive:					
Fun to eat	40	60	45	24	21
Modern brand	30	45	59	29	30
Popular brand	41	61	62	24	38
One of my favourites	28	42	53	30	23
Instrumental:					
High quality	48	72	74	42	32
Worth paying more for	16	24	50	22	28

Questions

1 Would you say Smiths did enough strategic communications research upon which to build its advertising strategy? If not, what other information could have been useful to prepare its campaign?

2 No pre-test research results are reported. If you were asked to conduct pre-tests, what types of pre-tests would you use, and what would you try to find out?

3 Do you think that the post-tests that Smiths conducted are appropriate? What do you think of the recall and attribution results that are reported? What else could have been measured?

4 Are the campaign evaluation tests appropriate? Should they have focussed on other types of tests or questions? If yes, which ones?

5 Have the objectives of the campaign been met? Are the results of the campaign impressive in all respects? If the latter is not the case, what could be the reason?

Based on: Effie Book Belgium 2002, AC Nielsen Scantrack, Research & Marketing, CBEM.

References

1 Rossiter, J.R. and Percy, L. (1987), *Advertising and Promotion Management.* New York: McGraw-Hill.

2 Pickton, D. and Broderick, A. (2001), *Integrated Marketing Communications.* Harlow: Financial Times/Prentice Hall.

3 Ferrée, H. (1989), *Groot Inspiratieboek voor Creatieve Reclame (Great Inspiration Book for Creative Advertising).* Deventer: Kluwer Bedrijfswetenschappen.

4 Fill, C. (2002), *Marketing Communications: Contexts, Strategies and Applications.* Harlow: Financial Times/ Prentice Hall.

5 van Raaij, F.W. (1989), 'How Consumers React to Advertising', *International Journal of Advertising,* 8(3).

6 See also: de Houwer, J. (2001), 'A Structural and Process Analysis of the Implicit Association Test', *Journal of Experimental Social Psychology,* 37, 443–51; Maison, D. (2002), 'Using the Implicit Association Test to Study the Relation Between Consumers' Implicit Attitudes and Product Usage', *Asia Pacific Advances in Consumer Research,* 5.

7 For an overview of physiological tests; Hansen, F. (1998), 'Advertising Research: Testing Communication Effects', in McDonald, C. and Vangelder, P. (eds), *ESOMAR Handbook of Market and Opinion Research.* Amsterdam: ESOMAR, 653–724.

8 De Cock, B. and De Pelsmacker, P. (2001), 'Emotions Matter', in *ESOMAR, Excellence in International Research.* Amsterdam: ESOMAR, 63–88.

9 Aaker, D., Kumer, V. and Day, G. (2001), *Marketing Research.* New York: John Wiley & Sons.

10 Aaker, D., Kumer, V. and Day, G. (2001), *Marketing Research.* New York: John Wiley & Sons.

11 Zinkhan, G.M. and Gelb, B.D. (1986), 'What Starch Scores Predict', *Journal of Advertising Research,* 26(4), 23–6.

12 Duncan, T. (2002), *IMC. Using Advertising and Promotion to Build Brands.* Boston: McGraw-Hill/Irwin.

13 Rossiter, J.R. and Percy, L. (1987), *Advertising and Promotion Management.* New York: McGraw-Hill.

14 Due to confidentiality requirements, the country and companies involved are not given.

15 Due to confidentiality requirements, the name of the supermarket is not given.

16 For modelling approaches in advertising research: Leeflang, P., Wittink, D., Wedel, M. and Naert, P. (2000), *Building Models for Marketing Decisions.* Boston: Kluwer Academic Publishers; Hanssens, D.M. Parsons, L.F. and Schultz, R.L. (2001), *Market Response Models. Econometric and Time Series Analysis.* Norwell, MA: Kluwer Academic Publishers.

Chapter 9

Sales promotions

Chapter outline

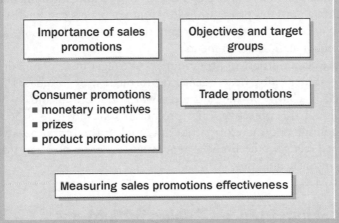

Importance of sales promotions

Objectives and target groups

Consumer promotions
- monetary incentives
- prizes
- product promotions

Trade promotions

Measuring sales promotions effectiveness

Chapter objectives

This chapter will help you to:

- Understand why sales promotions are an increasingly important instrument in the communications mix
- Learn about the various types of promotions and their objectives and target groups
- Distinguish between the various consumer and trade promotion tools, and their advantages and disadvantages
- Learn about the techniques to measure sales promotions effectiveness

Introduction

Unlike many other instruments in the communications mix, sales promotions are a category of techniques aimed at increasing sales in the short run, and therefore mostly used for a short period of time. Essentially, sales promotions are 'action communications' to generate extra sales, both from existing customers purchasing more products and by (temporarily) attracting new customers, on the basis of a temporary incentive or deal. The main characteristics of promotions are that they are limited in time and space, they offer better value for money and they attempt to provoke an immediate behavioural response. Although in sales promotions lead and lag effects can be distinguished, their effectiveness can be evaluated more directly than that of advertising and many other marketing communications instruments.

Although the main purpose of promotions is to trigger immediate sales, they can also be used more strategically, i.e. to generate, through trial purchases and subsequent learning effects, a change in the attitude towards the brand and, as a result, brand loyalty. In spite of this objective, sales promotions are often regarded as a threat to the long-term image and therefore profit potential of the brand because too frequent promotional actions give the brand a reputation of 'cheapness' and destroy the perception of its intrinsic qualities.

The growing importance of sales promotions

Sales promotions are becoming an increasingly important instrument of the communications mix.[1] In 1980 American companies spent 44% of their advertising and promotions budget on advertising. Twenty years later in the US, still more money is spent on promotions than on advertising.[2] A similar situation exists in Europe. In the UK, for instance, estimates suggest that promotion budgets exceed advertising spends. Some sources claim that the advertising to sales promotion expenditure ratio has evolved from 60:40 in the mid-1980s to 30:70 in favour of sales promotions.[3] This evolution can be attributed to a number of factors (Figure 9.1).

In an increasing number of product categories, more and more brands and product lines are offered. For the consumers it is becoming increasingly difficult to distinguish brands on the basis of their intrinsic qualities. Furthermore, functional differences between brands have become less important. Therefore, manufacturers find it increasingly difficult to differentiate their brands on the basis of advertising. Promotion is seen as a useful tool to attract the attention of target groups and to 'seduce' them into buying their brands. It is increasingly difficult to reach the consumer effectively by means of advertising. Individual ads get lost in communications clutter, and are hardly noticed by the majority of consumers. Therefore, marketers are looking for other tools to attract the consumer's attention to their brands.

Consumers, at least for certain fast-moving consumer product categories, are less brand loyal, and are becoming increasingly price-conscious.[4] This results in an increased response to material incentives, such as promotions. The majority of buying decisions take place within the retail outlet. An increasing number of product or brand purchasing decisions are essentially impulse-buying decisions. Since communications efforts are

Figure 9.1 Factors affecting the increasing use of sales promotions

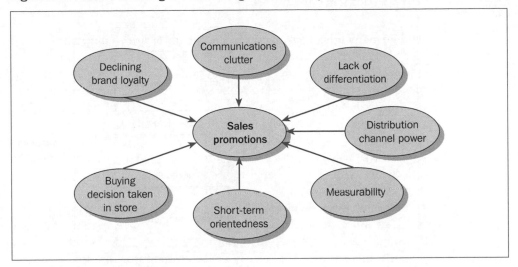

most effective at the time and place when and where the consumer makes his or her decision, in-store promotions become more attractive tools of persuasion.

Companies are becoming increasingly short-term oriented. However, the effects of traditional advertising campaigns only become visible in the long run. Product managers who want to see immediate results from their communications efforts will therefore be tempted to use promotion tools rather than long-term thematic advertising campaigns. The result of a promotion campaign can be more easily measured than that of an advertising campaign. Advertising is often aimed at obtaining intermediate effects, such as awareness and favourable attitudes, eventually leading to increased sales. Promotions are aimed at an immediate behavioural response, which can be readily measured. The immediate availability of results for most product managers is a very welcome characteristic of promotions. Finally, distribution channels are becoming increasingly powerful. Many brands are jostling for shelf space and, as a result, retailers are in a position to decide which brands will obtain shelf space under which conditions. Often, promotional tools are used to persuade the trade channel. Furthermore, the distribution channel is taking an increasing part in the promotional activity of manufacturers.

Objectives and target groups

Based on the initiator of the promotions and his target groups, several types of promotions can be distinguished (Figure 9.2). The initiator of the promotions can be either the manufacturer or the retailer. Promotions can be aimed at three types of audiences: distributors, the salesforce and the end consumer. Normally, retailers only promote to end consumers, whereas manufacturers can target their efforts at all three target groups. This results in four types of promotions:

- consumer promotions by manufacturers;
- consumer promotions by retailers;

Figure 9.2 Basic types of sales promotions

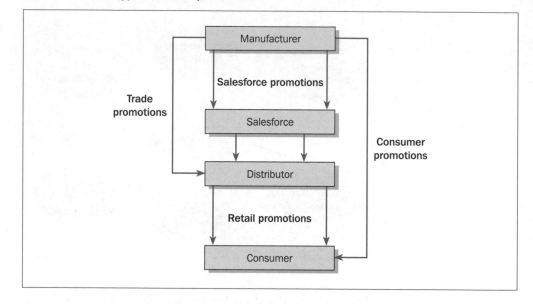

- trade promotions by manufacturers, aimed at distributors;
- salesforce promotions by manufacturers.

The first two types are essentially similar in nature, since they are aimed at the end consumer. Specific tools of retail promotion are discussed in Chapter 12 on in-store communications.

From trade to consumer promotions?

Recently there have been reports that, especially in food marketing, trade promotions are tending to gain in importance at the expense of consumer promotions. This evolution is attributed to the previously mentioned intensified battle for shelf space and the growing power of the distribution channels. However, a trade promotion survey of the food industry in the US showed that, on average, the allocation of funds between trade promotions and consumer promotions has not significantly changed between 1997 and 2002. The relative importance of trade promotions has only marginally decreased by two points to 49% of the total promotion and advertising expenses in 2002. The share of advertising has remained stable at 24%; consumer promotions have increased in importance to 27%. There are indications, however, that marketers are trying to monitor all their promotion efforts to ensure more impact. In trade promotion, this means that there is a shift in budgets from generic ads and displays to co-marketing partnerships with retailers (e.g. in-store events like demonstrations and recipe programmes), in which the latter also have to invest. Shifting the promotion focus from trade to consumer promotions does not necessarily work. For instance, Heinz suffered share and volume declines as a result of shifting its efforts to 'keep the consumers in the forefront'. It had to acknowledge that many of its products benefit more from trade efforts than from consumer-oriented campaigns.[5]

Figure 9.3 Objectives and target groups of consumer promotions

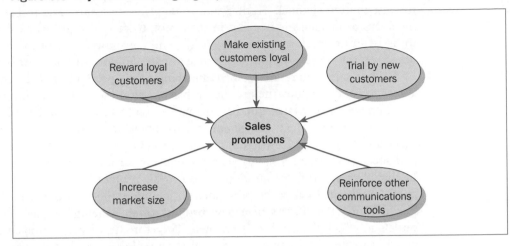

Consumer promotions can have several objectives and target groups[6] (Figure 9.3). Potential new customers can be attracted to try the product. Inducing trial by new customers is one of the most important objectives of a promotion campaign. This 'horizontal' effect results from brand-switching (i.e. consumers of competing brands purchase the promoted brand), or from attracting consumers who have never tried the product category before. The latter group is seldom inclined to try a product on the basis of consumer promotions alone. Trial promotions are particularly important when launching a new brand or a new item in a product line. When a retailer opens a new store, trial promotions (in this case by the retailer) can be an important tool to generate store traffic, in other words to make consumers enter the store.

Existing customers can be made loyal, and loyal customers can be rewarded for their loyalty. For a marketer it may be more important (and certainly less expensive) to retain a (loyal) customer than to convince a competitor's client to switch brands. Therefore, promotions are frequently aimed at inducing repeat purchase or rewarding loyal customers to stop them trying a competitor's product on promotion.

Promotions can be used to increase market size, as such, by stimulating the use of an entire product category. Promotions of this type are particularly suitable for market leaders who benefit most from a growing market or from a market without seasonal fluctuations. Examples are last-minute offerings, or selling ice cream during winter. Another way of inducing this 'vertical effect' of market growth is to increase sales with existing consumers. Consumer 'basket-filling' (e.g. by giving discounts when large volumes are purchased) not only increases sales, but also serves as a buffer against competitors' actions. As long as the consumer has sufficient stock of the product he or she may be less inclined to try a competitor's promotional efforts.

Finally, promotions can serve as reinforcers of other communications tools. An advertising campaign can have a greater impact if a promotion is included. The response to a direct mailing campaign may be much more effective if the mail is linked to a promotional offer. This symbiotic effect is often counted on in mail order catalogue selling.

The effect of marketing efforts are increasingly dependent on the co-operation of the distribution channel. To that end, trade promotions are used to persuade channel members to include the product in their mix, to give it appropriate shelf space, and to assist in promoting the product to the end consumer. One of the most important objectives of trade promotions is to gain the support of the distribution channel, both wholesaler and retailer, when launching a new product. In order for an end consumer to be able to buy the product, it has to be on the shelves in sufficient quantities and in a sufficiently large number of retail stores. Since the number of new brands is increasing steadily, the trade channel has to choose which ones to carry in their assortment and to promote. In that case trade promotions precede consumer promotions, and successful trade promotion is a prerequisite for an effective new product launch. In that respect, trade promotion is also 'trial' promotion in the sense that the distribution channel has to be persuaded to include the new product in its assortment. Furthermore, the success of a new product often depends on the number of retail outlets in which the product is on shelf. Therefore, trade promotions are often aimed at intensifying distribution in terms of the number of outlets in which the product is available.

For existing products, it is useful to keep the trade channel motivated to sell the brand. Trade promotions are aimed at maintaining shelf space or at inducing the retailer to promote the product by means of retailer promotions. One way to motivate the trade channel to push the product is by increasing its stock. Full warehouses induce the trade to pay more attention to selling the products in stock, i.e. to give them more shelf space and to promote the products actively themselves. On the other hand, trade promotions can be used to decrease the stock of a product in the trade channel rapidly, e.g. when a new product launch is being prepared.

In a more general sense, trade promotions are used to keep the distribution channel loyal to a product (category). Much as in the case of 'rewarding' the consumer for loyalty to a brand by means of consumer promotions, the distribution channel may be rewarded for its loyalty in giving shelf space to a product by means of trade promotions.

The salesforce is an integral part of the distribution effort, since they are the first link in the distribution channel. As a result, offering them incentives to market the product well is a vital first step in any marketing strategy. The most important objectives of salesforce promotions are to induce the salesforce to approach new customers, more specifically members of the trade channel, to try the product, or to increase the volume purchased by existing customers. In industrial marketing situations, new final customers can be the target.

The salesforce can also be encouraged to push new or existing brands as part of an integrated short-term sales promotions effort, or as a support to an advertising campaign. As in consumer promotions, a synergetic effect between salesforce promotions and other communications tools, such as advertising, can be established. Finally, the salesforce can be motivated to help the distribution channel to improve the exposure of the brand, by giving it more and better shelf space, keeping the shelves filled, checking stocks, and pushing and improving the use of displays and other in-store communications material.

Depending on the objective of the promotions, a number of specific tools can be used. An overview of consumer and trade promotion techniques is given in the following sections.

IMC promotions

Promotions can be very creative, and can result in synergetic effects with other communications tools. Two examples of so-called offbeat promotions illustrate this.[7]

■ As a promotional stunt for **Dare**, a perfume brand, the Daring Adventure Programme was launched. Women were invited to write a story about their most intimate and adventurous dates. The winning stories were published in a booklet that was given as a premium to all buyers of Dare perfume. The campaign attracted a lot of media attention, trial purchase and consumer involvement.

■ **Odor Eaters** insoles organise a contest every year to award a prize, the Order of the Golden Sneaker, to the most stinking shoes. The name of the owner of the shoes is cited in the Hall of Fumes, and receives a cash prize. The shoes are exhibited in stores selling Odor Eaters. Again, the campaign results in a lot of publicity, consumer involvement and store traffic.

Consumer promotions

Depending on the type of incentive, three categories of consumer promotions can be distinguished, i.e. monetary incentives, product promotions and the chance to win a prize (Table 9.1).[8]

Table 9.1 Consumer promotion tools

Monetary incentives	Chance to win a prize	Product promotions
■ Price cut on the shelf	■ Contests	■ Sampling
■ Coupons	■ Sweepstakes and lotteries	■ Free in mail
■ Cash refunds		■ Premiums
■ Extra volume		■ Self liquidators
■ Savings cards		■ Savings cards

Monetary incentives

Different types of monetary incentives can be used, but they all lead to an improved price/quality perception by the consumer by lowering the price of the product.

The most direct monetary incentive is the price cut on the shelf in which the consumer gets an immediate discount when buying the product. This is the most immediate and simplest price promotion for the consumer, the manufacturer and the retailer. It can be used to generate trial, stimulate repeat purchase behaviour and for 'basket-filling' purposes. The advantage for the consumer is that the price cut is immediate and unconditional. The manufacturer can easily and quickly organise sales promotions of this type, and it does not lead to extra workload for the retailer. Furthermore, price cuts on the shelf almost invariably lead to additional turnover.

On the other hand, there are a number of disadvantages, the most important being the potential damage to the image of the product and the store. Although promotions always run the risk of damaging a brand's high-quality image, this is more specifically the case with immediate and directly visible price cuts. Consumers may doubt the quality of the product or the store in which too many price cuts are offered. When price cuts are used too frequently, the company runs the risk of selling discounts rather than products. Furthermore, too frequent price cuts influence the consumers' expectations of the normal price of a product: no price cuts may be perceived as price increases. Price cuts can be very expensive for both the manufacturer and the retailer. Large extra volumes may be required to compensate for the loss of margin per unit. Therefore, although the promotion campaign may be successful in terms of extra volume or extra trial, its profitability may be far from impressive.

Coupons are vouchers representing a monetary value with which the consumer can get a discount on a specific product. Coupons may be inserted in print ads, in direct mailings, or in newspapers and/or magazines. They can also be offered on-pack, in-pack or near-pack, or be distributed after a previous purchase. Normally, coupons have a limited lifetime. The percentage of coupons distributed that are used when buying a product is called the redemption rate. Coupons have been a promotional strategy for more than 100 years. By 1965 in the US more than 350 manufacturers were distributing 10 billion coupons annually. In 2001 it was estimated that 3,000 manufacturers distributed 310 billion coupons. Redemption rates are, on average, lower than 2%.[9] To increase the redemption rate and lower the cost of coupon distribution, more targeted procedures can be used, as illustrated below.

Database technology improves the effectiveness of sales promotions

Computer technology, barcode scanning and individualised store cards can be used to generate powerful databases, on the basis of which tailor-made couponing campaigns can be organised.[10]

- In Dahl's Food Supermarket, customers can become a member of the **Vision Value Club**. The computer chip in the individual store card immediately registers the purchases at the checkout, and the consumer can, by means of a touch screen, immediately check which coupons are available, and print the ones he or she is interested in.

- A similar system has been tested by Prisunic (Lille, France). By means of interactive touch-screens throughout the store and a personal store card the consumer can immediately print the coupons he is entitled to on the basis of his past purchasing pattern. Suggestions can even be made as to a combination of purchases of e.g. food items that give the opportunity to obtain extra coupons.

- A number of manufacturers of fast-moving consumer goods organise mailings in Belgium under the name of **Sophie's Shopping Club**. Consumers are asked to fill in a questionnaire on their buying habits. The response rate was 12%, and 70% of the target group recall having received the mailing. Based on their answers €30 million of personalised coupons were distributed, the redemption rate of which was 9%, far better than in a traditional couponing campaign.[11]

As a promotional tool, coupons can serve a number of objectives, of which stimulating trial is a very important one. Couponing has the advantage that the consumer gets an immediate discount, provided that he or she has noticed and is prepared to use the coupon. The consumer does not have to do much to enjoy the promotion. Manufacturers can target a couponing campaign very well, in specific media and/or retail outlets, and for specific product categories and towards well-defined target groups. The retailer also benefits from couponing in the sense that it often generates extra sales. A problem with couponing is that it is often difficult to predict the redemption rate, and thus the couponing budget. Furthermore, instead of inducing trial, couponing may only have the effect of 'subsidising' already loyal customers. The latter is not necessarily a disadvantage, since 'basket-filling' by existing customers may be the primary objective of a couponing action. If the consumer is not price-sensitive, he or she will probably not notice the coupon or not use it, in which case the promotion action will be ineffective. Finally, the co-operation of the retailer is necessary since couponing means more work at the checkout.

The Procter & Gamble zero-couponing strategy

Procter & Gamble is one of the largest coupon distributors. In 1992 the company announced a new strategy. It decided to spend 50% less on couponing, and to adopt an EDLP (Every Day Low Prices) strategy, dropping retail prices by US$2 billion. In January 1996 the company launched an 18-month no-coupon test in a carefully chosen part of the state of New York, where 90% of the shoppers were known to use coupons. The vast majority of other manufacturers, retailers and wholesalers believed that this was a viable strategy, and some of them followed Procter & Gamble's lead. However, the no-coupon strategy was very unpopular among consumers. Many consumers considered coupons as 'an inalienable right'. Consumers in the test region started boycotts, public hearings and petition drives. Signs saying 'save our coupons' appeared in front gardens, and the local media were flooded with complaint letters to editors. The protests even made it into the national media. Public officials joined the protests, claiming that Procter & Gamble was the company of 'profit and greed' that hurt 'average Joe'. A resolution was voted to ask Procter & Gamble to abandon its strategy. Petitions with more than 20,000 signatures were sent to the company. After only 14 months, the company pulled the plug on its no-coupon test in April 1997. A settlement was agreed upon whereby US$4.2 billion worth of coupons was distributed that could be redeemed at any supermarket in the region by any consumer or for any food item. However, Procter & Gamble did not admit any wrongdoing. It still claimed that during the test period consumers received at least equally good value for money, without the cost and inconvenience of coupons. Nevertheless, the sales of Procter & Gamble were flat during the test period, while on average the use of coupons of competitors of Procter & Gamble and different product categories increased substantially. The company's experience has triggered new methods to distribute coupons. Instead of inserting them in media, more and more coupons are made available through shelf dispensers at the point of sale, in frequent buyer and loyalty programmes, in combination with free samples at the store, through direct mailings, the internet, or electronically at the checkout.[12]

Cash refunds are discounts offered to the consumer by means of refunding part of the purchase price after sending a proof of purchase. The refund is transferred to the customer's bank account. A cash refund is very similar to couponing in that it is mainly a trial-inducing promotion technique in which the consumer receives a price discount. Like couponing, the consumer has to do something, not by collecting coupons, but by sending back the proof of purchase.

Normally, cash refunds result in a more substantial discount than coupons. Therefore the resulting trial purchases tend to be higher. Furthermore, contrary to direct price cuts and couponing, the consumer has to pay the full price at the checkout. As a result, the consumer is less easily conditioned to expect lower prices and price expectations are less easily adjusted. As in the case of coupons, cash refund actions can be put in place very rapidly, and can be targeted to specific items of the product range. The main advantage for manufacturers is that the redemption of proofs of purchase enables them to build up a customer database. As compared to couponing, refunds do not result in extra work at the checkout. Therefore retailers prefer refunds to coupons.

Similar to couponing, it is difficult for the manufacturer to predict the success of a refund action, and hence the budget required. Again, there is the risk that existing customers will be subsidised instead of new customers being attracted. The main disadvantage for the consumer is that it takes more trouble to get the discount, especially if it means saving a number of proofs of purchase before part of the price is refunded. Sometimes the consumer has to wait a considerable time before the discount is refunded. Misunderstandings may occur if the consumer expects an immediate discount at the checkout or if it is not clear what part of the package the consumer has to send back to obtain the refund. The retailer may run the risk that the 'old' packages, of which no part of the price is refunded, are difficult to sell.

In **product plus** or **extra volume promotions** an extra quantity of the product is temporarily offered at the same price. In fact extra volume promotions are very similar to other types of price promotions since the price per unit of volume decreases. Promotions of this type are mainly used to induce 'basket-filling' by regular users. Consumers are not tempted to try a product for the first time if it is offered in larger volumes, quite the contrary. On the other hand, regular users may be attracted to the savings per unit proposition, and therefore buy more of the product.

Promotions of this type are very attractive for consumers since the advantage is immediate and unconditional. It does not result in extra workload or costs for the retailer, except the problem of fitting larger pack sizes onto the shelves. In terms of organisation, the product plus promotion is a very simple tool for the manufacturer. Follow-up campaigns are not necessary, and the promotion can easily be communicated on-pack or via an advertising campaign. The disadvantage is that extra volume promotions tend to be quite expensive. Special packages have to be designed, logistic problems may arise, and the extra volume sold does not always compensate for the implicit price cut. Retailers may experience logistic problems too, and may find it difficult to sell old stock without product plus promotion. Furthermore, as a result of the basket-filling, retailers may see a fall in sales after the promotion, since consumers have all the product they need for a while, and are not inclined to buy the same product immediately after the promotion. If this promotional tool is used too often or for too long, consumers' expectations as to the normal price/quantity rate may be conditioned in the wrong direction.

Award-winning promotions

The Esprix awards in the Netherlands make an award for the best promotion and direct marketing campaigns. Here are two examples of 2002 winners:[13]

■ During a certain period of time, a special edition of the women's weekly magazine *Margriet* was given as a premium to every consumer who purchased a Nivea Vital product. This ▶

special edition entirely focussed upon the 1970s to offer the target group a nostalgic flash-back to the time they were young and to create the right atmosphere to make the target group aware of the importance of the appropriate product for mature skin (Nivea Vital). The idea is based on the appreciation of a generation and its specific needs. The sales of Nivea Vital increased by more than 40%, and the promotion campaign resulted in market leadership for the brand.

■ During the period before the release of a Harry Potter movie, Coca-Cola offered each family in the Netherlands a special six-pack of 1.5l bottles of Coke in a special and unique Harry Potter packaging format. The pack was cheaper than a normal pack of six bottles because of retailers' discounts. The box was used to creatively communicate the campaign in-store in most supermarkets. After a couple of months almost 200,000 Harry Potter Coca-Cola boxes were sold and became part of the decor of Dutch children's rooms. A unique packaging concept has successfully created a bond between the soft drink and its target group.

Monetary incentives may also be offered on the basis of repeat purchase of a brand or in a store. Savings cards, possibly combined with trading stamps, are promotion techniques on the basis of which customers receive a discount provided they have bought a number of units of the brand during a specific period of time, e.g. 'buy 10 items during one year, and you get a 20% discount when you buy the 11th item', or when trading stamps are handed in at the moment of purchase. This tool is often used by shops to stimulate store loyalty. The system is not very convenient for consumers, since they end up with dozens of saving cards in their wallet or purse if lots of brands or stores are using this type of promotion. If they forget the card, the item bought cannot be put on it. Furthermore, the discount is not immediate, it may take a long time before the consumer experiences the benefits of his loyalty. The advantage of the system is that the consumer is not conditioned to an immediate lower price. Moreover, promotions of this type (retention promotions) are very suitable for generating brand or store loyalty, since the benefit is dependent on repeat purchase. It is a very flexible promotion technique, since the number of trading stamps offered per purchase can be adapted to the objective at hand, e.g. to stimulate the sales of a specific item in a product range, double stamps can be offered. However, this promotional tool implies a long-term commitment by the manufacturer. If a large part of the budget is tied up in retention promotions, the short-term flexibility to react quickly to competitors' actions is lost. The system is widely used by shops of all kinds. The positive side-effect of using store cards is that the retailer can build up a consumer database and the purchasing history of each consumer can be tracked, and can be used to make future promotions more effective. Store cards, combined with scanning of barcodes of goods purchased, lead to powerful databases which are improving the ability of the retailer to understand consumer behaviour.

Contests, sweepstakes and lotteries

Contests differ from sweepstakes and lotteries in that in the former the participant can influence the outcome of the game. Creating a slogan or an advertising headline, recognising a voice or a piece of music, estimating how many people will send back a coupon, etc., are examples of contests. Lotteries and sweepstakes are based purely on chance. In a sweepstake, consumers receive a (set of) number(s), the winning ones of which are decided on in advance. This means that, if only 10% of the customers having received a set of numbers participate by buying a product, only 10% of the prizes have to be awarded. Sweepstakes are frequently used by mail order catalogue companies. In some countries some types of sweepstakes are forbidden by law.

Chance games are easy to organise, relatively cheap and appealing to consumers, depending on how gamble-prone they are, which is to a certain extent culturally determined. Consumers have much to win and nothing to lose. Therefore, contests and lotteries can be relatively effective promotion tools, provided the prizes are attractive enough. On the other hand, the benefit for the consumers is not unconditional or immediate. They have to participate actively to have a chance of winning. Chance games and lotteries are also plagued by 'professional players', a group of consumers obsessed by the possibility of winning something, and who therefore participate in all campaigns. There is only a very slim chance that this type of consumer will ever become loyal to the promoted brand. Furthermore, contests and lotteries are seldom capable of generating trial purchases. As a result, the potential of promotions of this type in attracting new customers or generating loyal ones is rather weak. Retailers are not particularly inclined to co-operate in promotions of this type since they do not generate long-term benefits for the store either. Finally, in most countries legal restrictions on contests and gambling exist, which result in either straightforward and thus not so creative contests, or near-illegal situations.

Contests as sales promotion tools

The Bavaria brewery realised that its slogan 'OK, now first a Bavaria' was no longer well known in the Netherlands. To counter this, Bavaria decided to launch a promotion campaign. The objective was not so much to increase sales, but to make the brand top of mind again. To this end a photo competition was organised. Although there is nothing special about organising a photo competition, it is unusual to organise a photo competition that convinced more than 10,000 consumers to respond without the possibility of earning big prizes. The promotion ran between May and September 1998. To make consumers aware of the contest, TV commercials, print advertisements, stickers, flyers, displays, beer mats and dispensers which were distributed in buses to holiday destinations were used. Consumers were encouraged to take holiday pictures on the theme of Bavaria and to come up with the funniest 'OK, now first a Bavaria' picture. Every week a winner was announced whose picture was used in an advertisement in the newspaper De Telegraaf. Every person who submitted a photo received a set of fridge magnets. Every winner received a photo book of the promotion and one winner received the winning prize of €2,450. Bavaria succeeded in mobilising a lot of tourists to take pictures on its theme. Bavaria regained its original brand experience and despite a price increase, its market share has increased in a stable to decreasing market. The promotion campaign won a Silver Esprix Award in 1999.[14]

L'Oréal rolled out a roadshow for its Maybelline brand. The 'Make-up on the Go Tour' travelled the UK from May until October 2002. A contest was organised for 16 to 24 year old girls, the prime target group of the brand. Girls winning the 'Face of Maybelline' contest in their region got an expenses-paid trip to New York.[15]

Product promotions

In product promotions the consumer is offered products free, either as an incentive to buy a product, or as a reward for having purchased it.

Sampling is a promotion technique that consists of distributing small samples of a product, sometimes in a specially designed package free of charge or at a very low cost. Sampling can be done in many different ways. The product can be distributed in every mailbox, or delivered at home. This technique is especially suitable for products with very broad target groups. If more specific targeting is called for, the sample can be mailed to the addresses of carefully selected target groups, or can be distributed at events where the target groups congregate, e.g. sports arenas or cultural performances. The sample can also be distributed in certain media, e.g. the scratch-and-sniff samples of perfume in magazines. The sample can be included in the package of a (complementary) product of the same product line. In the latter case only existing customers of the product line are being reached, to make them try an extension of the product line. Sampling can also be combined with demonstrations in or near stores. In fact, this is to a certain extent a combination of personal selling and consumer promotions. A sales-person at a demonstration stand tries to 'seduce' shoppers to try the product (usually food or drink), hoping that they will go on to buy it.

Sampling is the ideal promotion tool for generating trial, especially in those cases in which the product characteristics cannot be communicated very convincingly by means of advertising, and/or in those cases in which it is possible for a potential customer to get an idea of the product's benefits on the basis of trying it in small quantities. A possible disadvantage is that manufacturing and distributing small samples in large quantities, or demonstrations at supermarkets, may be quite expensive, and may lead to logistic problems for both the manufacturer and the retailer.

With free in-mail promotions, the customer receives a (nearly) free gift in return for a proof of purchase which has to be sent to the manufacturer. In that sense, promotions of this type are very similar to the cash refund, the only difference being that the consumer receives a gift instead of money. The main purpose of this type of promotion is not to generate trial, but to reward loyal customers, or to improve the link between the consumer and the brand. Moreover, such promotions can generate a lot of valuable information for the construction of a database on the interests and consuming habits of (potential) customers. This information can be used for future marketing action, and is one of the major advantages of this type of promotion. The disadvantages are that the consumer does not derive an immediate benefit, the logistics may be very expensive and time-consuming, and the benefit for the retailer is non-existent, since promotions of this type do not improve the link between the product and the store.

Premiums may be offered in-, on- or near-pack. They are small gifts that come with a product, e.g. a free glass when buying a bottle of cognac, or a pair of sunglasses when buying two bottles of sun lotion. Sometimes the package itself is a premium, like marmalade in a glass that can be used afterwards. Premiums tend to be successful, since for most consumers getting something for free is a powerful incentive. Such promotions can be used to generate impulse buying and trial, to reward existing customers and to stimulate repeat buying by offering a series of premiums that can be collected, like a set of glasses or stickers.

Consumers like this type of promotion because the benefits are immediately visible and easy to obtain. The budgetary implications for the manufacturer are clear in advance, and a premium can be easily combined with other types of promotions. Furthermore, there are no extra handling costs after the promotion campaign. The advantage for the retailer is that a premium campaign can generate extra store traffic and extra sales.

When are premium-based promotions effective?

To gain a better understanding of consumer reactions to premium-based promotions, an exploratory qualitative study among 12 consumers and a survey among 182 adult consumers were held in France. The results show that the consumer appreciation of this type of promotions is more positive when the premium is direct than when consumers can obtain it at a later point in time. Consumers also appreciate premiums more when the quantity of product to be purchased to obtain the premium is lower, when the value of the premium is mentioned, and when the interest in the premium is great. The more positive the consumer's brand attitude is, the more positive he or she is about the premium. Consumers that are characterised by deal-proneness and compulsive buying tendencies are also more likely to have a positive attitude towards premiums. Consumer's perception of the manipulation intent of the brand offering the premium is lower when the premium can be obtained directly, when the value of the premium is mentioned, and when the consumer is deal-prone and has an interest in the premium.[16]

If the consumer fails to respond to a premium, the whole campaign may fail. Furthermore, the wrong kind of premium may damage the long-term image of the brand. Finally, there is always the risk that only existing customers are subsidised, and that no extra trial or basket-filling results. The disadvantage for the manufacturer is that the production, handling and logistics costs may be quite substantial. The retailer may experience difficulties in displaying the product with the premium. Especially with near-pack premiums, shelf space has to be provided, and the retailer has to check for consumer fraud. As in other types of immediate purchasing incentives, the old stock of the product may be difficult to sell. If the premium is a product that is also being sold by the same retailer (a glass, sunglasses, etc.), sales of these items may fall.

Self-liquidators or self-liquidating premiums are presents that can be obtained in exchange for a number of proofs of purchase, and an extra amount of money. Sometimes self-liquidators can be obtained in the store, but more frequently they have to be ordered by mail. Similar to free in-mail promotions, self-liquidators are mainly used to stimulate repeat purchase and brand loyalty, rather than to generate trial. The advantage for the consumer is that he can obtain products of relatively high quality at a minimum cost. On the other hand, he has to go to some trouble to obtain a product, the quality of which is unknown. Indeed, it may be difficult to find a premium that is appealing to the target group. For the manufacturer, the follow-up of the campaign may be cumbersome, but valuable information about the consumer is obtained. If well communicated in-store, the campaign generates attention, to the benefit of both the manufacturer and the retailer.

Finally, savings cards and trading stamps may be used not only to offer consumers a discount some time in the future, but also to offer a gift. As such, the characteristics, advantages and disadvantages of these promotions are similar to savings cards with a cash incentive.

Premiums that make an impact

Every Dutch owner of a middle-of-the-range car of between three and six years old might have found a scratch ticket on their car during the months November and December 1998. Daewoo sampling teams visited car parks, shopping streets and office buildings in order to find possible candidates. The sampling team detected 650,000 cars and put a scratch ticket together with a Daewoo flyer on the window. The ticket contained the number of the registration plate. Up to €4,500 could be saved when the owner exchanged his old car for a new one. Furthermore, one lucky person could win a new Daewoo. The result of the promotion was that Daewoo sold 1,400 new cars in December, 70% above the objective. This is a remarkable result during a month in which sales traditionally are very poor, for within a few weeks the car is already a year old. Daewoo won a Bronze Esprix award for its campaign.[17]

During the release of the Twentieth Century Fox film *X-Men* in 2002, Kellogg's ran an in-pack promotion that for the first time offered a metal premium in the cereals market. Children could collect a set of six X-Men metal ID tags. Research had shown that children were very keen on the idea of real metal ID tags because they saw them as trendy and aspirational.[18]

Different manufacturers may also co-operate to generate synergies between their promotional efforts (joint promotions). Similarly, a single manufacturer can offer a joint promotion for two different brands of his own. One item may be offered as a premium for the other, purchase proofs of different products may be requested to obtain a self-liquidator or a free in-mail present, and discounts may be made contingent on the purchase of different items at the same time. To increase the benefits for both the manufacturer and the retailer, they can co-operate in the organisation of promotion campaigns. Retailers can pay part of the manufacturer's promotion budget, perhaps in return for exclusiveness of the campaign in their stores, or they can provide the necessary in-store communication to draw attention to a promotion campaign. In Table 9.2 an overview is given of the different consumer promotions techniques, their main objectives, advantages and disadvantages.[19]

Trade promotions

Different promotion tools can be used to motivate the trade. They are summarised in Table 9.3.[20] Off-invoice allowances are direct price reductions to the trade, for instance during a limited period of time. They are the simplest form of trade promotions. The trade may receive a discount per unit purchased or a discount after he or she has sold a certain volume of the product. Discounts may also be given after a longer period of time, when a certain volume of sales has been reached (discount overriders). Also the count-recount method is retrospective in that the stock of the manufacturer's brand is counted at the beginning and at the end of a period, and a discount, for instance per case sold, is given. A slotting allowance is a one-time, up-front fee that is charged by retailers before they allow a new product on their shelves to cover the start-up costs of entering a new product into their system. Manufacturers often contest these allowances because they feel that they are subsidising the retailer's business. Advertising/performance allowances are monetary incentives aimed at encouraging the

Table 9.2 **Objectives, advantages and disadvantages of consumer promotions**

Promotion objectives	A	B	C	D	E	F	G	H	I	J
Generate trial	+	++	++	--	--	--	++	--	++	--
Induce repeat purchase	+	+	++		++	--	--	++	++	++
Basket-filling	++	+	+	++	+		--		+	
(Dis)advantages										
Direct consumer benefit	++	++	--	++	--	--	+	--	++	--
Ease of obtaining benefit	++	+	--	++	--	-	++	--	++	--
Impact on brand image and brand loyalty	--	-			++	-		+		+
Manufacturer's workload and problems	++	+	-	-	+	--	-	--	-	--
Impact on consumer's price perception	--	-	+	-	--	+				+
Ease of targeting	--	++	++	--	++		+	++	-	--
Ease of budget planning	--	--	--	++	-	+	++	++	++	-
Database support	--	--	++	--	++	++	--	++	--	++
Immediate increase in sales	++	+		++	-				+	
Impact on store image and store loyalty	-				++	--			+	
Retailer's workload	++	-	+	-	-		-	--	-	

++ very positive   + positive   – negative   –– very negative

A price cut on shelf	**F** contests, sweepstakes and lotteries
B coupons	**G** sampling
C cash refunds	**H** free in mail
D product plus	**I** premiums
E savings cards	**J** self-liquidators

Table 9.3 **Trade promotion tools**

- Off-invoice allowances
  - Individual case bonus
  - Volume allowance
  - Discount overriders
  - Count and recount
  - Free merchandise
- Slotting allowances
- Advertising/performance allowances
- Co-operative advertising allowances
- Buy-back allowances
- Dealer contests
- Dealer loaders

retailer to advertise the manufacturer's brand and are provided when proof of the ad is produced. In fact, the manufacturer pays part of the advertising campaign of the retailer. In some cases, a percentage of everything the retailer buys from a manufacturer is put into a co-operative advertising fund. The dealer adds an agreed-upon percentage to the fund, and uses it to advertise the brands of the manufacturer. To stimulate the retailer to put a new brand or a renewed version of the product on the shelves, the manufacturer sometimes offers to buy back the 'old' product, or commits to buying back the stock of the new product that is not sold during a specific period of time. This is called a buy-back allowance. To motivate retailers to sell more of the manufacturer's product, a contest among them may be organised in which, for instance, trips or other prizes can be won. In some cases, additional materials (dealer loaders) are offered during a promotional campaign, for instance, a refrigerator during a soft-drinks promotion. After the promotion, the retailer can keep the extra equipment.

Trade allowances result in a higher profit margin for the wholesaler or the retailer. This higher margin can (partly) be used to offer a discount to the end consumer by means of retail promotions, or to stimulate sales by means of more shelf space or other in-store communications tools. In those cases the trade promotions can eventually result in a favourable effect on end consumer purchases. If the (volume-based) trade allowance is used by the retailer only to increase inventory temporarily, the trade promotions will not result in an increase in sales to the end consumer. Although trade promotions have become increasingly important as a result of the growing power of the distribution channel, their effectiveness largely depends on the incentives given to the retailer to pass on the benefits to the end consumers and to stimulate short-term sales in-store.

Measuring sales promotions effectiveness

Sales promotions can be pre- and post-tested. Sales promotions pre-testing is very similar to advertising pre-testing. Consumers may be exposed to sales promotions ideas, in a focus group setting or elsewhere, and may be invited to express their opinion about them. However, since the objective of most sales promotions campaigns is to provoke immediate buying behaviour, most promotions research will focus on behavioural response measures. Promotions are essentially aimed at stimulating trial purchase and at increasing sales with existing consumers. Therefore, effectiveness measures will focus on the evolution of sales compared with non-promotion periods, or on the comparison of different types of promotions as to their ability to generate extra sales.

When launching a new brand, or monitoring the sales evolution of an existing brand for which sales promotion campaigns are being used, the following analysis using consumer panel data can be carried out.[21] It is based on a decomposition of the market share of the brand as follows:

Market share = (attraction × conviction × domination × intensity)/shock absorption

Attraction   = Number of buyers of our brand/total number of buyers of the product category.

Conviction   = Number of loyal customers of our brand/number of buyers of our brand.

Domination   = Average volume of our brand purchased per loyal customer of our brand/average volume of the product category purchased per loyal customer of our brand.

Intensity = Average volume of the product category purchased per loyal customer of our brand/average volume of the product category purchased per buyer of the product category. If the intensity rate = 1, the loyal customers of our brand are buying the same amounts of the product category as the average buyer of the product category.

Shock absorption = Total purchases in volume of our brand by loyal customers/total purchases in volume of our brand.

The definition of a 'loyal customer' is based on repeat purchase within a specified period of time. All indicators are measured per period (monthly, bi-monthly, etc.). All measures are volume-based. The attraction rate measures the penetration of the brand and is a measure of the effectiveness of trial promotions. The conviction rate gives an indication of loyalty promotions effectiveness, more specifically the success of repeat buying promotions campaigns. The domination rate indicates to what extent loyal customers are truly loyal. The higher the domination index the more exclusively loyal customers are loyal to a brand. It is an indication of the effectiveness of loyalty and basket-filling promotions. The intensity rate indicates the extent to which the brand is capable of attracting heavy users of the product category. If this indicator is larger than one, our brand is capable of attracting a more than proportional amount of heavy users. As such it is also an indication of the basket-filling capacity of promotional campaigns. The shock absorption index indicates to what extent our brand is vulnerable to competitive campaigns. The higher the shock absorption rate, the more our sales are based on loyal consumers, and the less vulnerable our brand is to switching behaviour caused by competitive actions.

The effectiveness of promotions is often assessed by studying the evolution of sales over a period of time during which several types of promotions have been implemented. By studying the evolution of sales during the campaign, and comparing it to the sales level before and after the campaign, the extra sales volume generated by the campaign can be calculated. This type of analysis will also reveal potential 'sawtooth' effects, which follow the 'post-promotion dip' which is often the result of some types of promotions. Basket-filling promotions may induce consumers to buy large quantities of the product on promotion, after which they have enough stock for a number of weeks or months, and sales drop sharply in the post-promotion period. This phenomenon is illustrated in Figure 9.4. Obviously, if the only net result of promotions campaigns is that the post-promotion dip entirely compensates for the extra sales during the promotions period, the only thing that has happened is that the company has given up part of its profit margin. The success of a promotions campaign can be judged on the basis of the size of the positive difference between the extra sales during the promotions period and the drop in sales during the post-promotion dip.

In Figure 9.5 another example, based on retail panel data, is given of the baseline sales of a product, calculated on the basis of medium-term 'normal' sales, and the sales effect of promotions campaigns in subsequent months.

Obviously, the only relevant measure of promotions effectiveness is its long-term profitability.

Figure 9.4 The sawtooth effect of sales promotions campaigns

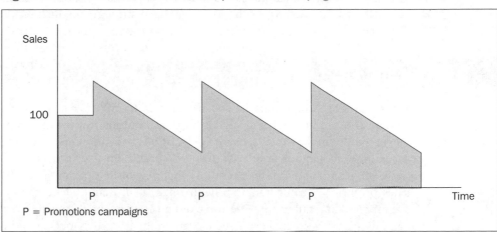

Figure 9.5 Baseline sales and the sales effect of promotions campaigns

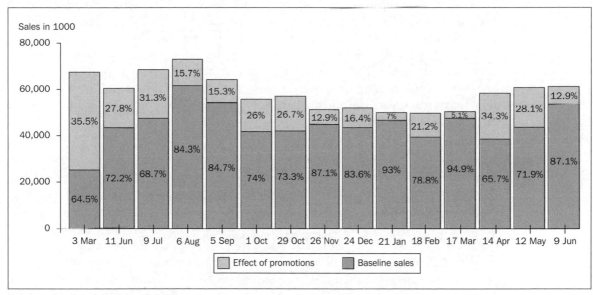

Based on: data from A.C. Nielsen Belgium.

Various studies lead to the conclusion that, although promotions may be effective in the short run, they result in negative effects in the long run. Competitive campaigns neutralise the short-term effects, and the only result is an increase in promotions costs for the same amount of sales, and stable, long-term market shares. Furthermore, promotions have the reputation of undermining the effect of more strategic marketing instruments, such as advertising and sponsorship, which try to build brand image in the long run. Therefore, some manufacturers increasingly rely on the 'every day low pricing'

(EDLP) strategy, aimed at maintaining a relatively low stable price for most of their products, as opposed to the 'high-low' (HILO) strategy in which frequent promotions are used.

Summary

Although sales promotions are sometimes used to influence business results in the long run, a sales promotions campaign is a category of instrument that is primarily used to increase sales in the short run. Sales promotions have become increasingly important as a result of communications clutter, less brand loyalty, the lack of differentiation between brands and the short-term orientedness of many companies. Different types of sales promotions campaigns can be distinguished, mainly depending on whether they are targeted at retailers, the salesforce or end consumers. By means of sales promotions, various objectives can be pursued: attracting new customers, making existing ones loyal, increasing market size, reinforcing other communications tools, and rewarding loyal customers. Consumer promotions can take different forms. Three basic categories can be distinguished: monetary incentives (coupons, extra volume, savings cards) prizes (competitions, sweepstakes and lotteries) and product promotions (sampling, free in mail, premiums). The choice between these specific techniques depends on the objectives of the sales promotions campaign. Are sales promotions effective? In the short run, a number of potential positive and negative results can be discerned. Promotions can increase trial, loyalty and profitability, but can also lead to deal-proneness, brand-switching, a post-promotion dip and negative effects on profitability. In the long run, the effects are unclear. The potential negative effect of sales promotions on brand image must be taken into account.

Review questions

1 Why are sales promotions becoming an increasingly important part of the marketing communications mix?

2 What are the objectives and target groups of sales promotions?

3 What are trade promotions used for?

4 What are the objectives of salesforce promotions?

5 Discuss the various tools of consumer promotions, their objectives and target groups, and the advantages and disadvantages for both the manufacturer and the retailer.

6 Describe the 'launch analysis' of a new product and how it can be used to assess the effectiveness of a sales promotions campaign.

Further reading

Cummins, J. and Mullin, R. (2004), *Sales Promotion: How to Create, Implement and Integrate Campaigns that Really Work*. Kogan Page Ltd.

Neslin, S.A. (2002), *Sales Promotion*. Marketing Science Institute.

Case 9

Fébrèze – safely eliminating odours

Fébrèze is one of Procter & Gamble's innovations in the fabric and home care market. After six years of research and testing, it was introduced in the US market in mid-1998, and proved to be very successful. Based on the US and UK test market results, P&G decided to enter the European market as well, launching Fébrèze in February 1999 in the UK, followed by France, Belgium and the Netherlands. This case study mainly concentrates on the launch of Fébrèze in the Netherlands and Belgium, which took place in March 1999.

In line with P&G's mission of manufacturing and marketing products 'that improve the lives of consumers around the world', Fébrèze tries to fill the need of removing odours from fabrics without having to wash them. In contrast with hard surfaces, like floors and counters, soft surfaces composed of fabrics are much harder to clean and take care of. These fabrics are everywhere: from upholstery, to carpets, curtains and canvas shoes. In fact, generally in Europe about 75% of the household surfaces that need routinely cleaning are made of fabrics. Fébrèze, a completely new product in the market, is an environmentally friendly spray that eliminates odours on fabrics. After using the spray, a fresh scent similar to a laundry detergent is left, which lasts a few hours to one or two days. Fébrèze is not intended to replace cleaning, but to refresh household items and clothing that are not dirty, but do not smell clean. Examples are pet odour in the sofa, cigarette or cigar smoke in curtains or clothes, and cooking smells in kitchen fabrics. Several of these product uses have been discovered during consumer testing. The women who were asked to test Fébrèze found all kind of uses for it around their homes. And the more they used it, the more possibilities they discovered. This made it increasingly difficult to develop a product that tackles all kinds of odours on all kinds of fabrics effectively.

Pre-tests in the Netherlands and Belgium

Before launching the product in the Benelux market, pre-tests were carried out to get an idea of how convincing and engaging the product was and how easy to remember. The pre-test results showed that recall of the strategic information in the advertisement was quite high: 77% for the Netherlands and 62% for Belgium. The level of how convincing and how engaging it was, was average. When respondents were asked for comments, they responded with statements such as 'Too good to be true', 'If it's true . . . !', 'Is the product safe for my fabrics, my family?' The objectives of another study were to identify trial barriers and credible third parties to help overcome trial barriers. The conclusions of the pre-tests were that, in the trial phase, first, P&G needed to get the product into the hands of consumers ('seeing/using is believing'); second, consumers needed to be reassured on safety (especially in the Netherlands); and third, the versatility of Fébrèze had to be stressed.

Communications strategy

In response to the results of the pre-test study, P&G decided to implement a strong trial plan, to include the word 'safety' in the selling line to reassure consumers on the safety aspect ('Fébrèze *safely* eliminates odours from fabrics'), and to use TV commercials 'Discover the Uses' fully focussing on the versatility of Fébrèze. The communications plan is shown in Case Figure 9.1.

The objectives of the advertising campaign were to:

1 Create an awareness rate of 80% after four months of advertising.

2 Generate trial by explaining the product/concept of Fébrèze, stressing its versatility, reassuring consumers on the safety aspect and telling them where they can find Fébrèze in the store (since it is a new product category).

3 Break through the media clutter by using 40-second TV ads in combination with a cut-down version of 10 seconds.

In different countries where Fébrèze had been launched, different selling propositions had been stressed. In the UK, one TV ad showed people in the living room spraying the product on the curtains which results in a cloud of freshness coming out of

Case Figure 9.1 The Fébrèze communications plan

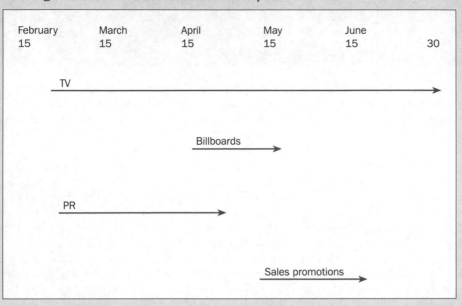

the curtains. Another ad shows the different possible product uses. In France billboards are used picturing clothes surrounded with a cloud of freshness. In the US one print ad illustrates how Fébrèze works its way into fabrics, leaving no trace. Another one shows a bottle of Fébrèze spraying all the possible product applications one after another: sofa, car, carpet, clothes and shoes.

Concerning the PR campaign, the problem of getting free media coverage was that even as a new product initially it was not very relevant to the press. Therefore, P&G had a research agency carry out an investigation on 'consequences of malodours in everyday life' with a special focus on newsworthy outcomes and differences in opinion between males and females, urban versus rural-dwelling people, and North versus South. Afterwards, a press conference was organised, both in the Netherlands and Belgium. First, the research agency presented the research results. Next, an external odour expert commented on the results and brought odours into a broader, more scientific context. Finally, the R&D and Marketing Department presented the Fébrèze concept. The research results confirmed that consumers think odours are important. About one in two consumers claim even to have left a room because of a bad odour. Futhermore, consumers realise that odours can have an influence on their social life (for example, bad odour as a reason for disliking someone). Odours are more important to Belgians than to Dutch people. Women as compared to men, and people under 50 as compared to older persons are more critical of odours, claim to perceive odours better and are more likely to think odours are important in their daily life.

Besides advertising and generating publicity, Fébrèze was also supported by a sales promotions campaign. The objective of the latter was to generate 30% household trial within the Benelux market. To this end samples of 100 ml bottles were distributed, among others, at the exit of supermarkets, with a leaflet stressing how to use Fébrèze correctly, how versatile and safe the product is, and that Fébrèze is available in 500 ml bottles to stimulate conversion. Three weeks after the sampling another sales promotions campaign was launched to prompt consumers to repurchase Fébrèze in a 500 ml bottle, consisting of a reduction of half a euro on every 500 ml bottle. By sustaining this price reduction, P&G could participate in the retailers' weekly brochures and the retailers could be more easily convinced to use POP material, such as displays. Furthermore, in-store product demonstrations were used. They demonstrated the product to consumers and mentioned that the product was on promotion. If the retailer did not carry a promotions programme, the consumers were given a coupon worth half a euro to persuade hesitant shoppers.

Results

One week after the start of the advertising campaign, the Benelux consumption was nine times higher than the week before. After two and a half months of advertising, awareness amounted to 60%. Only 3% mentioned safety as a barrier to trying Fébrèze. The PR campaign was quite successful as well: 60% of the Benelux shoppers aged between 20 and 49 were reached via free press and in-use shots (stills from the TV commercials) were frequently featured in the newspapers and magazines. According to P&G, the sales promotions campaign also proved to be effective. During the price reduction period, sales increased four-fold. The success rate of the product demonstrations ranged from good to excellent and mainly depended on the traffic of shoppers present in the store and the size of the supermarket.

Fébrèze has already been used by more than 25 million households around the world. The next challenge is to make this new product part of the daily cleaning routine of consumers.

Questions

1 What type of sales promotions did P&G use during the launch of Fébrèze?

2 Would you have chosen another type? If so, why?

3 Is it a good idea to launch a product like Fébrèze using price incentives?

4 Would you advise P&G to continue to use sales promotions after the introductory period? What are the advantages and disadvantages of repeated promotions?

5 How important do you think trade promotions versus consumer promotions were for introducing Fébrèze?

6 How would you advise P&G to test the effectiveness of its sales promotions?

Based on: Documents provided by Arnaud Demoulin, Customer Marketing Manager, Valérie Van Geel, Assistant Brand Manager, and Jochem De Boer, Assistant. Brand Manager, P&G Belgium–the Netherlands. A paper prepared by Ambrogio Foscarini, student of the Postgraduate Programme in Management, Free University of Brussels, Belgium. http://www.febreze.com/html/facts.html. Reproduced with permission of Procter & Gamble.

References

1 See also Papatla, P. and Krisnamurthi, L. (1996), 'Measuring the Dynamic Effects of Promotion on Brand Choice', *Journal of Marketing Research*, 33 (February), 20–35; Mela, C.F., Gupta, S. and Lehmann, D.R. (1997), 'The Long-Term Impact of Promotion and Advertising on Consumer Brand Choice', *Journal of Marketing Research*, 34 (May), 248–61.

2 Duncan, T. (2002), *IMC. Using Advertising and Promotion to Build Brands.* Boston: McGraw-Hill/Irwin.

3 Pickton, D. and Broderick, A. (2001), *Integrated Marketing Communications.* Harlow: Financial Times Prentice Hall.

4 McDonald, C. (1992), 'Finding Out How – Unleashing the Power of Single-Source Data to Explain the Marketing Mix', *Admap*, (December), 21–5; Pickton, D. and Broderick, A. (2001), *Integrated Marketing Communications.* Harlow: Financial Times Prentice Hall.

5 *Advertising Age*, 24 March 2003.

6 See also www.incentivesatwork.com

7 Doyle, K. (1991), 'Offbeat Programmes', *Incentive*, (December), 21–4.

8 See also www.bcentral.com

9 Slater, J. (2001), 'Is Couponing an Effective Promotional Strategy? An Examination of the Procter & Gamble Zero-couponing Test', *Journal of Marketing Communications*, 7(1), 3–10.

10 De Pelsmacker, P. (1994), 'Een reis Langs de Nieuwste Vormen van Winkelpuntcommunicatie' ('A Journey to the Latest Forms of In-Store Communication'), in Van Camp, E. (ed.), *Marketing en Communicatie in de 21ste Eeuw: A Brave New World? (Marketing and Communication in the 21st Century; A Brave New World?).* Roeselare: Roularta Books, 76–85.

11 *De Morgen*, 28 January 1999.

12 Slater, J. (2001), 'Is Couponing an Effective Promotional Strategy? An Examination of the Procter & Gamble Zero-couponing Test', *Journal of Marketing Communications*, 7(1), 3–10.

13 www.esprix.nl, 9 June 2003.

14 *Esprix Jaarboek* (1999), 60–1.

15 www.pandionline.com, 9 June 2003.

16 D'Astous, A. and Jacob, I. (2002), 'Understanding Consumer Reactions to Premium-based Promotion Offers', *European Journal of Marketing*, 36(11), 1270–86.

17 *Esprix Jaarboek* (1999), 60–1.

18 www.pandionline.com, 9 June 2003.

19 See also www.incentivesatwork.com

20 Duncan, T. (2002), *IMC. Using Advertising and Promotion to Build Brands.* Boston: McGraw-Hill/Irwin; Brassington, F. and Pettitt, S. (2003), *Principles of Marketing.* Harlow: Financial Times/Prentice Hall.

21 GfK Belgium.

Chapter 10

Direct marketing

Chapter outline

Direct marketing as a marketing communications technique

Direct marketing objectives and target groups

Direct marketing media and tools

Relationship marketing

Measuring direct marketing effectiveness

Chapter objectives

This chapter will help you to:

- Understand what direct marketing communications are, and why they are increasingly important in marketing communications
- Get an overview of the objectives and target groups of direct marketing communications
- Acquaint yourself with the direct marketing media, tools and techniques
- Understand why database marketing is so important, and how a database should be managed
- See how direct marketing communications can contribute to relationship marketing
- Measure the effectiveness of a direct marketing communications campaign

Introduction

The success of direct marketing, not only as a marketing philosophy, but also as a set of communications techniques, originates from the corner shopkeeper's philosophy of having close and personal contact with customers, knowing everyone's needs and wants, providing them with the best solutions to their problems and giving them excellent after-sales service. This makes them happy and loyal customers. The growing opportunities offered by technology, automation and database-supported marketing intelligence systems, and the reductions in computer hard- and software prices have encouraged marketers to execute their marketing activities with an emphasis on efficiency and quantifiable objectives. Direct marketing activities do not require huge production costs like, for instance, television commercials, and consequently are more accessible to all kinds and sizes of companies. They are also very flexible, highly selective (easy to target) media. Knowledge of customer habits and needs and other detailed market information are considered to be highly valuable tools for marketing strategy development. As there is less and less difference between products, consumers are finding brand loyalty increasingly irrelevant. Manufacturers have to look for communications tools that motivate consumers to product trial and give them incentives to keep using their brands. These changes have led to the growing importance of one-to-one communications and relationship marketing, based on lifetime bonding of customers. Direct marketing has given added value to this kind of marketing activity in comparison to traditional mass marketing.

With the fast-growing internet penetration in the new millennium the number of e-mail addresses has been increasing at a fast pace, allowing direct marketers to develop e-mailing campaigns that are more flexible, and above all much cheaper than traditional direct marketing media. E-marketing and e-mailings will be discussed in Chapter 11, E-communication.

Direct marketing as a marketing communications technique

The definition of direct marketing has gone through various changes. In the beginning (the 1960s) it was considered as a type of distribution (direct selling through a different channel), as used by mail order companies. In the 1970s direct marketing became a marketing communications tool with emphasis on feedback and optimising response rates on mailings and other direct marketing tools. In the 1990s long-term relationship building and increasing customer loyalty ('retention marketing') became the main issues in direct marketing.[1]

Direct marketing means contacting customers and prospects in a direct way with the intention of generating an immediate and measurable response or reaction. 'Direct' means using direct media such as mailings, catalogues, telephone or brochures, and not through intermediaries such as dealers, retailers or sales staff. An immediate response is possible via answering coupons, phone or a personal visit of the customer to the store or retailer. In order to make a direct contact with customers and prospects, a database is required. Databases can be considered as the heart of direct marketing. Some issues on database marketing are explored below.

Table 10.1 The difference between mass and direct media

Mass media	Direct media
■ Segmenting	■ Individualising
■ Recall, recognition and image measurement	■ Response measurement (per client)
■ Mass one-way communications	■ Targeted two-way communications
■ Market share	■ Customer share

There are a number of fundamental differences between direct marketing communications and media and traditional mass media communications. They are shown in Table 10.1. The basic philosophy of direct marketing is to consider each customer as an investment. Identification of each customer means you can target the most appropriate communication in an interactive way. Customers are personally addressed and are able to respond. Data involved with these transactions are stored in the database and may be used to establish long-term relationships by adapting a company's offer to the needs of the customer. Consequently the main goal of a direct marketer is to increase customer share (i.e. the quantity and frequency of purchases of each individual customer) rather than market share.

The importance of direct marketing in European countries has consistently been increasing during the last decennium. Even during the past economic recession years direct marketing expenditures kept rising. Within Europe, Germany is the largest direct marketing market, although second placed UK is gaining share. The importance of direct marketing varies considerably in different European countries. In the Netherlands, direct marketing expenditures exceed those of traditional advertising (117.7%) whereas in Greece direct marketing expenditures are only 9% of traditional advertising spends. In Denmark this percentage is 78.4% while in Sweden it is 48.7. The breakdown of total direct marketing expenditure per European country in 2001 is shown in Figure 10.1.[2]

During the last decade direct marketing has moved from a typical and traditional mail order company activity to an important communications tool of banks, insurance companies, not-for-profit organisations, supermarkets, car manufacturers, etc.

Objectives and target groups

Direct marketing may be the appropriate communications tool for direct sales, sales and distribution support, and customer loyalty and retention.

Direct sales

Direct marketing communications may be used as a direct sales channel or distribution technique: selling products and services without face-to-face contact with intermediaries (salespersons, dealers or retailers). The best example is the mail order business. Catalogues are mailed to prospects and orders are taken by phone or by mail. The success of mail order sales varies across Europe. The total turnover of mail order operators exceeded €52.4 billion in 2001, representing a 17.1% increase from 1996. Turnover per capita in the European Union was €132 in 2001. Germany (€265) has the highest

Figure 10.1 Total direct marketing expenditure in Europe, 2001

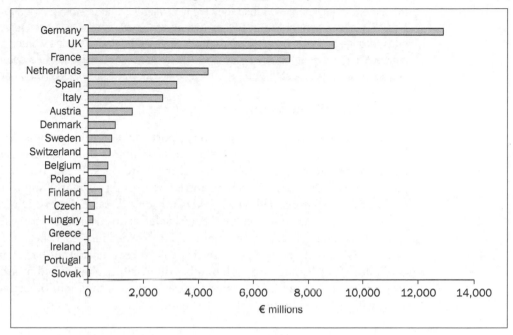

Based on: FEDMA (2002), *Survey on Direct and Interactive Marketing Activities in Europe.* Reproduced with permission of the Federation of European Direct Marketing, www.fedma.org.

turnover per capita, followed by the UK (€221), Austria (€183) and Switzerland (€143). The lowest per capita turnover figures in 2001 were Hungary (€7), Italy (€14) and Slovakia (€15).

As the roots of direct marketing lie in the mail order industry, many authors argue that the real strength of direct marketing, as illustrated by mail order success stories, still relates to what they call 'transactional direct marketing' or selling. The database compiled by companies allows them to segment their target groups by needs and values and to maximise the probability of response. It also allows marketers to develop profiles of the most profitable customers, and hence target new prospects more efficiently. This efficiency at transaction marketing is what has driven marketing's growth and many marketers leave direct marketing at that 'direct sales level'.[3]

Egg: direct selling of banking products

New financial services organisations and brands such as the European online bank Egg (www.egg.co.uk) have been developed to function as direct sales businesses. Egg initially started in the UK in 1998 where it is now serving over two million customers and has been operating in France since 2002. Egg offers a range of direct banking services including credit cards, savings, loans and mortgages. It also provides its customers with top-of-the-range online banking facilities and even TV banking. With the Egg Money Manager, clients can see all their online accounts in one place, whether they are held with Egg or not. Having an Egg account also offers other benefits: customers can even e-mail money to their friends – all they

▶

need is the friend's e-mail address. Egg's products and services are specifically tailored to fit the direct marketing medium and they are simplified so that customers require less advice as part of the decision-making process. This considerably improves response and conversion rates through building consumer confidence. On the other hand, the new brand had to be independent and therefore could not leverage the heritage or awareness of its parent company. It had to build its own customer base and generate awareness and trust on its own terms.[4]

Sales or distribution support

Direct marketing can also be used to support the activities of the sales team, dealers or retailers. In this case, although the actual selling is done by intermediaries, direct marketing tries to prepare, stimulate and facilitate sales. It can also be used to follow up sales. For instance, the Dutch airline KLM uses direct marketing to motivate independent travel agents to sell KLM tickets for long-distance flights. Direct marketing is also often used to support personal sales. Sales visits are rather expensive, but a high frequency of contacts has to be maintained or even increased because of the highly competitive market environment. In this case direct marketing has a funnel function (see Figure 10.2). Reducing a high number of possibles to a limited number of qualified prospects (to be visited by the sales representative) is the main objective. Direct marketing will take over some of the sales team's tasks to reduce costs.[5]

Figure 10.2 Direct marketing as a sales supporting tool

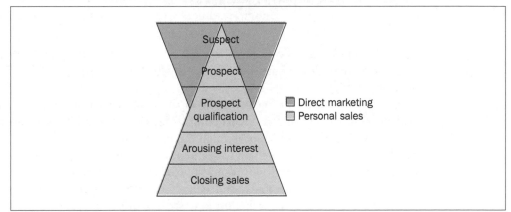

Direct marketing by Hewlett-Packard

Hewlett-Packard tried to increase its market share in the Dutch PC notebook market in 2001 by developing a direct marketing campaign that, unlike most campaigns, did not focus on primary product features but stressed Hewlett-Packard's facilitating role in home-working. The campaign, which consisted of a mailing and the minisite www.hphomework.nl with lots of practical content for home- and teleworkers, aimed to help people find the right 'work–life balance' and in the process build brand preference among notebook buyers. As a result of the campaign, Hewlett-Packard's market share in the Netherlands for notebook PCs rose from 4.2% at the beginning of the direct marketing campaign to 6.1%, all in one year. The HP Homework campaign created by Publicis received a Silver Esprix award for best direct marketing campaign in 2002.[6]

Customer retention and loyalty building

Direct marketing is also the appropriate tool to improve relations with customers and increase their satisfaction and loyalty. Customer loyalty is important for different reasons. One study involving 27 brands showed that the most loyal customers (12%) are responsible for 69% of the sales figure of a brand.[7] Others claim that lack of loyalty slows company performance by 25%–50%. Customer switching is costing British companies an estimated sales loss of £100 billion each year and another £100 billion to win back lost customers. Relationship marketing has two positive effects: customer retention, in combination with gaining new customers, leads to a higher number of customers. Second, the longer they stay, the more profitable they become. The return per customer will increase, operational costs will decrease, positive word-of-mouth will lead to new customers and loyal customers are less price-sensitive. Figure 10.3 shows how profits increase year on year thanks to the different effects of customer loyalty.[8]

Corporate expenditures on loyalty programmes are booming. The top 16 retailers in Europe, for instance, spent more than €1 billion in 2000 on loyalty initiatives. Nevertheless, the role of direct and database marketing in achieving higher levels of customer loyalty is not undisputed. A fair amount of academic research seriously doubts that loyalty schemes, magazines or other tactical initiatives make much difference. Emotional loyalty is said to be only a reality when personal interactions take place.[9] Moreover, large-scale and longitudinal studies have found that the relationship between loyalty and profitability is much weaker than proponents of customer relationship marketing (CRM) and loyalty programmes claim. One study discovered little or no evidence to support the hypothesis that customers who purchase steadily from a company over time are cheaper to serve, less price sensitive or effective at bringing in new business by positive word-of-mouth advertising. Instead of focussing on loyalty alone, a trend among many marketers, companies will have to measure the relationship between loyalty and profitability in order to identify the really interesting consumers. To track the

Figure 10.3 Profit per client as a function of customer retention

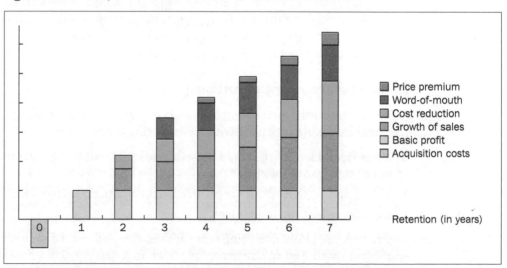

performance of its newly instituted loyalty programme one US high-tech corporate service provider set up a costing scheme to measure all costs for each customer during five years. The results took them by surprise. Half of the customers who had regularly been buying for at least two years (the company thought these could be called 'loyal' customers) barely generated profit while about half of the most profitable customers were buying high-margin products in a short time, before completely disappearing.[10]

Whiskas is leading the premium segment of the cat food market. To sustain this position it was essential to lead a direct dialogue with the consumer to strengthen brand loyalty and increase the lifetime value of the brand users. Using direct response television advertising, addresses of owners of kittens in Germany were collected at the earliest possible age of the cat. The dialogue programme consisted of a welcome package providing relevant information to make life with the cat more comfortable and convenient in the first year of the cat's life, together with distributing product samples (see Plate 18). After this welcome package, addresses were transferred to the Whiskas loyalty programme, ensuring four contact moments per year. The cat owners receive a quarterly full-colour, 22-page magazine with content that is closely linked to the core brand values: best possible care and nutrition for the cat and responsible cat ownership because 'nobody knows cats better than Whiskas'. The programme led to a significant increase in brand preference and buying intention, and above-average response rates.[11]

Direct marketing media and tools

To meet the communications objectives different direct marketing media and tools can be used. Two types may be discerned: addressable and non-addressable media. They are presented in Figure 10.4.

Although it may seem a paradox, direct marketing communications can also make use of mass media or non-addressable media, but the difference with mass communications is that they are used to generate a direct response among receivers of the message. Direct response advertising (direct response print ads, television and radio advertising) makes up an important part of the advertising activity. For instance, in the US approximately two-thirds of all advertising is response-generating.

Direct response print advertising

Direct response print advertising or coupon advertising means placing an advertisement in a newspaper or a magazine with the following characteristics:

- direct feedback from the reader (respondent) to the advertiser by returning a coupon or calling a phone number;
- a clear link between the response (feedback) and the message advertised;
- identification of the respondent.

Direct response print advertising is not addressable and not individually targeted at one single consumer. The advertisement is placed in a mass medium (newspaper or magazine). The primary goal of direct response ads is to select interested consumers or companies (in a business-to-business context use) out of a large audience. Direct response

Figure 10.4 Direct marketing media and tools

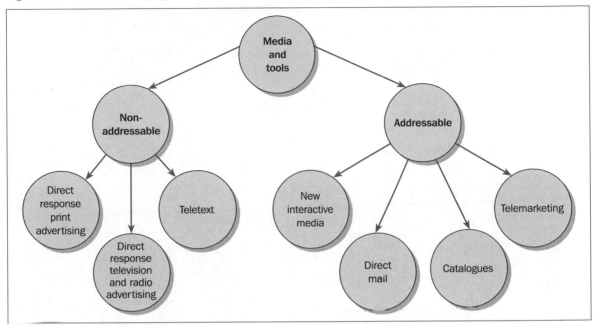

advertising is also a good way to provide interested consumers and prospects with more information than can be 'packed' in a traditional ad. By responding with an answering coupon, the interested potential customer can obtain more detailed information. Ads with a coupon seem to be quite effective in that they are able to produce up to 20% better attention scores than other ads.

Thanks to the directness and feedback of direct response ads some interesting research on effectiveness can be carried out. In the first figure the impact of print ad format (full-page or part-page) on response success is shown.[12] The results lead to the conclusion that doubling the ad format will not lead to a 100% growth in response.

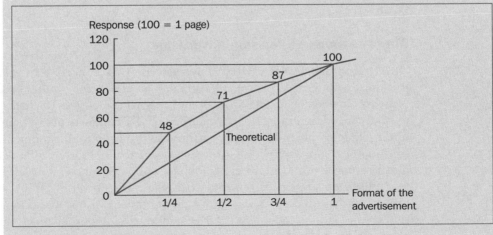

Increasing the frequency of a direct response ad will rarely lead to a rise in response figures. A second ad published shortly after the first one will most of the time have a lower response rate. The first exposure will reach the majority of the interested audience. This is shown in the next figure.

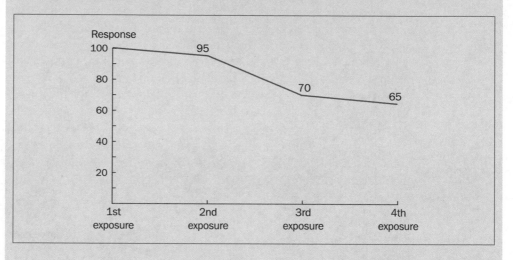

To incite readers to react to a direct response print ad, usually three different techniques are combined:

- *Motivational information*: information that gives the readers a reason to react. The visual and headline used in the ad are important because they draw the attention of the readers and have 15 or 20 times more chance to be seen than the rest of the ad. Visuals and head-lines should get the attention and give motivation to read the rest of the ads. Motivational information is information appealing to the needs of the readers.

- *Activating information*: this informational content of an ad stresses what the reader should do to react and how he or she can react. Active language (words like 'now' and 'quick') and clear response instructions ('come', 'call', 'cut') are crucial.

- *Facilitating instruments*: these will help the reader to react and will break down potential problems and barriers. Examples are: a dotted line around a coupon, the picture of scissors, a phone number that is easy to remember etc.

Direct response television advertising

Direct response television (DRTV) uses television as a medium to generate reactions. It is thus, with regards to principles and key success factors, quite comparable to print response advertising in newspapers and magazines. In the US half of all TV commercials include a response phone number. DRTV commercials are principally used for direct selling or information enquiry purposes (both 40%), for competitions (21%) and for sampling, gifts and shop visit invitations (each 10% use).[13] Quite often, different direct response propositions are combined in one commercial or DRTV is integrated in a multi-step strategy to generate extra sales. The power of DRTV as a sales tool is proved by the success of teleshopping programmes (for instance, Home Order Television on the German cable station DF1) or even teleshopping channels (like QVC, Home Shopping Europe or Polonia 1).

Direct response television commercials are different from traditional television advertising or direct response ads in a number of ways. The first is the choice of a response method. Providing the possibility to react by phone will create more response than a simple mail-answering method. The phone number will have to stay long enough on screen to allow viewers to memorise the number. Visual and auditory support and repeating the phone number will also increase response. Another difference with traditional television ads is that direct television advertising is more efficient during the cheaper broadcasting hours. Traditional TV advertising has as its main objective to be seen by as many viewers as possible. DRTV commercials want to generate the highest and most profitable response. Broadcasting DRTV spots in the morning and afternoon is the most efficient way to do so because they will lead to the largest percentage of viewer response. The reason for this is that viewers do not want to be disturbed during prime time while they are watching their favourite programmes and shows. Calls for action at those broadcasting hours will be less successful.

Direct response radio advertising

Similar to direct response TV advertising, direct response radio advertising is an interactive form of radio advertising, aimed at generating direct behavioural responses from the listening audience using the phone, post or internet. Although direct response radio advertising can be used both for mass and niche markets in a consumer or business-to-business environment, content analysis of broadcast commercials has shown that services like banking and insurances and the tourism industry in particular use this kind of advertising. Compared to other advertising media, radio suffers from characteristics such as external pacing, volatility and lack of attention. However, it also has some advantages. It is relatively cheap both in renting and production costs as the average costs of a radio-GRP tend to be five to ten times lower than the average costs of a TV-GRP. Radio advertising is also a selective medium, allowing advertisers to limit reach to certain geographic areas or demographic and lifestyle groups, as the specialised music and news programming of radio stations usually attracts specific audiences. Radio is also a very flexible medium to advertisers as commercials can be delivered shortly before the first broadcast. The last advantage is its availability to a broad public in any place, at any time. Although radio advertising has been lacking attention as a direct response medium for a long time, more recently there is a growing awareness of the powerful role radio can play in direct marketing. The growing penetration and use of mobile telephones is facilitating response to advertising in cars and other places where a fixed phone line is not available. However, research has shown that it is less effective and efficient to broadcast direct response radio commercials between 7 a.m. and 9 a.m., and between 4 p.m. and 6 p.m.; those broadcast between 2 p.m. and 4 p.m. were most effective. Spots broadcast on Monday, Tuesday and Wednesday were also significantly more effective than those broadcast on other days of the week. Position in the commercial break and total length of the commercial break had no implications for the effectiveness.[14]

Teletext

Advertisers may rent one or more teletext pages to spread their message and generate response. The popularity of this medium is different from one country to another and depends on the tradition of commercial teletext broadcasting. In the UK, for instance, teletext is widely used by advertisers since ITV teletext is heavily used by the British public.

Addressable media are media by means of which it is possible to communicate individually with each customer or prospect. The most important addressable media are direct mail, telemarketing and catalogues.

Direct mail

Direct mail are written commercial messages, personally addressed and sent by mail. A direct mailing usually consists of an envelope, a sales letter accompanying a brochure and an answering card. Pros of direct mail are the selectivity, the opportunity to personalise messages, flexibility in the use of very creative ideas, and the ability to communicate fast, target specific groups and customise messages and offers. The con is that the response to mailings is usually rather low. This is due to the 'clutter' and the resulting 'junk mail' image of direct mail. Direct mailing is still the most frequently used direct medium and the high number of mailings per capita (Figure 10.5[15]) stimulates receivers to be very selective in what mailings they open and wish to read.

Switzerland is the most frequently mailed European country with an average of 234.5 addressed mailings per capita. Belgium, the Netherlands and Finland are also mail-intensive countries. Poland, Slovakia, Hungary and the Czech Republic are the least direct mailed countries with less than 14 addressed mailings per capita in 2001.[16]

Figure 10.5 Addressed direct mail per capita in Europe, 2001

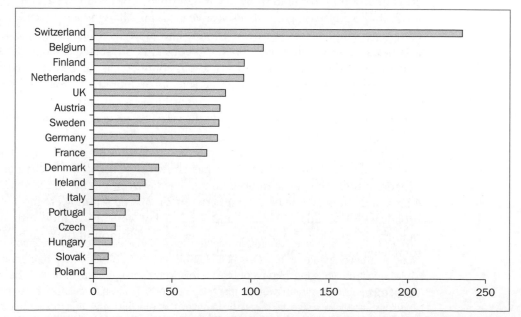

Based on: FEDMA (2002), *Survey on Direct and Interactive Marketing Activities in Europe.* Reproduced with permission of the Federation of European Direct Marketing, www.fedma.org.

Early in 2001 Citroën introduced its model C5, a big, higher-mid-class car, especially popular in business fleets. The new model is a dynamic, safe and comfortable car with a good price/quality ratio. However, these claims were already frequently used by Citroën's main competitors, Renault Laguna and Ford Mondeo, which both relaunched in the same year as the C5. The direct marketing and e-mail campaign for the C5 had as its main objective to put the brand in the considered set of makes when someone in the target group was in the orientation and information phase of the buying cycle. By asking more and more personal information (stepwise) and using this gathered data in the one-to-one personalised follow-up mailings, Citroën created a complete customised experience that made the car look more vivid and personal. As a result, 30% of the Citroën C5 sales originated from the database that was created during this direct mail and e-mail campaign.[17]

Every direct marketing or mailing campaign will require a different success measure according to the initial marketing or communications goals.[18] A classic illustration of this is a company selling a Caribbean island through a direct mailing campaign. A brochure with an accompanying letter was sent to 500 key prospects each having enough money, being eager for privacy and being sun worshippers. Only one response was received but it led to the sale of the island, making the direct mailing campaign 100% effective.

RSGB Mailmonitor is providing a measure of effectiveness in the UK based on a panel of 1,350 households selected on a nationally representative basis. The table shows that even if response is not immediate, a mailing could be effective at a later stage.

Reactions to mailings in the UK (based on the RSGB Mailmonitor)

	Number of items (m)	% of direct mail
Total direct mailings	1,411.44	100.00%
Kept for future reference	292.73	20.74%
Read, threw away	198.73	14.08%
Read carefully, threw away	91.18	6.46%
Placed an order	68.88	4.88%
Passed to someone else	34.72	2.46%
Entered competition	20.32	1.44%
Made appointment/visit	6.49	0.46%
Telephoned for quote	1.97	0.48%
Any action	**714.99**	**51.00%**

Reproduced with permission of Centaur Communications Ltd.

According to this monitor, half of the mailings resulted in one reaction or another. But response rates seem to vary considerably from one industry to another. In 1994 the market with the best response rates to its mailings was the food and beverages industry with 23.6% response. There are three main reasons why this industry had an astonishingly high response rate compared to the other markets. First, until now direct mailings had not often been used in this industry and would therefore account for a higher attention and reaction rate. Second, food and beverage items have a small cost per item which makes the barriers for trial lower. Third, most mailings in this market have a relatively simple message. Across the different consumer product markets an average response rate of 5.7% was calculated. In terms of individual mailings, analysis suggested that the smaller the mailings and the more targeted the direct mailing campaign, the higher the response rate is likely to be.[19]

Telemarketing

Telemarketing may be defined as any measurable activity using the telephone to help find, get, keep and develop customers.[20] The use of telemarketing as a direct marketing medium has increased enormously. Total European telemarketing expenditures were €12.3 million in 2001, an amount that has steadily grown over the last decade. Developing markets are Greece and Slovakia, with growth rates of +275% and +400% respectively in 2001. However, these markets are still very small compared to the biggest telemarketing spenders, the UK (€4.7 million) and Germany (€3 million).[21]

Telemarketing may be considered as a number of different activities that can be defined on the basis of two dimensions, i.e. the party taking the initiative (inbound versus outbound telemarketing), and the extent to which it is used as a sales-generating versus a sales-supporting direct marketing tool (Table 10.2).[22]

Table 10.2 The different functions of telemarketing

	Sales-generating	Sales-supporting
Inbound telemarketing	▪ Taking orders	▪ Product and company information ▪ Customer service, helpdesk ▪ Complaints service
Outbound telemarketing	▪ Tele-sales	▪ Organising meetings/dates for the salesmen ▪ Tele-prospecting ▪ Updating commercial databases ▪ Supporting other marketing communications ▪ Generating traffic ▪ Tele-factoring

Based on: Walrave, M. (1995), Telemarketing: Storing op de Lijn? (Telemarketing: Badly Connected?). Leuven/Amersfoort: Acco.

Outbound telemarketing means that the marketer is taking the initiative to call clients or prospects; inbound implies that interested customers or prospects are using the phone to contact the company and ask for product information, order a product, ask for help with a problem or file a complaint. Outbound telemarketing means outgoing telephone calls (from the marketer's point of view) and inbound incoming calls. Using telemarketing to take orders is especially common in mail order companies or for direct response advertisers. Telesales involve actively calling consumers or companies with the purpose of selling products or services. Tele-prospecting is searching for prospects by phone. Two other uses are controlling and actualising databases and settling dates for the sales team. Telemarketing might also be a good way of creating synergetic media effects when it is used together with other marketing communications activities. For instance, the response to a direct mailing might be increased by calling to announce the arrival of the mailing. Telemarketing can be used to generate more traffic at the point-of-sales or to collect debts (tele-factoring). A survey of France Télécom revealed that 35% of French companies use the phone for active sales (telesales) purposes; 44% used the phone to take orders; 53% to set dates and meetings.

The phone is the most direct of all direct media tools and has some advantages. It is a flexible, interactive and quick medium. A telemarketing campaign may be launched at any moment and its effectiveness is very easy to track immediately. On the other hand, it is quite a hard-selling and intrusive medium and with its costs being 10–20 times higher than a mailing it is a rather expensive tool. However, costs should be gauged against response figures to make a correct evaluation.

Catalogues

A catalogue is a list of products or services presented in a visual and/or verbal way. It may be printed or electronically stored on a disk, a CD-ROM or a database. Although customers are not able to feel, try, smell, taste, etc. the product in a catalogue, it does give them the freedom to go through the catalogue, choose among a wide range of products and save time.

There are different types of catalogues.[23] Reference catalogues are an extensive overview of all products with their characteristics, references and prices. This kind of catalogue is typically nothing more than a purely technical description of the products or services range. They are more used in industrial markets and are appropriate if a relationship with a customer has already been developed. The hard-selling catalogue is a sales-generating tool that should be able to sell without further involvement of a salesperson, a dealer or distributor. These catalogues are used by clothing, soft- and hardware, books and CD mail order companies. Just like the reference catalogues they have a functional sales goal. Other types of catalogues are more supporting sales and used as guidelines or helping tools during a sales conversation or during a shop visit. For instance, the Ikea catalogue is used as a guide during a stroll in Ikea shops. A second goal of these catalogues is to invite and stimulate people to visit the store (traffic-generating objective).

New interactive media

New media are often a combination of existing media such as telephone, cable, television and computers into new applications. That is why they are also called multimedia. Interactive media are characterised by the fact that they deliver tailor-made information to the users at the moment that the user wants to have this kind of information. In other words, the user is directing the information process. Media such as CD-I, CD-ROM, internet, interactive teletext, websites and e-mail are the most important new interactive media. In Chapter 11 these techniques will be explored in more depth.

Database marketing

A database is a collection of interrelated data of customers and prospects which can be used for different applications such as analysis, individual selection, segmentation and customer retention, loyalty and service supports.[24] The minimum requirements of a good marketing database are personal customer data, transaction (purchase history) data and communications (received mailings, incentives, marketing actions and market reactions) data. The database could also file which products, company departments and salespersons are involved with a certain marketing action. In fact, a database stores three kinds of data: market information, relationship data and company data (Figure 10.6).

Figure 10.6 The marketing database

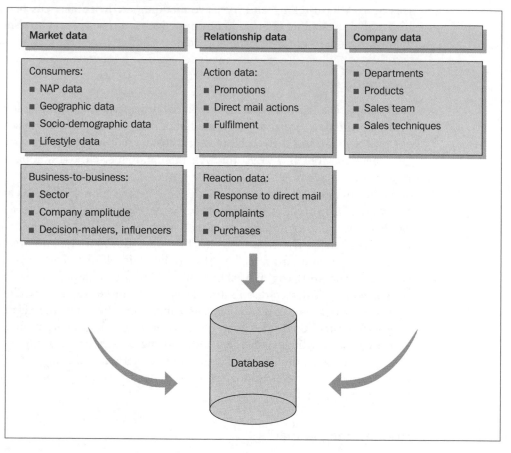

They are mostly stored in a relational database, such as Access and Oracle, that use SQL (structural query language) to make links between individual data.

There are two possible sources of data:[25] internal and external. Most companies already have the basic information needed to start a database:[26] order and invoice information, such as customer names, addresses, account numbers, purchase data, method of payment, etc. These customer files are internal data which may be the first basis to start up a database. External data are all types of lists compiled outside the company which can be bought or hired for direct marketing purposes. Examples are subscriber lists of newspapers and magazines, or databases segmented on lifestyle and consumption habits.

The success of any direct marketing campaign depends heavily on the quality and structure of the database used. The effectiveness of direct marketing campaigns will increase with improved targeting. The latter means that individuals may be reached with a relevant message improving response and reducing irritation levels. Repeat business and new business are the key factors to company growth. The former will need communications with the current loyal customers. Those heavy users are often small in number and thus only accessible through direct marketing targeting. Strategic use of the database and accurate segmentation based on the registered consumer profiles will be crucial to these goals. For new business success depends on the ability to identify potential customers with the correct profile to be hot prospects for the kind of products or services the company has to offer. Learning from the current customers and keeping all kinds of useful information about these customers in a database will make it easier to make a good list of prospects. For example, Seagram (a liquor company) knows that two-thirds of all American adults will never drink liquor. It would be a waste of money to invest in mass marketing and advertising. Creating a database to identify potential new customers would be a better investment.

As the marketing database is a crucial instrument of direct marketing communications, it is important that it is correctly managed. Most of the data will quickly expire and frequent updates are required to prevent the database from losing its value. There are five potential pitfalls for a marketing database:

■ *Incompleteness*: some data are not collected for all records in the database. This may be due to a bad data collection procedure or to a compilation based on different sources.

■ *Data expiration*: some data expire quickly, for instance, function (job title) and home address may rapidly change, but the name of the customer usually stays the same during his or her entire adult lifetime.

■ *Unreliability*: some data might be false because the source is not trustworthy. For instance, data collected through the internet sometimes contain many fictitious names and addresses.

■ *Inconsistency*: some data are not automatically changed, although they are linked to others, for instance a phone number is not adapted to a newly entered home address.

■ *Duplications*: two or more identical records may be stored due to different spellings resulting in two or more of the same mailings to customers and prospects, which might irritate them and is costing money to the direct marketer.

At least one person in the organisation should be appointed to manage the database in order to avoid these mistakes.

To launch Scandinavian Airlines' new website, www.scandinavian.net and to get 70,000 regular travellers to register in the on-line database and move customers to internet booking, Scandinavian Airlines started a direct mail campaign to frequent flyers throughout the Scandinavian countries and Finland. Internal address databases were analysed and divided into several target groups. The most interesting groups (the most frequent travellers) received a mailing referring to a demo-booking sequence on the internet, giving a pedagogic introduction to the new services. All who completed the demo booking participated in a draw for 100 return trips to New York City. A combination of addressed mails and banner ads were used but traditional direct mail turned out to be ten times more cost-effective than the internet banners. A total of 98,000 registered as site members within the first four weeks of the campaign. The value of on-line booking immediately rose by 250%. Response rates from Sweden, Finland, Denmark and Norway were similar, with the lowest response being 13% and the highest 17.8%. For this campaign Scandinavian Airlines received a Best of Direct Marketing Silver Award.[27]

The growing importance of one-to-one marketing[28] has made it clear that generating and managing customer information has moved from a strategic opportunity to a strategic

Figure 10.7 Five stages in the use of database marketing

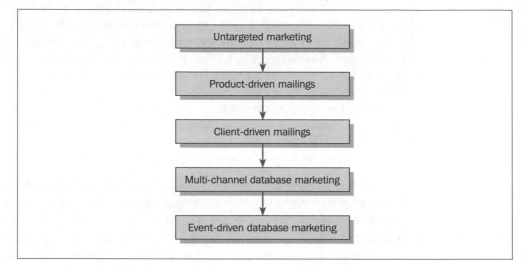

Based on: Bügel, M.S. (1997), 'Van Direct Mail naar Event-Driven Marketing' (From Direct Mail to Event-Driven Marketing), *Tijdschrift voor Strategische Bedrijfscommunicatie*, 3(2), 98–106.

necessity. Companies that are the first to detect and answer customer needs with the right product or service at the right moment, offered through the right channel have a substantial competitive advantage. A file with address data is not enough to support marketing decisions and drive customer loyalty programmes. More sophisticated database techniques have to be used. In Figure 10.7 five stages in the use of database marketing are shown:[29] from the use of the database as a file with addresses (untargeted approach) to the use of database marketing to get the right product through the right channel at the right moment to the customers (event-driven database marketing).

Stage 1: Untargeted marketing

Often, the starting point of database marketing in a company is the phase in which a company uses a database of prospects. They are selected on certain criteria to fit with the target group of the product or service the direct marketer will promote in the mailing sent to this broad group of potential customers.

Stage 2: Product-driven mailings

The disadvantage of the first step in database marketing is that the criteria to determine who will be addressed are constituted by the marketer. Sometimes when the wrong criteria are chosen the mailing can be ineffective. The second step in database marketing is to choose the target group on the basis of a test action instead of mailing a predetermined target group. This second step is based on response scoring models. A sample of potential prospects is mailed and response profiles are compared to non-response patterns. The result of this comparison is a model of customer characteristics with a predictive value for response. This model is then used to give a score (the likelihood of response or, in other words, the need of every customer for the product or service offered in the mailing) to every potential prospect. Those prospects for whom the estimated returns (based on response chance) would be higher than the mailing cost are then selected for mailing. Product-driven database marketing uses customer information to select the right customers for a certain product or service. This is a more targeted form of direct marketing offering more relevant propositions to consumers and lowering mailing costs for the direct marketer.

On the other hand, there are two cons: too much focus on action-driven mailings could lead to cannibalisation of the sales of other products or services, i.e. stealing sales from some of the other products of the company. Furthermore, incentives and loyalty systems used in these product-driven mailings could subsidise consumers who would have bought the products without these incentives. This has a negative influence on profits.

Stage 3: Client-driven mailings

To take the negative aspects of product-driven database marketing into account, a measure for individual client relationship value can be developed. The decision to contact certain customers will depend on the change in this relationship value rather than the profits on individual actions. Only customers who increase their relationship after a certain action are targeted. This introduces the concept of lifetime value[30] or the expected return a certain customer will deliver during the years he or she has a relationship with the company. This implies an estimation of the lifetime of a client as well as the profitability of every individual customer (share of wallet).[31] In this stage the direct marketer tries to target the right customers with the right products.

Stage 4: Multi-channel database marketing

This database marketing technique integrates the knowledge on channel sensitivity into marketing activities. Some prospects are more open to direct mail than others. In this approach actions to sell the same kind of products or services are sent through different sales channels (direct sales, personal selling, etc.). Which combination of sales channels will be used depends on the sensitivity of every individual customer and the costs of each channel. Both types of data are stored in the marketing database. Multi-channel marketing uses the database to offer the right product to the right client through the best channel.

Stage 5: Event-driven database marketing

In stage 4 products and services are promoted and proposed during the action period. But consumers' needs are not always felt during this action period. The chance of a mailing arriving just in time, i.e. when the consumer actually considers a certain purchase, is slim. By the time he is planning the purchase there is only a slight chance that he will remember the mailing and the action of competitors could get more attention. To avoid this, it is necessary to adjust the timing of mailings and other marketing actions to the moment when customers' needs become prevalent. Needs often arise as a consequence of certain events in the life of a customer (marriage, buying a house, birth of a child, moving, etc.), or they are related to the relation between the client and the company (e.g. an information request two weeks ago, for a bank: €2,500 on a customer's account, etc.). In event-driven database marketing customers are actively followed to detect changes in needs and to offer them the right products at the right moment (through the right channel). Smart chip cards, internet and call centres may be used to keep track of these changes. Instead of traditional promotion planning done by a marketer, all actions take place at the most effective moment for each individual client.

Privacy concerns

With the rising use of databases linked to the growing desire to get to know individual customers, consumers are concerned about what companies know about them and how those companies obtain and use personal information. The primary source of consumer privacy concerns revolves around personal or individual-specific data such as names, addresses, demographic characteristics, lifestyle interests, shopping preferences and purchase histories. Growing numbers of marketers are assimilating and using information from (and about) individual consumers and renting or exchanging data or lists describing habits and characteristics of individual consumers. A survey has found that consumers are most willing to provide marketers with demographic and lifestyle information and least willing to provide financial information (such as annual household income, the kind of credit cards they possess and the two most recent credit card purchases) and personal identifiers. On the other hand, the majority of respondents were willing to share their favourite hobbies, age, marital status, occupation or type of job and education. Although most consumers understand the need for financial information when purchasing on credit, a request for income information, particularly from a non-financial or non-insurance service marketer, has a profound negative effect on purchase intentions. Most consumers desire more control over information collection and use. They want to control what companies do with their information as well as control the number of catalogues and the amount of advertising material they receive. Apart from the control of information disclosure, privacy also has to do with control over unwanted intrusions such as telemarketing, unwanted direct mail or unsolicited commercial e-mail (spam). The internet channel in particular has fostered a new set of privacy concerns resulting from the ease with which data in this channel can be collected, stored and exchanged. Additional consumer concern results from the volume of spam due to the low absolute cost and waste inherent in sending commercial e-mails. Nevertheless research has shown that consumers are more likely to request name removal from telephone lists than e-mail lists. But on the other hand, removal from e-mail lists is more desired than postal mail lists.[32]

Relationship marketing[33]

Marketers still tend to spend more and exert more effort on gaining new customers than on keeping the current customers satisfied and loyal. An estimation revealed that the part of marketing budgets assigned to promotional activities aimed at attracting new customers is five times greater than the budget spent on current customers.[34] But the efforts involved in attracting new customers are much higher than those required to keep the current customers loyal. In fact, some claim that companies can realise profit increases of 35%–85% just by decreasing customer loss by 5%. Moreover, the profit per customer will also increase the longer a customer stays with the company. This is the result of diminishing acquisition costs, lower operational and service costs per client per year, combined with a rise in the average yearly purchases per loyal client, declining price sensitivity and, last but not least, positive word-of-mouth (more referrals) attracting new customers cost-effectively.[35] Direct marketing plays a crucial rule in building and maintaining profitable relationships with customers.

In relationship marketing a marketer's challenge is to bring quality, customer service and marketing into close alignment, leading to long-term and mutually beneficial customer relationships.[36] In other words, the direct marketer tries to create and maintain relationships of value. For example, Harley-Davidson created the Harley Owners Club which has about 200,000 members worldwide. Besides motorbikes, Harley-Davidson also offers an insurance programme, a travel agency, an emergency roadside service, two magazines, member competitions and 750 local chapters. Nestlé regularly sends information to young mothers. It employs qualified dieticians to operate its customer service lines and runs a chain of baby cafés to cater for families away from home.

The fundamental importance of relationship marketing is related to the principle that customer satisfaction, loyalty and profitability are correlated. Lifetime value, or the net present value of the profits a company will generate from its customers over a period of time (usually 4–5 years), is an important concept for the direct marketer involved with relationship or retention marketing. By computing the average lifetime value of its customers, the company will be able to determine how much it can invest in attracting and making loyal potential new customers. Not all customers should be made loyal.[37] It makes no sense building up a loyal but unprofitable relationship. With the Pareto principle in mind, 80% of time and promotional efforts should be allocated to 20% of the customers. To identify these customers the information assembled about the customer's past behaviour will help the direct marketer select the right customers for further loyalty development. Apart from traditional socio-demographic and psychographic segmentations, customer portfolio segments can be measured in terms of number of customers, number of purchases (frequency of purchase), recency of purchases and contribution to sales and profits (monetary value).[38]

During a relationship, customers can progress from being a prospect to being a customer, client, supporter and, at the top of the loyalty ladder, an advocate (see Figure 10.8).[39] The latter are so involved with the organisation that they are very loyal and influence others by positive word-of-mouth. The relationship direct marketer wants to encourage its customers as far up the loyalty ladder as possible.

Customer loyalty will be won by being better than competitors (offering superior products and services) or by loyalty strategies. There are two strategies to stimulate customer loyalty: a rewarding strategy and a relationship strategy. The former implies rewarding loyal behaviour by giving 'hard' advantages to reinforce and maintain customer loyalty. Examples are frequent flier programmes, gifts, prizes or money. Rewarding strategies are targeted to rational calculating customers. But, as these rewards are easy to copy or exceed by competitors, they are rarely the best strategy when they are not used in combination with a relationship strategy. The latter consists of creating tight relations with customers by gathering information about each individual customer and using it intelligently by providing soft, personalised and customised advantages. Examples are sending targeted and relevant messages, special events for customers, etc. These relationship strategies are targeted at affective-oriented customers. For instance, someone calls a local florist and orders a bouquet for his mother's birthday; the next year he gets a postcard from the florist three weeks before his mother's birthday which

Figure 10.8 The loyalty ladder

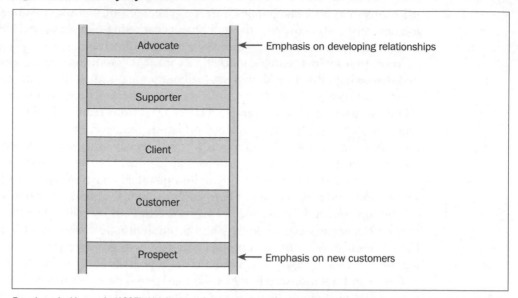

Based on: Jenkinson, A. (1995), *Valuing Your Customers: From Quality Information to Quality Relationships Through Database Marketing*. London: McGraw-Hill.

reflects the number and type of flowers he ordered last year and with the message that it only takes one phone call to send her flowers again. Which of the strategies should a direct marketer choose? Rewarding programmes are effective to use as a first step in the process of building a close relationship. They will bring in customers in the programme. However, this will not be enough to keep customers loyal.

A marketer introducing a loyalty programme should consider the following strategic points involved with sharing value with customers.[40] To profit from loyal customers, marketers should offer the best value to the best customers: the clients creating most profit should benefit from this situation, which will make them even more loyal and profitable. For instance, a company could consider offering lower prices to its loyal customers. Unfortunately, most companies forget this and deliver products or services of the same quality to all customers. The value created by a customer loyalty programme should lead to higher returns than costs. A reward programme may never be a cost and should not attract price- or promotion-sensitive customers of competitors instead of rewarding loyal clients. Rewards should concentrate on stimulating desired behaviour (loyalty, word-of-mouth) and discourage unwanted, unprofitable behaviour (customer defection). Loyalty programmes are long-term actions and not short-term promotions and long-term advantages should be communicated rather than promoting switching behaviour. Loyalty programmes should attract valuable customer segments and discourage less valuable segments by being self-selective and individually correcting. For example, MCI's Friends and Family loyalty programme offered 20%–50% discount on calls to a specified network of friends and family. The proposition is most attractive to heavy users of long-distance calls, a core segment for MCI.

In the customer's mind, five elements determine the value of a loyalty programme: cash value, the number of options, aspiring value, relevance and convenience. The value should be calculated as a percentage discount on the amount a consumer has to spend to be able to get the reward. A free trip to a Caribbean island or a new car has a higher aspiring va. than a discount on a phone bill. Customers should also be able to choose from differen benefits. A programme is only relevant if the aspired benefit is within reach; if it takes years to collect the necessary air miles to make a free trip it will not be of any relevance to a customer. If it takes a lot of administration, whether for the customer or the retailer, a loyalty programme has a small chance of success. This is what is meant by 'convenience'.

Measuring direct marketing effectiveness

Direct marketing and interactive marketing are behaviour-oriented in nature, and therefore research into the effectiveness of direct and interactive marketing campaigns will invariably be tests of 'counting' behavioural response. The number of people responding to a free telephone number in a direct response television commercial, the number of people returning a coupon included in a print ad or the number of people placing an order as a result of a direct marketing campaign, are examples of effectiveness tests.

Evidently, all communications effectiveness tests are aimed at subsequently improving the communications effort. In direct marketing, which is essentially database-driven, the optimisation of a direct mailing campaign can be based on response scoring models, i.e. a procedure in which a number of indicators of behavioural response in the past are combined. A well-known response scoring model is the RFM-model. For all customers in a database, three behavioural response parameters are measured:

- *Recency*: the time elapsed since the last purchase;
- *Frequency*: the frequency with which a customer places an order;
- *Monetary value*: the average amount of money a customer spends per purchase.

Obviously, the shorter the time elapsed since a customer placed an order, the more frequently he or she buys something, and the higher the average amount of money spent, the more positive the expected response is following the next mailing campaign.[41] For each of the three variables a number of categories can be defined, and each category can be given a 'value' or score, representing the importance of each category for future response. This is illustrated in Table 10.3.

Table 10.3 The RFM model

Recency	Score	Frequency	Score	Monetary value	Score
Last 6 months	100	Once a year	0	Less than £100	0
7–12 months	80	Between 2 and 4 times a year	30	More than £100	20
13–24 months	60	More than 4 times a year	70		
25–36 months	30				
37 months or more	0				

To evaluate the effectiveness of direct mailing campaigns, response percentages and cost per response are two possible criteria. But a mailing can also be evaluated by means of traditional hierarchical communications objectives, as illustrated in the table below.

		Private (%)	Business (%)
Recall	■ spontaneous	29	16
	■ aided	44	44
	■ not recalled	27	40
Reading	■ entirely	12	9
	■ browsed	29	28
	■ not yet	24	16
	■ not read	8	7
Attitude	■ very interesting	13	11
	■ a bit interesting	11	10
	■ not interesting	15	14
	■ don't know	2	2
Response	■ planned to react	8	6
	■ no intent to respond	10	9
	■ don't know yet	6	6

Evidently, the values attached to each category are to a certain extent arbitrary, but can also be derived from the analysis of past response behaviour. The RFM-values can now be used selectively to mail those members of the target group that have the highest score on one or two of the three factors, or on a combination of all three. It can, for instance, be decided to mail only those customers that have a score of at least 80 on the recency value, as well as a score of 30 on the frequency factor, or only to mail those database entries that have a combined score of at least 100. Response scoring models can improve the effectiveness of mailing campaigns. It remains advisable, however, to pre-test a campaign before sending it out to a sample of target group members.

Recent publications have criticised the RFM score model as a poor way to measure loyalty. One problem is that patterns of buying behaviour for frequently purchased goods are different than those for infrequently bought goods. RFM ignores the average time between purchases as a key variable, while the probability that someone who is within historic range of buying frequency will buy again in the future is higher than for someone who is way past the average time between two purchases. RFM analysis would determine that someone who buys more frequently and has bought recently to be the more loyal and therefore direct marketing activities and investments would be targeted at the wrong profile of customers. Take, for instance, two customers, Mr Smith and Ms Jones, who both start to buy goods from a company in month 1. During the first year they purchase at different rates: Smith buys again in the second, sixth and eighth month, whereas Jones purchases again in the eighth month. A simple RFM analysis suggests that Smith is more loyal and thus more interesting for direct marketing investments than Jones because his purchases are more frequent and recent. But Smith usually buys every 2.3 months and yet by month 12 he hasn't bought anything for four months. Jones, too, hasn't bought anything since month 8, but she normally doesn't purchase anything for seven months. On this basis, the chance that she will buy again in the future is higher than for Smith.

This is a case of 'event-history modelling'. In its simplest form, the formula to calculate the probability that a customer will keep on buying is t^n, with n the number of purchases the customer made during a period (in this case a year), and t the fraction of the period represented by the time between his first and last purchase. Unlike RFM, this model is particularly good at predicting how soon a customer's buying activity will drop off and might prevent heavy overinvestment in profitable but disloyal customers.

The second main disadvantage of a scoring model such as RFM is that the monetary value is mostly based on revenue rather than profitability. The cost of servicing customers who buy only small quantities of low-margin products often exceeds the revenue they bring in. Therefore revenue, the average profit earned on each customer, must be brought into the analysis. By multiplying the probability figure for each period (e.g. a quarter) by the historical average profit number, the sum will be the estimated profit for each customer over the next year.

After analysing customers' profitability and the projected duration of the customer relationship, all customers can be placed into one of the four categories in the matrix shown in Figure 10.9.

Figure 10.9 Reinartz and Kumar's matrix for categorising customers and relationships

	Short-term customers	Long-term customers
High profitability	**Butterflies** High profit potential Actions: ■ Aim for transactional satisfaction and milk accounts ■ Cease investments soon enough	**True friends** Highest profit potential Actions: ■ Communicate consistently ■ Build attitudinal and behavioural loyalty by delighting them
Low profitability	**Strangers** Lowest profit potential Actions: ■ Make no investments in these relationships ■ Make profit on each transaction	**Barnacles** Low profit potential Actions: ■ If share of wallet is low, focus on up- and cross-selling ■ If size of wallet is small, impose cost controls

Source: Reinartz, W. and Kumar, V. (2002), 'The Mismanagement of Customer Loyalty', *Harvard Business Review*, (July), 86–94.

Summary

Direct marketing communications are an increasingly important instrument of the communications mix, and have the unique characteristics of being able to reach the consumer personally and directly, and immediately measure the effects. Direct marketing can serve a number of objectives, such as direct sales, sales and distribution support, and customer retention and loyalty enhancement. Direct marketing uses a multitude of tools and media. Some of them are non-addressable mass media instruments, such as direct response print and television ads and teletext. Others are addressable or personalised, such as direct mail, telemarketing and catalogues. A prerequisite for successful direct marketing communications is building, maintaining and managing a marketing database which enables the company to collect individualised information on all its customers and prospects, and use it in one-to-one marketing communications campaigns. Depending on the sophistication of data collection and data use, five types of databases and direct marketing techniques can be distinguished. Given the fact that keeping existing customers loyal is far less expensive than gaining new customers, relationship marketing, using databases and direct marketing techniques, becomes increasingly important. Based on database information on customer response to previous campaigns, several techniques, such as the RFM model, have been developed to assess the effectiveness of direct marketing communications campaigns.

Review questions

1 Why is direct marketing becoming increasingly important?

2 What are the typical characteristics of direct marketing communications, and to what extent do they differ from mass marketing communications?

3 What are the objectives and tasks of direct marketing communications?

4 How can mass media advertising be used in a direct marketing communications campaign?

5 Compare the various media and tools of addressable direct marketing communications. What are the advantages and disadvantages of each tool?

6 How can telemarketing be used as a direct marketing communications tool?

7 How important is a database for direct marketing communications and how can it be managed?

8 What are the stages in the evolution of database marketing use?

9 What is the importance of relationship marketing and how can direct marketing communications techniques contribute to customer loyalty?

10 How can the RFM model be used to measure the effectiveness of a direct marketing campaign?

Further reading

Bush, R., Smith, R. and Cresswell, P. (2003), *The B2B Handbook: A Guide to Achieving Success in Business-to-Business Direct Marketing*. London: Base One.

Gentle, M. (2003), *The CRM Project Management Handbook. Building Realistic Expectations and Managing Risk*. London: Kogan Page.

Molineux, P. (2002), *Exploiting CRM: Connecting With Customers. (The Management Consultancies Association Series)*. London: Hodder & Stoughton Educational.

Mullin, R. (2003), *Direct Marketing: A Step-by-Step Guide to Effective Planning and Targeting. (Marketing in Action Series)*. London: Kogan Page.

Stone, M., Band, A. and Blake, E. (2003), *The Definitive Guide to Direct and Interactive Marketing: How to Select, Reach and Retain the Right Customers*. London: Financial Times Prentice Hall.

Tapp, A. (2001), *Principles of Direct and Database Marketing*. London: Financial Times Prentice Hall.

Thomas, B. and Housden, M. (2002), *Direct Marketing in Practice*. Oxford: Butterworth-Heinemann.

Warwick, M. (2003), *Testing, Testing, 1, 2, 3: Raise More Money with Direct Mail Tests*. Hoboken, NJ: Jossey Bass Wiley.

Case 10

Direct marketing at Tesco – 'Join the Club . . .'

Tesco is a fast-growing UK-based international retailing group, operating almost 2,000 stores in 10 markets (including Eastern Europe and South-East Asia). Its core business is food retailing, of which it holds a 16.7% market share in the UK. With a turnover of €33.67 billion in the UK, Tesco is not only market leader, but also one of the most profitable retailers in its home market. With an international turnover amounting to €41.15 billion, Tesco is ranked seventh among the world's biggest food retailers. According to Tesco's Chairman, Terry Leahy, the company's 'organic growth is stronger than that of any other international retailer'.

The leading British grocer operates four different types of store: hypermarkets (Tesco Extra), supermarkets (Tesco Metro), convenience stores and petrol station stores (Tesco Express). The food retailer also operates a successful on-line shop (Tesco.com), which was introduced in 1996 on a small-scale basis, and slowly expanded to cover almost the entire UK by 2000. Tesco's virtual store managed to achieve its breakeven point in 2001, making a profit of €17.74 million in 2002. Expansion of the on-line business to other countries (including the US through a joint venture with Safeway) is on its way.

Tesco ClubCard

With the mission 'to create value for its customers, to earn their lifetime loyalty' (see Case Table 10.1), Tesco launched its ClubCard in February 1995. The innovative magnetic-strip card allowed customers to collect points and save money. For every pound spent, they would receive one point, worth one penny. Rapidly, around 14 million customers signed up to the programme and Tesco overtook J. Sainsbury's as the UK's leading grocery retailer.

However, Tesco's loyalty programme turned out to be much more than a mere points reward scheme.

Case Table 10.1
Tesco vision and values

Vision	To create value for customers to earn their lifetime loyalty
Values	No one tries harder for customers Treat people how we like to be treated
Brand promise	Every little bit helps

Source: Tesco Annual Report, 2002.

Indeed, Tesco's ClubCard has caused a considerable stir in the marketing world. Tesco recognised that the most valuable asset provided by the card is consumer insight. In a recent interview for the *McKinsey Quarterly* (2002), David Reid, Tesco's Deputy Chairman, acknowledges the strategic importance of the loyalty cards, stating that without them 'it would be like flying blind'.

Indeed, the cards collect all sorts of information on Tesco's customers, from shopping frequency to shopper basket contents. This valuable information sheds more light on its shoppers' driving forces which permits Tesco to develop more appropriate strategies to meet the needs of individual customer groups. For instance, this caused Tesco to adapt the product ranges stocked in different stores to the particular types of customers patronising them. Sophisticated insight, gained from analysing ClubCard data also allows Tesco to target specific awards more accurately. Thus, Tesco can direct high-rate saving schemes at families, discounts on holidays at elderly people and free 'Me Time' pampering sessions at women. Such a targeted approach saves the company over £300 million a year. Direct marketers have always known that good targeting is the key to efficiency and effectiveness.

Tesco's *ClubCard Magazine*

Tesco introduced its *ClubCard Magazine* with the following aims:

- To create a fun, information-packed magazine that communicates core Tesco brand values and services;
- To engender lasting brand loyalty and contribute significantly to customer awareness of new areas;
- To increase take-up of other Tesco ventures, especially non-food.

At Forward Publishing, they realised very quickly that you can't talk to someone in their twenties in the same way that you would to a person in their sixties. A single magazine just wouldn't do. And what better way to make use of the vast amount of customer information that Tesco has accumulated than to craft perfectly targeted magazines for people at different life stages?

From the ClubCard data, five life stages could be identified and different copies of the *ClubCard Magazine* were developed for each of them. In the magazine the latest products, ranges and services are introduced and practical features, hints and tips are offered – all adapted to the target audience. The *ClubCard Magazines* are mailed in spring, summer and autumn to the 7.5 million customers who earn over 250 ClubCard points on their purchases over a 12-week period. Every Christmas a newsstand size bumper issue is distributed to stores. Soon Tesco's *ClubCard Magazine* reached the highest circulation of any magazine in Europe. Incredibly, the circulation is 95% higher than the highest-selling women's newsstand titles.

The magazines also offer great targeted advertising opportunities to a wide supplier base. Brand-tracking after each mailing provides a clear picture of sales growth. Receiving increasing advertising support as a result of their success, the targeted *ClubCard Magazines* proved to be an important communication tool for Tesco.

Taking it one step further with Tesco Lifestyles

The marketing services consultancy agency 'Dunnhumby', which handled the initial trial, launch and continuing development of Tesco's loyalty programme, introduced 'Tesco Lifestyles' in 2001, a major new lifestyle customer segmentation based on the extensive ClubCard data. Shopper basket analysis and lifestyle information (e.g. family orientation, calorie consciousness, environmental concern, etc.) allowed them to give Tesco's ClubCard holders a Lifestyle code, enabling highly detailed targeting of quarterly ClubCard statement mailings. This way, key customer groups, such as the 50,000 vegetarians shopping at Tesco, could be targeted even more effectively and given special attention. Not only life 'stage' but also life 'style'-based magazines were developed (such as *Tesco Recipe Magazine* and *Tesco Vegetarian Magazine*) – see Case Figure 10.1 and Case Tables 10.2 and 10.3.

The data-mining skills of marketing consultancy agency 'Dunnhumby' were valued so highly at Tesco that it decided to acquire a majority shareholding in the company in 2001. From that moment on, Tesco could start sharing consumer profiles from its ClubCard database with its suppliers. The success of Tesco ClubCard had awakened interest in direct marketing among fast-moving consumer goods manufacturers, who could also use this valuable information to profile the buyers of their product categories. This would also allow more accurate targeting of their offers and promotions. These promotions could be targeted via Tesco-owned media channels, such as the quarterly statement mailings or mailing campaigns to selected 'clubs' within ClubCard (such as wine lovers, pregnant women, mothers with newborns or toddlers, etc.). According to a recent statement provided by 'Dunnhumby' (November, 2002), the latest ClubCard quarterly statements now contain more than four million coupon variations and produce a sales uplift in the region of £30 million. It also claims that sales effectiveness of new stores has been increased by 50% since 'Tesco Lifestyles' was introduced because of the ability to optimise the product range to better match potential shoppers' lifestyles and because of better customer targeting of marketing activity.

Nestlé Purina, one of the UK's biggest pet food manufacturers, was the first to take this opportunity to join forces with Tesco and in April 2003 launched a co-branded direct marketing campaign aimed at building customer loyalty, both to the Felix cat food range and to the Tesco supermarket chain. The mailing, targeted at thousands of consumers profiled from Tesco's ClubCard data, was sent in a Tesco-branded envelope and included a booklet entitled 'Keeping your cat purrfect . . . with a helping hand from Tesco and Felix', offering tips on keeping cats healthy and comfortable. The direct marketing campaign also featured a series of discounts on Felix-branded products as well as promotional material on Tesco Personal

Case Figure 10.1 Tesco's lifestyle-based customer segmentation

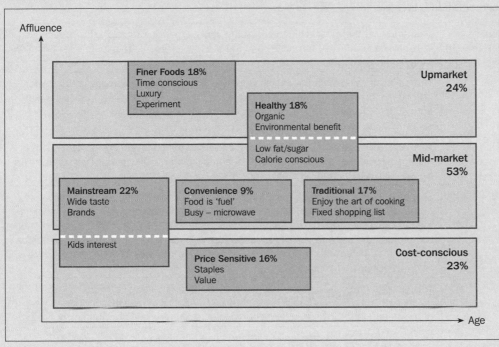

Source: Tesco/Dunnhumby.

Finance pet insurance products and Purina Pet-Care services.

Customised communications: Coupons@Till

Another innovative media channel introduced by Tesco in 2002 is the till receipts delivered to customers at the cash register. Through 'Coupons@Till' shoppers can receive customised coupons printed on their till receipt. These highly personal coupons are based on the customers' actual purchase history as recorded through the ClubCard scheme. Although this system may help reduce mailing costs, according to *Precision Marketing* (May 2002) its biggest benefit is that it will enable Tesco to provide even more targeted offers.

Building relationships at store level

As 30% of a retailer's customers appear to be responsible for 75% of its sales (*Financial Times*, 9 November 1996), it may be worthwhile for store managers to communicate with their highest-spending customers in a more personal way. The information provided by ClubCard data at store level could be used to identify these large spenders. Tesco encourages, for example, parents-to-be to sign up to its Baby Club at a point in time when they are likely to increase their spending in this area considerably. In an attempt to build a profitable long-term relationship with this group, Tesco provides them with a targeted magazine and special customised offers. At the individual store level, this relationship can be even

Case Table 10.2

Tesco lifestyle segmentation

Upmarket (24%)	Customers who are very health-oriented in terms of food, and real gourmets, enjoying finer foods.
Mid-market (54%)	Mainly families, contemporary mainstream or with kids, and time-conscious people that lead a busy lifestyle and therefore need quick and easy food. These customers are slightly traditional and health-oriented.
Less affluent (23%)	Price-sensitive customers, slightly traditional. They look for value and buy working-class brands.

Source: Tesco/Dunnhumby

Case Table 10.3

Tesco lifestyle segmentation – lifestyle groups

Price Sensitive (16%)	This group are the most likely to buy 'value' lines either due to necessity or because they provide good value for money and are the least affluent. They purchase a narrow range of products which tend to be processed and canned rather than fresh.
Mainstream (22%)	This segment represents the middle ground in terms of grocery shopping and is more likely to contain families with children at home. They have a trust for brands despite not being particularly affluent, which may be partly driven by pester power and, as such, tend not to be adventurous.
Traditional (17%)	This segment contains customers with a traditional outlook, who are predominantly older, however their affluence levels have some variation. They prefer traditional meals based around meat and vegetables and enjoy cooking and baking.
Convenience (9%)	These customers like convenience in food preparation and for them the microwave is an important feature in the kitchen. They tend not to be adventurous; however, there are differences in household composition and affluence reflected in the variety of food they consume. They can be families with older children who buy convenience in order to cater for different meals being consumed at different times or younger adults for whom cooking is a chore.
Healthy (18%)	This group is driven by different elements of health and dieting but with varying points of focus. There are traditional attitudes to healthy living which include plenty of roughage, households who buy diet foods or customers driven by organic foods.
Finer Foods (18%)	This segment is the most affluent and upmarket but displays different levels of adventurousness and has different requirements in terms of convenience. Some of these customers are fairly traditional, high spenders whilst others enjoy cooking but don't always have the time.

Source: Tesco/Dunnhumby.

further developed as it pays to market to this valuable group on a more individual basis (e.g. by sending birthday cards, organising special events, etc.). Based on store-level ClubCard information, store managers can also personally telephone defecting or dissatisfied customers.

Facing the loyalty wars . . .

According to Tim Mason, Marketing Director of Tesco Stores, one of the greatest management insights derived from the ClubCard data is the 'Fallacy of Averages' as a basis for understanding customers and marketing to them. As a result of its ClubCard programme, the Tesco supermarket chain has managed to be at the forefront of customer knowledge for several years now and it has been using this information very successfully. Therefore Tesco has been elected as the company which makes the best and most innovative use of direct marketing techniques in a Top Client Companies survey conducted by *Precision Marketing*, the UK's weekly business magazine devoted to targeted, accountable and responsive marketing

(*Precision Marketing*, June 2003). However, as the other supermarket chains follow Tesco's successful example and adopt their own customer cards and loyalty programmes, the company will be faced with a new challenge: to stay ahead in the loyalty wars . . .

Questions

1 What are Tesco's objectives with its ClubCard?

2 How does Tesco differentiate between its customers? (Consider the ClubCard magazines, the quarterly ClubCard statements, Coupons@Till, etc.)

3 Evaluate the information stored in the ClubCard database. What different types of data are kept? In what way is Tesco able to use its ClubCard database, considering the five stages in database marketing development?

4 How does Tesco's ClubCard data enhance Tesco's efficiency and effectiveness in communicating with its customers?

5 What methods are available to measure the effectiveness of the Nestlé Purina and Tesco co-branded direct marketing campaign?

6 Do you think Tesco's customer card is a good means for creating loyalty?

7 What is the challenge Tesco is currently facing and what can it do to stay ahead?

Case prepared by Malaika Brengman, Limburgs Universitair Centrum. *Based on:* Cuthbertson, R. (2003), 'Every Little Helps: Interview with Crawford Davidson, Director of ClubCard at Tesco, UK', *European Retail Digest*, (March), 37, 26; Child, P. (2002), 'Taking Tesco Global', *McKinsey Quarterly*, 3, 2002, http://www.mckinseyquarterly.com/article_page.asp?ar=1221&L2=21; Dunnhumby, (2002), 'Tesco ClubCard Case Study', November; Kleinman, M. (2001), 'Tesco to Offer Profiles of ClubCard Customers', *Marketing*, 2 August 2002; Knox, S. (2002), 'Building Customer Relations in the Value Chain', Cranfield University School of Management; http://www.marketing.unsw.edu.au/PDFFiles/Simon_Knox_presentation.pdf; 'Tesco Plays its ClubCard Right', *Marketing Week*, 3 November 1995; 'The Loyalty Wars', *Brand Strategy*, 24 December 2002; 'Tesco ClubCard Shake-up to Pave Way for Mail Cutbacks', *Precision Marketing*, 3 May 2002; Mauri, C. (2001), 'Card Loyalty. A New Emerging Issue in Grocery Retailing', Working Paper n° 42, Bocconi University School of Management, http://www.sdabocconi.it/dr/file/wp42.pdf; Peck, H. (2002), 'Tesco ClubCard Forever?', Cranfield School of Management, August; M+M Eurodata; LZ NET; M+M Planet Retail; Forward Publishing website; documents provided by Nigel Lawrence (Dunnhumby).

References

1 Hoekstra, J.C. (2002), *Direct Marketing: Van Respons tot Relatie (Direct Marketing: From Response to Relationship)*. Groningen: Wolters-Noordhoff.

2 Federation of European Direct Marketing, (2002), *Survey on Direct and Interactive Marketing Activities in Europe*. www.fedma.org.

3 Tapp, A. (2001), 'The Strategic Value of Direct Marketing: What Are We Good At? Part 1', *Journal of Database Marketing*, 9(1), 9–15.

4 Shannon, R. (2002), 'Grasping the Direct Marketing Advantage', *Journal of Financial Services Marketing*, 7(1), 75–9.

5 Goldberg, B.A. and Emerick, T. (1999), *Business-to-Business Direct Marketing*. Direct Marketing Publishers.

6 www.esprix.nl

7 Baldinger, A.L. and Rubinson, J. (1996), 'Brand Loyalty: The Link Between Attitude and Behavior', *Journal of Advertising Research*, 36(6).

8 Reicheld, F.F. (2001), *The Loyalty Effect: The Hidden Force Behind Growth, Profits and Lasting Value*. Boston: Harvard Business School Press.

9 Tapp, A. (2001), 'The Strategic Value of Direct Marketing: What Are We Good At? Part 1', *Journal of Database Marketing*, 9(1), 9–15.

10 Reinartz, W. and Kumar, V. (2002), 'The Mismanagement of Customer Loyalty', *Harvard Business Review*, (July), 86–94.

11 Federation of European Direct Marketing, *Best of Europe Cases 2000/2001*.

12 Bird, D. (2000), *Common Sense Direct Marketing*. London: Kogan Page.

13 Vergult, C., De Wulf, K. and Van Vooren, E. (1997), *DRTV, Technische Kenmerken en Beleving. Op Zoek naar Succesfactoren (DRTV, Technical Characteristics and Responses. In Search of Success Factors)*. Research report, Direct Marketing Research Centre, Ghent: Vlerick Leuven Gent Management School.

14 Verhoef, P., Hoekstra, J. and Aalst, M. (2000), 'The Effectiveness of Direct Response Radio Commercials. Results of a Field Experiment in the Netherlands', *European Journal of Marketing*, 34(1/2), 143–55.

15 De Rijcke, J. (2000), *Handboek Marketing*. Garant: Leuven, Apeldoorn.

16 Federation of European Direct Marketing, (2002), *Survey on Direct and Interactive Marketing Activities in Europe*. www.fedma.org.

17 www.esprix.nl

18 Bell, F. and Francis, N. (1995), 'Consumer Direct Mail – Just How Effective Is It?', *Seminar on Advertising, Sponsorship and Promotions: Understanding and Measuring the Effectiveness of Commercial Communication*. Madrid: ESOMAR publications.

19 Croft, M. (1994), 'Food for Thought', *Precision Marketing*, 5 December, 14–15.

20 Liederman, R. (1990), *The Telephone Book. How to Find, Get, Keep and Develop Customers*. London: McGraw-Hill.

21 Federation of European Direct Marketing, (2002), *Survey on Direct and Interactive Marketing Activities in Europe*. www.fedma.org.

22 Walrave, M. (1995), *Telemarketing: Storing op de Lijn? (Telemarketing: Badly Connected?)*. Leuven/Amersfoort: Acco.

23 Van Vooren, E. (1994), *Direct Marketing Actieboek: Bondige Tips voor Business-to-Business Marketers (Direct Marketing Action Book: Shorthand Tips for Business-to-Business Marketers)*, Zellik: Roularta Books.

24 Tapp, A. (2001), *Principles of Direct and Database Marketing*. London: Financial Times Prentice Hall.

25 Tapp, A. (2001), *Principles of Direct and Database Marketing*. London: Financial Times Prentice Hall.

26 Katzenstein, H. and Sachs, W.S. (1992), *Direct Marketing*. New York: Macmillan.

27 Federation of European Direct Marketing, *Best of Direct Marketing 2000/2001*.

28 Peppers, D. and Rogers, M. (1996), *The One-to-One Future: Building Relationships One Customer at a Time*. London: Piatkus Books.

29 Bügel, M.S. (1997), 'Van Direct Mail naar Event-Driven Marketing' ('From Direct Mail to Event-Driven Marketing'), *Tijdschrift voor Strategische Bedrijfscommunicatie*, 3(2), 98–106.

30 Hughes, A. (2000), *Strategic Database Marketing: The Masterplan for Starting and Managing a Profitable Customer-based Marketing Program*. Hightstown: McGraw-Hill.

31 Peppers, D. and Rogers, M. (1996), *The One-to-One Future: Building Relationships One Customer at a Time*. London: Piatkus Books.

32 Phelps, J., Nowak, G. and Ferrell, E. (2000), 'Privacy Concerns and Consumer Willingness to Provide Personal Information', *Journal of Public Policy & Marketing*, 19(1), 27–41; Milne, G. and Rohm, A. (2000), 'Consumer Privacy and Name Removal across Direct Marketing Channels: Exploring Opt-in and Opt-out Alternatives', *Journal of Public Policy & Marketing*, 19(2), 238–49.

33 De Wulf, K. (1998), 'Relationship Marketing', in Van Looy, B., Van Dierdonck, R. and Gemmel, P. (1998), *Services Management: An Integrated Approach*. London: Financial Times Pitman Publishing.

34 Bunk, R. (1992), 'Fluktuation Minimieren. Was Kunden Bindet' ('Minimise Fluctuations. It Keeps Customers Loyal'), *Absatzwirtschaft*, 4, 36–47.

35 Riechheld, F.F. and Sasser, W.E. (1990), 'Zero Defections: Quality Comes to Services', *Harvard Business Review*, (September/October), 105–11.

36 Christopher, M., Payne, A. and Ballantine, D. (1994), *Relationship Marketing: Bringing Quality, Customer Service and Marketing Together*. Oxford: Butterworth-Heinemann.

37 Reichheld, F.F. (2001), *The Loyalty Effect. The Hidden Force Behind Growth, Profits and Lasting Value*. Boston: Harvard Business School Press.

38 Curry, A. and Curry, J. (2000), *The Customer Marketing Method. How to Implement and Profit From Customer Relationship Management*. Riverside, NJ: Simon & Schuster Inc.

39 Jenkinson, A. (1995), *Valuing Your Customers: From Quality Information to Quality Relationships Through Database Marketing*. London: McGraw-Hill.

40 O'Brien, L. and Jones, C. (1995), 'Do Rewards Really Create Loyalty?', *Harvard Business Review*, 73(3), 75–82.

41 David Sheppard Association, (1999), *The New Direct Marketing. How to Implement a Profit-Driven Database Marketing Strategy*. Berkshire: McGraw-Hill Education.

CHAPTER 11
E-communications

Chapter outline

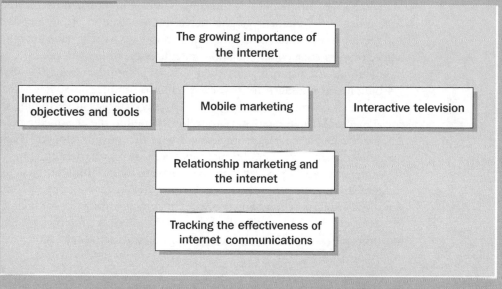

The growing importance of the internet

Internet communication objectives and tools

Mobile marketing

Interactive television

Relationship marketing and the internet

Tracking the effectiveness of internet communications

Chapter objectives

This chapter will help you to:

- Assess the importance of the internet and other new media as interactive communications tools

- Distinguish the different types of internet communication objectives and tools related to different communications objectives

- Understand the internet as an advertising medium, its success factors, and the different types of internet advertising

- Learn about new evolutions such as mobile marketing and interactive digital television

- Understand how the internet contributes to relationship marketing

- Learn how the effectiveness of internet communications can be measured

Introduction

Mass marketing communications techniques have dominated communications strategies for decades. Gradually, direct marketing principles have been adopted that allow access to each member of the target group on an individual basis. The next stage in this evolution is the trend towards real interactivity, i.e. not only is the marketer capable of communicating with his or her target group on a one-to-one basis, but also individual members of the target group are capable of responding to, and interacting with, the sender of the message. Although some direct marketing communications techniques also allow a certain degree of interactivity, the increasing penetration of internet and mobile phones and the rise of new interactive media such as interactive television are bound to change the nature of marketing communications interactivity. Moreover, people's media attention is fragmenting. For instance, more than 75% of UK adults have a mobile phone and some 1.4 billion text messages are sent every month. Among the 50% of UK households that now have an internet connection, over 30% say that they are watching less television as a consequence. So, marketers have to follow them into the new media they are consuming. Among these new media, the internet is by far the most developed. The internet is fundamentally different from traditional, and even direct, marketing communications tools: consumers can go all the way from awareness to interest to desire to action, all within the same medium and within the same session.[1] Although the internet has the capability to support all aspects of company processes (including logistics, e-commerce, e-procurement, etc.), this chapter will specifically focus on the use of the internet for marketing communications purposes. Also mobile marketing and interactive television are briefly discussed.

The growing importance of the internet

The internet refers to the computer network infrastructure enabling the exchange of digital data on a global scale. Worldwide 171.6 million hosts[2] are interconnected through cable and telephone networks. Through historical developments (the internet was first a military tool developed to make communication possible in case of nuclear wars and was later adapted by academics to share and exchange information) and intentional efforts, nowadays the internet is a unique, independent medium that is not owned or operated by a commercial or government body. Although the internet is also the network serving e-mail applications, news servers (newsgroups), ftp (file transfer), gopher (pure text-based information exchange) etc., it is often used as a synonym for the World Wide Web (WWW), the interactive and graphical communication medium invented by Tim Berners-Lee, physicist at the European Centre for Nuclear Research (Cern).[3] The Web is characterised by the use of hypertext mark-up language (HTML) that allows documents consisting of text, icons, sounds or images to be shared by different users, regardless of the computer operating system they use. The hyperlinks (text- or image-based) make it possible to navigate quickly through documents and pages by simple mouse-clicking. The growth of the WWW can be attributed to the user-friendly, consumer-operated pages utilising this hypertext capability.[4]

In March 2003 there were, on a global scale, 31.6 million domain names[5] (an indication of the number of websites). Worldwide, more than 650 million people (200 million of whom are in Europe) are connected to the internet. Scandinavian countries have the highest share of their inhabitants on-line in Europe, with penetration rates of more than 60%. When looking at absolute figures, Germany (38 million on-line), the UK (29 million) and Italy (23 million) are the largest European players.

Wired marketers gain the edge[6]

With internet audiences growing at a fast pace in every European country, it may come as no surprise to learn that on-line advertising is growing faster than any other marketing channel. Across the European markets on-line advertising has grown to 1.3% of media spend with market shares double that in France and five times that in parts of Scandinavia. Total advertising spend across Europe grew by about 2% in 2002, but the growth in on-line has been about 10 times faster as the internet industry completed its full recovery, triggered by the setback in confidence in 2000–2001. Europe's emerging markets in Greece and Eastern Europe are also accelerating fast and benefiting from the standards and research developed in the US and UK. Although different factors are driving growth in each country, a common resurgence in confidence in the internet industry has pushed on-line back up media planners' schedules. Analysts at Forrester Research calculate the European on-line ad market to have been worth €787 million in 2002 with a further €57 million of investment in other interactive channels, including iTV and wireless. They see the interactive market rising at a steady rate to reach €5.2 billion by 2006, with on-line still accounting for the lion's share. This evolution follows an increasing number of web users and web penetration rate in most countries.

Europe's web advertising market – 2002	Web advertising spend as % of traditional ad spend	Web advertising spend (€ millions)	Web users (thousands)	Web penetration of total population
Austria	0.6%	12	4,089	61%
Belgium	0.9%	17	4,383	53%
Denmark	1.3%	20	3,227	61%
Finland	1.1%	11	2,756	66%
France	1.0%	97	18,635	39%
Germany	0.8%	147	37,897	55%
Greece	0.0%	1	720	7%
Ireland	0.5%	3	1,180	41%
Italy	0.4%	34	23,189	48%
Luxembourg	1.9%	3	258	67%
Netherlands	1.2%	37	7,796	61%
Norway	2.5%	41	2,357	66%
Portugal	0.4%	9	3,245	40%
Spain	1.0%	37	10,622	32%
Sweden	5.0%	86	4,930	68%
Switzerland	1.1%	32	3,888	66%
UK	1.2%	198	29,315	61%
Total Western Europe		**787**		

Source: Forrester Research 2003.
Note that national IABs use different methodologies for collecting and reporting on data.

Internet communications objectives and tools

Basically the e-marketer can focus on four specific marketing goals when turning to digital tools:

- *Generating brand awareness*: putting or reinforcing the brand in the evoked set (i.e. the set of brands that is considered when the need or desire for the product or service arises) of consumers.

- *Shaping brand image and brand attitudes*: defining, reinforcing or changing the set of associations that differentiate the brand from competing products and improve consumers' knowledge and judgement about a brand.

- *Generating trial*: attracting new buyers to the brand by attracting brand switchers (i.e. consumers of competing brands) or consumers who have never tried the product category before. Trial stimulation implies an increase in the brand penetration rate in a certain market.

- *Creating loyalty*: influencing consumers' buying behaviour in the sense of increasing the number of satisfied and committed buyers. Striving for customer loyalty is also a cost-saving strategy as research indicates that the cost of attracting new customers can be as much as six times greater than the cost of retaining customers.

Generating traffic to a website is often stressed but is not actually a marketing communications end goal, except for e-commerce sites for which traffic is essential. Of course it is important to engage customers by the e-marketing actions that a company undertakes, but in the end site traffic will have to lead to one of the four objectives defined above.

Marketers have a large number of different e-marketing communications tools at their disposal. The multimedia capabilities of the net allow advertisers to use content, graphics, movement, audio and video. Almost every traditional communications tool has an on-line twin, take for instance e-coupons or on-line contests and seminars. Since almost every internet user has his or her own e-mail address, marketers can build a direct communication line with customers and prospects at lower costs than traditional direct marketing.

Brand websites

Brand websites are sites with specific brand-related information and/or services. A brand site can be used to communicate with the target groups and also as a platform that enables interaction with, or between, customers or the collection of individual customer data, for instance by letting them subscribe to receive e-newsletters. Brand sites can also form brand attitudes and enforce the positioning of the brand (Plate 19). For instance, the Swedish car make Volvo uses its website Volvocars.com to stress the concern for safety by making associations with lifestyle, people and attributes. The 'Volvo safe my life' club and 'Volvo Safety Showroom' on http://vcc.volvocars.se/safety/ promote Volvo's reputation for, and dedication to, safety.[7] Heineken, the Dutch brewer, develops brand websites for different countries stressing the theme 'enjoying'.[8]

Brand websites are essential to sustain or increase effectively the loyalty of user groups. A brand website is necessary for 'maintenance communication' all year round,

24 hours a day, with loyal customers and brand lovers. If heavy users of a brand feel bonded with the brand and the company, they will also expect to find more product information on the internet and might even want to contact the people behind their favourite product. However, merely having a website is in most cases a waste of budget since only the leading brands supposedly benefit from spontaneous traffic towards their brand sites. Brands with a moderate or low unaided brand awareness are likely to be disillusioned by the reach of their website. Hence, websites need continuous traffic-generating efforts. Successful traffic generators are on-line advertising, search engine optimisation and including the URL on corporate media (stationery such as business cards, letter headings and brochures), on packaging and in off-line advertising. The way a site is marketed has a substantial impact on the types of customers it attracts. Loyal customers are attracted by referrals, whereas 'butterflies' are attracted by promotional discounts and general untargeted banner advertising.[9]

Websites have become a favourite marketing tool for many brands. For instance, the German car brand BMW created www.bmwfilms.com, a site that is not linked to the company's main corporate site, solely to promote the launch of the Z4 roadster through the creation of unique content. The website shows several short movies created by celebrity Hollywood action filmmakers such as John Woo and Tony Scott. To view the movies website visitors have to leave their names and e-mail addresses. This example illustrates that a brand site does not have to be continuously hosted but can be used for a short period during a product launch. These temporary sites are also called micro-sites. A micro-site is a small website that exists for a specific purpose, and often doesn't contain more than fives or six pages. Companies often buy a specific URL related to the launch or promotion of a new product or service and then use the micro-site to enhance brand experience. Retailers frequently use micro-sites to highlight certain goods out of their massive assortment. Because of the many possibilities of adding content, audio, video and interaction, micro-sites have many advantages over banners and other standardised ad formats. But just like a standard brand or company site, micro-sites need promotion to get found and noticed by the target group. Micro-site-based campaigns have a limited shelf life that is comparable to any other advertising campaign. Each Playstation2 game has its own micro-site, giving consumers a direct experience of the game. The sites act as satellite sites to the main Playstation2 site, giving immediate access to gamers. When a game becomes obsolete, the micro-site is easily removable without affecting the main website.[10] For companies selling low-interest or impulse-buy products, or fast-moving consumer packaged goods such as soft drinks and candy bars, micro-sites are an interesting alternative to large and expensive websites that often demand enormous efforts to generate traffic to them.

Search engine optimisation

The biggest issue with having a brand or company website is to attract visitors to the site. Unlike traditional advertising with its interruptive nature, on-line marketing communications often require an action from the consumer as the internet is a pull medium. To find this traffic marketers use a combination of off-line and on-line marketing communications techniques. One specific on-line technique is to improve the listing in search engines. As 47% of web users tend to use search engines to find on-line information and the top 10 search query results get 78% more traffic than the others, this so-called 'search engine optimisation' is important to

▶

many companies, not least to on-line stores and e-commerce sites. Some web agencies are specialists in registering sites in top and niche search engines and in improving their rankings at the engine. For this purpose they use specific metatags, page titles, reciprocal linking, hidden keywords and multiple domain names as these are the factors that influence search engine robots' behaviour. Another way of increasing search engine share-of-voice is keyword buying, one of the on-line advertising techniques explained below.[11]

Online advertising

Online advertising can be defined as commercial messages in standard formats on specific rented spaces on websites of other companies. Different formats can be discerned, among which the banner is the best known. Banners are graphic images used as advertisements. Several standard formats (defined by number of pixels) exist: some are known as buttons (very small rectangles or squares), rectangles and skyscrapers (a thin and small format, typically along the right side of a web page). Apart from banners and their variants, other forms such as pop-ups and interstitials exist. Pop-ups are banners that appear in a separate window on top of or beneath (in which case called pop-unders) the visited website. Interstitials are ads that appear temporarily when loading a new web page. Sometimes they cover part of the browser; sometimes they take over the entire screen. Superstitials are additional pop-up browser windows that are opened when a new web page is opened; they are very intrusive and irritating. Interstitials can be static (an image file) or dynamic. In the latter case they often consist of a so-called rich media ad, i.e. an ad using animated content such as audio/video, Flash, Java, etc. to create special effects, interaction, or moving or floating ads. The floating ad that moves over the browser in an animated way and is usually very effective in getting the attention of the website visitor is also called 'shoskele' or overt. Rich media technologies such as Enliven (see unicast.com for cases) and Bluestreak (see bluestreak.com for expandable banners, for example) allow marketers to create banners that include games, contests, purchasing and other interaction within the banner.

A specific type of targeted on-line advertising is keyword buying. This is advertising on large search engines such as Google that is triggered by specific keywords and search terms and which appears alongside the search results. These 'smart ads' ensure higher impact and low waste for advertisers looking to target genuine potential customers. This type of advertising uses the unique benefits of the Web as a pull medium.[12] Another smart way of linking is affiliate marketing or affiliate networking. This is often used by on-line retailers. Amazon.com, the on-line book and CD shop, employs this technique most successfully, with more than 300,000 affiliates who offer small banner advertisements on their sites that direct the visitors to their sites to the Amazon site. The network also includes major portals such as Yahoo!. Each partner earns up to 15% commission every time a customer clicks on the banner and buys at Amazon. To Amazon this affiliate network accounts for a quarter of its revenues.[13]

The cost of on-line advertising differs substantially between the different formats, with pop-unders, banners and skyscrapers the cheapest and rich media ads, interstitials and keyword buying the most expensive. Of course this strongly correlates to the effectiveness and impact of each ad format. Table 11.1 shows the performance and the level of irritation of each ad format.[14] It is remarkable that the level of effectiveness in

Table 11.1 Performance of, and viewers' annoyance at, on-line advertising formats

Ad format	Performance*	Irritation*
Banner	*	*
Rectangle	**	***
Skyscraper	**	**
Pop-up	***	*****
Pop-under	**	****
Rich media ad	****	****
Interstitial	****	****
Keyword buying	*****	*

* The number of stars in the columns represents the general performance and annoyance caused for each ad format.

Based on: Elkin, T. (2003), 'Size matters; so does prize', *Advertising Age,* January, 13; Dynamic Logic (2001), 'Branding 101: an overview of branding and brand measurement for online marketers', (March), www.dynamiclogic.com

general strongly correlates with the perceived annoyance of an ad format by site visitors. Only keyword buying proves to be very effective without being irritating. Irritation by ad formats cannot be ignored because of its possible negative effect on brand attitude. Although larger ads are noticed more and communicate better, they are also often too disruptive for consumers, for instance due to their slow download. Consumers might take away a negative perception of the ad and, in consequence, of the advertised brand.[15]

Lancaster, a global cosmetic brand, launched its first on-line promotion campaign for its new pure skin care product line in Spain. The Lancaster website is very basic and, in fact, not much more than an on-line store and the brand did not have local websites to promote its global brand. The on-line campaign was preceded by a traditional media campaign in typically glossy magazines. Although the main goal was to increase the number of sales, it also had other objectives: launching the new skin care product, creating a client database and driving users to selected retail outlets. Lancaster placed banners on major websites for women to target Spanish women aged between 17 and 35. The click-through rate of this campaign was 2.4%, a good result thanks to the right targeting. The campaign was supported by a micro-site offering a product presentation, an automated on-line test and free advice from the dermatology department. Thousands of on-line consultations with the dermatologist through e-mail created a highly reliable database of potential customers, since users obtained feedback on their personal skin problems.

Less standard advertising formats are advertorials, content sponsorship and anchor deals. Advertorials are informative ads with an editorial approach but also a clearly identified advertiser. They can be used to communicate product and services news or attributes, third party endorsements, research or trends and can include visuals and links to the site of the advertising company. The content of the advertorial should be informative and engaging to reinforce messages in traditional media. They can also be linked to promotional activities where consumers are encouraged to read content to win prizes. Advertorials improve the opinion about the sponsoring company and increase awareness, influence image and encourage interest.

Content sponsorship consists of placing an advertiser's message in an area on a website that stands out from other advertisements, for instance a fixed and exclusive presence in a chosen section that is relevant to the advertiser's brand. Area and topic sponsorships are the two most common types. Procter & Gamble has a long tradition of associating products with content and content syndication dating back to radio days and early 1950s television (the first 'soaps' were initially sponsored by P&G which explains their name). For its Bounty brand, P&G used a modernisation of the same concept via on-line content sponsorship of 'Real Families, Real Fun' which featured a real-life view of family activities. The programme gathered input from a nationwide panel of young families by offering home projects, recipes, trips and entertainment ideas. The programme was launched on several portals and category sites and ran for six months. All programming carried the message 'this editorial programme is made possible by Bounty' and the content was syndicated, resulting in higher exposure across the Web. The programme was linked to Bounty's new website, launched simultaneously with 'Real Families, Real Fun'. By clicking on the Bounty logo, families could learn what the brand had to offer them.

Anchor deals represent the presence of a brand on certain content sites and portals as a supplier of brand-related content continuously for a long period. In exchange for co-branding on all Pepsi bottles, in-store displays and so on, Yahoo! handled all the technical assistance for the Pepsistuff.com website. The site became the centrepiece of the most successful campaign Pepsi ever ran. Consumers logged on to the site by entering a code found under the caps of Pepsi bottles. Each code was worth 100 points and could be redeemed for prizes such as DVDs and digital rewards (music downloads, credits at Yahoo! auctions, etc.) More than 50% of redeemed prizes were digital, saving Pepsi lots of money. Pepsi also saved $10 million by not having to print prize catalogues and the anchor deal with Yahoo! resulted in 2.9 million people providing their name, e-mail address, zip code and date of birth, a valuable database for organising polls, launching new products such as the Pepsi Blue (the new Pepsi-with-berries fusion launched in Spring 2003) and promoting the music celebrity endorsement with Britney Spears and Shakira.

Response rates for banner ads are lower than those for direct mail. The average click-through rate is between three-tenths and five-tenths of 1% (i.e. three to five responses for every 1,000 people who see the ad), and this rate continues to decrease despite new audio and video techniques that should contribute to a bigger impact and better attention-getting.[16] Thanks to the precise measurement possibilities of banners (click-through rates), some research and testing was done to improve their effectiveness. The following tips should be taken into account when developing banner advertisements:

- *Consider placement of the banners*: just like in traditional advertising, well-thought-out media planning is a must as the more relevant an on-line advertisement is to the audience, the better it will work. Some sites, and pages within sites, will perform better than others. Not only page views (audience reach), but also selectivity (which target groups are reached at a certain site) and specific contextual content (domains of interest in the website) should be considered. To create brand awareness, sites with a large reach, such as MSN, should be considered. To shape brand attitudes, these sites should be supported with others that have a more specific context, endorsing the image. To generate trial, a

▶

combination of contextual sites, sites with selective audiences (that have the right profiles) and sites with a large reach are advised. Targeted banners based on the content of the website also get better response rates. Research has also shown that the attitude of visitors towards the website where the ad is placed will affect their attitude towards the advertising.[17]

■ *Consider frequency of exposures*: traditionally a rule of thumb was that after three exposures the ad effectiveness would drop. Research has shown that although click rates tend to drop (from 2.7% to less than 1% after four contact moments), brand awareness through on-line advertising still increases after the third and fourth exposure.[18] For instance, Travelocity, an on-line provider of travel services, noticed an increase in brand awareness of 44% among people who were exposed to its banners four times or more.[19]

■ *Make the ad more goal-oriented with a call to action and create a sense of urgency*: as in all direct response communications, a clear 'reason to click' should be pointed out. Without a reason to click, such as prizes to win or discounts to be obtained, a user will not have an incentive to leave the site he or she is surfing. Adding limiting time indications such as 'now' will also have a positive effect on response figures. Call to action phrases will lead to a rise in click-through rates of 15%.[20]

■ *Add trigger words*: words like 'free' and 'click here' will increase response rates. Using the latter actually led to a five times larger click-through than for the same banner without these words. This was also confirmed by a more recent study:[21] the 'click here' version of the banner had a response rate of 11.13% compared with 2.87% for the normal banner. The reasons for this astonishing finding could be twofold: 'click here' is, of course, a call to action; on the other hand, it could be that inexperienced net users do not know that a banner may be clicked unless told.

■ *Make animated, well-coloured banners with limited text and keep the message simple*: the keywords used on a banner are very effective when they are well perceived and clearly linked to a certain brand or company and will lead to higher response rates. One study[22] found a 25% increase in response rate when using animations, 18% when using cryptic messages, 16% when asking questions.

■ *Consider placement of logos*: the performance of banners and skyscrapers appears to be driven to a large extent by the placement of the advertiser's logo within the ad. Awareness and persuasion metrics indicate that skyscrapers with the logo at the bottom perform worst, while skyscrapers with the logo at top and bottom perform best.[23]

On-line events and seminars

Even face-to-face communications tactics such as exhibitions, trade shows and events have been translated to an on-line environment. Victoria Secret, the American undergarment brand, introduced one of the first commercial on-line events in 1999 when it held its web-based fashion show. It was announced in advertisements in the *New York Times*, TV commercials during the Super Bowl football game and other traditional advertising media. The on-line event drew 1.2 million visitors, an 82% increase in web traffic. In subsequent years the on-line fashion shows were continued. On-line seminars, with experts that first give an exposition and afterwards participate in chat sessions, are also becoming more common in business-to-business markets and professional segments. As broadband penetration increases, bandwidth problems will disappear and on-line events, workshops, seminars and narrowcasts will gain popularity as they save time and money both for the organisers and the participants and allow a much wider and more international reach.[24]

Advergames and on-line games

On-line games are a rich media type of brand-related on-line entertainment used as a tool for brand interaction and experience. In other words, advergames use interactive game technology to deliver embedded messages to consumers. The advertising message can then become an integral part of playing the game. Advergames are often used in combination with e-mail and viral marketing campaigns as their entertainment value increases the value perception of the mail receivers and tends to evoke consumer responses beyond their own personal interaction, such as forwarding the message to friends and relatives. In this way advergames can reach up to four times the initial number of gamers through referrals. Games can drive traffic to websites, for instance candy producer Nabisco's website dedicated to games, Candystand.com, is attracting 3.5 million visits per month, with each visit lasting on average half an hour. Games can also be used to expand the company's marketing database while engaging consumers in a bit of fun, like Guinness did on its brand site when launching the Extra Cold sub-brand.[25] Subscription-based on-line games, like the Cap'n Crunch game of Quaker Oats, are an effective way of capturing data and constructing an opt-in database of names and e-mail addresses.[26]

Advergaming seems to be one of the new trends in internet advertising that by 2005 could generate about $1 billion, according to a Forrester report. This is mainly because one of the problems of internet advertising is the user's willingness to click away from a website or from a message. Games present enticing content that encourages consumers to click on the advert (in this case the game).[27] A survey found that 60% of 25–34 year olds and 56% of 35–44 year olds play an on-line game once a week, proving that this medium is effective not only to computer-game minded youngsters. In 2002, 35.1 million people worldwide played on-line games and this figure was expected to grow to 105 million in 2005.[28]

Although the costs of creating an advergame exceed those of rich-media banners, interaction time and brand immersion should be considered as well. On-line games and advergames are tools that permit the on-line marketer to build brand awareness and brand image through a more interactive user experience.[29] For example, players of the Jurassic Park III game played for an average of 19 minutes, which is obviously a guarantee of a bigger mind-share among the target groups. The retention value of advergames is said to be 10 times higher than the retention value of traditional broadcast commercials. They allow voluntary self-induced exposure to brand communications and are a non-intrusive and non-interruptive way of internet advertising. Depending on the approach, a high percentage of players don't even see the game as 'advertising'.[30] Advergames are also used to teach consumers the prime benefits of a product and increase their brand knowledge by making a brand's core values and attributes central in the on-line game. Nike launched a 3D game that demonstrated the different performance features of the Nike Shox basketball shoe, from which the gamer could chose in the opening sequence of the game.

Viral marketing

Quite often the success of advergames and on-line games strongly depends on the strength of on-line word-of-mouth advertising, also called 'word-of-mouse' advertising. Viral marketing is the set of techniques that is used to spur brand users and lovers, game participants or advocate consumers among the target group to promote their favourite brand to friends and relatives. They are put to work to spread the word about the brand or product by using e-mail, SMS, 'tell or send to a friend' buttons or other referral tools on websites. Viral marketing attempts to harness the strongest of all consumer triggers: personal recommendation. Viral marketing uses the snowball principle and the typical network nature of the internet strongly supports the quick exponential growth in the message's exposure and its influence in a rather effortless way. Just like viruses, viral marketing strategies take advantage of rapid multiplication to explode the message to thousands or millions of 'victims'. One of the first and probably most successful viral campaigns was set up by Hotmail. By simply using the free web-based e-mail package, consumers hawked the message as every message they sent contained a Hotmail ad ('Get your own private free e-mail at http://www.hotmail.com'). Hotmail grew to 12 million accounts in its first year, 1996. Compared to the results of its print campaigns (100,000 new subscribers) this result was impressive.[31]

Member-get-member action can also be considered as a viral technique when its goal is to enlarge an e-mail database in a very short time. An example of this kind of viral action was the Dove Moments campaign for the Unilever brand in the Netherlands. Using the website dovemoments.nl, visitors could request a 'Dove moment' (a package of Dove samples) for a friend (referral) by composing a personalised e-letter. A hundred thousand sample packages were delivered in the first month of the campaign, resulting in a new database of the same size in only one month.[32] Other typical viral examples are screensavers (remember the Bud Frogs and Dancing Hamsters/Babies), e-cards and rich media e-cards, and funny commercials, pictures or cartoons. According to a survey, 81% of those who receive viral messages pass them on to at least one other person, and almost half of those receivers are likely to pass the message along to two or three other people.[33] Finally, for 68% of surfers, word-of-mouth is the top source for learning about new websites, which puts referrals and viral marketing in second place after search engines (74%) and above links on other sites (65%), ads (46%) and on-line advertising (45%).[34]

HP uses 'fishy' tactics

Hewlett-Packard developed an engaging interactive application that encouraged the use of the multiple original print (MOP) function on HP printers as opposed to printing a single copy and taking photocopies. The MOPy Fish is a lifelike virtual pet goldfish swimming around the user's desktop in its own aquarium. To survive, just like a Tamagotchi, the fish needs regular feeding and attention. Each day MOPy Fish owners are rewarded points and each time they use the multiple print option on their PC they gain 20 points. The points can then be exchanged on the HP website for aquarium accessories which in turn enhance the environment of the fish. MOPy Fish is an example of strategic viral marketing that successfully increased awareness and use of the multiple original print function, drew users to the HP website and created a

▶

digital one-to-one relationship between HP and its customers. Only a few months after the launch the pet fish was downloaded more than 16 million times and it is in the *Guinness Book of Records*.

On-line contests and sweepstakes

Related to on-line games are the internet versions of contests and sweepstakes. They are particularly effective for generating enthusiasm, building name recognition and rewarding long-time customers. On-line contests often have an off-line component, for instance in TV or radio ads to get attention or on packaging, leaflets, etc. to communicate the contest. Sometimes codes such as access codes or lottery numbers are distributed either in or on packaging but relate to the brand's (promotional contest) website. A contest should arouse a customer's interest and demand interaction. E-contests can just draw winners at random (sweepstake) or ask for a certain skill or creative involvement (contest). For example, Heineken held a beer-mat contest asking participants to create and design their own beer mat. Just like advergames, on-line contests seem to be growing in popularity.[35] Keys to success are an appropriate play value of the contest and appropriate incentives to participate. The latter is determined by the business a company is involved in and the goal of the contest. For instance, if the objective of the contest is to create a customer database, a company should offer one of its products as the prize. This relevancy will attract the right entrants, since providing an incentive to people who can and will buy your products and services should be the goal. A contest or sweepstake with a high number of participants might look successful at first sight but if it attracts the wrong people, those who enter any contest just to win something, the campaign won't be effective and customer acquisition costs will rise. Prizes should also create a sense of value, uniqueness and emotional appeal to winners. If the prize is large enough or attractive enough, people will take the time to enter and fulfil requirements such as registration and they will even tell their friends and colleagues about the contest. Of course, contests and sweepstakes will only work if people know about them, and if you want people to come back regularly, it will be necessary to award prizes on a daily or weekly basis.[36]

Frozen dessert retailer Häagen-Dazs created interest around its new dessert, the Dazzler, with an on-line contest and promotion. With every purchase in a Häagen-Dazs outlet, consumers received a game card during a two-month period. On the card was a code that when entered on the Häagen-Dazs website took customers to a game page where they could play an on-line match-and-win game. Site visitors had to select three of the nine 'Dazzlers' on the page, which revealed a prize. If the three prizes revealed were the same, the visitor won that prize. Häagen-Dazs was giving away $11 million worth of prizes, including a three-year Jaguar XK8 lease, $5,000 shopping sprees, free ice cream for a year and gift certificates for the Banana Split Dazzler. Contest participants were asked to register with information such as age, zip code, and e-mail address to enter the contest.[37]

E-sampling and e-couponing

Companies (especially those in the consumer packaged goods business) can use the internet as a means of promoting their products by sampling or couponing, for instance banner advertising leads consumers to a data-capture page where they leave their details to receive samples or coupons. Traditionally, brands had a few options for reaching consumers with a **sample**: sampling at events, on street corners, in the mailbox, with newspapers or magazines, on door hangers, and in-store sampling. Now the internet adds a new way of sampling (combined with mail addresses) at a lower cost per converted person because of the opt-in request. E-sampling gives marketers the option to carry out extremely accurate one-to-one demographic, geographic and psychographic targeting, whereas traditional sampling is often based on convenience targeting (street corners, shop) or neighbourhood clusters (mailbox sampling). There is also less waste or duplication as 'one sample item per household' can be controlled and consumers make a conscious choice to request a sample themselves. As targeted users can be part of a marketing database that tracks their behaviour and engages them over time, e-sampling is less of a one-shot and more part of a CRM campaign. Companies can also get real-time, instant consumer feedback on usage and likeability of the sample without high costs or much effort.[38] For some businesses e-sampling can be completely handled on-line, for instance software companies providing free downloads or demo versions of their software, often with an expiration time of 30 to 60 days. On-line music and book stores like Amazon allow their customers to sample 30-second clips of music or fragments of books before ordering.[39]

E-coupons are the on-line equivalent of print coupons and can be redeemed on-line (on e-commerce sites) or printed. They can be delivered via e-mails or via a website. Just as with e-sampling, they offer the ability to monitor the user's online shopping behaviour (if redeemed on-line) and can reach an audience that would not bother to cut out print coupons in newspaper or magazine advertisements. Apart from these advantages, on-line couponing can also save money compared to the off-line printing costs and advertising costs. E-couponing also makes it possible for the advertiser to experiment with split/run tests (choosing which offer/design combination has the best response results and then quickly adapting the coupon's value or message) and to make immediate and automatic responses by tailoring the coupons to the demographic profile of the consumer. Research found that about 30% of the web population uses on-line coupons.[40]

To build awareness and encourage trials of the new Pert Plus Shampoo, Procter & Gamble created a high-profile on-line marketing campaign for the product targeted at 18 to 49 year old males and females. The campaign included a micro-site, 25 banners, pop-up windows, a sweepstake, e-sampling and an opt-in e-mail marketing programme. Internet users could request samples, enter the sweepstakes and send referral e-mails to friends, all from within the HTML banners and pop-ups without leaving the site they were on. Other banners drove traffic to the mini-site (pertplus.com) and to customised content sponsored areas at Sony and E! Online. A video banner featured part of the 'Sinkboy' television commercial, in which the wacky character Sinkboy runs around Miami attempting to wash people's hair with the new Pert Plus. P&G also tested referral sampling: an e-mail-based referral system that allowed internet users to request a shampoo sample, enter the sweepstakes and send a 'hint' or funny e-mail to a friend suggesting that it was high time he or she washed his or her hair. Recipients of that e-mail could then easily request a sample of Pert Plus. If entrants indicated that they were willing to receive further information (opt-in), a survey about their shampoo usage was sent to them.

E-mail marketing

The one 'killer' application that is most used by internet users is e-mail. Globally, around four billion e-mail messages are sent daily. Just as in traditional direct marketing, e-mail marketing can be used inbound and outbound.[41] In fact, e-mail marketing is basically not much more than using the internet and e-mail for direct marketing practices. The net provides speed, flexibility and low costs compared with traditional direct marketing media and customisation and full individualisation are much easier and cheaper. With these features, e-mail marketing usage has grown significantly during the last five years. According to Jupiter Research, the average number of commercial e-mail messages that US on-line consumers receive per year will increase from 40 in 1999 to more than 1,600 in 2005.[42] Forrester Research estimates that the total spending for e-mail marketing services in the US reached $3.4 billion by the end of 2003; DoubleClick projects a growth rate for e-mail marketing that is nearly twice the rate for other on-line marketing tactics. One of the clear reasons for this surge in volume and spending is that e-mail marketing is more effective in terms of response than traditional direct mail or other web campaigns such as banners or interstitials. Click-through rates of commercial e-mails range between 2% and 10%, and response figures of 32% are achieved for highly targeted personalised messages and up to 18% for e-mail newsletters. Banner click-through rates are still far below 1% and a traditional average direct marketing response rate is 2%.[43] Moreover, it is estimated that an e-mail marketing campaign costs between 60% and 65% less than a traditional postal direct marketing campaign by eliminating postage, paper and printing expenses. This also implies that e-mail made it possible to start using direct marketing for lower-cost items and that communicating with less frequent buyers now is profitable.[44] E-mails reach their destination within a few seconds of sending, and responses will also typically arrive within 48 hours of a communication. Compared to the usual six weeks response time for a traditional direct mail campaign, this speed of delivery and response is clearly another advantage of e-mail marketing.[45]

Marketers also appreciate the easy and inexpensive way of tailoring messages to groups of customers or even individuals. Content of e-mails and newsletters can be customised to specific customer interests and needs and running tests on small samples to refine messages before finally mailing them to the entire target market is cheap. Research has shown that personalisation has profound effects on results. The average click-through rates can be expected to double when messages are fully personalised. Personalisation effects grow over time: where impersonal e-zines (electronic magazines sent by e-mail or e-newsletters) are still able to reach curious people, only the personalised ones seem to be able to continue attracting the attention of readers.[46]

Measurement and tracking of e-mail marketing effectiveness can be carried out automatically and if necessary at a detailed level. There's also a link with viral marketing as it is easy for receivers of a promotional e-mail message to pass it along to other readers simply by forwarding it to friends or relatives who they think might be interested in the offer.

Privacy and legal issues were once a hot and controversial issue in the e-mail marketing industry but now most markets have restricted and regulated the use of commercial e-mails, spam (unsolicited e-mails) is forbidden in Europe and opt-out possibilities should be offered in each message sent, creating a good environment for permission-based programmes. Still, permission and privacy must be cornerstones of every e-mail marketing programme. Successful e-mail campaigns are based on thrust. 'Opt-in' means that users have voluntarily agreed to receive commercial e-mails about topics that they find interesting. They do so by subscribing on websites and checking a box. 'Opt-out' means that users have to uncheck the box on a web page to prevent being put on an e-mail list. 'Opt-in' is better than 'opt-out' as the quality of the database or list will be better.[47] Companies should always stress the purpose of collecting addresses and guarantee that the information will not be disclosed to third parties or misused. However, the real threat for e-mail marketing is overuse due to its low cost and reputation for outperforming other on-line actions and traditional direct marketing. Some analysts predict that response rates will seriously be driven down due to each consumer's inbox being flooded by thousands of commercial messages and massive opting-out. Another limitation of the new direct marketing medium is the lack of good opt-in e-mail databases. Supply is limited which results in companies renting the same lists, with bombarded and tired consumers as a consequence. Often the first and most difficult challenge for marketers who want to launch an e-mail campaign is to create a good target database of prospects and customers.[48] The second challenge is then to deliver the right content as low relevance of content and high mailing frequency both incite consumers to unsubscribe from a mailing list. A survey among 1,000 e-mail users concluded that the preference in e-mail content differs between males and females. Men are more interested in thematic content such as compelling news and information while for women promotional content like discount offers and samples are welcome.[49]

Ten dos and don'ts when using e-mail marketing

1 Personalise all e-mail messages to lift response rates and decrease the number of unsubscribers by including the recipient's name and company and tailoring content based on the customer's interests, preferences, behaviour, demographics or requested information.

2 Invest in the e-mail database by using every contact moment (sales, calls, bills, etc.) and every communication to give customers the opportunity to provide their e-mail address and to select the type of information they want and when they want to receive it. Make signing up for e-mail newsletters easy to do and verify customer name and address information in real time. Don't ask more than seven questions on the subscription page and don't ask for information outside the scope of what you are delivering.

3 Test the best period to send e-mails by comparing response rates for e-mails sent in the morning, evening, specific day, weekend, etc.

4 Compose short, clear and compelling messages with a clear subject line and state the offer in the first lines of the message. Don't reuse the same content and use links to draw readers to the company's website.

5 Choose HTML messages whenever possible (depending on the percentage of people in your list that can receive HTML instead of text-based e-mails). They allow the use of compelling images and custom fonts, and the embedding of audio and streaming video. Click-through rates on HTML e-mails are also two to five times higher than on text-based messages.

6 Complement the e-mail marketing programme with an ad banner strategy to service each customer's interests and needs.

7   Use customer feedback on e-mail campaigns to fine-tune products and the way they are delivered.

8   Deliver the content that you had promised and the receiver expects. For instance, if they signed up for a personalised 'just for me' newsletter, don't send untailored mails. Stick to the frequency that was promised. Less than one a month is probably too infrequent to maintain the continuity of the relationship and more than one a week is usually a bit much.[50]

9   Develop a company's own voice and style and stick to the e-mail template, maintaining brand consistency in every message.

10 Create and communicate a privacy policy and keep respecting the privacy of your customers.[51]

Aberlour, a Scottish brand of single malt whisky, used an e-mail marketing campaign to build awareness among the target group and generate pre-Christmas sales of its 10-year-old single malt whisky. Apart from this it wanted to test a previously untried market: women buying whisky as a gift for their husbands or friends. The last campaign objective was to build a database of whisky enthusiasts who gave their permission for further activities and communications. Aberlour bought two e-mail lists, both of which matched the profile of the typical whisky drinker. A sequential e-mail campaign rolled out over a two-week period consisted of three stages: an initial invitation to enter a prize draw and win a case of whisky, a reminder e-mail to everyone who didn't respond to the first e-mail and a final e-mail to all prize draw losers with a follow-up drive-to-retail offer. As a result, over 10% of the cold list were permissioned to Aberlour's database, the drive-to-retail offer achieved a 1% conversion rate and over 95% of the entries volunteered further profiling information.

Mobile marketing

By the end of 2001, there were over 850 million mobile phone users worldwide compared to 500 million e-mail users. During the past decade mobile phones have evolved from devices reserved for a select group to mass-market necessities and fashion accessories. Markets in Europe are slowly reaching saturation and while mobile phones dominate the wireless scene, other devices such as PDAs (personal digital assistants) – with 6.5 million sold worldwide in 2002 – will contribute to the growth of mobile marketing communications.[52] In Europe, Scandinavia has leapt ahead in the ratings (for example, 87% penetration of mobile phones in Finland) but several other countries such as Austria and Italy have exceptionally high rates of mobile use (respectively 92% and 90%) and mobiles are on average owned by 80% of the European population. The percentage of mobile users is higher in the UK than in France or Germany and the UK's mobile owner tends to be younger than in many other European countries.[53] Nowadays SMS (short message system) is widespread and well used by people of all ages. The number of SMS users varies, from 97% of 15–17-year-old mobile users, over 88% of 35–44-year-old mobile users to 38% of the 65+ age group. The average number of SMS messages sent per month, over all user groups, increased from 44 in 2000 to 56 in 2002. This popularity emerged despite major shortcomings such as lack of colour, graphics, audio, video and the limitation of 160 characters per message.[54]

Mobile marketing or wireless advertising consists of all the activities undertaken to communicate with customers through the use of mobile devices to promote products and services by providing information or offers. It typically consists of commercial or sales promotional messages sent to mobile phones by using permission-based SMS or MMS (multimedia messages such as digital pictures, audio tunes and video), advertising or WAP/i-Mode advertising (internet advertising viewed by the internet connection of the mobile device). Mobile marketing will be more productive and useful to marketers in the near future when time- and location-based information services as well as real MMS will become widely available and popular (supported by GPRS and 3G technology). Location-aware advertising messages (for instance, you receive a wireless coupon on your mobile phone or PDA that is related to a shop or restaurant in your immediate neighbourhood) are expected to create five to ten times higher click-through rates compared to internet advertising messages. A study revealed that the degree of acceptance of SMS marketing is significantly influenced by the level of exposure and the knowledge that marketing messages are controlled by a known and trusted service provider. In this respect, SMS advertising is considered as acceptable as TV and radio advertising.[55]

SMS marketing campaigns

- *SMS contest and sweepstakes linked to codes on packaging or in advertising*:
  - Tiger, a premium import beer brand in Shangai competing with Budweiser, wanted to stimulate interest at retail level and increase brand stickiness (i.e. foster brand loyalty) as well as sales by using an SMS quiz. The campaign was tied to consumption: each purchase of a Tiger beer gave a voucher that allowed people to play a quiz game based on World Cup soccer. The game offered prizes, entertainment and soccer news. It had a 95% conversion rate and over two games per player were played. The action sold €100,000 of extra beer.
  - McDonald's build a GSM database in the UK with an SMS campaign. Within its french fries boxes there was a special code that customers could send through SMS to win thousands of prizes such as TV sets, DVD boxes, DVD players, MP3 players, etc.). The campaign was supported by a website and in-store communications and flyers in 1,200 McDonald's outlets. A GSM database of over 220,000 subscribers was built in only ten weeks. McDonald's now obtains 30% response rates on mobile marketing campaigns on this permission-based database.
- *Permission-based alerts*: marketing messages proactively pushed to a consumer's device. Most often this involves an SMS or WAP alert that may include relevant content accompanied by an ad. This model is best executed on an opt-in basis where the user grants permission to the marketer to deliver such ads.
- *Lead generation using mobile marketing*: Mercedes-Benz used rich media e-mails and SMS text messaging to attract qualified prospects to test-drive the new Mercedes Benz C car. A substantial database of prospects was built and 18% registered for a test-drive while half of them gave permission to be contacted by SMS in the future.

SMS has many advantages as a marketing tool. It is still considered a novelty and a more personal and engaging form of communication than e-mail. Just like e-mail, SMS is instantaneous, but it has an even faster and wider reach than e-mail as the mobile device usually accompanies the user and SMS can be received anywhere, at any time. It also allows for more precise targeting as every mobile phone is tied to one single person, whereas computers are often shared. Recipients are also able to call back immediately for further information when prompted by an SMS message. Production costs and lead times of SMS messages are negligible. The average response rate to commercial SMS messages is 10% to 15% while an average campaign cost is only €24,000.[56] As SMS actions are quite intrusive, they should always be launched on an opt-in basis, which implies that they should be regarded as a complement for other marketing communications. In most cases it needs a traditional medium (above-the-line, packaging, etc.) to broadcast the invitation to participate. An SMS message is most appreciated when the content is appealing (an offer, a game, an incentive, a contest) and attractive. The most effective wireless campaigns are sweepstakes. An instant-win contest is a good way to acquire a database of consumers.

Until now we can conclude that the power of SMS marketing is outperforming that of direct mail and e-mail, but on the other hand this is easily explained by the use of voluntary opt-in databases and the fact that SMS campaigns are not yet a very common marketing technique, giving it a unique aspect with not much advertising clutter negatively influencing the effects. It can be predicted that the effectiveness of SMS campaigns will decline as the number of campaigns increases.

When using mobile marketing techniques, a lot of legal and moral implications have to be taken into account. The Mobile Marketing Association (MMA) is the key institute regulating the mobile industry. The key guidelines of the MMA code of conduct can be summarised as follows:

1 Consumers must have given explicit consent to receive messages prior to any communication being sent.

2 Every communication must clearly indicate who the message is from.

3 Every communication must have clear opt-out options.

Other legal instruments (e.g. the Data Protection Act) require companies to treat consumer data fairly. It should clearly be indicated to consumers how often they will receive messages and what types of messages will be sent.[57]

Interactive television

Interactive (digital) television, or i(D)TV, is television content that gives viewers the ability to interact with programmes and to use a number of interactive services such as t-government, t-banking, t-commerce, t-learning, information, games, video-on demand and communication (t-mail), all supported by a set-top-box.[58] The new medium offers some new possibilities for marketers as they are now able to move buyers through the complete buying process. Interactive advertising, for example, allows viewers to ask for extra information about products and services, receive coupons or samples and even buy a product, all with one push of a button. iDTV will also enhance the possibilities of understanding the viewing behaviour of the target group as well as developing personal relationships with viewers and making tailored interactive advertising content adapted to the needs of the viewers.[59] Apart from interactive commercials, the iDTV medium provides advertisers with other possibilities:

- *Programmercials or programme sponsoring*: for instance a tour operator sponsors a travel programme on iDTV that gives viewers the opportunity to receive more information about a destination, order a catalogue or book a holiday;
- *Advertising messages or logos on the electronic programme guide*, visited on average five to ten times by the iDTV viewer;
- *Linking with certain t-services*, for instance the *Financial Times* sponsoring the t-banking application on iDTV;
- *Bannering during programmes*;
- *Walled gardens*, a kind of website created specifically for iDTV, and linked with an interactive commercial or an iDTV programme, for instance through product placement.[60]

The impact of digital television for marketers is considered important because the market penetration of televisions is so much higher than that of personal computers. Forrester predicts that by 2006 the number of Europeans watching iDTV will be higher than the number of internet users. As technology develops further, the distinction between the PC, TV and telephone will completely blur. This is called media convergence.[61]

Relationship marketing and the internet

The basis of loyalty programmes consists of collecting data that are related to the customer's behaviour. What kind of customer is he or she? What does he ask for? What does she buy? What interests do they have and how can we tailor our e-communication to his or her wants? Customer profiles drive what the website looks like, which e-mails he or she receives, what kind of offers he or she receives, etc. The Web is not about fragmenting audiences but about creating one-to-one relationships for marketers and increasing the bond between consumers and producers. The internet is well suited for the evolution towards an individualised, tailored value proposition. It offers addressability, two-way continuous interactivity, customisation capabilities, on-demand availability and seamless transactions. Marketers can leverage interactive media to identify self-selected users, enhance loyalty by providing value-added services, use what they learn about their customers to customise existing products or create new products and services, and start an ongoing on-line communication with customers. E-mail communication with customers is more personal and intimate than the traditional letter with glossy brochure. When a customer sends an e-mail to a company, the person who replies to the e-mail suddenly becomes the representative for the whole company.[62]

An increasing proportion of contact with customers is conducted via the Web rather than the phone. E-CRM focusses on the electronic relationship with customers and allows marketers to deliver cheaper and faster CRM (customer relationship marketing). Although the initial software investments can be high, the automation and personalisation of the marketing dialogue with the customer imply significant savings and faster response. E-CRM is a web approach to synchronising customer relationships across communications channels, business functions and audiences. It empowers customers to access tailored information and services that are tied to products in ways that are less expensive and more convenient than traditional ways. E-CRM represents a shift from employees taking care of customers directly to allowing customers to use self-service tools that make them an active part of the buying and servicing process.

The internet is a good instrument for this e-CRM as it enables companies to find out more about each customer and thus to empower customers to control the process. E-CRM-initiated websites, intranets and extranets let customers obtain the tailored information they need before making a purchase or help them solve problems in an after-sales-service site without help from more costly sales and support staff or call centres. The core issue in CRM and e-CRM is to collect the right data and turn that data into useful information to leverage customer service, marketing and sales. The salesforce can benefit from the fact that the internet qualifies sales leads and shortens the sales cycle. Marketers learn what promotions work best and how their target group reacts to advertising, and better understand the needs, desires and consumer behaviour of their customers. Customer service is supported by customer-care sections on the website or extranet that are available 24 hours a day without extra costs. The essence of CRM is to have a single comprehensive database with a complete history of the prospect or customer that can be accessed from any of the customer touch points (sales, call centre, personalised website and customer service).[63]

Communities on the internet

Many people long to be accepted, loved and taken seriously. Communities are groups of people with common interests that interact. The internet created an interesting environment for hundreds of thousands of communities as it is a global medium that enables interaction every day, 24 hours a day. That and the desire to learn and share experiences attract people to virtual on-line communities. Communities on the internet revolving around particular interests, task or hobbies provide information that is added by the site visitors themselves. As involvement with communities is high, they typically consist of very loyal and often returning community members who develop a sense of ownership and participate in ongoing discussions. Virtual communities can be built around a website with bulletin boards where members post comments, moderated or unmoderated e-mail discussion lists, newsletters and chat rooms. To consumers these on-line communities feel accessible, autonomous and independent of the 'big manufacturers'. As consumers become more aware of marketing techniques such as PR there is a difference between the trust placed in a magazine's opinion and that of a group of people who share their point of view in a community.

For companies there are several reasons why communities on the net are interesting. Creating communities and on-line forums and monitoring posts is an opportunity to get continuous and instant feedback on customers' opinions, views and criticisms about the company, its products and its competitors. Apple's customers are highly loyal and make a definite choice to buy an Apple computer. They belong to the community of Apple lovers and are opposed to other PC users. Apple's on-line customer support service incorporates formal Apple staff input as well as customer discussions and content. The effect of involving users in service

▶

support within the company's branded website reflects positively on the company's image and reinforces customer loyalty. For companies marketing low-interest products and for companies that are in contact with their customers infrequently (buyers of cars and houses, for instance) it is better to be where the customers are to be found when they are dealing with product-related subjects. These can be communities for parents like www.parentsoup.com or for people interested in cars like www.edmunds.com. The context suddenly makes the low-interest or low-frequency products much more relevant and interesting.[64] Also it is often easier for a company to go where the customers are already than to try to entice them over to the company or brand's own website.

Today there are different types of communities on the net:

- **Geographic communities** that share a physical place in which all the visitors have an interest, for instance www.aok.dk on Copenhagen.

- **Demographic communities** aimed at different age groups, such as the Danish youth communities www.kult.dk, www.chilinet.dk and www.thirdage.com, and the grey population or communities aimed at parents like www.parentsplace.com or www.libero.se of the Swedish company SCA.[65] Visa card launched a very successful community called www.rankit.com, narrowly targeted at young students having their own place for the first time. On the site they can find advice on how to stretch their money with tips from users on best restaurants, music venues, etc.

- **Subject-oriented communities** such as www.espn.com which is oriented to sports or www.diabetes.dk, a community created by the world's largest producer of insulin for diabetes patients in order to communicate directly with the end users. Site visitors get their own area with diary, calendar and a place to put their own diabetic data. Local versions of the community are built in 25 other markets on the same platform.

- **Branch-oriented communities**, for instance www.duuninet.fi, a very successful community for the building industry in Finland or www.freightmarket.dk, a Danish community targeted at companies interested in transporting goods over long distances.

- **Function-oriented communities** aimed at certain job functions, such as www.cnet.com for IT employees.[66]

Assembling internet users into like-minded groups has three major advantages for marketers: it collects people into easier-to-reach target markets or cohorts, it creates bonds which engender goodwill and loyalty and it allows a company to listen to its customers through a kind of real-time observational research.[67]

Tracking the effectiveness of e-communications

The company website is a way to reach customers directly and deliver information to them, take their orders and build relationships. The net is also a medium used to place advertising and to create a direct communication line with customers and prospects. For these reasons it is important for marketers to know how their website and on-line marketing campaigns are performing and how they can improve the effectiveness and efficiency of their site and digital strategy. As the internet is an interactive and computer-supported medium, all information about site traffic is stored on the net server in server log files. Analysing these files is one way of tracking website performance.

Assessing the effectiveness of e-marketing involves finding answers to questions like:

- Are the marketing objectives identified in the e-marketing strategy being met?
- Are the marketing communications objectives identified in the e-marketing plan achieved?
- How effective are the different promotional tactics used?[68]

Measuring website effectiveness

The most basic method of using feedback to measure site effectiveness is by asking for **feedback on the website**. This can be done by asking visitors to leave a contact e-mail address or by inserting a feedback form on one of the web pages. Both methods will only elicit the most extreme (negative and positive) reactions, and are not representative of the site audience. Moreover, little feedback may be expected. Including a feedback form may provide more detailed feedback and more direction as specific questions and categories of information can be included in the feedback form.

Each time a user clicks on a link or interacts with a site, the server of that site will automatically add data into a number of computer files called **server logfiles**. Metrics that logfile analysis can deliver are:

- the number of hits: a request for a file on a web server – not very useful and not reliable as every text or graphic file that is included in a web page is considered as one hit;
- the number of page views: a request for a total page;
- entry and exit pages;
- the number of unique visitor sessions: visits during a period of, for example, 20 minutes;
- the number of unique visitors (if combined with cookies);[69]
- visitor frequency report (repeat visitors);
- session duration: the length of time a visitor spends on a site;
- country of origin;[70]
- browser and operating system used;
- referring URL and domain (where the visitor came from).

To really find out who visits a website and what his or her evaluation of the site, the brand and the sales effects are, **visitor surveys** (on-line or off-line) are necessary. Surveys may give socio-demographic, psychographic and webographic (with regard to the use of the internet) profiles of visitors. They can also measure attitudes, satisfaction and intentions, and are a good way of tracking the effectiveness and success of a website. InSites Consulting (www.insites-consulting.com), a leading European internet research agency, developed a model to evaluate the performance of a website using scientifically tested questionnaires and constructs, adaptable to specific research questions and needs (see Figure 11.1). In pre-testing, usability testing and post-testing of websites, qualitative market research techniques such as focus groups and in-depth interviewing can be used in conjunction with quantitative internet panel surveys to add research insights to the website visitor surveys. Website users' input should be integrated with the design process to ensure targeted and effective website building.

Figure 11.1 Assessing website marketing performance: the InSites Consulting model

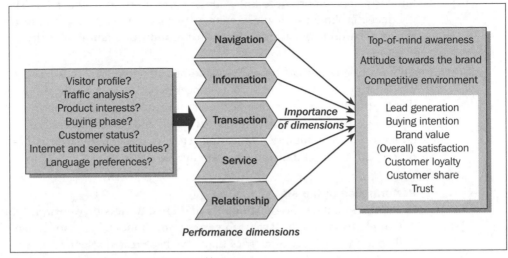

Performance dimensions

Source: developed by InSites, www.insites-consulting.com.

The InSites Consulting model[71] to measure website effectiveness consists of different parts that permit an in-depth assessment of the site based on an on-line questionnaire filled out during the site visit:

User profile of the website

The user profile is described in terms of (firm) demographics and webographics (such as internet experience and usage, type of connection, etc.) as well as a personal/professional or socio-demographic profile (such as customer, function, role in the decision-making unit, dealer, employee, etc.). This information is crucial in order to detect the extent to which the site attracts the right visitors: does the 'anticipated target group' correspond to the 'actual target group'?

Traffic analysis and generation

In-depth information can be gathered concerning the way users of the site arrive at the site (traffic analysis). What is the performance of the different traditional media used to attract visitors to the site? How many and which visitors are redirected from other (sub)sites (dot-com – local sites)? In addition, this section will also provide insights into the motives for the site visits.

Product interest, knowledge and buying phase

Visitors to the site will be asked to provide insights into their area(s) of interest. More specifically, with which product categories and information are they concerned? From the (on-line) marketing and sales viewpoint, it is also important to ascertain which stage of the buying cycle visitors have reached. Have visitors to the pages recognised a product need, are they processing information about the products, are they currently comparing supplier and product information, do they wish to order products or are they just seeking after-sales service and feedback?

Current customer status

Similarly, it is important to know about current product ownership (such as number of products, looking for new products or replacement of an existing product), customer status, relation towards the company or brand (for example, loyalty).

Content needs and attitudes for value-added services

The customers' interest in several concepts for on-line applications (such as on-line demos, product configuration, accessory information, etc.) can be tested. Furthermore, different attitudes towards on-line marketing and service through the internet (such as e-mail offers, community application/references, attitude towards brand banners and others, call-me-back buttons, etc.) are measured.

Performance of the site

In order to analyse the functionality and effectiveness of websites, InSites Consulting will apply its comprehensive web performance model. The model is multidimensional and contains a variety of metrics that have been tested scientifically.

1 Navigation

- *Design* and *layout*: the extent to which users perceive the site as visually attractive;
- *Content readability*: the degree to which users consider the texts easy to read;
- *Structure*: the extent to which visitors perceive that navigation through the site is simple;
- *Technical reliability*: the degree to which users perceive the site to be free of technical problems;
- *Technical advancedness*: the extent to which users find that advanced technical applications are integrated into the site;
- *Web page processing speed*: the extent to which users perceive that pages load quickly.

2 Information

- *Availability of relevant information*: the degree to which visitors find that there is enough relevant information on the site;
- *Information credibility*: the extent to which users judge the information to be credible;
- *Information recency*: the extent to which users consider the information to be up to date.

3 Transaction

- *Information search usability*: the extent to which users consider that the product/ service they want to buy can be easily reached on the site;
- *Transaction process information*: the extent to which users perceive that the site offers clear and sufficient information on the rest of the buying cycle;
- *Product/service assortment*: the degree to which visitors perceive that the site offers a broad range of products/services;
- *Product/service quality*: the extent to which users perceive that the quality of the product/service corresponds to what they expect.

4 Service

- *Contact possibility*: the extent to which users consider that the company can easily be reached for voicing questions, feedback and complaint;
- *Responsiveness*: the extent to which users feel that the company (will) respond(s) swiftly to questions, feedback and complaints.

5 Relationship

- *Website personalisation*: the extent to which users perceive that the site takes their personal wants and needs into account.

Competitors and brand awareness

Do visitors to our site also visit the competitors' sites? What is their overall assessment of these sites in comparison to the site information on our site? These questions allow the company to find out to what extent visitors are loyal to the site. Simultaneously, the company will ascertain which on-line position it holds in relation to its main competitors. In addition, the top-of-mind awareness and branding perception within the industry will be assessed among visitors.

Marketing effectiveness and customer behaviour

This monitor can provide insights into the degree to which visitors are becoming interesting leads (for example, intention to contact dealer or sales representative/company), whether they intend to buy a certain product, how they value the brand, how satisfied they are with the website, etc.

By relating the web performance metric scores to these marketing effectiveness variables, InSites Consulting provides an understanding of the commercial importance of the different site features. For example, based on correlation and regression analyses, the importance of site design for satisfying users or the weight of information credibility for spurring customer loyalty will become clear. By comparing the performance on several web dimensions with their importance, a web performance quadrant will enable the company to focus on the major problem areas of the website.

Measuring the effectiveness of on-line advertising

The effectiveness of banner advertising depends on different aspects: the location of the banner, and the message content and execution. How relevant is the website on which the banner is posted to the target audience? A banner ad for a CD company will probably be more effective when placed in a music-related website. This is very similar to the case of traditional advertising that is likely to be more effective when placed in media that target the relevant customer group well. Again, much like in traditional advertising, the quality of the banner for attracting attention and its placement on a web page will have a great impact on its effectiveness.

Although, as a consequence of the interactive nature of the medium, web advertising effectiveness measurement will be based on the behaviour of web users, a certain hierarchy of effects can be defined: internet users may be exposed to a message, they may engage in looking for more information 'behind' the banner and they may even click through to the web page of the advertiser. Based on this distinction, different types of ad effectiveness measures can be defined:[72]

- **Graphical ad impression** is the delivery of a graphical advertisement to a browser.
- **Cached/textual ad impression** is the delivery of an advertisement to a browser that has cached the advertisement, has graphics turned off or does not support graphics.

Both of the above measures, often added to obtain **total ad impressions**, are in fact exposure measures. Furthermore, since in the internet environment it is unlikely that an ad is seen by different people at the same time, it is also a measure of the number of contacts made by an ad.

- **Click-through** is a click by a user on an advertisement. As such, it can be compared with the response to a direct response ad in traditional media.
- **Ad transfer** is the successful arrival of a user at the advertiser's website. Evidently, most click-throughs will result in ad transfer. This measure can be considered an indication of the number of people who are really motivated to visit an advertiser's web page.

In web ad tracking, the above-mentioned indicators are often summarised into the following rates:

- **Graphical click-through rate**: total number of click-throughs divided by total number of ad impressions for graphical advertisements;
- **Total click-through rate**: total number of click-throughs divided by total number of ad impressions;
- **Ad transfer/total impressions**: total number of ad transfers divided by total number of impressions;
- **Ad transfer/click-throughs**: total number of ad transfers divided by total number of click-throughs.

Impression, click-through and ad transfer can be measured for different banners used by the same advertiser, and on a daily basis, to track web ad effectiveness.

For e-couponing, e-sampling and mobile marketing, **conversion and response rates** are the most important metrics.

Apart from these measures, the most important issue for marketers is what happens after users click-through an on-line advertisement or visit a website. Does the on-line marketing strategy lead to conversion? What is the effect of the e-marketing campaign on brand equity and purchase intention? For e-commerce sites, purchase behaviour is easy to link to e-marketing tactics, but for most companies and businesses the effects on sales are difficult to trace as they often take place in the off-line distribution system. Using post-campaign research that consists of an initial tracking of brand awareness, brand image and intention to buy before the campaign and a post-campaign survey tracking the same metrics can deliver this kind of information.

Summary

In large parts of Europe the internet reaches more than half of the population. Mobile phone penetration is even higher and interactive digital television is expected to penetrate even further within a few years. As a consequence, consumers' media attention is fragmenting and marketers will have to follow them into the new digital media. They therefore employ a number of e-marketing tactics that all contribute to the communications objectives: creating brand awareness, shaping brand attitudes, generating trial and sustaining loyalty. Brand websites are essential for most brands to support brand image and communicate with customers. Merely having a website is not enough and other off-line and on-line advertising tools such as search engine optimisation will be required to drive traffic to the site. Because of the time and budget involved, more and more companies tend to create temporary mini-sites called micro-sites to draw users and bring a new product or service to their attention. On-line advertising is on the rise in Europe and new ad formats regularly see the light. Although rich media ads, pop-ups and skyscrapers perform better than traditional banners, these new formats affect budgets and often cause irritation. Keyword buying and content sponsorship are formats that are known to work on their strengths: relevance to the target group. New ad types that are very popular due to their customer engagement and impact are advergames or on-line games. Although the cost of this kind of interactive advertising tends to be much higher than for other ad formats, the interaction time leads to a higher brand immersion. Related to these games are viral marketing actions, which make good use of the network characteristics of the net community, on-line contests, and e-sampling and e-couponing, which have a number of advantages over their off-line counterparts. The same is true for e-mail marketing, the digital form of direct marketing communication, which has recently been joined by action-driven mobile marketing communications to the cellphones of consumers. A new era for marketers lies ahead when looking at the commercial developments in interactive digital television in Europe. Finally, the internet, as an intrinsically interactive medium, can also be used to develop and sustain customer relationships, for instance via customer service pages on the net or virtual communities. The effectiveness of e-communications can be assessed by the use of logfile analysis, customer feedback forms and visitor surveys.

Review questions

1 How is the internet and on-line advertising market in Europe evolving?

2 How can a brand or company website contribute to a marketing plan?

3 Discuss the different kinds of on-line advertising and compare them in terms of performance, cost and irritation.

4 What other e-marketing tools are available? For which communication objective would you choose them?

5 What is meant by 'viral marketing'?

6 What are the dos and don'ts of e-mail marketing?

7 Explain the added value of mobile marketing to an e-marketing plan.

8 How can marketers benefit from a new evolution such as interactive digital television?

9 How can the internet help to develop relationships between a company and its customers?

10 What use are virtual communities to a company or brand?

11 How can the effectiveness of e-marketing tactics be tracked?

Further reading

Chaffey, D., Mayer, R., Johnston, K. and Ellis-Chadwick, F. (2003), *Internet Marketing. Strategy, Implementation and Practice.* Essex: Financial Times/Prentice Hall.

Parasuraman, A. and Zinkhan, G. (eds) (2002) Special Issue on 'Marketing to and Serving Customers Through the Internet: Conceptual Frameworks, Practical Insights and Research Directions', *Journal of the Academy of Marketing Science*, 30(4), Fall.

Strauss, J., El-Ansary, A. and Frost, R. (2003), *E-Marketing. 3rd Edition.* New Jersey: Prentice Hall.

Case 11

Sony® CLIÉ™ – leading the handheld revolution

Sony Corporation was founded in 1946 in Tokyo by two men: Masaru Ibuka, an engineer, and Akio Morita, a physicist, who invested the equivalent of €1,430 to start a company of 20 employees repairing electrical equipment and attempting to build their own electrical products. The latter was first successful in 1954 when Sony launched Japan's first transistor and the first all-transistor radio in the following year. Since then few companies have matched Sony's track record for inventions and innovations. Significant developments include the first colour television in 1968, the colour video cassette recorder (or 'VCR') in 1971, the Sony Walkman™ portable stereo cassette player in 1979, the 3.5-inch micro floppy disk system in 1989, an electronic camera in 1981, the world's first compact disc (or 'CD') player in 1982, the first consumer camcorder in 1983, 8mm video in 1988, the first digital VCR in 1985, the MiniDisc™ media format in 1992, the DVD media format in 1997, the Memory Stick™ flash memory card in 1998, and so on, through to the present day. Today Sony manufactures audio, video, communications and information technology products for consumer and professional markets. In more than 55 years since the company was established, it has grown from 20 employees to over 180,000 people worldwide. Sony is an international company; Akio Morita recognised from the beginning that his company needed to consider the whole world as its marketplace and not to restrict activities to Japan alone. For the fiscal year ended 31 March 2003, Sony Corporation recorded consolidated annual sales of $62.28 billion, of which 28% was obtained in Japan, 32% in the US, 22% in Europe and 18% in other geographic areas. In Europe, Sony recorded con-

solidated annual sales of €13.88 billion. Morita insisted that the Sony brand name be prominent on all the company's products. The Sony brand name comes from two other words: '*sonus*', Latin and the root for the English words 'sound' and 'sonic', and 'sonny boy', a popular expression in Japan at the time of foundation, which was used to describe a person with a free and pioneering spirit. As Sony products allow consumers to immerse themselves in whatever form of entertainment and communication they fancy, the Sony brand is about freedom, no limits, empowerment, imagination, autonomy, creativity and choice. This is represented by Sony's recent corporate slogan, 'You make it a Sony'.

Sony Information Technology Europe (I.T.E.), a European business unit

In 1960 Sony arrived in Europe, first with a presence of sales companies in Switzerland, the UK, Germany and France, later with manufacturing and Research & Development. There are now nine factories plus R&D sites in Europe accounting for almost half of the electronics products sold in the European continent. Since 1999 the headquarters of Sony Europe, responsible for the company's European electronics business, are in Berlin at the landmark Sony Center at Potsdamer Platz. They registered consolidated sales of €8.62 billion for the fiscal year ended 31 March 2003. Sony I.T.E. is a European business unit, established in April 1997 to set up Sony's European PC business (with the brand name 'Sony VAIO') and to market Sony computer displays (of which sales in Europe started in 1991) in Europe. I.T.E.'s main task is to lead the business, co-ordinate and support the activities of the local sales companies in striving to implement network applications using VAIO notebooks, computer monitors, digital still cameras, camcorders and the CLIÉ handheld devices. Since 1998 Sony I.T.E. operations have been centralised in Brussels and presently it has 240 employees working on business planning, marketing, engineering, operations, finance and control. The same year VAIO notebooks were introduced in the UK, Germany, Austria, Switzerland and France. The notebooks entered the Netherlands and Italy in 1999 and 2000 respectively. In February 2001 Sony introduced the CLIÉ handheld, Sony's PDA (personal digital assistants), into the European market.

CLIÉ's market situation

Sony entered the PDA handheld market at the end of 2000, challenging Palm's Palm Pilot PDA, and brought the CLIÉ handheld to Europe the next year in 2001. The word 'CLIÉ' originally was an acronym for Communication, Link, Information and Entertainment. Compared with other personal digital assistants, it integrated the Memory Stick flash memory card, Sony's proprietary format memory card, with the size of a stick of chewing gum. During the past years, new versions of the CLIÉ brought high-resolution colour displays, an integration of audio players for ATRAC3 and MP3 files, digital cameras, as well as the so-called 'CLIÉ Gear' accessories, i.e. accessories adding value to the handheld such as a Bluetooth™ module, a game controller, a mini keyboard and a camera module. By the autumn of 2002 Sony I.T.E. had a complete CLIÉ handheld product line-up ready to offer a solution for each 'share of wallet' to the European market. Entry models, such as the SJ30 and SL10, as well as high-end models (CLIÉ's all-in-one star model NR70V) and the two mid-range models from the T-series (T675c and T625c) targeted at business professionals complemented each other in a European product portfolio of five products. This range together with the CLIÉ Gear formed solutions that should convince the handheld buyer market to prefer the CLIÉ handheld over a competitor product. Key competitors for the CLIÉ handheld in the PDA market were Palm, Compaq (iPaq), HP and Toshiba. Apart from these players, Smart Phones could also be considered as a part of the mobile devices market. In September 2002, the CLIÉ handheld was in the top five brands for the total European market. In France, CLIÉ handhelds had a very strong position and was number two in

the market. Germany was a tougher market and the CLIÉ handheld was at number six, and in the UK CLIÉ handhelds had climbed up to number three.

The CLIÉ handheld was clearly targeted at young professional people with a busy and demanding workload. This target group, irrespective of whether they were working for themselves or for a company, was increasingly spending time away from their desks, cubicles or offices. As work increasingly became flexible, the line between work and leisure was blurred. Sony wanted to create a specific lifestyle that was not only applicable to geeks and gadget-lovers but also to consumers who were looking for more in a handheld than just good specs.

Objectives and target group of the on-line campaign

To communicate that CLIÉ handhelds had a full and complete line-up able to offer both entry and high-end products to the market, an on-line marketing campaign was planned. The campaign had to target both a business style- and a lifestyle-oriented audience and make use of emotional triggers that would make the target group feel part of the specific lifestyle that the 'CLIÉ' brand represented. The diverse product portfolio of CLIÉ handhelds evidently led to a dichotomy of target groups. The SL10 and SJ30 were bought by a younger audience who might be first-time PDA users, for instance students, while the T-series and NR CLIÉ handhelds were bought by professional business people who could afford this type of high-end product. The CLIÉ Gear accessory catalogue showed the same differences: the game controller targeted a younger audience or professionals who enjoyed playing games after work, while the Bluetooth Module was, due to its considerable price of €200, for the more affluent. The overall target audience of the on-line campaign was finally set to the 25–35 year olds, mainly males and early adopters. Although the campaign was quite product-oriented, showcasing the product solutions, the strong lifestyle element of the CLIÉ handheld had to be taken into account to target the media placements. Apart from making consumers aware of the product portfolio and the added value of CLIÉ Gear accessories, the campaign also had to support and increase the CLIÉ brand awareness as a secondary communication objective.

Campaign creation and media planning

The on-line marketing campaign started mid-October 2002 and ran until mid-December 2002, a two-month period chosen to keep the attention span along the Christmas period. A majority of rich media ads was preferred as these ad formats had proven to be the most effective from former campaigns and would allow higher levels of animation to showcase the product USPs. Transparent Flash banners (type 'shoskele' or overt), expandable banners, skyscrapers and sound-supported banners for CLIÉ handhelds with audio-functions were used with a few different messages (audio, gaming, Gear accessories, etc.). (See Plate 20.) The landing page for the on-line ads was in most cases Sony's CLIÉ micro-site offering, for instance, an accessories selector. For some countries language-depended homepages were used as landing pages. The on-line campaign was deployed in the three key European markets, Germany, the UK and France, and also ran in Austria, Switzerland and the Netherlands. In **Germany** a Flash animated transparent ad (shoskele) ran on telecom, technology and IT portals such as Xonio.com, Tecchannel.de and Golem.de but also on lifestyle-oriented content sites (Playboy.de, gq-magazin.de) and on a business magazine site (manager-magazin.de). For the **United Kingdom** banners, skyscrapers and pop-up Flash movies were inserted on technology news site zdnet.co.uk. Banners (with the frequency-per-user session capped at three contacts) were shown on the sports and the tickets and travel section of the world's (and UK's) largest on-line trading platform, eBay. Skyscrapers were also inserted on lastminute.com across the travel and sports category and banners within the sport and music section of ticketmaster.co.uk (the UK's largest ticketing agent) and on Guardian.co.uk, one of the UK's top on-line newspapers. Overlayz/eyeblasters promoted the CLIÉ handheld in the UK via timeout.co.uk, and additional advertorials were used to position the brand as a must-have accessory for both the professional businessman and the tech-savvy and style-conscious consumer alike. On Freeserve.co.uk, one of the UK's top ISPs (internet service providers), keyword impressions were bought for PDA-related keywords: PDA, personal digital assistants, hand-held, handheld computer and 'CLIÉ'. In **France** pop-ups were bought on all 25–34 year old categories of 01net.fr, a high-tech site. A transparent Flash was put on lemonde.fr and lesechos.fr, both on-line versions of the leading daily newspapers.

Results
Overall the on-line marketing campaign delivered over 6.6 million advertising messages and generated

64,572 visitors to the CLIÉ website. For a breakdown per country see Case Table 11.1. The broader site selection (including lifestyle areas) proved effective. In Germany the business site performed best. French pop-ups performed very well in terms of CTR with technology and trendy sites delivering better results than business sites. The UK campaign performed well in both technology and up-market lifestyle sites.

Case Table 11.1
Local market results

	Germany	UK	France
Impressions served	2,037,024	1,801,118	1,331,357
Clicks delivered	10,050	27,438	11,519

Germany
Manager-magazin.de, the financial/business site, was the most successful site with the highest CTR and the lowest CPCT (cost per click through). This indicated that the response of the business audience was key for the CLIÉ handheld. Communicating product attributes to a lifestyle audience seemed to be more difficult and might have needed more time or a different creative strategy. When selecting sites, it is important to consider not only reach but also affinity and quality. In Case Table 11.2 the performance of each creative format in Germany is shown.

United Kingdom
Timeout was the best performing site, delivering nearly 50% of total clicks with a very low CPCT. Banners served against PDA-related keywords on Freeserve performed far better than general banners (CTR of 0.95% versus 0.15%). Websites using a variety of ad formats and positioning produced very effective consumer response overall. In Case Table 11.3 the performance of each creative format in the UK is represented.

Case Table 11.2
Performance of the ad formats in Germany

	Banners	Skyscrapers
Impressions served	1,905,977	131,047
Clicks delivered	9,175	875

Case Table 11.3 Performance of the ad formats in the UK

	Banners	Skyscrapers	Pop-ups	Overts
Impressions served	1,099,812	318,592	40,105	170,360
Clicks delivered	835	548	575	18,748

France

Specific niche sites such as 01net (technology) and Novaplanet (hype/trendy) performed very well in terms of CTR and as such demonstrated strong interest levels. Activity on business and news sites will continue to be relevant as these sites offer PDA downloading content and information and hence there is an obvious affinity with the target audience and product. In Case Table 11.4 the performance of each creative format in France is represented.

Conclusion

Although we only went into detail for three key European markets, it is clear that there are big differences from market to market. Sony's on-line communications about CLIÉ still primarily appealed to a business audience and consumers still need to be educated about the product benefits of a handheld. Different creative executions should be used to reach the different audiences among the target group. The internet proved to be a key communication medium for the CLIÉ brand. On-line campaigns that used richer ad formats were good in showcasing the product features, resulting in engaging the targeted users.

Questions

1 For the CLIÉ handheld, on-line marketing campaigns are the key communication strategy. When considering the target group, market situation, markets (countries) and communication objectives, can you underwrite this strategy? How do you evaluate the specific on-line media planning in the key European markets of the CLIÉ handheld?

2 In which country was the on-line campaign most successful according to your calculations? What could be

the reasons for these differences? Which creative ad formats obtained the best campaign results when looking across the different markets? Does this match with your expectations? Why?

3 Suppose the next challenge for the CLIÉ handheld is to focus less on product features and stress the lifestyle positioning. What kind of e-marketing tactics would you advise? Why? Would e-mail marketing be a part of your on-line communications plan? How would you tackle this?

4 The on-line marketing campaign for the CLIÉ handheld in Austria that went live simultaneously with the other countries was a big success. The campaign was built on one sole banner and ran for just one month (compared to the two-month campaigns with various ad formats in the other countries). Nevertheless the campaign obtained the lowest cost per click through. What factors could have influenced this good result?

5 Do you think mobile marketing or interactive digital television should be considered as a part of the e-marketing plan by the CLIÉ handheld's marketers? What kind of marketing actions would you propose in these new media?

6 Sony VAIO, Sony's notebook brand, has a Club VAIO website dedicated to subscribed VAIO owners only. Do you think the CLIÉ brand could also benefit from this kind of website? Explain why or why not.

7 How was the effectiveness of the on-line campaign for CLIÉ handhelds measured in this case? What other metrics could be useful when paying attention to the communication objectives of CLIÉ handhelds? What would be the best way to obtain these kinds of metrics?

Source: www.sony-europe.com; texts and internal documents provided by Danny Cools, Sony I.T.E. Reproduced with permission of Sony I.T.E.

Case Table 11.4 Performance of the ad formats in France

	Banners	Skyscrapers	Pop-ups	Overts
Impressions served	316,720	161,640	228,558	624,439
Clicks delivered	624	2,020	3,127	5,748

References

1 Butterfield, L. (2003), *AdValue. Twenty Ways Advertising Works for Business*. Oxford: Butterworth-Heinemann.

2 Based on Network Wizards Internet Domain Survey, (January 2003), http://www.isc.org/ds/WWW-200301/index.html.

3 Samiee, S. (1998), 'The Internet and International Marketing: Is there a Fit?', *Journal of Interactive Marketing*, 12(4), 5–21.

4 Peters, L. (1998), 'The New Interactive Media: One-to-one, but Who to Whom?', *Marketing Intelligence & Planning*, 16(1), 22–30.

5 Based on SnapNames State of the Domain Q1 (2003) research, https://www.sotd.info/sotd/Member.aspx.

6 Meadows-Klue, D. (2003), 'Wired Marketers Gain the Edge', contributed for this book on behalf of the IAB Europe.

7 Kania, D. (2001), *Branding.com. Online Branding for Marketing Success*, New York: McGraw-Hill.

8 Vlugt, B. (2001), 'Beer-to-consumer', www.emerce.nl, 3 May.

9 Reicheld, F. and Schefter, P. (2000), 'E-loyalty, Your Secret Weapon on the Web', *Harvard Business Review*, July/August, 105–13.

10 Adams, R. (2003), *www.advertising. Advertising and Marketing on the World Wide Web*. Cambridge: The Ilex Press Limited.

11 Strauss, J., El-Ansary, A. and Frost, R. (2003), *E-Marketing. 3rd edition*. New Jersey: Prentice Hall.

12 Adams, R. (2003), *www.advertising. Advertising and Marketing on the World Wide Web*. Cambridge: The Ilex Press Limited.

13 Strauss, J., El-Ansary, A. and Frost, R. (2003), *E-Marketing. 3rd edition*. New Jersey: Prentice Hall.

14 Elkin, T. (2003), 'Size Matters; So Does Prize', *Advertising Age*, January, 13.

15 Dynamic Logic (2001), 'Branding 101: An Overview of Branding and Brand Measurement for Online Marketers', (March), www.dynamiclogic.com.

16 Duncan, T. (2002), *IMC. Using Advertising & Promotion to Build Brands*. New York: McGraw-Hill.

17 Bruner, K. and Kumar, A. (2000), 'Web Commercials and Advertising Hierarchy-of-effects', *Journal of Advertising Research*, January/April, 35–44.

18 Dynamic Logic (2001), 'Beyond the Click: Insights from Online Advertising Research', (June), www.dynamiclogic.com.

19 Dynamic Logic (2000), 'Travelocity Successfully Uses Online Advertising to Boost Brand', (November), www.dynamiclogic.com.

20 Hofacker, Ch. and Murphy, J. (1998), 'World Wide Web Banner Advertisement Copy Testing', *European Journal of Marketing*, 32(7/8), 703–12.

21 Hofacker, Ch. and Murphy, J. (1998), 'World Wide Web Banner Advertisement Copy Testing', *European Journal of Marketing*, 32(7/8), 703–12.

22 Hofacker, Ch. and Murphy, J. (1998), 'World Wide Web Banner Advertisement Copy Testing', *European Journal of Marketing*, 32(7/8), 703–12.

23 Dynamic Logic (2002), 'Bigger Ads do not Guarantee Effectiveness', (November), www.dynamiclogic.com.

24 Strauss, J., El-Ansary, A. and Frost, R. (2003), *E-Marketing. 3rd edition*. New Jersey: Prentice Hall.

25 *Interactive News*, August 2002.

26 Prensky, M. (2002), 'The Motivation of Gameplay', *On the Horizon*, (August).

27 Adams, R. (2003), *www.advertising. Advertising and Marketing on the World Wide Web*. Cambridge: The Ilex Press Limited.

28 Jupiter MMX, 2003.

29 Abcnews.com, November 2002.

30 Pintak, L. (2001), 'It's Not Only a Game. Advergaming Set to Become a Million Dollar Industry', 23 May, www.turboads.com/richmedia_news/2001rmn/rmn20010523.shtml.

31 Neuborne, E. (2001), 'Viral Marketing Alert!', *Business Week*, (March).

32 Adformatie Online (2001), 'Veel Respons op Dove Moment' ('Much Response to Dove Moment Campaign'). http://www.adformatie.nl/nieuws/Nieuws20001-06-26.html#item11027.

33 Jupiter MMX, 2002.

34 DBT Database & Internet Solutions (2001), 'Viral Marketing', December, www.dbt.co.uk.

35 Strauss, J., El-Ansary, A. and Frost, R. (2003), *E-Marketing. 3rd edition*. New Jersey: Prentice Hall.

36 'Supermarket sweep', *Advertising Age, Direct & Database Supplement*, October, 16, 2000 and various online sources: www.kcustom.com/articles/winemover.htm, www.kresch.com/articles/art012.htm, www.the-marketing-agency.com/sweepstk.html (2003).

37 Saunders, C. (2001), 'Häagen-Dazs Launches Web Promotion for New Dessert', *Internet News*, June, www.internetnews.com/IAR/article.php/788831.

38 *Internet Sampling: Reaching Consumers* (2001), Congress presentation, 10th Annual Conference on Global Electronic Marketing (GEM), 8/22/01, San Diego, USA, www.gmabrands.com/events2001/gemcon/weiss.pdf.

39 Strauss, J., El-Ansary, A. and Frost, R. (2003), *E-Marketing. 3rd edition*. New Jersey: Prentice Hall.

40 ACP (Association of Coupon Professionals) (2001), *A Guide to Internet Coupons*, www.couponpros.org.

41 Chaffey, D., Mayer, R., Johnston, K. and Ellis-Chadwick, F. (2003), *Internet Marketing. Strategy, Implementation and Practice*. Essex: Financial Times/Prentice Hall.

42 Logan, J. (2001), 'Dialog Marketing Elevates E-mail Efectiveness', *Customer Interaction Solutions*, 20(5).

43 Waring, T. and Martinez, A. (2002), 'Ethical Customer Relationships: A Comparative Analysis of US and French Organizations using Permission-based E-mail Marketing', *Journal of Database Marketing*, 10(1), 53–69.

44 Rapp, S. and Martin, C. (2001), *Max-e-marketing in the Net Future. The Seven Imperatives for Outsmarting the Competition in the Net Economy*. New York: McGraw-Hill.

45 Furger, R. (2000), 'E-mail's Second Shot', *Upside*, 12(4), 160–8.

46 Postma, O. and Brokke, M. (2002), 'Personalisation in Practice: The Proven Effects of Personalisation', *Journal of Database Marketing*, 9(2), 137–42.

47 Strauss, J., El-Ansary, A. and Frost, R. (2003), *E-Marketing. 3rd edition*. New Jersey: Prentice Hall.

48 Khera, R. (2002), 'E-mail Marketing Primer: 12 Tips for Successful Campaigns', *The Magazine for Magazine Management*, 30(9), 53.

49 EMarketer (2002), 'Does Permission E-mail Marketing Push Consumers to Purchase?', *eMarketer e-zine*, October, 28.

50 DoubleClick (2002), 'Best Practices in E-mail Marketing', Presentation at InSight 2002.

51 Waring, T. and Martinez, A. (2002), 'Ethical Customer Relationships: A Comparative Analysis of US and French Organizations using Permission-based E-mail Marketing', *Journal of Database Marketing*, 10(1), 53–69.

52 Sadeh, N. (2002), *M-commerce: Technologies, Services and Business Models*. New York: John Wiley & Sons.

53 Plant, S. (2002), 'On the Mobile: The Effects of Mobile Telephones on Social and Individual Life', www. motorola. com.

54 Huberland, X. (2003), 'Developing New Services Based on Mobile Business: SMS/MMS Case: From "person to person" to "mobile business" ', *Proceedings of the Mobile Marketing Congress: The Added Value*, TMAB, 18 March Brussels, Belgium.

55 Enpocket Insight (2002), 'Consumer Preferences for SMS Marketing in the UK', www.enpocket.com, August.

56 FEDMA and Forrester (2001), *The Marketer's Guide to SMS*, December.

57 De Kerckhove, A. (2002), 'Building Brand Dialogue with Mobile Marketing', *Advertising and Marketing to Children*, July–September, 37–42.

58 Wise, T. and Hall, D. (2002), *Pause or Play? The Future of Interactive Services for Television*. Accenture.

59 Lekakos, G. (2002), *An Integrated Approach to Interactive and Personalized TV Advertising*, Athens University of Economics and Business.

60 Bernoff, J. (2002), *Smarter Television. The Forrester Report*, (July).

61 Pickton, D. and Broderick, A. (2001), *Integrated Marketing Communications*, Essex: Prentice Hall/Financial Times.

62 Smith P.R. and Chaffey, D. (2002), *eMarketing Excellence: The Heart of eBusiness*, Oxford: Butterworth-Heinemann.

63 Allen, C., Kania, D. and Yaeckel, B. (2001), *One-to-One Web Marketing. Build a Relationship Marketing Strategy One Customer at a Time*. New York: Wiley Computer Publications.

64 Rowan, W. (2002), *Digital Marketing. Using New Technologies to Get Closer to Your Customers*. London: Kogan Page.

65 Jobber, D. and Fahy, J. (2003), *Foundations of Marketing*. Berkshire: McGraw-Hill.

66 Lindström, M. and Andersen, T.F. (2001), *Brand Building on the Internet*. London: Kogan Page.

67 Duncan, T. (2002), *IMC. Using Advertising & Promotion to Build Brands*. New York: McGraw-Hill.

68 Chaffey, D., Mayer, R., Johnston, K. and Ellis-Chadwick, F. (2003), *Internet Marketing. Strategy, Implementation and Practice*. Essex: Financial Times/Prentice Hall.

69 Weima, K.W. (2002), *Webvertising. Tools voor een Effectieve Campagne (Tools for an Effective Campaign)*. Alphen aan den Rijn: Kluwer.

70 Chaffey, D., Mayer, R., Johnston, K. and Ellis-Chadwick, F. (2003), *Internet Marketing. Strategy, Implementation and Practice*. Essex: Financial Times/Prentice Hall.

71 www.insites-consulting.com (2003).

72 Bhat, S., Bevans, M. and Segupta, S. (2002), 'Measuring Users' Web Activity to Evaluate and Enhance Advertising Effectiveness', *Journal of Advertising*, 31(3), 97–106.

Chapter 12

Point-of-purchase communications

Chapter outline

Objectives and tools of point-of-purchase communications

Effectiveness of point-of-purchase communications

Other point of purchase factors:
- Store image
- Store organisation
- Product presentation
- Store atmosphere
- Packaging

Chapter objectives

This chapter will help you to:

- Understand why point-of-purchase communications are important
- Learn about the tools and objectives of point-of-purchase communications
- Learn how effective the various tools of point-of-purchase communications can be
- Get an overview of other aspects of the point-of-purchase environment, such as store image, store organisation, product presentation, store atmospherics and packaging

Introduction

Point-of-purchase (POP) communications are a very powerful tool as they reach consumers at the point when they are making the decision which product or brand to buy. Purchase intentions often do not result in an actual purchase because of situational factors such as out-of-stocks, competitive brands that are on promotion and attention-grabbing displays. Furthermore, many consumers seem to make choices at the point of purchase and do not know in advance what brand they are going to buy. They spend more and more time on the road and out-of-home, which makes it harder for traditional media to reach them.

Point-of-purchase communications are most effective when they form part of an integrated communications plan, which means that, for instance, they reflect what consumers have seen on TV or billboard ads, and correspond with PR efforts or sponsorships.[1] Indeed, it has been shown that, for instance, when advertising and POP communications are combined, as compared to using advertising only, sales increase by more than 100%.[2] Also the combination of POP and a price cut appears to have enormous advantages over and above the use of POP or price cuts only.[3]

After having discussed why point-of-purchase communications are important, the objectives and tools will be highlighted, and attention will be devoted to the effectiveness of point-of-purchase communications tools. Finally, other aspects of the point-of-purchase environment such as store image, store atmospherics, store organisation, product presentation and packaging will be briefly discussed.

The importance of point-of-purchase communications

The Point-of-Purchase Advertising Institute (POPAI) conducted a consumer buying habits study in several European countries.[4] To this end, the POPAI institute used entry–exit interviews, meaning that the consumers were interviewed twice, once before entering the store (to measure the planned budget and the planned purchases), and again after leaving the store (to measure the budget spent, the actual purchases and the perception of POP material).

Purchases can be classified into four categories. In the case of **specifically planned purchases** the consumer has bought the specific product and brand she intended to buy before entering the store. **Generally planned purchases** assume that the purchase of the product, but not a specific brand, was planned before entering the store. **Substitute product or brand purchases** occur when the consumer intended to buy a specific product or brand, but actually purchased another product or brand. **Unplanned purchases** are defined as the purchases that the consumer did not plan in advance. In Europe an average of 67.2% of brand purchase decisions are made in the store, which is comparable to the in-store decision rate of 72% for American consumers (Table 12.1).[5] The number of in-store decisions are highest for younger and higher-income consumers, larger households and consumers accompanied by children.

In this table the numbers of unplanned purchases are exaggerated. All the purchases that one really needs, but did not think of in advance, are also considered as 'unplanned'. For example, some consumers do not write a shopping list in advance, but

Table 12.1 Purchase classification

	UK	France	Italy	Netherlands	Denmark	Belgium
Specifically planned	24.5%	24.0%	58.0%	20%	23.5%	31%
Generally planned	8.0%	12.0%	19.0%	24%	16.0%	9%
Substitute product or brand	3.7%	6.0%	6.0%	4%	7.7%	4%
Unplanned	63.8%	58.0%	17.0%	52%	52.8%	56%

Source: POPAI Europe (1998), *The POPAI Europe Consumer Buying Habits Study*. Co-ordination by Retail Marketing In-store Services Limited, Watford, Herts: POPAI Europe. Reproduced with permission of POPAI Europe.

walk down all the aisles to spot what they need. In any case, POP communications can be very effective, given the substantial in-store decision incidence of consumers.

Objectives and tools of point-of-purchase communications

Point-of-purchase or POP advertising, also called in-store, point-of-sales or POS advertising, can be defined as any promotional material placed at the point of purchase, such as interior displays, printed material at shop counters or window displays.[6] However, it also includes in-store broadcasts, video screen demonstrations, shopping-trolley advertising, shelf talkers, coupon dispensers, wastepaper baskets and interactive kiosks (devices by means of which the consumer can interactively retrieve information about the shop and the products in the shop). POP communications are not only concerned with POP advertising. The store image, store design, the scent and the music in the store, the way the products are placed on the shelves and the packaging of the products form an integral part of POP communications. In short, POP communications involve all the aspects of the store and the store environment that can signal something to customers about the quality, price or product assortment, whether it is initiated by the retailer or by the manufacturer (Plate 21).

POP communications can serve several objectives or functions (Figure 12.1). An attractive exterior store design may **attract consumer's attention** and may differentiate the store from its competitors, so increasing the likelihood that the consumer will enter the store. Fashion retailer Hugo Boss, for example, installed a 106-inch screen in its

Figure 12.1 Point-of-purchase communications objectives

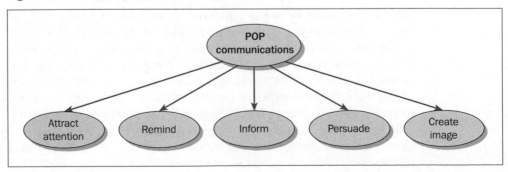

Regent Street store in the UK to show Hugo Boss's latest collections as well as fragments of sponsored sporting events. According to the retail manager the screen can be seen from the other side of the street and really attracts people to the shop because it brings a sense of excitement to the store environment.[7] In supermarkets eye-catching displays may attract attention to specific products and may induce the consumers to buy a product they did not intend to buy before entering the store. Effective POP material should remind consumers of ongoing or previous advertising, PR, sales promotion or other campaigns, reinforcing the communications message. Because of the high amount of advertising clutter today, consumers have difficulty remembering the different messages and often confuse brands. POP material is a good tool to aid consumers in this. Apple, for example, used pictures of Gandhi, Amelia Earhart, Jim Henson and Einstein on branded banners to help brand their new vendor shops in compUSA locations (shop in the shop system). These celebrities perfectly illustrate Apple's unique selling proposition and remind people of the baseline used in all advertising, 'think differently'.[8]

Besides reminding, POP material can also inform consumers. Detailed information on a VCR or a computer can be shown on large displays, the store's design may signal the intended target groups, or an interactive display may help consumers decide on what kind of wine is best served with certain meals. Procter & Gamble, for example, used an interactive kiosk called the Oil of Ulay/Tesco Consultant to launch its Oil of Ulay Colour Collection range. By means of touch screen technology consumers are asked to enter details on eye, hair, skin colour and skin type. The Oil of Ulay/Tesco Consultant then suggests products from its Ulay range, such as lipsticks, foundation, eye shadow and mascara. According to P&G, Oil of Ulay Colour Collection reached market leadership in the UK cosmetics market within a month.[9]

Another objective of POP communications is to persuade consumers, to influence their decision-making at the point of sale and to trigger impulse purchases. Finally, POP communications serve to help with building an image, both of the retailer and the products sold.

No hot Nikes at Foot Locker any more

Nike was founded in 1972 and Foot Locker in 1975. Foot Locker started with a new concept: a store devoted to athletic shoes only. This aroused Nike's interest and Nike wanted very badly to get in there. Selling its shoes in an athletic shoe store would rub off on its own image. In the beginning, Foot Locker was hesitant since it did not want to sell 'unbranded footwear' and Nike was still unknown at that time. Over the years the two companies grew together and were able to benefit from each other's strengths. Nike's ad campaigns triggered demand for its shoes and Foot Locker's extensive network of stores made the shoes available everywhere for the consumers. Nike got prominent displays in Foot Locker stores and Foot Locker got Nike's newest models. This allowed Foot Locker to grow five times as fast as its competitors. To drive sales, Foot Locker began to aggressively discount its products over the last few years. Nike, on the other hand, wanted to preserve its image of cutting-edge fashion king. This led to a dispute between the two companies that began in the beginning of 2002. When Nike posed rigid terms on the selection and price of shoes it would sell to Foot Locker, Foot Locker announced a cut in its Nike order by 15% to 25% in the hope that Nike would reconsider its terms. Nike responded in the opposite way: it slashed its planned shipments to Foot Locker by 40%, withholding its most popular and newest sneakers. Consumers can no longer find Nike's hottest shoes at Foot Locker, shoes that Nike is selling to Foot Locker's competitors now. Moreover, Nike's campaigns ▶

are no longer driving consumers to Foot Locker's stores. All this induced a serious drop in sales, a negative impact on its image and an enormous marketing challenge for Foot Locker.[10]

In order to be able to communicate the store, the products and the brands offered effectively, market segmentation and a clear understanding of the characteristics of target groups are essential components of a marketing communications strategy. For example, with fashion clothing the most important attributes seem to be price, quality, product selection and service offered by the personnel.[11] However, different target groups will prefer different levels of these characteristics. Knowing the exact preferences of your target groups is essential to fine-tune the interior and exterior design of the store, the POP material present in the store, the product assortment and the overall image of the store. For example, the fashion retailer catering to wealthy women must design his store in a way that looks exclusive and expensive. On the other hand, if you want to communicate that you have low prices and that consumers can get bargains, it may not be a good strategy to have the products neatly arranged by size or colour. A chaotic mélange and large price displays attracting bargain hunters like a magnet seems to be a better strategy to communicate the bargain possibilities.[12]

House of Fraser turns into House of Segments

The objective of the House of Fraser is to become the best upper-mass-market department store chain in the UK, ranking between Harvey Nichols and Debenhams. The chain wants to get rid of its problems of former years, among which are low sales densities, and an unclear definition of its customer base. The embodiment of this new approach is a £12 million, 81,000 sq. ft outlet in Nottingham, opened in October 1997. House of Fraser and the design company Kinnersley Kent Design worked together to identify the target customer groups. The main target group remains the quality classic market consisting of people who like details and wear brands like Jaegar. But the new strategy also seeks to target fashion lovers, smart careerists, label lovers and smart dressers. For each segment, profiles were drawn, including the first and second choice brands. Smart careerists, for example, are more likely to purchase Planet or Mondi, while fashion lovers are expected to be in favour of DKNY, Oasis or French Connection. The design company tried to reflect the personality of each consumer segment in the physical environment. To this end, large boards were made picturing the images of the targeted segment, as well as colour pallets, and materials (limestone, maple, glass, etc.) that would reflect the segment's personality. Those boards were used to ensure consistency and to give concession operators (such as Tommy Hilfiger, Bobbi Brown, CK, Versace, etc.) an idea of the offering. Translating this into the global store environment, while retaining the House of Fraser identity, was done by blurring the edges of the different departments especially designed for the targeted segments. Instead of circulating through the racks, consumers have to follow walkways and can have a glance at what the department has to offer through display units containing cut-out circles filled with glass.[13]

The effectiveness of point-of-purchase communications tools

In-store communications have an enormous potential impact on the consumer. Several studies show that displays and shelf talkers are able to trigger purchase responses, sometimes even when the price reduction is negligible.[14] Therefore, POP material is receiving growing interest and is used more and more often. Special product presentations on existing shelves, displays, billboards and pallets are most often used. According to POPAI, these are also the POP materials that are remembered by most consumers (see Figure 12.2). In another study, about 1,000 US shoppers were asked to indicate the POP elements to which they pay particular attention when grocery shopping and the POP elements that have motivated them in the past to buy a product or brand they had not planned to purchase beforehand.[15] Figure 12.3 summarises the results. According to the consumers, in-store samples seem to be particularly effective. More than two in three respondents claim that these attract attention and have in the past persuaded them to buy the product or brand. Moreover, 68.3% say they try in-store samples almost every time they are available, while 26.3% say they do this occasionally. Of course, trying a sample is not the same as buying a product. Some 13% admit to buying the product or brand almost every time they try a sample, while about 73% claim to buy the tried product occasionally. Besides in-store samples, coupons, on-pack promotions and displays are also deemed very effective. It is interesting to know that according to this study, 50% of the grocery shoppers who use shelf coupon dispensers most frequently use the coupon for brands they have not tried before, while a quarter use the coupon only if it is for the brand they intended to buy.[16] Other studies have also demonstrated the effectiveness of shelf coupon dispensers. It has been found, for example, that consumers tend to respond even more easily to shelf coupons than to price reductions of the same amount.[17] Floor ads or floor graphics and shopping cart ads

Figure 12.2 POP awareness in supermarkets

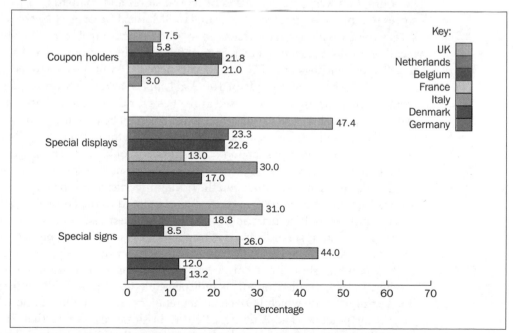

Source: POPAI Europe (1998), *The POPAI Europe Consumer Buying Habits Study.* Co-ordination by Retail Marketing In-store Services Limited, Watford, Herts: POPAI Europe. Reproduced with permission of POPAI Europe.

Figure 12.3 Attention and purchase motivation of different POP elements

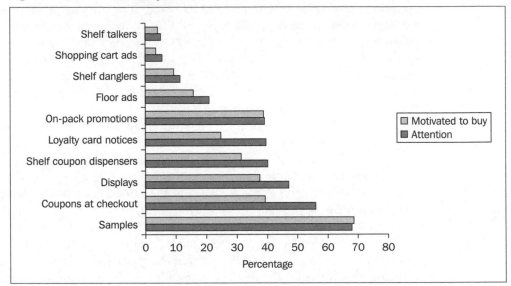

also appear to work, sometimes even better than assumed by the respondents of the foregoing US study. Nestlé, for example, tested its floor graphics in Germany. To this end, floor graphics were placed in aisles of six test stores and compared to six similar control stores without floor graphics. According to 3M, the developer of Nestlé's floor graphics, sales were 23% higher in the test as compared to the control stores. Furthermore, brand recall of products advertised by means of floor graphics amounted to 47%, as compared to 19% for wall posters and 10% for shelf stickers.[18] Walls promoted its Solero ice cream by means of shopping cart ads in 100 Asda supermarkets. The most memorable image from a recent television ad was used as the basis for the poster. It featured a man with an iceberg capping his head eating a Solero ice cream. The baseline read 'the mind cooler'. One in four trollies were decorated with a poster on the outside, as well as on the inside, so that both the trolley pusher and other shoppers could see the message. The cost of the campaign was estimated at 63 pence per 1,000 exposures. Sales of Solero were monitored in 32 Asda stores, half of which ran the trolley advertising campaign. The results showed a sales increase of over 20% in the test as compared to the control stores.[19]

The spot where POP material is installed also exerts an influence on purchase behaviour. In a US study, in-aisle displays resulted in 58% unplanned purchases, as compared to 61% for displays at the end of aisles and 64% for displays placed at the checkout.[20]

POP material should not only work for the consumer, it should also work for the retailer. Indeed, retailer support is indispensable for a good POP campaign. Therefore it is useful to know which POP elements retailers are in favour of and what they think of current practice. The American POPAI Institute discovered that 70% of retailers prefer POP displays with a mobile element rather than static displays. The reason is that movement is more likely to attract the attention of shoppers. According to retailers, moving displays as compared to no POP support result in a sales increase of 83%. Also interactive kiosks look very promising. However, about 90% of the interactive projects over the last decade failed. More attention should be devoted to setting clear objectives and to developing the appropriate content. The kiosk should be placed in a quiet corner rather than in a crowded, noisy aisle. Moreover, it should be clear to the customer what the kiosk is for, how it can help the customer and how the customer can make use of it.[21]

Retailers recognise the importance of POP communications, but unfortunately they experience many shortcomings in current practice. As the greatest weaknesses they mention that the displays often are inappropriate for the channel of trade, are of the wrong size, are poorly built and are unattractive.[22] Retailers' advice on how to improve POP communications is summarised in Table 12.2.[23] Marketers, on the other hand, have complaints about retailers. The most important ones are summarised in Table 12.3.[24] Clearly, a good relationship and open communication between retailers and manufacturers can solve many problems. Manufacturers should not only focus on their own needs

Table 12.2 Suggestions to improve POP

1 Strive to be classy and not gaudy.
2 Gather more information from sales staff.
3 Avoid cheap-looking solid white bases.
4 Get your POP designers out into the field more often.
5 Keep in mind that you have to clean around these displays.
6 Use materials that will not look shop-worn after a week.
7 Better seasonal timing of POP.
8 Have a dummy display first to trouble-shoot it for design errors.
9 Produce smaller sizes with an option to utilise multiples (fit together) if the space is available.
10 Discuss the programme with our visual merchandising personnel as well as the product merchants.

Based on: 'P-O-P Times/POP Design Trends Survey 1998', in P-O-P Times, The News Publication of Point-of-Purchase Advertising, Display and Packaging (December 1997), 4. Reproduced with permission of Hoyt Publishing Company.

Table 12.3 Complaints about retailers

1 They are lazy, stupid and don't want to merchandise properly.
2 Every retailer has different rules.
3 Their willingness to accept POP initially is not matched by a willingness to implement it at the store level.
4 They are slow decision-makers – they make unreasonable delivery schedule demands.
5 They will knock out our POP for any vendor with a higher profit margin.
6 You cannot depend on them to place it in the proper location.
7 They are more worried about slotting fees than sales.
8 When only half empty, a display is thrown away.
9 The last one in the door wins the space.
10 No concern for the abuse of displays by competitors.

Based on: 'P-O-P Times/POP Design Trends Survey 1998', in P-O-P Times, The News Publication of Point-of-Purchase Advertising, Display and Packaging (December 1997), 4. Reproduced with permission of Hoyt Publishing Company.

and profits but also on those of the retailers. Collaborating with retailers to increase category sales instead of just the manufacturer's own sales, differentiating the POP programme for different stores to give the retailer a unique programme, communicating and working with retailers to find out what works for them and what does not can raise goodwill enormously and lead to real partnership.[25]

Other point-of-purchase factors

Besides the use of specific tools, there are a number of other angles and aspects of POP communications.

Store image

Store image can be defined as 'an individual's cognitions and emotions that are inferred from perceptions or memory inputs that are attached to a particular store and which represent what that store signifies to an individual'. It consists of both affective and cognitive factors.[26] The way the store is organised, the way the personnel dress and behave, the quality of the merchandise, the POP advertisements, the service, the location, price levels and the store's reputation all combine to form the image of the store and its products.[27] However, the attributes of store image and the importance of specific attributes are industry- and situation-specific. Cleanliness may be an essential aspect of store image for food retailers, while it may be less crucial for fashion shopping. The situation, such as the purpose of a store visit, may also alter the importance of store attributes. Store location may be less of a determining factor in recreational than in urgent shopping trips.[28]

Merrell Outdoor Footwear: a rugged business

Merrell Outdoor Footwear wants to create a natural store image reinforcing a natural, durable footwear brand personality. To this end, Merrell launched an aggressive POP programme focussed on the rugged outdoors. It included POP features such as mountain profiles, ice axes, climbing ropes, mountain nails, bleached wood and gun metal to stress the rugged, natural orientation.[29]

Related to store image is the concept of store personality. While store image refers to a mental representation of all dimensions that are associated with a store, store personality is limited to dimensions that reflect human traits.[30] A scale for store personality which consists of the following five factors:[31]

1 Enthusiasm (welcoming, enthusiastic, lively, dynamic).
2 Sophistication (chic, high class, elegant, stylish).
3 Unpleasantness (annoying, irritating, loud, superficial).
4 Genuineness (honest, sincere, reliable, true).
5 Solidity (hardy, solid, reputable, thriving).

Different consumer segments will appreciate a different store personality and a different store image. Indeed, a store cannot appeal to, or be an ideal store for, all people. Tailoring a store's characteristics to the psychological and physical needs of a selected target group is the key to making their store impressions and shopping experiences as satisfactory as possible, and in trying to convert casual entrants into loyal customers.[32]

Store organisation

How a store's total space is divided into areas or departments can have an enormous impact on its profitability. First, a retailer should try to maximise the space devoted to selling activities and minimise the non-selling space (customer services, inventory, repair counter, etc.) in order to get a high space productivity. The ratio between selling and non-selling space is usually 4 to 1. Second, the allocation of space determines to a large extent the store atmosphere, which can have an influence on the willingness of consumers to shop in the store. After dividing the total space into selling and non-selling areas, product categories have to be assembled in natural groupings. A logical grouping facilitates the location and comparison of products, making the shopping experience more enjoyable for the consumer. Furthermore, consumers apparently allocate a certain time to shopping. If they find what they need quickly, they appear to spend the rest of the time browsing around which increases the likelihood of additional purchases.[33] Next, a retailer has to decide where to place the different merchandise groupings in the store. Two important criteria for merchandise location are consumer buying behaviour and merchandise compatibility. With regard to the former, low involvement products, for which consumers are not willing to spend time looking, will be placed in high exposure areas, such as major aisles, checkouts, etc. High involvement, or speciality items on the other hand, can be placed in less accessible areas since the consumer is willing to devote more effort to finding them. Furthermore, frequently purchased items can be located in such a way that consumers are led past as many other products as possible.[34] Merchandise compatibility concerns the location of related products in the same area. White wine can be located near the fish department, spaghetti sauces near the pasta, ties near shirts, etc.[35]

Scanning data reveal interesting insights for store organisation

Customer and loyalty cards and scanning applications are gaining ground all over the world. Albert Heijn, a Dutch chain of supermarkets, has launched a customer card that provides personal offers. In the UK, supermarkets experiment with cards that give the customer advantages even outside the store. Delhaize in Belgium is considering publishing a magazine with different offers depending upon customers' family situation. Store cards combined with scanning data are important sources of information. Supermarkets know whether you drink beer or wine, whether or not you use condoms, whether or not you are a vegetarian, whether or not you have pets, whether you buy vegetables or fruit in their store, etc. They even know whether or not you have been shopping elsewhere. If you buy pet food on a regular basis and then do not do so for a few weeks, supermarkets know that you have been buying it elsewhere. Scanning data offers a lot of strategic information on target groups and individual consumers. Besides that, it can also be used for store organisation. The Belgian supermarket GB, for example, has reorganised its home collection department on the basis of scanning data. The data showed that consumers usually buy a bath robe, bath towels and a bath carpet at the same store visit. In order to service the customer better, these products are now arranged in each others' vicinity.[36] Another example ▶

can be found in the American night shops. By means of scanning data, it was found that consumers who buy babies' nappies often buy beer at the same time. An explanation for this odd finding was found through a survey. Women often realise in the evening that only one nappy is left for their lovely baby. Fortunately, their husbands are still at work, so they can ask them to stop at the night shop. The fathers make the purchase, but are a bit embarrassed to do so or think they deserve a little treat. Therefore they decide to treat themselves to beer. American night shops have reorganised their shops and have put the beer next to the babies' nappies.[37]

Studies show that particular store layouts are very attractive to consumers. Consumers seem to walk through the store, for example, in a counter-clockwise direction. They try to avoid turns and like to continue to walk in the direction they are going.[38] Furthermore, customers usually look to and buy products situated on their right-hand side. Broad aisles and aisles on the walls are most preferred and, as a consequence, are visited by the majority of the shoppers.[39]

The way a store is organised can have impressive implications for marketers. If consumers fail to locate desired products, this may produce feelings of frustration and anger. This probably induces very low satisfaction levels, and may even lead to a premature interruption of the search process. The shopper may opt for a substitute product and/or for another store in the future, which results in lost revenues.[40]

Product presentation

After store organisation has been taken care of, attention should be devoted to the way products and brands are presented to the consumer and how the shelves are filled (see Plate 22). Shelf management is not easy. The most important aspects that have to be considered are the product assortment, the space allocated to each product and the shelf position. The retail assortment (product lines, brands, styles, services, etc.) has to match consumer needs.

A common practice in shelf management is that shelf space is allocated according to market share or retail margin. However, space allocation based on market share is an example of circular reasoning, since shelf space depends on market share, which in itself partly depends on shelf space.[41] Recent shelf space allocation models also include product profitability for each item, demand interdependencies (a fixed amount of shelf space requires that an increase in the space of item X may raise the sales of X, but the decreased shelf space of item Y may at the same time cause a fall in the sales of Y), inventory levels and product stock-outs.[42] Stock-outs can be a serious problem. A study indicated that about 41% of the consumers confronted with a stock-out purchase a different size of the same brand; one-third bought a competitive brand; 14% went to another store to find the stocked-out brand; 13% delayed the purchase.[43] However, across studies the percentage of consumers visiting another store in case of stock-out ranges from 6% to 83%, partly depending on the product category. Those percentages increase when the item is missing on a second purchase occasion.[44] With promotional advertising, stock-outs of advertised items are a recurrent problem. Such stock-outs may generate negative feelings in the consumer, especially in those people who have made a special trip to the store to buy a bargain.[45]

Concerning shelf position, there seems to be general agreement that products positioned at eye level generate the best results. The second best position is probably immediately to the right of the brand leader or the visually most dominant brand on the shelf. The reason for this is that consumers watch the shelf in the way they read; as a consequence their eye is most likely to move from the most visually dominant brand to the right and downward.[46] Most complete product lines with regard to sizes and colours are usually placed at eye level, while assortments with missing elements appear in lower racks.[47] Another rule is to put high-margin products on the most visible shelves, while cheap products are placed on the floor rack. Other criteria to take into account are the weight of the products (put heavy products on the floor) and the turnover of the products. Products that sell very well need to be frequently replenished. Such products need to be positioned at an easily accessible place.[48]

Store atmospherics

Atmospherics can be defined as the effort to design buying environments to produce specific emotional effects in the buyers that enhance their purchase probability,[49] since atmosphere is apprehended through the senses. The dimensions of store atmosphere are shown in Figure 12.4. Taste is not considered a meaningful dimension of the store atmosphere since one cannot taste an atmosphere. However, in-store 'degustations', a sales promotion instrument, may be regarded as an atmospheric dimension for food retailers.

The atmosphere adds a valuable characteristic to the product and mainly serves three functions.[50] First, the atmosphere can generate attention by using specific colours, music, etc., which make a store stand out. Second, the atmosphere creates a message by using the atmospheric characteristics in such a way that they express, for example, the intended store audience. Third, the atmosphere creates affect by arousing people, which may tip the scale in favour of buying certain products or brands.[51]

An experiment in a British supermarket revealed the following.[52] Four French and four German wines were put on the supermarket's wine shelves. On days that French accordion or Gallic favourites such as the 'Marseillaise' or can-can music was played, Beaujolais and Côtes du Rhône sold extremely well (40 French versus 8 German bottles), while on the days that German, side-splitting Keller music was played, the German wine sales rose (12 French versus 22 German bottles). Interviews revealed that consumers were certain that the kind of music did not influence their purchase. Also in a

Figure 12.4 Dimensions of store atmosphere

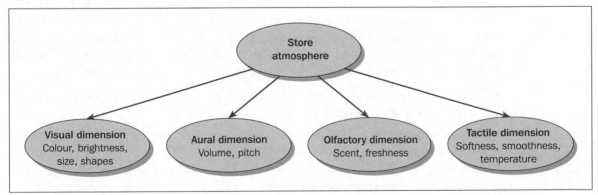

restaurant setting it has been shown that when visitors' preferred music is playing they stay significantly longer in the restaurant and spend significantly more on both drinks and food.[53] With regard to aroma, the link between aroma advertising and increased sales still has to be proved. However, according to The Aroma Company's Simon Harrop's experience, a pleasant aroma induces a better response than no aroma, or worse, an unpleasant smell.[54] One study[55] showed that products in a scented shop were perceived to be better than identical goods in an unscented shop, while another study found that a scented versus an otherwise identical unscented store induced more positive evaluations of the store and of the merchandise, increased the intention to visit the store, increased the intention to purchase some of the products and lowered the perception of the time that consumers had spent in the store.[56]

The majority of the atmospherics research seems to support the relationship between store atmospherics, emotions and consumer behaviour. Some practitioners even say that 'fifty % of consumers' decisions are made because of the environment they are in'.[57] Therefore, a good understanding of store atmospherics and store dynamics is very important, both for the manufacturer and the retailer.

Packaging

Besides protecting the product and making distribution easier, packaging fulfils several communications functions, such as attracting brand attention, identifying the brand and the product, facilitating brand and product recognition, and informing consumers of price, ingredients and product use.[58]

As for advertising in general, the packaging should try to attract and keep the consumer's attention to be effective. In order to do so, the package should possess an attention-grabbing colour, an unusual size or form, or be novel or complex. Recent multimedia techniques are a useful tool to design and test new packages. However, paying attention to the packaging is one type of consumer response; a positive packaging evaluation is another. Research shows that packages that deviate considerably from what is standard for the product category indeed attract a lot of attention, but they also lead to negative package evaluations. Moderate package deviation seems to be the best trade-off in serving the purpose of drawing attention and generating favourable evaluations.[59] It is important to realise that shoppers on average spend only five to seven seconds glancing at a package. Therefore, although some complexity might be favourable to attract attention, the package or label should not be too complex. The point of difference of the brand should be made clear at a glance and should not require shoppers to read the full label or to read the back label. Putting too many messages on the label might increase the likelihood of shoppers missing every benefit statement.[60] Furthermore, although the new multimedia techniques can be very helpful in modernising packaging, marketers should try to avoid the 'seven packaging sins' and pay attention to the following:[61]

- Define the objectives you want to reach with the new packaging: on what criteria should it score more positively than the current packaging?
- Define the priorities for the different characteristics (conspicuousness, recognition, product expectations, etc.) of the package.
- In testing, both the old and the new packaging should be tested to find out which aspects have improved or deteriorated.

- In testing, both the own and the competitive packaging should be tested to learn own strengths and weaknesses.
- Test the product concept and brand image in order to discover what the package signals to the consumer.
- Test before the package development has begun.
- Test alternative packages in order not to have to start all over again when the test appears to be negative.

In a study by P.I. Design International, results indicate that children's favourite colours are: purple, red, yellow, blue and green. Children disliked light, dark, smudgy and sophisticated colours. The use of over-large colour blocks was perceived as boring. Using foil and blister packaging seemed to be attractive to kids. The same study advised not breaking through standard flavour colour codes such as pink or red for strawberries, brown for chocolate, etc. It helps children to understand and recognise what they prefer. Multi-packs may also lead to confusion and should be transparent, permitting children to see exactly what is inside. Children like bubble typographs and find straight refined fonts cold and unfriendly. Colourful and exciting funny illustrations are preferred to realistic photographs. Children find the latter typical for adults and, as a result, dull.[62]

An important conclusion from recent research is that packaging can influence consumer behaviour long after the actual purchase has been made. It appears that larger pack sizes encourage greater usage volume per usage occasion, although there is, of course, a limit on how much detergent or pasta a consumer wants to consume at one time.[63] One reason for this greater usage volume seems to be the lower perceived unit cost of larger packages. Another explanation is that, because of the large package, consumers are less worried about running out of the product.[64] Besides an encouragement to use more, larger packs sometimes also induce people to consume the product more frequently, simply because of the presence of the product in the household inventory.[65]

Summary

Point-of-purchase communications are a powerful marketing tool, since they reach consumers at the moment when, and the place where, they are taking decisions. Since a majority of consumers make buying decisions at the point of purchase, in-store communications are of crucial importance. Point-of-purchase communications have to be particularly well integrated with sales promotions and distribution strategies. The objectives of in-store communications are to attract the consumer's attention, to remind him or her of ongoing or previous advertising, to inform, to persuade and to build an image of the brands on shelves. Several instruments of in-store communications can be used, such as shelf displays, floor graphics, trolley advertising, moving displays and interactive kiosks. Besides these specific communications instruments, store image, store organisation, store atmospherics and product presentation are also important. They all add to the impression a consumer has when making buying decisions in store. Finally, packaging is an important tool of in-store advertising.

Review questions

1 Why are point-of-purchase communications so important, given consumer buying behaviour?

2 What are the tools and objectives of point-of-purchase communications?

3 How effective are the various point-of-purchase tools?

4 How can store image influence sales?

5 What is the importance of store organisation and product presentation?

6 How do store atmospherics help to achieve communications objectives?

7 In what way can packaging influence buying behaviour?

Further reading

International Journal of Retail and Distribution Management

In-Store Marketing

Journal of Retailing

Liljenwall, R. and Maskulka, J. (2002), *Marketing's Powerful Weapon: Point-Of-Purchase Advertising*. Washington, DC: Point-Of-Purchase Advertising International.

P-O-P Times

The Promotion Marketing Association, (http://www.pmalink.org/research/).

Case 12

POP in the c-store – the case of Red Bull

No longer are convenience or c-stores just great pit stops for filling up gas tanks; they have become an easy alternative to grocery stores. A recent study shows that only 12.4% of customers stop at a c-store because they need gas, while about one in three stop because they are hungry or thirsty. A couple of years ago, the convenience stores redefined themselves by adding several products. Nowadays many c-stores offer quick-serve meals, dry cleaning services, express mail counters, pharmacies and internet access, besides the food, snacks and drinks they used to offer. About 75% of the c-stores have a petrol distributorship, while more than 40% run a branded food service programme. Due to the high number of different items that are for sale, c-stores have become overcrowded with signage and POP-material.

Customer segments

C-stores try to offer convenience by being a little of everything to everybody. They target males and females, teens and grown-ups. This makes in-store marketing a really difficult task. The segments differ, the time of shopping differs (see Case Figure 12.1), but the reason remains the same: convenient shopping. Of all purchases at c-stores 30% are planned and 20% are made on impulse. The key is to have POP material that stimulates the different consumers, while not making the relatively small shops 'over-cluttered'.

Different needs

Supermarkets differ substantially from c-stores (Case Table 12.1). Although c-stores have recently grown from an average of 2,400 square feet to an

Case Figure 12.1
When do shoppers visit c-stores?

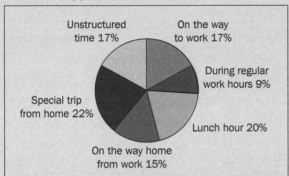

Reproduced with permission of Hoyt Publishing Company.

average of 3,800–4,400 square feet, the proportion of square feet to the number of available products (different stock-keeping units, SKUs) is rather small. Therefore, although recently more space has become available for in-store material, most of the manufacturers' POP displays are too big. So, displays that are accepted in grocery stores and supermarkets will not even be considered in c-stores. The reason for this is that the square footage needed for the display can generate far more sales from other products. Furthermore, since c-stores' *raison d'être* (impulse buying),

is different from that of supermarkets, c-stores do not need smaller versions of supermarket POPs, but specially designed POP material which they currently often make themselves. Besides space, time is another challenging aspect of c-stores. Visitors do not have the time to browse through the store or interact with displays. This speed flows over to the retailers who change their window signs and internal POP material every week. Therefore, they ask for flexible POP items, as well as a lot of variety which makes it stand out and be noticed by the customers.

Main characteristics that c-store retailers value in POP are convenience and ease of placement. Case Table 12.2, based on *P-O-P Times' Trend Report* (1999) shows c-stores' least and most preferred POP material. POPAI's 2002 study indicates that advertising at the cash register and on the outside window enjoys a particularly high recall.

The Miller Brewing Company is one of the first manufacturers to come up with hundreds of POP items developed especially for c-stores. The items began to appear in c-stores in spring 1999. Items include metal branded pricing signs, curb stickers, metal curb signs, cooler signs, beer bottle cooler door handles and a 'faux display'. The latter is 'a vacuum-formed plastic cube, which, when seen from the road, looks like a mass stacking of 12-packs of Miller cans'. Another way of attracting attention seems to be the use of gas pump talkers, which formed part of a very successful campaign launched by Red Bull.

Red Bull
One of the key market segments that Red Bull targets is motorists, hence c-stores seemed an especially attractive distribution channel for the product. However, at the beginning of 1998 Red Bull was a new and unknown product. Since oil companies are not obliged to stock the product, Red Bull distributor's (Ubevco)

Case Table 12.1
Most important differences between c-stores and supermarkets

Aspects	Differences
Space	Space is much more crucial for c-stores than for supermarkets
Time	Customers are more in a hurry in c-stores than in supermarkets
Flexibility	Because of the quick replacement and reorganising of POP material in c-stores, they need to be more flexible
Variety	A lot of POP in such a small space in c-stores requires more variety to be noticed
Functionality	C-stores are looking for functional rather than aesthetic POP material

Case Table 12.2
Most and least preferred POP material

Most preferred POP	Least preferred POP
Translites for menuboards	Coupon dispensers
Case stackers	Electric signage
Shelf organisers	Sidekicks
	Pallet displays

Case Table 12.3

Sales increase in Fina sites that stocked the product before the campaign

Fina convenience stores	Sales increase
Site 1	167%
Site 2	180%
Site 3	530%

Case Table 12.4

Awareness rates of Red Bull for different types of POP techniques

Medium	Awareness rate
Average for other outdoor media	26%
Average for gas pump talkers	80%–90%
Lowest for gas pump talkers	50.8%

first worry was to get Red Bull into the already over-crowded c-store. To this end, it announced a major c-store campaign in the UK in the hope that this might persuade the c-market. The campaign mainly consisted of having covered fuel nozzles, also called sqawkers or gas pump talkers. Pump talkers are attached to gas hoses by means of durable, self-locking hose clamps. In fact, they function as a kind of mini-billboard while customers are filling their car up. The advantage of gas pump talkers is that they have a completely captive audience for the three minutes it takes for the average 25-litre fill. Red Bull's gas pump talkers read as follows. 'Tired? Red Bull [a picture of the can] revitalises mind and body. Improves concentration, improves reaction times, improves endurance. Caution: Do not drink when you want to sleep.' The campaign ran in Elf, Total, Q8, Murco, Repsol and Maxol stores. For the first campaign, 182 Fina sites agreed to collect data. Of these 182 sites only three had stocked Red Bull before the one-month campaign started. Compared to the month prior to the campaign, sales jumped enormously (see Case Table 12.3). The 179 other Fina sites did not stock Red Bull prior to the campaign. However, 152 of them put Red Bull on their shelves before the end of the campaign, which increased Ubevco's distribution by 85%.

Red Bull's communications campaign not only consisted of gas pump talkers, but also used sampling, sponsoring of the Sauber Petronas Formula One team, and an in-store campaign consisting of a free Formula One poster for every can of Red Bull bought. The whole campaign had a significantly positive impact on awareness (Case Table 12.4), and both distribution and sales. However, Red Bull is most pleased with the gas pump talkers. Compared to the cost of other forms of outdoor media, gas pump talkers are relatively cheap, costing £50 to cover all the fuel hoses on one forecourt during one month.

According to the company supplying the gas pump talkers, the talkers are also more effective than other outdoor media tools.

Red Bull is really sold on the medium. It immediately invested in subsequent campaigns in the UK and started planning a huge pan-European programme, starting with a big entry in the German market. Later on, other POP materials were also developed (see Plate 23).

Meanwhile, several manufacturers, such as Nestlé and Dr Pepper, have followed Red Bull. Gas pump talkers are becoming a popular technique worldwide.

Questions

1 Do POP communications serve the same functions in a c-store as in a grocery store or supermarket?

2 Why do you think c-stores change their POP material more frequently than supermarkets?

3 More and more people pay at the pump. What is the major advantage and disadvantage of this trend for c-stores? How does this influence their need for POP material?

4 Would you advise a c-store to use atmospheric elements, or do you think this is less important for c-stores than for supermarkets or other retailers?

5 How could the Red Bull campaign have been made even more effective?

Based on: Cosgrove, J. (2002), 'Convenient POP. POPAI's latest advertising study details what works and what doesn't in convenience stores', *Beverage Industry*, May, 38–40; 'Convenience Store, You've come a long way, baby', 1999. *P-O-P Times, The News Publication of Point-of-Purchase Advertising, Display and Packaging*, 12, 4, 46–55; Special report, 'Ambient Media is Providing Retailers and Suppliers with Yet Another Way of Advertising Their Products Instore and Influencing Consumers' Buying Decisions', 1998. *In-Store-Marketing* (January), 32; 'Marketing at the Gas Pump', 1997, *P-O-P Times. The News Publication of Point-of-Purchase Advertising, Display and Packaging*, 10, 12, 34; Case prepared by Malaika Brengman, Limburgs Universitair Centrum.

References

1 Chadwick, P. (2003), 'POP Dos and Don'ts', *Promotions & Incentives*, April, 45–7.

2 Leeds, D. (1994), 'Accountability is In-Store for Marketeers in '94', *Brandweek* (14 March), 17.

3 Tellis, G.J. (1998), *Advertising and Sales Promotion Strategy*, Reading, Mass.: Addison-Wesley.

4 POPAI Europe (1998), *The POPAI Europe Consumer Buying Habits Study*, Co-ordination by Retail Marketing In-store Services Limited, Watford, Herts: POPAI Europe; POPAI (1995), *Measuring the In-Store Decision Making of Supermarket and Mass Merchandise Store Shoppers*, Englewood Cliffs, NJ; POPAI.

5 POPAI Europe (1998), *The POPAI Europe Consumer Buying Habits Study*, Co-ordination by Retail Marketing In-store Services Limited, Watford, Herts: POPAI Europe; POPAI (1995), *Measuring the In-Store Decision Making of Supermarket and Mass Merchandise Store Shoppers*, Englewood Cliffs, NJ: POPAI.

6 Rosenberg, J.M. (1995), *Dictionary of Retailing and Merchandising*. New York: John Wiley & Sons.

7 'Boss Switches to Interactive CD System' (1998), *In-Store Marketing* (January), 6.

8 ' "Think Different" Boutiques Boost Sales' (1998), *Point of Purchase Magazine*, 4(3), 56.

9 'Procter & Gamble Backs Health and Beauty Product Launch with Twin Interactive Kiosk Strategy' (1997), *In-Store Marketing* (October), 7.

10 Tkacik, M. (2003), 'Rubber Match: In a Clash of Sneaker Titans, Nike Gets Leg Up on Foot Locker', *Wall Street Journal*, 13 May.

11 Birtwistle, G., Clarke, I. and Freathy, P. (1998), 'Customer Decision Making in Fashion Retailing: A Segmentation Analysis', *International Journal of Retail & Distribution Management*, 26(4) (http://www.europe.emerald-library.com/brev/08926db1.htm).

12 Kotler, P. (1973), 'Atmospherics as a Marketing Tool', *Journal of Retailing*, 49(4), 48–64.

13 'House of Change' (1997), *In-Store Marketing* (October), 22–3.

14 Inman, J.J. and McAlister, L. (1993), 'A Retailer Promotion Policy Model Considering Promotion Signal Sensitivity', *Marketing Science*, 12, 339–56; Inman, J.J. and Winer, R.S. (1998), *Where the Rubber Meets the Road: A Model of In-Store Consumer Decision Making*, Working Paper, Report no. 98–122, Cambridge, MA: Marketing Science Institute.

15 *Grocery Incentive Study 2002*, The Promotion Marketing Association, (http://www.pmalink.org/research/CDPgrocery_F.asp).

16 *Grocery Incentive Study 2002*, The Promotion Marketing Association, (http://www.pmalink.org/research/CDPgrocery_F.asp).

17 Dhar, S.K. and Hoch, S.J. (1996), 'Price Discrimination Using In-Store Merchandising', *Journal of Marketing*, 60, 17–30.

18 'Building the Nesquik Brand' (1998), *In-Store Marketing* (March), 28.

19 'Special Report: Ambient Media is Providing Retailers and Suppliers with Yet Another Way of Advertising Their Products in Store and Influencing Consumers' Buying Decisions' (1998), *In-Store Marketing* (January), 32–3.

20 Inman, J.J. and Winer, R.S. (1998), *Where the Rubber Meets the Road: A Model of In-store Consumer Decision Making*, Working Paper, Report no. 98–122, Cambridge, MA: Marketing Science Institute.

21 'Special Report: Touchscreen Kiosks, Trolley Displays and Talking Shelves – Interactive Multimedia is Coming to a Shop Near You. But is it Working?' (1997), *In-Store Marketing* (September), 25–31.

22 'Does P-O-P Measure up?' (1997), *P-O-P Times, The News Publication of Point-of-Purchase Advertising, Display and Packaging* (December), 36–52.

23 'Backroom Brawling' (1997), *P-O-P Times, The News Publication of Point-of-Purchase Advertising, Display and Packaging* (December), 4.

24 'Backroom Brawling' (1997), *P-O-P Times, The News Publication of Point-of-Purchase Advertising, Display and Packaging* (December), 4.

25 Botsford, D. (2002), 'Getting the Retail Support You Want', *Brandweek*, 43(22), 19.

26 Brengman, M., Geuens, M. and Faseur, T. (2002), 'Capturing the Image of Second-hand Stores: Investigating the underlying image dimensions', *Asia Pacific Advances in Consumer Research*, 5, 387–93.

27 Zimmer, R. and Golden, L.L. (1988), 'Impressions of Retail Stores: A Content Analysis of Consumer Images', *Journal of Retailing*, 64(3), 265–91.

28 Birtwistle, G., Clarke, I. and Freathy, P. (1999), 'Store Image in the UK Fashion Sector: Consumer versus Retailer Perceptions', *International Review of Retail, Distribution and Consumer Research*, 9(1), 1–16.

29 'Merrell Uses Equipment Replicas for Imagery' (1999), *POP Times, The News Publication of Point-of-Purchase Advertising, Display and Packaging*, 12(4), 1, 16.

30 D'Astous, A. and Lévesque, M. (2003), 'A Scale for Measuring Store Personality', *Psychology & Marketing*, 20(5), 455–69.

31 D'Astous, A. and Lévesque, M. (2003), 'A Scale for Measuring Store Personality', *Psychology & Marketing*, 20(5), 455–69.

32 Lewison, D.M. (1997), *Retailing, 6th edition*, Englewood Cliffs, NJ: Prentice Hall.

33 Miller, R. (2002), 'In-Store Impact on Impulse Shoppers', *Marketing*, November 21, 27–8.

34 Inman, J.J. and Winer, R.S. (1998), *Where the Rubber Meets the Road: A Model of In-Store Consumer Decision Making*, Working Paper, Report no. 98–122, Cambridge, MA: Marketing Science Institute.

35 Lewison, D.M. (1997), *Retailing, 6th edition*, Englewood Cliffs, NJ: Prentice Hall.

36 'De Supermarkt Weet Wanneer Je Vreemd Gaat' (The Supermarket Knows When You Are Doing It Somewhere Else) (1998), *De Morgen*, 14 March, 70.

37 'Het is Bewezen: Wie's Avonds Luiers Koopt, Drinkt Blond Bier' (It Has Been Proven: Persons Who Buy Diapers in the Evening, Drink Blond Beer), (1998), *Intermediair*, 24 (9 June), 19.

38 Spies, K., Hesse, F. and Loesch, K. (1997), 'Store Atmosphere, Mood and Purchasing Behavior', *International Journal of Research in Marketing*, 14(1), 1–17.

39 Van der Ster, W. and van Wissen, P. (1987), *Marketing & Detailhandel, 4th edition*. Groningen: Wolterns-Noordhoff.

40 Titus, P.A. and Everett, P.B. (1996), 'Consumer Way Finding Tasks, Strategies, and Errors: An Exploratory Field Study', *Psychology and Marketing*, 13(3), 265–90.

41 Mulhern, F.J. (1997), 'Retail Marketing: From Distribution to Integration', *International Journal of Research in Marketing*, 14(2), 103–24.

42 Mulhern, F.J. (1997), 'Retail Marketing: From Distribution to Integration', *International Journal of Research in Marketing*, 14(2), 103–24; Urban, T.L. (1998), 'An Inventory-Theoretic Approach to Product Assortment and Shelf-Space Allocation', *Journal of Retailing*, 74(1), 15–35.

43 Emmelhainz, M.A., Stock, J.R. and Emmelhainz, L.W. (1991), 'Guest Commentary: Consumer Response to Stockouts', *Journal of Retailing*, 67, 138–44.

44 Borin, N. and Farris, P. (1995), 'A Sensitivity Analysis of Retailer Shelf Management Models', *Journal of Retailing*, 71(2), 153–71.

45 Mulhern, F.J. (1997), 'Retail Marketing: From Distribution to Integration', *International Journal of Research in Marketing*, 14(2), 103–24.

46 Young, S. (2002), 'Winning at Retail', *GCI*, August, 61–4.

47 Lewison, D.M. (1997), *Retailing, 6th edition*, Englewood Cliffs, NJ: Prentice-Hall.

48 Van der Ster, W. and van Wissen, P. (1987), *Marketing & Detailhandel, 4th edition*, Groningen: Wolterns-Noordhoff.

49 Kotler, P. (1973), 'Atmospherics as a Marketing Tool', *Journal of Retailing*, 49(4), 48–64.

50 Kotler, P. (1973), 'Atmospherics as a Marketing Tool', *Journal of Retailing*, 49(4), 48–64.

51 Mehrabian, A. and Russell, J.A. (1974), *An Approach to Environmental Psychology*. Cambridge, MA: MIT Press.

52 North, A.C., Hargreaves, D.J. and McKendrick, J. (1999), 'The Influence of In-Store Music on Wine Selections', *Journal of Applied Psychology*, 84(2), 271–6.

53 Caldwell, C. and Hibbert, S.A. (2002), 'The Influence of Music Tempo and Musical Preferences on Restaurant Patrons' Behavior', *Psychology & Marketing*, 19(11), 895–918.

54 'Special Report: Ambient Media is Providing Retailers and Suppliers with yet Another Way of Advertising their Products in Store and Influencing Consumers' Buying Decisions' (1998), *In-store Marketing* (January), 29–33.

55 Ethridge, M. (1996), 'We Follow Our Noses to Stores', *Akron Beacon Journal* (20 January), B1.

56 Spangenberg, E.R., Crowley, A.E. and Henderson, P.W. (1996), 'Improving the Store Environment: Do Olfactory Cues Affect Evaluations and Behaviors?', *Journal of Marketing*, 60 (April), 67–80.

57 Miller, R. (2002), 'How to Exploit POP Around the Globe', *Marketing*, August, 27.

58 Schoormans, J.P.L. and Robben, H.S.J. (1997), 'The Effect of New Package Design on Product Attention, Categorization and Evaluation', *Journal of Economic Psychology*, 18(2), 271–87.

59 Schoormans, J.P.L. and Robben, H.S.J. (1997), 'The Effect of New Package Design on Product Attention, Categorization and Evaluation', *Journal of Economic Psychology*, 18(2), 271–87.

60 Young, S. (2002), 'Winning at Retail', *GCI*, August, 61–4.

61 'De Zeven Verpakkingszonden' (The Seven Packaging Sins) (1999), *Marketing Mix Digest*, 34(3), 5.

62 Clark, S.H.L. (1997), 'How Packaging Works with Children', in Smith, G. (ed.), *Children's Food Marketing and Innovation*. London: Chapman & Hall, 119–25.

63 Wansink, B. (1996), 'Can Package Size Accelerate Usage Volume?', *Journal of Marketing*, 60(3), 1–14.

64 Folkes, V., Martin, I. and Gupta, K. (1993), 'When to Say When: Effects of Supply on Usage', *Journal of Consumer Research*, 20 (December), 467–77.

65 Wansink, B. (1994), 'Antecedents and Mediators of Eating Bouts', *Family and Consumer Sciences Research Journal*, 23 (December), 166–82.

Chapter 13

Public relations and sponsorship

Chapter outline

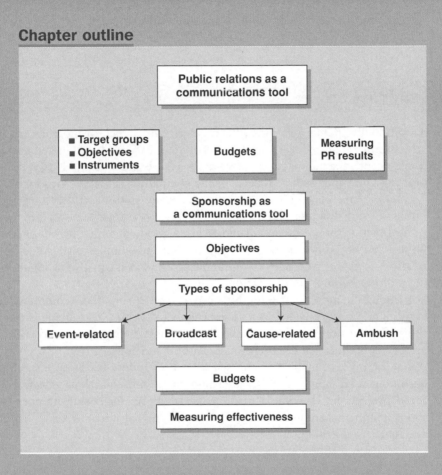

Chapter objectives

This chapter will help you to:

- Understand the role of marketing public relations in the company's communications effort
- Get an idea of the strengths and weaknesses of public relations
- Distinguish the target groups, objectives and instruments of public relations
- Distinguish a number of public relations budgeting techniques
- Learn how to measure public relations effectiveness

▶

- Understand the role of sponsorship in the communications mix
- Distinguish the target groups and objectives of sponsorship
- Learn about the different types of sponsorship, such as event-related sponsorship, broadcast sponsorship, cause-related sponsorship and ambush marketing, and their advantages and disadvantages
- Select sponsorship proposals on the basis of a set of relevant criteria
- Measure the effectiveness of a sponsorship campaign

Introduction

Traditionally, public relations (PR) is an activity which in most companies has been structurally separated from marketing communications. It originated in the function of 'press agent', the main activity of whom was to bridge the gap between the company's point of view and media coverage of the company's activities. Gradually, press agents became a vital part of the company's communications efforts targeted at various publics or stakeholders, and the activity of 'press relations' evolved into the 'public relations' function. Staying in touch and creating goodwill with all types of company stakeholders has become an extremely sophisticated and complex task. And, although public relations is mainly a corporate communications tool, it can also be an important instrument of marketing communications.

Although in most companies the share of sponsorship in the communications budget is still limited, worldwide it is an increasingly important instrument of the communications mix. Not only are sponsorship budgets increasing, sponsored events and causes are becoming more and more diverse. Although 'spouse-driven projects' still exist, the degree of professionalism in the selection and follow-up of sponsorship projects is becoming increasingly sophisticated and the communications effectiveness of sponsored projects has become a major concern. In an increasing number of companies sponsorship has acquired the status of one of the cornerstones of the communications and marketing strategy.

Public relations as a marketing communications tool

Public relations is a communications tool that is used to promote the goodwill of the firm as a whole.[1] It is the projection of the personality of the company, the management of reputation.[2] Public relations is the planned and sustained effort to establish and maintain good relationships, mutual understanding, sympathy and goodwill with (potential) customers and with secondary target groups, also called publics, audiences or stakeholders.[3] It is those efforts that identify and close the gap between how the organisation is seen by its key publics and how it would like to be seen.[4] Publicity is the term used to decribe the free media coverage of news about the company or its products, often as a result of PR efforts.

Public relations is different from most other marketing communications in a number of ways. Marketing communications tend to be commercial and short-term. Few marketers will jeopardise short-term benefits for the sake of long-term returns. Although public relations executives recognise the importance of customer satisfaction and profits, their main concern is the long-term goodwill towards, and reputation of, the company as a whole. They want people to respect their organisation. As a result, marketers will always have to keep PR people focussed on marketing objectives. On the other hand, public relations professionals will have to challenge marketing people in terms of the effects of their actions on a broader public. Good public relations lay the groundwork, create the platform for successful marketing communications.

The privacy issue and two big brands

In March 2003 Benetton and Philips announced that Philips was going to help Benetton embed computer chips in the clothes it sells, enabling individual garments to be tracked, potentially beyond the point of sale. This initiative was announced at a time when the following things also happened:

- The US government confirmed that it was going to mine commercial databases for clues about terrorist organisations;

- The movie *Minority Report* with Tom Cruise featured talking billboards that track wherever you go;

- The US government threatened to block flights to America by European airlines that refuse to give the US government access to passenger lists;

- Surveys indicate that a majority of consumers do not believe commercial companies are handling personal information about their customers in a confidential way.

Within two days a consumer privacy group was calling for an immediate worldwide boycott of Benetton. CASPIAN, Consumers Against Supermarket Privacy Invasion and Numbering, warned the public that Benetton could easily link the serial number in your sweater to credit card information, and that this information would be available to anyone with access to the Benetton database. A number of consumers expressed their concern about the initiative. A website calling for a Benetton boycott and posters featuring messages such as 'I'd rather go naked' quickly appeared. Less than three weeks later Benetton announced that it was 'reconsidering', and no chips were currently present in the garments produced. Philips removed all traces of the press release from its website. Companies should be increasingly aware of the perceptions of the general public, pressure group activities, and the potential damage to the image of the company that occurs as a result of PR initiatives that do not take major concerns of these publics into account.[5]

Although advertising, sales efforts, direct mailing on the one hand, and public relations – more specifically the publicity generated by PR activity – on the other, can both have a similar influence on the reputation of a company and its products, there are a number of specific characteristics of public relations.

PR targets important stakeholders and difficult-to-reach audiences such as opinion leaders, financial analysts and investors. Many of them are not interested in advertising or direct mailing, and even avoid it, or are very sceptical towards it.[6] Furthermore they are shielded from salespersons by their assistants. On the other hand, they are often interested in news and may be reached indirectly by the media exposure generated through PR activity. PR professionals can advise companies on important trends and on the consequences of corporate activities on marketing effectiveness. PR can present the company as a good citizen and as such contributes to the corporate image and reputation of the company and its products.

PR plays an important role in guiding the company through crises without too much damage to its reputation. Often, advertising and sales promotions are strictly regulated by governments. PR offers the opportunity of more message flexibility. PR is often relatively cost-effective because the media coverage generated is free. Getting media coverage often enables the company to reach a variety of audiences and a large number of people at a fraction of the cost that would have been required in an advertising campaign.

The most important advantage of PR and the resulting media exposure over other marketing communications tools may be that the former is generally considered to be more objective and therefore more believable in the perception of the target groups. News is also generally more exciting, or is presented as such. Other marketing communications, on the other hand, are paid for by the company, and the public are aware of that. This results in a certain cynicism about the bias in the message. As a result, PR is capable of breaking through the communications clutter more effectively.

The major weakness of PR is the lack of control over the content of the press coverage of news releases. Evidently, the media have other priorities and other sources, and the published story may be quite different from the information disseminated by the PR department. The context and style of the original message may be substantially changed or completely lost. In advertising, for instance, the company has full control over the content of its communications. With PR, journalists act as gatekeepers: if a story is perceived as having not enough 'news value' it may not be published, especially in a period in which there is other important news to cover. The timing of ads and sales promotions are fully controlled by the company. The effectiveness of PR is hard to measure. Often, exposure measures, such as the amount of media coverage, are used, but they hardly say anything about the long-term effect of PR efforts on company goodwill or sales. Measuring the effectiveness of advertising is often more straightforward.

Public relations is of growing importance for companies. In the US three out of four companies have a PR department. The number of people working in PR is estimated to be 145,000. The growth of the PR industry is estimated to be in double digits.[7] In recent years, the UK PR market has grown by approximately 20% per year.[8]

Target groups, objectives and instruments of marketing PR

Marketing PR is targeted at commercial stakeholders, such as distributors, suppliers, competitors and potential customers, and can be defined as a direct support of marketing communications.

Sometimes a distinction is made between direct and indirect PR. Direct PR activity is directly aimed at (potential) customers of interest, while indirect PR tries to reach them through other publics. Thus, employees, and in particular, the media can be considered as indirect PR audiences. Keeping good relations with the media and other opinion leaders is not important as such. It is their role as intermediate groups between the company and its (potential) customers that makes them important PR target groups.

Although employees can be a direct target group of PR activity, they are an important intermediate public too, because they are often in close contact with other audiences such as the general public, customers, suppliers and distributors, etc. It is therefore vital that they are 'spreading the good news' about the company. Therefore, internal PR should create goodwill with the employees to motivate them to do so.

Finally, a specific type of PR activity is crisis management or crisis communications. It may involve different types of audiences, internal as well as external.

KBC on-line: involving employees in an advertising campaign promoting on-line banking

KBC is one of the major Belgian banks. In 2000 it decided to launch an advertising campaign to stimulate on-line banking by switching regular customers to KBC-on-line, a service that is free of charge and by which KBC customers can carry out their banking activities electronically. The on-line activation is done during a visit to the bank office. The duration of the campaign was from early 2000 to February 2003. During the first stage of the campaign, awareness and interest was built with the slogan 'Always your banker at hand'. The second stage focussed upon the adoption of the new product: 'Don't be the last one to become a KBC on-liner'. During the last stage, the KBC on-line customer was reassured: 'Everything under control with KBC on-line'.

Especially during the early stages of the campaign, there was the risk that employees would not buy in to the on-line idea. They may have been offended by the fact that they would be replaced by a computer, and they may have feared that, in the long run, their jobs could become redundant. Therefore, KBC involved the employees in the campaign in different ways. In the first stage of the campaign, the focus was on the importance of the availability of the personal banker. In television spots, billboards and print ads, customers are shown in various circumstances, literally holding the hand of what appears to be their personal banker. The message is conveyed that on-line banking enables you to do your banking business wherever and whenever you want, but at the same time it stresses the point that human contact is indispensable. The mailings to customers were sent out from the local branches to increase the link between the bank office and its employees on the one hand, and the customers on the other. Each campaign stage and tool contained an opportunity (both for the employees and the customers) to engage in a personal conversation. All personnel received the campaign material six weeks before the start of the campaign so they could prepare themselves for an efficient personal follow-up to the mail. The campaign took into account the potential negative fallout of advertising campaigns on the motivation of the employees, and tried to integrate internal PR and external communication to avoid negative side effects. The campaign was a considerable success and won a Belgian Gold Effie Award in 2003.[9]

Ariel and the Palestinians

'We cannot tolerate that, without our permission, political messages are linked with one of our products' was the official reaction of Procter & Gamble to a campaign run by the Palestine Action Platform. This pressure group launched a print advertising campaign in which a fist holds a bloodstained Palestinian shawl, accompanied by the slogan: 'How will Ariel get this clean?' The purpose of the campaign was to make the public aware of the Palestinian problem and

▶

the alleged role of the Israeli Prime Minister, Ariel Sharon, using Procter & Gamble's well-known brand of washing powder. The campaign appeared in national newspapers, and Procter & Gamble first sent friendly letters to the organisation and to the media, asking them to stop the campaign immediately. The action group was not impressed, and continued its campaign: 'It is obvious that only Mr Sharon is implied, not P&G'. Procter & Gamble then threatened to start legal action if the campaign was not stopped. The company stated that 'we as a company do not want to take a stand on the political situation in the Middle East. Therefore we do not tolerate that our brand name, for which we are responsible, is used in this manner.' By that time all major media had covered the dispute.[10] Eventually, the campaign was withdrawn. Sometimes companies are confronted with unexpected publicity that can damage their reputation or that of their brands. Fast and well-balanced PR activity is then called for.

Marketing PR can be used to support the launch of a new product, for instance by inviting the trade press to test-drive a new car, or to see to it that a new CD gets enough 'airplay'. It can also be used to support and revive existing products, for instance by means of creating an event when the 50th shop is opened, or after the first 100,000 cars of a certain model have been sold. Sponsorship and special events can be used as PR tools to improve the relationship with suppliers and distributors, by offering free tickets for sports or arts events. Restaurants may invite journalists from the specialised press to encourage them to write a positive article, and as a result boost sales. All these examples illustrate that marketing PR is an activity that is largely integrated with both corporate PR and other tools of the communications mix.

Sales and marketing PR

The sales team can be motivated to feed the PR department with interesting stories that can be a starting point for marketing-derived and marketing supporting PR activity. The following sales events can be considered:[11]

- *Prestige orders*. These can be orders from famous companies or contracts relating to special projects that are themselves in the news;
- *Problem-solving orders*. Sales of products that have provided the solution for a particularly demanding need;
- *Added value contracts*. The product has made the life of customers and employees more agreeable;
- *Unusual orders*. Products used at famous locations or in places of interest;
- *Sympathetic associations*. Selling products in a situation of strong human interest appeal or related to a good cause of general interest.

Since the media are the most important intermediate public, developing and maintaining good contacts with radio, television and the (trade) press is often extremely important. Indirectly, media PR is aimed at generating favourable publicity about the company, its products and brands, and more generally all events and projects that support the image of the company and its marketing objectives.

Good media PR can result in positive comments during the introduction of a product, can create goodwill for the company's activities and can generate publicity for a range of organisational events, activities and sponsorship programmes. In the aftermath of the Class A moose test problems (some journalists questioned the car's safety), Mercedes was able to neutralise the bad publicity quickly by means of careful PR campaigns directed at the specialised press (see also Plate 24). Obtaining media attention for sponsorship projects can generate publicity that is, in terms of media exposure, worth much more than the initial investment in the event. In times of crisis, the media are a crucial audience in order to avoid or neutralise negative 'fallout' from the crisis event. Bad handling of media relations caused the Perrier problem (benzene in Perrier mineral water) to evolve into a major wave of bad publicity that resulted in enormous image and commercial damage to the brand and the company.

The instruments of media PR are press kits and press releases, and their audiovisual counterparts Video News Releases (VNR) and Radio News Releases (RNR). A press kit is a set of documentation, containing photos, reports and a press release, which are sent to journalists or presented at a press conference. A press release is a document that contains the material that the company would like to see covered in the press. VNRs and RNRs are audiovisual news releases put on video or audio tape and sent to the TV or radio stations free of charge for unrestricted use.[12] They are composed in such a way that excerpts can be broadcast immediately, thereby assuring that the message reaches the audience undistorted.

By means of press conferences and interviews the company can comment on the issues that it considers important and try to present them as 'news'. However, in this over-informed society, not a lot of things are 'news'. Companies should avoid falling into the 'marketing myopia' trap as concerns the news value of 'important' company events. What is news to a certain medium depends on the characteristics of the message and the medium itself, and on the way the news is presented.

Marketing PR budgets

Public relations should be operating within the same discipline that applies to other business functions. This implies that a budget has to be fixed, and that measurable objectives should be defined. Different budgeting techniques can be applied.[13]

Budgets may be based on historical comparison, i.e. on what has been spent in previous periods, possibly adjusted as a function of changed circumstances. New product launches may result in increased budgets; less competition may imply lower budgets. Overall, this method seldom leads to sound budgeting. Maybe the historical starting figure was inappropriate, or the company is doing so well that the PR budget can easily be reduced. Most importantly, there is a lack of strategic focus: by not taking into account the changing environment, great PR opportunities or dangerous threats calling for PR action may be overlooked. In the resources costing method management decides what resources are needed (an extra press officer, or an event co-ordinator) and calculates the costs implied. This method suffers from similar weaknesses to the previous one, although PR needs are to a certain extent taken into account.

In action costing a PR programme or activity is planned, and the cost to carry it out is calculated. This method has the virtue of starting from the task to be accomplished, but lacks long-term perspective. The competitive tendering method is very similar to the previous one. A PR programme is decided on and different PR agencies are requested to file a proposal and a budget. In the **income proportion** method a pre-specified proportion of margin or sales is devoted to PR. This method suffers from the same weakness as the historical comparison method. There is a lack of strategic focus, and the PR budget grows with sales – generally a situation in which less PR activity is needed. On the contrary, if there is a decline in sales, PR budgets decrease at a time during which they may be needed most. In **industry comparison** the industry average is used as a benchmark to decide the PR budget. Again, there is a lack of strategic focus, and no link with a pre-specified task.

In the **capitation rating** or **achievement targeting** method, audiences to be reached and objectives to be achieved are defined. For instance, a 30% awareness and a 70% favourable attitude with the general public by the end of the year may be the goals. Experience with other communications tools, such as advertising and direct mailing, may be used to calculate the budget required to achieve these objectives. This method is probably one of the most useful. However, as for all marketing communications activities, public relations is not an exact science, and the objectives to be achieved are often long-term oriented. Therefore it is difficult to set a PR budget. However, PR agencies increasingly face situations in which they are paid by results rather than on a mark-up basis.[14]

Measuring public relations results

Similar to most other communications instruments, the effectiveness of a public relations campaign can only be measured if clear objectives have been defined. These objectives have to be measurable and related to the PR activity. This implies that short-term or long-term awareness, opinion and/or attitude or goodwill changes will have to be measured with the targeted publics. Evolution of sales or market share are seldom good indicators, since they are not the main target objectives of PR activity. Furthermore, they are to a large extent influenced by other instruments of the marketing and communications mix. The result of public relations activity can be assessed by means of three categories of performance measures: input, output and achievement indicators:[15]

■ *Input indicators* measure PR efforts, such as the number of news stories disseminated, the number of interviews given, trade meetings organised, supermarkets visited or brochures sent. Input indicators measure efforts and not results. Therefore they are largely insufficient as measures of PR effectiveness. Nevertheless, they can be useful, since they can give a first indication of the activity undertaken.

■ *Output indicators* measure the result of the PR activity in terms of media coverage or publicity. Examples of such measures are the press space or television time devoted to the company, its events or brands, the length of the stories, the tone and news value of the headlines, readership/viewership levels, opportunity to see, tone of coverage, etc. Again, although output measures may be useful indicators of the result of PR activity, they do not give any information on how well the real objectives have been achieved.

■ *Achievement indicators* measure the extent to which a pre-specified objective has been met with a public of interest. They are very similar to some of the measures that are being used in the assessment of advertising effectiveness. Examples include: the share of the target audience that has been reached, changes in awareness and knowledge, changes in opinions and attitudes, evolution of the image and goodwill of the company and its products, and the extent to which behaviour has changed.

Sponsorship as a marketing communications tool

Sponsorship can be defined as an investment in cash or kind in an activity, in return for access to the exploitable commercial potential associated with this activity.[16] The company promotes its interests and brands by tying them to a specific and meaningfully related event or cause.[17] It is a thematic communications instrument with which the sponsor assists the sponsee in realising his or her project. In return the sponsee co-operates in realising the communications objectives of the sponsoring company. If the latter is not the case, the investment of the 'sponsor' is nothing more than altruism, charity, patronage or benefaction.

Generally speaking, sponsorship shares two of the fundamental objectives of advertising, i.e. the generation of awareness about the product or company, and the promotion of positive messages about the product or company.[18] However, there are a number of important differences between the two, the most important one being that advertising allows greater control over the content and the environment of the message. Advertising messages are explicit and direct, and advertisers can decide when and where to place their ads. On the other hand, although sponsorship results in a less cluttered promotion of their products, companies also have less control over sponsorship, which makes their messages more indirect and implicit. As a result, in order to make sponsorship effective, accompanying communications efforts are called for.[19] Indeed, sponsorship can be described as a 'mute non-verbal medium', as opposed to advertising, in which messages are created using visuals, vocals and context.[20]

On the other hand, sponsorship is less cluttered and financially more attractive. It can be considered a cheap form of advertising. However, sponsorship may be less effective in gaining attention as a result of the distraction factor: spectators are primarily involved with the sponsored event (a soccer game or a work of art) and pay less attention to the environment of the event, such as the sponsor.[21] Indeed, exposure to a sponsor's name or logo is not the same as sponsorship effectiveness. Furthermore, in some cases the sponsor is closely associated with a popular sponsored event or cause, which may turn out to have a strong positive effect on corporate and brand image. Sponsorship is also easy for the consumer to understand: it essentially works on the basis of association between sponsor and sponsee. Advertising, on the other hand, often requires elaborate processing of the message.[22]

Sponsorship is different from event marketing, which, in turn, is a type of PR activity.[23] Certainly, sponsorship can be integrated into a PR campaign. During the world championship cycling in Valkenburg (1998), Rabobank was one of the structural sponsors. It invited about 5,000 guests, mainly employees and customers of Rabobank in the Netherlands and elsewhere. Invitations to cultural events, for instance to see David Bowie at the Seat Beach festival in Ostend and the musical *Oliver* in one of the 12 large theatres in the Netherlands, are examples of corporate hospitality, integrating sponsorship into a PR campaign by Nashuatec.[24] Event marketing can be defined as using a number of elements of the promotion mix to create an event for the purpose of reaching strategic marketing objectives. An example of event marketing is the Camel Trophy.

Finally, sponsorship should be distinguished from value marketing. Value marketing or societal marketing can be defined as a strategy in which a company links its activities to a philosophy of general societal interest. The company positions itself on the basis of a value system that is often not product-related. For instance, the international cosmetics company The Body Shop tries to combine fair business, social conscience and profit-ability. It produces environmentally-friendly products, based on natural ingredients, that are not tested on animals and which are sold in recycled or recyclable packaging. Raw materials are bought from Third World countries at fair prices. Sponsorship can be part of the value marketing strategy, but it is by no means its only instrument.[25]

American Express: a pioneer in value marketing

American Express was one of the first companies that recognised the beneficial effects of value marketing. In 1983 it launched a campaign to raise money for the restoration of the Statue of Liberty. American Express made a donation of one cent every time someone used its credit card. The number of new cardholders grew by 45% and card usage increased by 28%. The company has continued its value marketing efforts. In April 2001, for instance, it created the Community Business Programme to help smart business owners gain access to the resources they need to start or grow. Together with its partners, the Association for Enterprise Opportunity and Count-me-in for Women's Economic Independence, American Express serves an under-served and underfunded group of small businesses and entrepreneurs. The company created the Community Business Card, a credit card for small business owners, which allocates 1% of all cardholder spending to one of the microenterprise development partners. They, in turn, provide small loans and training for entrepreneurs in need. The company receives significant recognition from consumers and other interested parties. As such, the programme reinforces American Express's reputation and future business.[26]

In 1984 the worldwide sponsorship market was estimated at US$2 billion. The esti-mate for 2001 is US$24.6 billion. Total sponsorship expenditures in Europe amounted to €7.4 billion in 2001, compared to €6.5 billion in 2000. Worldwide, the annual growth of sponsorship between 1990 and 1999 is estimated at between 10% and 15%. In the 1990s, the annual growth of advertising and sales promotion was only 6%. As a result, the relative importance of sponsorship in communications budgets has, on aver-age, increased to 7%.[27] In some countries (Italy, South Africa and Australia), more than 13% of the advertising budget is spent on sponsorship.[28] Furthermore, part of the advertising budget is directly sponsorship-related in that it supports and leverages the sponsorship efforts (see below). It is fair to conclude that sponsorship is an increasingly important instrument of marketing communications.

UPS supports Olympic sponsorship with worldwide advertising campaign

UPS is the world's largest express carrier and delivery company. It entered the European market in 1988. It did not make a profit in Europe during the first 10 years. In 1996 UPS made the fundamental decision to revamp its European operations. It decided to become an official partner of the 2000 Olympics in Sydney. Research identified four weaknesses:

▶

low awareness of the Olympic sponsorship, low awareness of brand and service capabilities, an undifferentiated brand position, and the fact that potential customers were unaware of UPS as an enabler of global commerce. UPS launched a global campaign to redress this situation by leveraging its association with the Olympics in a relevant way. The Olympics provided a unique opportunity to associate UPS with the core Olympic values of trust, integrity, ambition and success. The creative execution of the campaign compared UPS with the Olympics: 'If UPS are good enough to deliver for the Olympics, they must be good enough for us'. The campaign showed UPS employees demonstrating their commitment to preparing to represent their country. The advertising campaign was implemented throughout Europe and worldwide, and stretched from the national trials to the games themselves, with special focus on key business periods March–May and the weeks before and during the summer Olympics in September 2000. Fifty-four campaigns ran in the US, Latin America, Asia and Europe, using global, pan-European and national media vehicles. Besides television, radio spots, magazine advertisements and outdoor advertising, sponsorship of key news programmes was also used. Research showed that UPS awareness increased by 5% to 10% in most countries, and so did most-often usage of UPS by 3% to 20%. Year-to-year revenue growth was 4% during the first quarter of 2001. The international export volume grew by 17%, led by Europe with a 25% increase. The UPS example shows that sponsorship programmes need to be accompanied by major investments in other communication campaigns to secure maximum impact.[29]

There are a number of reasons why sponsorship is of increasing importance. First, there is a feeling that traditional mass media advertising is becoming increasingly expensive, increasingly irritating and, as a result of communication clutter, less effective. Sponsorship is believed to have the power to escape this clutter, to isolate the brand from the competition and to get the message across at lower cost, although some predict that sponsorship clutter may become equally widespread. Furthermore, sponsored events are increasingly broadcast, thereby leveraging the initial investment of sponsorship. Overall, media, especially television programme sponsorship (see below), is increasingly accepted, and substantially improves the levels of coverage of, and impact on, broad target groups.[30]

Due to increased leisure, sports and cultural activities, new sponsorship opportunities are emerging. Governments are less and less inclined to finance culture and other social activities, so forcing cultural and social organisations to look for financial support from private companies. Finally, legal constraints on tobacco and alcohol advertising are forcing the companies involved to look for other communications strategies to get their message across. Sponsorship is an obvious substitute to build awareness and image.

Target groups and objectives of sponsorship

Since sponsorship is explicitly linked to an event, audiences can be contacted as active participants in the event (soccer players or musicians), as live spectators who attend events (fans or visitors of a museum), and/or as media followers of the event. In Table 13.1 the results of a study on sports sponsorship in Canada are shown, illustrating the wide range of audiences that are targeted and their relative importance.[31] Obviously, depending on the objectives and the target groups of the global communications campaign,

Table 13.1 Sports sponsorship target audiences in Canada

Audience	Mean importance (on 7-point scale)
Potential customers	5.79
Existing customers	5.62
Local community	5.60
General public	5.16
Business community	4.37
Workforce	4.33
Distributors	3.21
Shareholders	3.18
Suppliers	3.09
Ethnic groups	3.05
Government	2.74

Based on: Thwaites, D., Anguilar-Manjarrez, R. and Kidd, C. (1998), 'Sports Sponsorship Development in Leading Canadian Companies: Issues and Trends', *International Journal of Advertising*, 17(1), 29–50. Reproduced with permission of NTC Publications Limited.

sponsorship projects will be selected that are best capable of reaching the desired target groups. For instance, products targeted at up-market demographic segments will sponsor tennis, golf and the arts, while brands targeting youngsters will focus on popular music festival or programme sponsoring.

World Cup sponsorship and brand perception

Does major investment in sports sponsorship actually benefit brand owners? This seems to be primarily the case amongst young consumers. The impact of sports sponsorship on other age groups is much more limited. In 2002, NOP World questioned 1,001 people from a representative sample of the UK population on behalf of the Superbrand organisation to test brand awareness and brand perception of the sponsors of World Cup soccer. Within the 15–24 year old range, 40% of people said that they would feel more confident about a brand if it sponsored high-profile sporting events such as the World Cup. Only 19% of the 25–34 year olds and 18% of the 35–44 year olds feel more confidence in a sponsoring brand. This percentage even lowers to 13% of the 45–54 year olds, and a mere 6% of the 55–64 year olds. For the over 65s, this percentage increases slightly to 11%. The impact of high-profile sporting events appears primarily to impress the younger age groups.[32]

In Table 13.2 an overview is given of the objectives of marketing-related sponsorship. Mainly awareness building, and to a certain extent image building, seem to be the objectives that sponsorship is most suited to achieve. These effects only become visible in the long run. Indeed, sponsorship effectiveness studies indicate that sponsors are not recognised better than their non-sponsoring competitors immediately after the sponsored event.[33] A direct increase in sales or market share is not the primary objective of sponsorship, although, for instance, a beverage supplier can obtain the sole rights for selling beverages at an event, and in this way boost sales. Linking a brand's name with a relevant event or cause is often used to improve the image with a specific target group of interest. Volvo sponsoring golf and tennis, and Adidas sponsoring, amongst others, soccer, are examples of this.

Table 13.2 Marketing objectives of sponsorship

Awareness building	■ Increase awareness with actual customers
	■ Increase awareness with potential customers
	■ Confirm market leadership
	■ Increase new product awareness
Brand image	■ Alter perception of brand
	■ Identify brand with particular market segment
Sales/market share	■ Induce trial of new product
	■ Increase sales/market share

One of the most important motives in sponsorship is the leveraging effect of the media coverage of the event. In some cases, as in tobacco or alcohol advertising, the ban on regular advertising leads to a situation in which sponsorship is the only way to obtain mass media exposure. But a lot of other sponsorship initiatives count on the 'bullhorn effect' of media coverage too. Sponsorship is indeed becoming more and more broadcast-driven, as illustrated in Table 13.3, in which the results of a British study are shown.

Table 13.3 Objectives of sponsorship

Objectives	*% Agreement*
Press coverage/exposure	84.6
TV coverage/exposure	78.5
Promote brand awareness	78.4
Promote corporate image	77.0
Radio coverage/exposure	72.3
Increase sales	63.1
Enhance community relations	55.4
Entertain clients	43.1
Benefit employees	36.9
Match competition	30.8
Fad/fashion	26.2

Source: Erdogan, Z.B. and Kitchen, P.J. (1998), 'The Interaction Between Advertising and Sponsorship: Uneasy Alliance or Strategic Symbiosis?', in Kitchen, P.J. (ed.), *The Changing World of Corporate and Marketing Communication: Towards the Next Millennia, Proceedings of the 3rd Annual Conference of the Global Institute for Corporate and Marketing Communication*, Strathclyde Graduate Business School, 144–55. Reproduced with permission of Professor Philip Kitchen, The Queens University of Belfast.

Types of sponsorship

Sponsorship budgets can be directed towards different types of projects. In Figure 13.1 the main sponsorship types are shown. Four basic categories can be distinguished. Event-related sponsorship is the best-known category. Companies may sponsor a soccer competition, a team, an athlete, shirts or even a match ball, a golf tournament,

Figure 13.1 Types of sponsorship

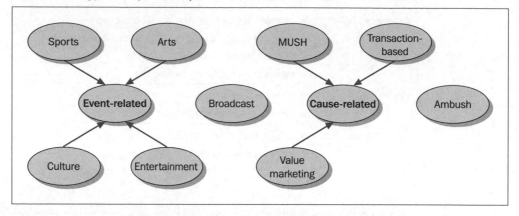

skiing or a baseball game. They can lend their support, in cash or kind, to an exhibition, a series of concerts, a philharmonic orchestra or an artist. Or they can sponsor a rock concert, a beach festival or an annual traditional crafts exhibition. Broadcast or programme sponsorship is a more recent phenomenon, at least in Europe. A brand can sponsor a sports programme, the weather forecast or a 'soap'. Cause-related sponsorship may be the oldest form of sponsorship, or rather charity. Rich people donating money to schools, the poor or other good causes is a phenomenon that has existed for centuries. The difference between those activities and cause-related sponsorship is that the latter is not just charity, but is integrated in the company's communications strategy. MUSH stands for Municipal, University, Social, Hospital sponsorship, and is a synonym for sponsorship of good causes. Transaction-based sponsorship (sometimes called cause-related marketing or point-of-purchase politics) is a type of sponsorship in which the company invests a pre-specified amount of money in a 'good cause' every time a consumer buys one of the company's products. Value marketing has been defined in the first section of this chapter. Sponsorship is only one aspect of value or societal marketing. Finally, ambush or parasitic marketing is a planned effort by a company to confuse the consumer regarding its affiliation status and to associate indirectly with an event in order to gain at least some of the recognition and benefits associated with being an official sponsor.[34] A company may be a minor sponsor of an event, but by spending considerable budgets on advertising support it creates the impression of being an important sponsor.

Traditional event-related sponsorship still accounts for the bulk of the expenditures. On average, in Europe 75% of all sponsorship is devoted to sports, mainly soccer and Formula One,[35] and 16% to arts and culture. The majority of the rest is spent on broadcast sponsorship.

Event-related sponsorship

The opportunities and advantages of event-related sponsorship are multiple. Compared to advertising it is a cost-effective instrument in terms of reaching a particular audience. Given the variety of events in terms of targeted audiences, it is an excellent tool to reach broad as well as very specific market segments in terms of demographic and psychographic characteristics. Sponsorship of opera, exhibitions or rock concerts, and of cultural events in general, is usually very selective in terms of the market segment reached, while some sports sponsorship is capable of exposing broad target groups to the sponsor's message. Extensive media coverage of sports events leads to high levels of exposure of broad target groups to the sponsor's name. For instance, as far as cycling is concerned, 18.4% of managers and executives watch this sport regularly on television, as well as 18% of farmers, 16.5% of civil servants, 16.5% of blue-collar workers, 12% of pensioners and 9% of housewives.[36] Heineken sponsored the Rugby World Cup worldwide. It was estimated that in the UK, 83% of all men were exposed to the Heineken brand name, each of them at least 22 times.[37]

Event sponsorship is also flexible in achieving different kinds of objectives. It can increase awareness with actual and potential customers, improve the company's image and the image of the company's products.

It is a tool in relationship building, it can be a platform for advertising campaigns, database building and sampling, and it is efficiently capable of avoiding advertising bans. For instance, as far as the latter is concerned, in a 1984 survey it was – sadly – found that the cigarette brands that were most widely recalled by children were those brands that were most commonly sponsoring televised sporting events.[38]

On the other hand, event sponsorship, and more particularly sports sponsorship, has a number of disadvantages and poses a number of threats. Spending large amounts of money on sponsorship can cause trouble with employees, especially if they are not properly informed about the relevance and economic justification of the sponsorship strategy. A company sponsoring a sportsman or woman or a team can alienate fans of the opponent.

Furthermore, unlike television sets and newspapers, sportsmen and women lead their own lives, and sometimes attract media attention that is not always favourable to the sponsor. The drugs scandal revealed in the Tour de France of 1998 was not particularly welcomed by the teams' sponsors, although Festina, the Spanish brand of timepieces and main sponsor of one of the offending teams, did not seem to suffer too much from the negative publicity. But even without such incidents, if the team or the sportsperson does badly, this can reflect negatively on the sponsor's image. Not surprisingly, a clean image is one of the main criteria on the basis of which sports or sports teams are selected for sponsorship.[39] Finally, although sports sponsorship can be used to transcend cultural, linguistic and geographic boundaries, some sports, like bull fighting, camel wrestling and dwarf throwing, are unfit for global brand sponsorship because they are culturally unacceptable in a number of countries.

Obviously, arts and cultural sponsorship is fundamentally different from sports sponsorship. First of all, arts audiences are different from sports audiences. The former are typically older and more affluent, and generally less numerous. The arts attract less media coverage and publicity, and are more suited to niche market segments than sports. However, some argue that the arts are increasingly attractive as sponsorship objects because of the increasing costs and saturation of sport sponsorship. Furthermore, a Toshiba study reveals that four times as many people visit museums and galleries as attended league football matches. Nevertheless, arts sponsors are believed to pursue corporate image and relationship and hospitality objectives rather than marketing goals. That makes arts sponsorship more of a PR tool than a marketing communications instrument.[40]

Integrating sponsorship into the marketing communications mix

For years Coca-Cola has been sponsoring big sports events all over the world. Obviously the World Cup in France could not be left out. Besides Coca-Cola's global approach to events like this, local adaptations were allowed. The Dutch agency localised Coca-Cola's sponsorship strategy as follows. Dutch teenagers could win a ticket to the World Cup for three bonus points and a good motivation, not as an international player, but as ball boy or girl, or as player in the games taking place just before the kick-off. Furthermore, Coca-Cola organised a fan day. For five bonus points Dutch fans could come to the Amsterdam Arena to wave their football heroes goodbye. For this successful localisation of a global sponsorship Coca-Cola received a nomination at the Esprix 1999, an award for exemplary Dutch Direct Marketing and Sales Promotion campaigns.[41]

Broadcast sponsorship

Broadcast or programme sponsorship is an increasingly important phenomenon. In the UK, broadcast sponsorship is estimated to be growing by approximately 15% per year.[42] In some countries, as in Belgium, government-owned television channels are not allowed to broadcast advertising messages, but are allowed to have their programmes sponsored, which makes broadcast sponsoring an extremely visible phenomenon. Broadcast sponsorship differs from plain advertising in a medium, in this case television, in that the sponsor has an influence on the content of the sponsored programme. Different types of broadcast sponsorship can be distinguished. Mentioning the name of a sponsor in a television programme is called billboarding: 'this programme was produced with the kind co-operation of company X'. Product placement involves the sponsor's product being used during the programme, and it is deliberately shown to the audience. Inscript sponsoring is a specific form of product placement. The sponsoring brand becomes part of the script of the programme. For instance if a programme is sponsored by a telecom company and the presenter asks the live audience to switch off their mobile phones, this establishes a connection between the sponsor and the programme. In prize sponsorship, the sponsoring company pays for awards or prizes, and is mentioned in the programme. In case of programme participation, product placement and billboarding are combined. The television channel produces a programme in close co-operation with a sponsor, for instance a tour operator that sponsors a travel programme, and pays for the prizes to be won in a contest during the programme.[43]

Product placement

In many cases, making movies would be impossible without product placement contracts between companies and movie producers. In the Bond movie *Die Another Day*, 20 brands are promoted by means of product placement. The total value of these contracts is estimated to be €45 million. James Bond (Pierce Brosnan) is civilised, appeals to both men and women, likes luxury and techno-logy, and is popular around the world. Halle Berry, who features as the Bond girl Jinx, appeals to youngsters. Companies try to associate their image with the attractive features of the movie characters. Bond shaves with a Philishave Sensotec, drinks Finlandia vodka, wears an Omega Seamaster watch, and again drives an Aston Martin, after a couple of BMW-dominated Bond movies. Jinx drives a Ford Thunderbird in the same colour as her bikini (a special Thunderbird

▶

007 series is also being made), uses the new Revlon lipsticks Mission Mauve and Hot Pursuit Pink, and wears a Swatch. Other product placers are Samsonite, Sony and British Airways.[44]

Product placement can be very effective, depending upon a number of moderating factors. A UK study of the impact of 10 cases of product placement in films resulted in the following conclusions:[45]

- Product placement leads to an increase in brand salience;
- Familiarity with a product category may have an inverse effect of product placement on brand salience;
- Prior exposure to the film may have an inverse effect upon salience;
- Liking of, and attention to, the film often increases brand salience;
- People with a high degree of self-monitoring (wanting to behave as they perceive others expect) exhibit higher levels of brand salience than people with a low degree of self-monitoring after exposure to a product placed in a film.

Of all sponsorship types, broadcast sponsorship is closest to advertising and for that reason is capable of achieving similar objectives of awareness and image building. Furthermore, famous television actors featuring in the sponsored programmes can be used as celebrity endorsers in subsequent advertising campaigns, thus leveraging the sponsorship effort. Broadcast sponsorship is perceived positively by the public. Sponsors are closely tied to the programme itself. In fact, they are physically part of it, to the extent that viewers even believe that sponsors actively participate in making the programme. Furthermore, sometimes the endorsing brand has a better image than the programme itself. Therefore, if the sponsor fits the programme well, this can lead to very positive carry-over effects between the two. Programme sponsorship also works in a different way. The long-term association between a likeable programme and a sponsor may lead to a very strong and positive brand image. Finally, broadcast sponsorship, as opposed to advertising, is perceived to benefit everyone. This has a major positive impact on viewer's acceptance of such sponsorships.[46]

Cause-related sponsorship

Cause-related sponsorship is a combination of public relations, sales promotions and corporate philanthropy, based on profit-motivated giving to good causes. MUSH sponsoring comes closest to traditional sponsoring in that money is given to good causes in return for exposure and image-building linkage with the good cause sponsored. Transaction-based sponsorship (sometimes called cause-related marketing) is different in that a company's contribution to a designated cause is linked to customers' engagement in revenue-producing exchanges with the firm.

Although the objectives of cause-related sponsorship are to a certain extent the same as those of other sponsorship activity, more emphasis is put on the impact on brand image as a result of the link between the brand and the good cause sponsored. Research has shown that effective cause-related sponsorship programmes can enhance brand image, and at the same time give customers a convenient way to contribute to non-profit organisations through their buying decisions. It is not only marketing professionals who believe that cause-related marketing can improve the image of their brands, consumers also seem to be interested. Studies indicate that as many as two-thirds of consumers are willing to take the company's contribution to good causes into account when taking a decision on which brands to purchase. A 2000 survey in 12 European countries indicated that two in five consumers bought a product because of its links to good causes. Cause-related marketing allows companies to attract and retain consumers, differentiate themselves from the competition and reach niche markets. A company wanting to engage in cause programmes successfully should be aware of the important principles of such activity: integrity, transparency, sincerity, mutual respect, partnership and mutual benefit. If not, the whole sponsorship programme will backfire, and the company will become known as insincere, opportunistic and lacking in credibility.[47]

Cause-related sponsorship programmes as a communications tool

In October 1999 ConAgra Foods, a company owning more than 80 household brands, launched Feeding Children Better, a cause programme to stop childhood hunger. By partnering with various anti-hunger organisations and using its extensive distribution, advertising and promotion resources, the company was able to bring more food into the charitable food distribution system and put child hunger on the agenda. Since the beginning of the programme, 50 Kids Cafes (places where kids can have a decent meal after school) have been funded, fresh food deliveries to relief organisations have increased dramatically and 29 trucks have been purchased for food banks with gifts from ConAgra. The programme received numerous sponsorship and non-profit awards.

Since 1995 Ford Motor Company has sponsored the Susan G. Komen's Breast Cancer Foundation. The support is not linked to Ford sales, but the company helps the organisation with donations, media support and in-kind gifts. The company also created the Ford Force, a united front of dealers, employees and the general public. More than 12,000 Ford employees and more than 3,000 dealers have participated in the activities of Ford Force. The results have been impressive, both for the Komen's foundation and for Ford. Website visits and toll-free telephone calls have increased dramatically, and there is a substantial increase in breast examinations. Ford has been able to create interest and sympathy among women, previously a lowly involved market segment.

Timberland, a lifestyle brand that sells footwear, apparel and accessories, and City Year, a national youth service organisation, have been partners for over 10 years. Timberland has donated more than US$ 10 million in grants and in-kind gifts since the beginning of the partnership. The partnership has helped to promote a service ethic among Timberland employees, who have contributed over 170,000 hours of community service. Timberland and City Year have co-ordinated numerous other service events and campaigns. Timberland also opened a City Year office in its headquarters. As a result, the company was voted by its peers as one of the '100 best companies to work for'.[48]

These examples illustrate that cause-related programmes can enhance corporate visibility and image, involve previously uninterested market segments and improve the commitment of the employees and future employees of the organisation.

A hybrid form of broadcast and cause-related sponsorship is the organised sponsorship of advocacy advertising on television. For instance, an insurance company could sponsor television spots in which parents are warned against situations that are potentially dangerous to children, such as water boiling on a stove, knives within reach, etc.

Ambush marketing

Ambush marketing occurs when an organisation deliberately seeks an association with a particular event without paying sponsorship fees, to persuade the audience that the ambusher is a legitimate or major sponsor. This can be done by sponsoring the media covering the event, by sponsoring subcategories within the event (one team or one player), or by overstating the organisation's involvement in the event by means of supporting advertising or sales promotion activity during the event.

Ambush marketers use several techniques, some of which are illegal, most of which are at least dubious, and some of which are legitimate. Ambush sponsors can use logos and brand names in non-authorised media: they can use sports logos and sports images without permission, exploit PR opportunities, sample non-official products or brochures, or run ambiguous advertising campaigns during the time of the event. They can co-operate with subsponsors of the event or with the media covering the event, or they can buy advertising spots or trailers that are embedded in an event that is, as such, sponsored by another company. They can publish 'congratulation ads' for athletes that have won a match or a medal or they can sponsor non-profit projects associated with the event.[49] Not surprisingly, official sponsors try to gain exclusive sponsorship and coverage of events in the media to prevent ambushers benefiting or the effectiveness of their own sponsorship efforts diminishing as a result of competitive action.

Ambush marketing in action

- Viewer recall and recognition scores for both sponsors and ambushers during the 1988 Winter Olympic Games revealed that the official sponsors were recalled more often than the ambushers in only four of seven product categories.[50]
- The spontaneous brand awareness of Sony rose by eight points to 61% during the 1991 Rugby World Cup. Sony was also mentioned as the main sponsor of this event. However, Sony was not the sponsor of the event itself, but of the ITV coverage.[51]
- When the Belgian top tennis player Kim Clijsters reached the final of Roland Garros in 2001, the insurance company Delta Lloyd, the official sponsor of the Belgian Tennis Federation, used her face in a newspaper advertisement the next day, referring to her performance. The federation had to intervene to prevent a lawsuit by the Clijsters management against the insurance company.
- To piggyback on soccer enthusiasm in the Netherlands, and in order not to allow Hyundai the advantage from being the official sponsor of the Euro 2000 European soccer tournament, Hyundai's competitor Daewoo launched an ambush campaign. Against a background of cheering soccer players, Daewoo advertised that car buyers would get a discount of €2,000 when buying a new Daewoo car. A judge ruled that this campaign was not a breach of the Euro 2000 'brand name'.[52]

Selection criteria

Selecting sponsorship proposals should be based on a careful comparison using appropriate selection criteria. They can be divided into three categories, listed in Table 13.4.

Depending on the type of company and the type of sponsorship projects, some criteria will be more important than others. But some of them should always be assessed as

Table 13.4 Assessment criteria for sponsorship proposals

Sponsored event or cause	Potential promotional spin-off	Budget
■ Type of event or cause ■ Quality level or image of the event ■ Target groups ■ Compatibility between sponsored event and company's promotional strategy ■ Strategic fit between event or cause and company or brand name ■ Uniqueness of sponsorship or place of the company in the list of sponsors ■ Length of impact ■ Geographic scope ■ Company's role in decision-making ■ Protection against ambush marketing	■ Event's own communications plan ■ Estimated media coverage ■ Quantity and quality of exposure ■ Fit between company's and event's communications strategy ■ Interest with employees ■ Corporate hospitality potential ■ Sales promotion spin-off potential ■ PR spin-off potential ■ Advertising spin-off potential ■ Amount of supporting advertising or PR activity needed ■ Chance of negative or no media exposure ■ Measurability and evaluation of effectiveness	■ Costs in cash or kind ■ Alternative investment for budget and expected return ■ Budget for supporting marketing activity ■ Time implications for own staff

important. Sponsorship budgets and supporting marketing budgets, compatibility with the company's strategic objectives, the strategic fit between the event and the company's or brand's name, image and target groups will always be important. On the other hand, media exposure and other spin-off potential and competitive considerations may be more important in sports sponsorship, while corporate hospitality potential and the interest to employees might be more important in an arts sponsorship project. Some companies may be more concerned about their corporate image (e.g. service or business-to-business marketers), while fast-moving consumer goods companies may be more interested in the commercial spin-off potential, like sampling at the event, or organising a lottery-on-pack to attend an event.

The criteria listed should be used as a starting point. However, the selection of relevant criteria and the grading of their importance will largely depend on the type of company and its overall communications strategy. The eventual short list of potential candidates for sponsorship will ultimately depend on the relative weights of the criteria used and the available sponsorship budget.

Sponsorship budgets

Obviously it is impossible to provide detailed guidelines as to the required budgets of a sponsorship campaign. Budgets should depend on the expected effectiveness or return in terms of exposure, communications effects and sales or market share impact (see below). As in communications campaigns in general, the objective-and-task method is called for. Sponsorship decision-makers should decide on the objectives they want to achieve, assess to what extent a sponsorship programme can contribute to these objectives and try to calculate how large an economically meaningful sponsorship budget should be. Needless to say, in most cases this is a cumbersome task.

However, sponsorship-linked budgets are not limited to the expenditures directly related to the sponsored event or cause, but also encompass all communications efforts and budgets that are spent leveraging the investments in the activity or cause. Buying the sponsorship rights is indeed 'just a licence to spend more money to leverage the initial investment'. For instance, Coca-Cola spent US$40 million to become an official sponsor of the 1996 Olympics, and an estimated $500 million to leverage this status.[53] A Canadian study revealed that only 37% of sports sponsors do not provide an additional support budget. But almost 20% allocate an additional budget of 50% of the sponsoring budget or more to communications support activities.

Indeed, there are different reasons why sponsorship should be supported by other media efforts. First, as has already been mentioned, sponsorship has its limitations. Very often brand awareness and brand image are supported, but other necessary communications and commercial objectives, like building knowledge about the brand and generating sales, will have to be achieved by means of additional communications support. But most importantly, the general principle of integrated communications also applies to sponsorship: the more it is supported by, and integrated in, the rest of the communications mix, the more effective it will be. For instance, among the sponsoring companies of the 1996 Olympics that also ran advertising on the events, 64% succeeded in creating the link. On the other hand, of the official sponsors that did not run advertising, only 4% created the link.[54]

Measuring sponsorship effectiveness

Similar to the measurement of the effectiveness of other communications tools, isolating the effect of sponsorship is complicated by a number of factors, such as the simultaneous use of instruments of the marketing and communications mix, the carry-over effect of earlier activities, creative management issues, the pursuit of multiple objectives and the discretionary nature of media coverage.

Sponsorship is to a certain extent similar to advertising in that one of its main objectives is to build brand awareness with specific target groups. Additionally, and equally important, brands try to improve their image by linking their name to the event sponsored. Furthermore, in a number of sponsorship projects, communications results are not only obtained during the sponsored event, but also as a result of their media coverage. Sponsorship research reflects these objectives and characteristics of this communications mix instrument.

Four types of sponsorship effectiveness can be distinguished: exposure, communications results, sales and market share, and feedback from participating groups. Two types of exposure can be distinguished: the number of people attending the event and the exposure resulting from the media coverage of the event. By counting the number of attendees at a sponsored event, and/or studying the composition of the audience present, the number of consumers reached and the frequency of their exposure to the brand name can be estimated. If the sponsored event is covered by the media, the number of lines, pages or times the brand name is mentioned, or the number of seconds it is shown on television or heard on the radio, can be calculated. On this basis, reach and frequency of exposure can also be estimated, as well as the monetary value of the exposure obtained. Evidently, frequency of exposure and reach only give an indication of the probability of having contacted parts of the target group, but nothing about the actual number of contacts, let alone of their quality or impact.

Second, **communications results** can be measured. In this respect sponsorship campaign effectiveness measurements are very similar to the advertising campaign tests discussed in Chapter 8 on advertising research: brand awareness, correct sponsor attribution, and the effect on the image of the sponsored event and the sponsoring brand can be measured. Besides increasing brand awareness, associating the brand with the sponsored event is the most important objective of a sponsorship campaign. As a result, measuring the percentage of the target group able to attribute correctly the name of the sponsoring brand(s) to an event is one of the most important measures of sponsorship effectiveness. In this type of test, a list of sponsored events is presented to a sample of consumers, who have to attribute (aided or unaided) the sponsors of the event. This results in an indication of the percentage of the target group that can correctly attribute sponsors to events, as well as measures of 'sponsor confusion'. Correct (aided and unaided) sponsorship attribution can be very low, while sponsorship confusion is in some cases stunningly high.

Additionally, the purpose of sponsorship is to associate the sponsoring brand or company with the sponsored event. Sponsorship research can therefore also focus on the link between the image of the brand and the event with members of the target group.

Although **increasing sales or market share** is not the primary objective of sponsorship, its long-term effectiveness can also be assessed by estimating the sponsorship's commercial impact.

Finally, sponsorship effectiveness can also be measured on the basis of **feedback from participating groups**. Given the nature of some types of sponsorship, its effectiveness primarily lies in the reaction of participants to corporate hospitality sponsorship projects or the opinion of employees about sponsorship programmes. This will particularly – but not exclusively – be the case in cultural or cause-related sponsorship.

Summary

Public relations is the management of reputation. Marketing PR is directed towards marketing audiences and mainly supports marketing communications objectives by means of newsletters, press releases, product events and meetings.

Sponsorship is an increasingly important instrument of the marketing communications mix. Sponsors often try to escape the advertising clutter by linking their name to an event, and hope for beneficial carry-over effects from the event on company and brand awareness and image. Four basic types of sponsorship can be distinguished. Event-related (culture and sports) sponsorship is best known. Cause-related sponsorship, or sponsoring good causes, is the oldest form. Broadcast sponsorship is a more recent phenomenon, but is growing fast. The youngest type is ambush marketing, whereby a company tries to benefit from an event it does not sponsor. Criteria that can be used to select projects can be event-related (type of event, quality level, target groups, uniqueness of sponsorship, fit with strategic objectives, etc.), spin-off related (indirect communications effects, media coverage, interest with employees, advertising and PR spin-off, etc.) and budget-related (cost in cash or in kind, time implications for staff, etc.). Sponsorship effectiveness can be measured on the basis of exposure, communications results, commercial results or on the basis of feedback from participating groups.

Review questions

1 What is the role of public relations in the communications mix, and what are its strengths and weaknesses?

2 Who are the target groups of public relations?

3 What are the objectives and instruments of PR activity?

4 Compare the different PR budgeting techniques and their advantages and disadvantages.

5 How can the effectiveness of PR campaigns be assessed?

6 What is the difference between sponsorship and advertising, public relations and value marketing?

7 How can sponsorship be used to reach a variety of marketing communications objectives in different target groups?

8 What are the advantages and disadvantages of the various types of event-related sponsorship?

9 How can cause-related sponsorship contribute to a company's communications strategy?

10 What criteria can be used to select sponsorship proposals?

11 How can the effectiveness of a sponsorship campaign be measured?

Further reading

Adkins, S. (1999), *Cause-related Marketing: Who Cares Wins*. Oxford: Butterworth-Heinemann.

Baines, P., Egan, J. and Jefkins, F. (2003), *Public Relations: Contemporary Issues and Techniques*. Butterworth-Heinemann.

Desanto, B. and Moss, D. (2001), *Public Relations: A Managerial Perspective*. Gower Publishing Co.

Duffy, N. (2003), *Passion Branding: Successful Sports Sponsorship*. John Wiley & Sons.

Grey, A.M. and Shildum-Reid, K. (2003), *The Sponsorship Seeker's Toolkit*. McGraw-Hill.

Haywood, R. (1998), *Public Relations for Marketing Professionals*. London: Macmillan Business.

Case 13

Sponsoring championship football – France 98 and Euro 2000

Football championships as strong brands

In recent years, the European and World football championships have been managed as high-profile events with sophisticated marketing communications campaigns, both from the point of view of the organising countries and the sponsors of the tournaments. Organising countries have positioned their championships as strong brands with unique core values, and have tried to attract sponsors that have the same core values. The sponsors of the championships have their own agenda and try to enhance the awareness and image of their brands among their target groups, piggybacking upon the worldwide interest for the football event. In a way, being a 'partner', or a structural sponsor, of a football championship is an exercise in co-branding. Sponsors start from the image and the core values that are being created by the organising countries, and try to position their brand images by developing sponsorship and other communications campaigns that are consistent with the brand values of the championship. In 1998 the World football championships were held in France ('France 98'); the European football championships in 2000 were held in Belgium and the Netherlands ('Euro 2000'). First, the core values of these championships are discussed, and then the strategy and sponsorship campaigns of the strategic partners of France 98 and Euro 2000 are highlighted.

The core values of the football championships France 98 and Euro 2000

France 98
The slogan of France 98 was 'The beauty of a world at play'. Through this core theme the organisers wanted to communicate that the championships were more than a series of football games. It is remarkable that, compared with other championships, the word 'football' did not appear in this core theme. The slogan of the 1996 championships in the UK was 'Football comes home', and that of Euro 2000 was 'Football without frontiers'. Three emotional cues were attached to France 98: universality, excitement and sharing. Universality referred to the fact that football is the most popular sport worldwide; excitement had to do with the atmosphere during the matches; sharing referred to the shared emotions during the games. These three core values were used throughout all communications about the championships. In building this brand, events and the media played an important role. On 14 September 1995, the media were invited to officially start the campaign, with exactly 1,000 days to go to the championships. At the end of 1995 the pools and calendar of the preparatory tournament were officially composed during an event at the Louvre. The official mascot was presented in 1996, and a contest was organised to find a name for it (Footix). One year before the start of the campaign, the official poster of France 98 was presented (with Ronaldo, Platini and children from around the

world). On 4 December 1997, the pools and calendar of the championship were composed at an event in a full stadium. The fact that France won the championship against super-favourite Brazil was, of course, a splendid apotheosis of four weeks of football. The organisation committee, the sponsors, FIFA (the international football organisation), the various cities in France where the matches were played and the media all worked together to consistently build the strong brand 'France 98'. The chaotic ticket sale was the only dark spot on the image of this football event.

Euro 2000
The European football championships in 2000 were jointly organised by Belgium and the Netherlands. The core theme of the tournament was 'Football without frontiers'. The co-operation between Belgium and the Netherlands stressed the international European character of the championships. Sharing exciting emotions was another core theme of the event. The public in the organising countries was critical about the decision to organise it in their countries, and they were particularly concerned about safety and traffic problems during the tournament. The communication campaign therefore used active media PR to stress the precautions taken to cope with these potential problems, and to convince the general public that everything was in place to organise an impeccable tournament. Numerous lifestyle events and tourist activities were organised to promote Euro 2000.

The sponsors of France 98 and Euro 2000
In Case Table 13.1, the official partners and suppliers of France 98 and Euro 2000 are presented. The implementation of their sponsorship campaigns is discussed in the next sections.

France 98
For *Coca-Cola* it was very important to be associated with the championships. The main objective of its sponsorship was to appeal to its target groups and keep brand preference at a high level. Coca-Cola wanted to show that it shares and understands its consumers' passion for football. Refreshment, both physical and emotional, during and after the match, was the core message of its campaign. Coca-Cola focussed its communications during the tournament on 12–19 year olds. Fans from more than 60 countries

Case Table 13.1 Partners and suppliers of France 98 and Euro 2000

France 98		Euro 2000	
Partners	Suppliers	Partners	Suppliers
EuroCard/MasterCard	Danone	Carlsberg	Adecco
Fuji Film	EDS	Coca-Cola	Adidas
Gillette	France Télécom	Fuji Film	Cisco
JVC	Hewlett-Packard	Hyundai	Connexxion
Philips	La Poste	JVC	KLM
Opel	Manpower	EuroCard/MasterCard	Lever Fabergé
McDonald's	Sybase	McDonald's	Nashuatec
Adidas		Philips	Nestlé
Snickers		Playstation	Total Fina
Coca-Cola		Pringles	Telfort
Canon		PSINet	
Budweiser		Sportal.com	

* Budweiser was replaced by Casio as a boarding sponsor in the stadiums because of a French law that forbids advertising for alcoholic beverages.

were involved in promotional activities and events. The championships were promoted in three continents; the promotion trip was sponsored by Coca-Cola. In that way, it shared the enthusiasm of the fans in countries such as Nigeria, Saudi Arabia, South Korea, England, the Netherlands and France. A number of country-specific activities were also organised. For instance, the Cup was first kissed by Ronald Koeman on Dutch soil, after which it made a trip through the Netherlands to allow fans to share the passion by holding the Cup for a few moments. On 7 June 1998 a big 'fan day' was organised in Amsterdam. Fans could greet their football heroes and wish them success on their trip to France. By joining a contest, boys and girls could win tickets or a position as ball boy or girl in one of the matches. Also in Belgium a contest was organised: participants had to guess how long it would take the Belgian goalkeeper to run around a football pitch. The winner received the lifelong right to a ticket for a match in the first round of the European championships, together with his or her partner, all costs paid by Coca-Cola.

As a sponsor of France 98, *Adidas* wanted to communicate that it was more than just a manufacturer of football products. At France 98, Adidas was a sponsor, a supplier of balls, ball boys and girls, and 12,000 volunteers, and the only licenser of the official World Championship outfit. By clothing top players like Kluivert and Zidane, it wanted to communicate that top football players are very selective about the material they choose to wear. The core target group of 12–19 year olds was reached through music television channels. For instance, Kluivert appeared on *The Music Factory* in a specially designated programme to talk about football and many other things. Adidas visited all youth tournaments in Belgium and Holland with a test centre for Adidas products. Near the Eiffel Tower an Adidas football village was built to organise a youth tournament during the championships.

Opel sponsored France 98 to support brand awareness and to make the brand image more dynamic. The championships were used to create an emotional bond between the brand and the customers in its European markets. The 1998 championship was also considered the highlight and the logical continuation of the Opel sports sponsorship strategy of the previous years. Together with Visa, in France Opel made 700 cars available to accommodate guests invited to the Opel Club. The Opel subsidiaries in every country could decide in which way they wanted to benefit from the France 98 event. In all European countries the subsidiaries could support the Opel sponsorship by means of various promotional campaigns, such as advertisements, sales promotions, dealer incentives, etc. In Belgium and the Netherlands, a limited series of the Corsa Worldcup was manufactured.

For *McDonald's* France 98 was an opportunity to express its sympathy with top athletes and a unique sports event. Through in-store activities and the creation of a World Cup meal in 75 countries,

McDonald's tried to carry over the fun and the excitement of the tournament to its customers. A Mc World Cup Special was offered with a spicy salsa sauce to make the association with Brazilian football. Furthermore, social programmes and local sports events were set up in various cities in France. Together with Fuji Film, the Young Photojournalist Contest was organised for children aged between 8 and 14 from the Netherlands, the UK, Italy and Argentina. The Mc Goal! Goal! Goal! campaign rewarded creative football with gifts to SOS Children's Village, the official social cause programme of FIFA.

A remarkable initiative was the sponsorship by *Snickers* of the Fair Play marathon between 4 December 1997 and 10 June 1998, which passed through 162 cities around the world. Every day two athletes ran half a marathon, totalling more than 7,000 kilometres. Around the marathon, 10,000 children were gathered through events and contests. Snickers also supported its sponsorship through extensive media advertising campaigns.

A new trend was the joint effort by the French Ministry of Youth and Sports and *Adidas, McDonald's* and *Danone* to organise a football tournament in 128 cities in France for boys born after 1984. The winning team in each city was combined with youth players from Brazil, Mexico and South Africa. The initiative aimed at stimulating integration, solidarity and sports. The campaign 'T'es jeune, t'es foot' was sponsored by *Coca-Cola* and *Crédit Agricole*. It tried to realise the dream of many boys and girls to participate in the championship as a volunteer or as a ball boy or girl.

Euro 2000

The sponsorship of Euro 2000 by *Hyundai* was part of an agreement to also sponsor the World Championships of 2002 in Japan and South Korea. For Hyundai, Euro 2000 offered an opportunity to improve its brand awareness and image in Europe because the brand name and logo of Hyundai were consistently exposed to the public, together with world-famous brands such as Coca-Cola, McDonald's and Playstation. During the tournament, Hyundai invested a lot in media campaigns to constantly draw attention to the brand in connection with Euro 2000. For instance, in May 2000 a television and poster campaign was rolled out to promote the Athos, Coupé and Accent models.

Coca-Cola was again an official sponsor of the European football championships in 2000. Together with the cities in which the tournament was organised, Coca-Cola developed a campaign, the communications tools of which were city maps, fan villages and vending machines. In that way, Coca-Cola tried to establish good contacts with local administrations. The brand image was also supported by means of street soccer tournaments and 'refreshment zones'. The latter were locations within two to five kilometres of the stadiums or in the historical centres of the cities (parking lots, metro stations, newspaper kiosks, tourist venues, etc.), where the brand name was extensively presented and unique brand events could be experienced. For instance, in Amsterdam fans could find refreshment against an ice wall, and could drink a Coke in a uniquely constructed ice bar.

Nashautec, one of the official suppliers of the tournament, wanted to communicate that it is more than just a manufacturer of copiers, printers and fax machines, but that it also sells hardware and software and consultancy. Nashuatec Benelux installed 450 'remanufactured' (used) fax and copy machines and printers, and 70 technicians to control the data flows at Euro 2000. It wanted to show that the machines worked flawlessly in the capable hands of the Nashuatec people. The company also invited 2,500 business contacts, and rolled out several image advertising campaigns.

Questions

1 To what extent are the sponsorship and support campaigns of the France 98 and Euro 2000 sponsors consistent with, and building upon, the core values of France 98 and Euro 2000? Discuss the campaigns of every sponsor described in the case.

2 Could the sponsors have organised other types of activities? Which ones? Try to think of other types of sponsorships and other types of communications.

3 Are there any companies or brands in the list that seem less compatible with football championships, given their objectives and target groups? Why?

4 How would you measure the impact of the sponsorship campaigns?

Based on: Lagae, W. (2003), *Marketingcommunicatie in de Sport*, Pearson Education Benelux.

References

1 Sirgy, J.M. (1998), *Integrated Marketing Communication. A Systems Approach*. Upper Saddle River, NJ: Prentice Hall.

2 Haywood, R. (1998), *Public Relations for Marketing Professionals*. London: Macmillan Business.

3 *Public Relations Practice – Its Role and Parameters* (1984), London: The Institute of Public Relations.

4 Haywood, R. (1998), *Public Relations for Marketing Professionals*. London: Macmillan Business.

5 http.://groups.yahoo.com/group/brandhut/ May 2003.

6 De Pelsmacker, P. and Van den Bergh, J. (1998), 'Advertising Content and Irritation: A Study of 226 TV Commercials', *Journal of International Consumer Marketing*, 10(4), 5–27.

7 Biurnett, J. and Moriarty, S. (1998), *Introduction to Marketing Communication*. Upper Saddle River, NJ: Prentice Hall.

8 Lages, C. (2001), *Dimensions of Public Relations Activity: An Exploratory Study*. PhD dissertation, University of Warwick: Warwick Business School.

9 KBC On-line, Effie Award. Belgium, 2003.

10 *De Morgen*, 3 April 2002.

11 Haywood, R. (1991), *All About Public Relations*. London: McGraw-Hill.

12 McCleneghan, J.S. (1998), 'Are VNR's all they're Cracked Up to Be?', *Public Relations Quarterly*, 42(4), 35–8.

13 Haywood, R. (1998), *Public Relations for Marketing Professionals*. London: Macmillan Business.

14 Gofton, K. (1997), 'Rethinking the Rules', *Public Relations – Supplement*, 6–10.

15 Haywood, R. (1998), *Public Relations for Marketing Professionals*. London: Macmillan Business; See also Moss, D., Vercic, D. and Warnaby, G. (2003), *Perspectives on Public Relations Research*. London: Routledge.

16 Meenaghan, T. (1991), 'The Role of Sponsorship in the Marketing Communication Mix', *International Journal of Advertising*, 10(1), 35–48.

17 Erdogan, Z.B. and Kitchen, P.J. (1998), 'The Interaction Between Advertising and Sponsorship: Uneasy Alliance or Strategic Symbiosis?', in Kitchen, P.J. (ed.), *The Changing World of Corporate and Marketing Communication: Towards the Next Millennia, Proceedings of the 3rd Annual Conference of the Global Institute for Corporate and Marketing Communication*. Strathclyde Graduate Business School, 144–55.

18 Hastings, G.B. (1984), 'Sponsorship Works Differently from Advertising', *International Journal of Advertising*, 3(2), 171–8.

19 Erdogan, Z.B. and Kitchen, P.J. (1998), 'The Interaction Between Advertising and Sponsorship: Uneasy Alliance or Strategic Symbiosis?', in Kitchen, P.J. (ed.), *The Changing World of Corporate and Marketing Communication: Towards the Next Millennia, Proceedings of the 3rd Annual Conference of the Global Institute for Corporate and Marketing Communication*. Strathclyde Graduate Business School, 144–55.

20 Meenaghan, T. (1983), 'Commercial Sponsorship', *European Journal of Marketing*, 7(7), 5–71.

21 Marshall, D.W. and Cook, G. (1992), 'The Corporate (Sports) Sponsor', *International Journal of Advertising*, 11(3), 307–24.

22 Bloxham, M. (1998), 'Brand Affinity and Television Programme Sponsorship', *International Journal of Advertising*, 17(1), 89–98.

23 Cornwell, T.B. and Maignan, I. (1998), 'An International Review of Sponsorship Research', *Journal of Advertising*, 27(1), 1–21.

24 Adfo Specialist Group (1999), *Rabobank Wielerplan (Rabobank Cyclism Plan)*, Adfo Sponsoring Cases no. 2, Alphen aan den Rijn: Samson; Adfo Specialist Group (2000), *Nashuatec en Oliver*, Adfo Sponsoring Cases no. 5, Alphen aan den Rijn: Samson.

25 See also: Abshire, M. (2002), *Consumer Product Manufacturers: Maintain Giving in Uncertain Times*. Corporate Philanthropy Report 17 (March), 1–11; Polonsky, M. and Macdonald, E. (2000), 'Exploring the Link Between Cause-related Marketing and Brand Building', *International Journal of Nonprofit and Voluntary Sector Marketing*, 5 (February), 46–57.

26 www.fdncenter.org/learn/faqs/html/cause_marketing.html, 23 May 2003; www.bsr.org, 23 May 2003.

27 Irwin, R., Sutton, W. and McCarthy, L. (2002), *Sport Promotion and Sales Management*. Champaign: Human Kinetics.

28 Meenaghan, T. (1998), 'Current Developments and Future Directions in Sponsorship', *International Journal of Advertising*, 17(1), 3–28.

29 Euro Effie 2002.

30 Quester, P. (1997), 'Awareness as a Measure of Sponsorship Effectiveness: The Adelaide Formula One Grand Prix and Evidence of Incidental Ambush Effects', *Journal of Marketing Communications*, 3(1), 1–20.

31 Thwaites, D., Anguilar-Manjarrez, R. and Kidd, C. (1998), 'Sports Sponsorship Development in Leading Canadian Companies: Issues and Trends', *International Journal of Advertising*, 17(1), 29–50.

32 www.nop.co.uk/news, 23 May 2003.

33 Quester, P. (1997), 'Sponsoring Returns: Unexpected Results and the Value of Naming Rights' in Meenaghan, T. (ed.), *New and Evolving Paradigms: The Emerging Future of Marketing, American Marketing Association Special Conference Proceedings*. Dublin: University College, 692–4.

34 Irwin, R., Sutton, W. and McCarthy, L. (2002), *Sport Promotion and Sales Management*. Champaign: Human Kinetics.

35 www.communicatiecoach.com, 23 May 2003.

36 Lagae, W. (1997), 'Het Pokerspel van de Professionele Wielsponsoring' ('The Poker Game of Professional Cycling Sponsorship'), in Duyck, R. and Van Tilborgh, C. (eds), *Aan Marketing Denken en Doen. Marketing Jaarboek (Thinking of and Doing Marketing. Marketing Yearbook)*. Zellick: Roularta Books, 86–94.

37 Brassington, F. and Pettitt, S. (2003), *Principles of Marketing*. London: Pitman Publishing.

38 Cornwell, T.B. and Maignan, I. (1998), 'An International Review of Sponsorship Research', *Journal of Advertising*, 27(1), 1–21.

39 Thwaites, D., Anguilar-Manjarrez, R. and Kidd, C. (1998), 'Sports Sponsorship Development in Leading Canadian Companies: Issues and Trends', *International Journal of Advertising*, 17(1), 29–50.

40 Farrelly, F.J. and Quester, P.G. (1997), 'Sports and Arts Sponsors: Investigating the Similarities and Differences in Management Practices', in Meenaghan, T. (ed.), *New and Evolving Paradigms: The Emerging Future of Marketing, American Marketing Association Special Conference Proceedings*. Dublin: University College, 874–86.

41 *Esprix Jaarboek*, 1999, 86.

42 Brassington, F. and Pettitt, S. (2003), *Principles of Marketing*. London: Pitman Publishing.

43 Floor, J.M. and van Raaij, W.F. (2002), *Marketing-communicatiestrategie (Marketing Communication Strategy)*. Groningen: Wolters-Noordhoff.

44 *De Morgen*, 16 November 2002.

45 Johnstone, E. and Dodd, C. (2000), 'Placement as Mediators of Brand Salience within a UK Cinema Audience', *Journal of Marketing Communications*, 6(3), 141–58.

46 Bloxham, M. (1998), 'Brand Affinity and Television Programme Sponsorship', *International Journal of Advertising*, 17(1), 89–98.

47 www.bsr.org, 23 May 2003.

48 www.bsr.org, 23 May 2003.

49 Lagae, W. (2003), *Marketingcommunicatie in de Sport*. Pearson Education Benelux.

50 Sandler, D.M. and Shani, D. (1989), 'Olympic Sponsorship vs "Ambush" Marketing: Who Gets the Gold?' *Journal of Advertising Research*, August/September, 9–14.

51 Smith, P.R. (1993), *Marketing Communication. An Integrated Approach*. London: Kogan Page.

52 Lagae, W. (2003), *Marketingcommunicatie in de Sport*. Pearson Education Benelux.

53 Sandler, D.M., Shani, D. and Lee, M.S. (1998), 'How Consumers Learn About Sponsors: The Impact of Information Sources on Sponsorship', in Meenaghan, T. (ed.), *New and Evolving Paradigms: The Emerging Future of Marketing, American Marketing Association Special Conference Proceedings*. Dublin: University College, 869–71.

54 Erdogan, Z.B. and Kitchen, P.J. (1998), 'The Interaction Between Advertising and Sponsorship: Uneasy Alliance or Strategic Symbiosis?', in Kitchen, P.J. (ed.), *The Changing World of Corporate and Marketing Communication: Towards the Next Millennia. Proceedings of the 3rd Annual Conference of the Global Institute for Corporate and Marketing Communication*, Strathclyde Graduate Business School, 144–55.

Name index

Subject index